Enjoy - Learn - B
In Loving Memor
Rebecca Berney Frances Fraser U.E.L.
Always her Daughter,
Love,
Frances Ann Loewen U.E.L.

Teaching Lessons of Loyalty:

The Society for the Propagation

Of the

Gospel's Mission to the Americans.

By

Ronald Leslie Cooksey

Published by arima publishing
www.arimapublishing.com

First published 2005

Copyright © Ronald Leslie Cooksey

The Author asserts the moral right to be identified as the author of this work

ISBN 1-84549-011-8

All rights reserved

This book is copyright. Subject to statutory exception and to provisions of relevant collective licensing agreements, no part of this publication may be reproduced, stored in a retrieval system, or transmitted in any form or by any means, without the prior written permission of The Author.

Cover images:
John Stuart, Courtesy of Library and Archives, Canada / C-011057
St Georges Cathedral, Courtesy of Thousand Island Publishers, Ontario.

Printed and bound in the United Kingdom and in the United States

Typeset in Palatino 11/16

This book is sold subject to the conditions that it shall not, by way of trade or otherwise, be lent, re-sold, hired out, or otherwise circulated without the publisher's prior consent in any form of binding or cover other than that in which it is published and without a similar condition including this condition being imposed on the subsequent purchaser.

arima publishing
ASK House, Northgate Avenue
Bury St Edmunds, Suffolk IP32 6BB
t: (+44) 01284 700321

www.arimapublishing.com

Table of Contents

PREFACE 5

CHAPTER

I	Missionaries to the Americans	15
II	The Americanization of the Church	63
III	The Search for Unity	113
IV	Bishops for the Americans	163
V	Helpless Dependence upon Britain	213
VI	Propagating Loyal Priciples	253

Notes on the Major Primary Sources 315

Bibliography 317

Index 333

PREFACE

The Church of England during the colonial period of American history has received its share of attention. In the nineteenth century the Church historiographers Francis L. Hawks and William Stevens Perry, and later William Wilson Manross, have related the story of the people who were responsible for leading the Church during its infant years. However, the task of examining the various efforts to extend the episcopate to the American colonies during the eighteenth century was left to Arthur Lyon Cross who published *The Anglican Episcopate and the American Colonies* in 1902.

Sixty years passed before Carl Bridenbaugh published the *Mitre and Sceptre: Trans Atlantic Faiths, Ideas, Personalities, and Politics, 1689-1775*. In this book he carried the work done by Arthur Cross to place the American episcopate at the centre of a dramatic trans-Atlantic conflict between Dissenters and Anglicans in their bid to settle their own peculiar social and political institutions upon America. Bridenbaugh concluded that the American Anglicans, supported from England by the prelates and the Society for the Propagation of the Gospel in Foreign Parts, were bent on foisting upon the colonies an ecclesiastical hierarchy complete with all the political privileges and trappings of the Old World.

In 1971, John Calam enquired into an area to which Bridenbaugh had given but scant attention. *Parsons and Pedagogues: The S.P.G. Adventure in American Education* examines the work of the Society for the Propagation of the Gospel from its inception in 1701 to the beginning of the Revolution, describing the role of the Society's clergy and schoolteachers in the colonies. The Society, according to Calam, set out with military thoroughness to teach the colonials subordination to Church and State, a mission which the Revolution proved to have been a dismal failure.

Both Bridenbaugh and Calam have had the advantage of a far greater range of source materials, printed and manuscript, than Cross, and they wrote after significant developments have taken place in the approaches to historical writing, but both have left much work to be done. Bridenbaugh has woven a fine network of interrelationships between the English and American Dissenters. However, he has only touched the surface of the wealth of correspondence in the archives of the S.P.G., relying heavily upon the small number of High Church Tories who were drawn to Trinity Church in New York for his view of the American Anglicans. He has ignored the scores of unknown clergy and missionaries of the Society who often disapproved of the New York High Churchmen's assumed role as spokesmen for the Church in the northern colonies. Calam's work, limited by its excessive use of the Society's published anniversary sermons and Abstracts of Proceedings, has given only a partly correct account of the Society's view of what it considered to be its role in America. He has assumed that the American clergy and schoolteachers were merely a mouthpiece for the English Churchmen. There was, however, a very serious divergence between the Society's aims and the view some of the clergy thought the Church should play in America.

Jonathan Boucher, one of the few Loyalist historians of the Revolution, emphasized an interpretation that many Loyalists held that the conflict over the American episcopate was central to the political disputes that led to American independence. Since 1797, when Boucher published the *View of the Causes and Consequences of the American Revolution*, the episcopal controversy has remained part of the historians' explanations of the aggravations and fears that compelled some Americans to revolt. For Cross, the religious disputes and the debate over the episcopate were of secondary importance in the process of estrangement between Britain and the colonies. Bridenbaugh and Calam attribute considerable importance to the activities of the Church of England clergy and the Society in convincing the Americans that they were the prey of a priestly and tyrannical cabal in London.

Anglican attempts to introduce the episcopate into America did intensify fears that a plot was afoot in England to subvert their freedom. The amazing growth of the Church during the first half of the eighteenth century had taken place in those colonies north and east of the Delaware, formerly the preserve of the Dissenters. At the turn of the eighteenth century, Anglicans were an insignificant few among the other denominations. They were even a minority among the Presbyterians, Quakers and members of the Dutch Reformed Church in the four counties of New York where the Church of England claimed a legal establishment. In New England they were generally to be found among the small group of royal office holders in Boston.

Anglican growth in these colonies owed much to the work of the Society for the Propagation of the Gospel. Its finance supported clergy and teachers, it provided Bibles, Prayer Books and literature from the beginning of the eighteenth century until the colonies finally separated from Britain. But while the Society's help was important, it was the Great Awakening that transformed the Church from the resented minority in New England and the negligible force in the middle colonies to the significant alternative to the Congregationalists and Presbyterians by the 1770's. In 1700, King's Chapel stood as a solitary reminder to New Englanders of the majesty of England's National Church. Seventy five years later it had become merely one congregation among over seventy in New England, some of whose churches added a graceful air with their elegant structures, steeples and peals of bells to the prospering towns.

The Church of England had become so serious a rival to the Congregationalists that one of its ministers, Ezra Stiles, could claim that the Anglicans in New England alone numbered over 12,000 in 1760. One of the Society's missionaries, a decade later, estimated that they were one in thirteen of the population. A study by Bruce Steiner ("New England Anglicanism: A Genteel Faith?" *William and Mary Quarterly*, XXVII, No. I (Jan., 1970), pp. 122-135) estimated the New England Episcopalian population as high as 25,000 in 1775. This figure might appear to be rather optimistic in a total population that probably amounted to no more than one half million. Though it bears some credibility when compared with the *notitia parochialia* that the Society's missionaries submitted half-yearly to London, reporting the population statistics of the various denominations in their parishes.

The proportion of Americans professing to be Anglicans in the middle colonies in the 1770's was smaller. The Great Awakening had made a less dramatic impact upon the non-Anglicans there, and the conservative branch of the Presbyterian Church, which emerged from the religious turmoil of the 1740's, could vie with the Church of England in offering a stable alternative to the religious extremes of the revival. Furthermore, immigrants from Europe and Ireland swelled the Dissenters' ranks on the Pennsylvania frontier and along the northerly reaches of the Hudson River in New York. John B. Franz ("The Awakening of Religion among the German Settlers in the Middle Colonies," *William and Mary Quarterly*, XXXIII, No. 2 (April, 1976), pp. 266-288) estimated that over one third of the total population of Pennsylvania were Germans in 1750. Though this figure includes numbers of Baptists, Mennonites and other sects, the preponderance of Lutherans and Calvinists, inadequately supplied by ordained ministers from Europe, offered a promising outlet for the Anglican clergy's missionary zeal. The Presbyterians in the middle colonies, and especially those in New York and New Jersey, remained the dominant religious group, always hostile to the pervasive presence of the Anglicans.

These Anglican encroachments in the northern colonies, particularly in New England, were fundamental in intensifying the colonists' fears for their religious and political liberties at the end of the Seven Years War, and they have formed the general framework for the studies of Bridenbaugh and Calam. However, two other works approached aspects of the colonial Church which have previously been ignored. Bruce Steiner's *Samuel Seabury 1729-1796: A Study in the High Church Tradition*, published in 1971, relates the story of Samuel Seabury's life and his final consecration as bishop in Scotland. Steiner refers to the New England Anglicans' "native roots" (p. 5). He acknowledges the difficulties Seabury had with his congregations at Jamaica, Long Island, rejecting the sacraments of baptism and communion (p. 67). But Seabury's experience was shared by many Anglican clergy who ministered to converts from the Quakers. Samuel Seabury the elder's church and service in 1739 were reminiscent of a Congregationalist meeting house and service where people did not kneel at prayer. He refers to the minister's soul-saving-from-eternal-damnation sermons. However, he goes no further.

In 1978, Frederick Vandever Mills Sr. published *Bishops By Ballot: An Eighteenth-Century Ecclesiastical Revolution*. He came much closer than Steiner in recognizing the American influence on the colonial Anglican Church. He refers to the southern Anglicans' fears that resident bishops might "interfere with established ecclesiastical practices and customs" in America (p.x). He saw that the "169-year existence of the Church in the relative freedom and isolation of America encouraged deviations from traditional English ecclesiastical polity."(p. xi) Vestry control of the Church, including tenure of office for ministers, and the democratic nature of conventions of clergy which settled affairs in the absence of bishops are all mentioned.(p.xi) He recognized Samuel Johnson's flouting English tradition by introducing lay readers into the Church. The zealots for the American episcopate were native-born converts to the Church and their "zeal for their adopted faith was a major motivating force behind" the drive for a resident American bishop. (pp. 8, 43, 53) He points out that the majority of New England clergy were native-born recruits from the Congregationalists. (p.7) However, all these promising observations of an American clergy being driven by very serious developments in a Church transplanted far from its origins receive little further attention.

The efforts of some Anglicans in the middle of the eighteenth century to strengthen the powers of the Crown and to secure a complete Anglican establishment were not motivated merely by their determination to saddle the colonies with a political and ecclesiastical structure more closely akin to that of England. They were also out to save their own Church from the slow drift into ecumenism which insidious environmental attrition and the absence of resident bishops in America seemed sure to guarantee.

The rapid growth of the Anglican population had been achieved almost entirely from among the Dissenters, and the majority of the Anglican clergy in the northern colonies were, like their congregations, apostates from the Congregationalists and Presbyterians. Innovations which these converts introduced into the Church, together with modifications in Church organisation and ritual, necessitated by an environment different from that of England, gradually transformed the American Church so much that some of the clergy began to wonder how long the Church could retain its distinctive character among the Dissenting sects. Hence the clergy's preoccupation with obtaining the episcopate for America acquires a meaning previously ignored. Without the episcopate the drift into dissent would continue, and the Anglican High Churchmen's dream of elevating the authority of royal government and England's National Church in the colonies would come to nothing.

The conclusion of the Seven Years War aggravated friction between Anglicans and Dissenters since it was clear that the expected proposals in Britain for reorganizing colonial administration could favour the Anglican Church. The recently acquired lands in North America would provide grants of land to support the Anglican clergy and bishops. The Dissenters were sure, and many Anglican clergy hoped, that the bishops would arrive empowered with political and civil authority. The fifteen years between the fall of Quebec and the colonists' revolt against Britain, however, demonstrated that the Anglican Church was far from being the unified institution that Bridenbaugh and Calam have described. The American clergy were not a monolithic contingent mouthing the sermons and publications of the Society for the Propagation of the Gospel; nor were they all bent on submitting themselves and their congregations to the autocratic dictate that governed the Church in England. The Revolution finally drove a wedge between the clergy, compelling them to show their political and ecclesiastical hue that bridged the two extremes between the High Church Tory and the Low Church Whig. Furthermore, the Revolution separated the clergy from the laity, most of who proved to be a great disappointment to the English prelates and politicians who had hoped to foster through the Church of England a loyal colonial citizenry. The Anglican Church in the northern colonies, and the century-long struggle to bring bishops to America, then, must be viewed in the light of the distinctly American character the Church had come to assume in the eighteenth century.

From this study I have substantially excluded the Church south of the Delaware River because in the two most populous colonies of Maryland and Virginia the Church enjoyed a legal establishment, which, until the middle of the eighteenth century embraced the majority of the population. The Church had been introduced with the first settlers at Jamestown, and in 1619 the House of Burgesses made provision for land and taxes to build churches and to support ministers. The Maryland Assembly, too, in 1703 made a similar provision for its clergy, though seventy years earlier Lord Baltimore had intended his proprietary colony to be a refuge for Roman Catholics.

From the outset, the Church in Virginia had come under the control of the vestries which had gained the right to present their clergy to the royal governor for induction. But even this procedure was generally ignored since the induction by the governor took away the vestries' right to dismiss their clergy – a privilege the laity preferred not to lose in a land where worthy clergymen were hard to find. Similarly, the Maryland parishes gained control of their clergy through the vestries, though the proprietor held fast to his right of presentation and induction until the Revolution.

The Church of England in Maryland and Virginia was part of the cultural heritage the settlers had brought with them. During the colonial period the laity had reduced the episcopal power to that of ordaining and licensing the Church ministry. Even the Bishop of London's traditional right to supervise the clergy's conduct fell into disuse as the vestries acquired the right to hire and dismiss their ministers; consequently, the Church in the Chesapeake displayed none of the missionary zeal that characterized the Church to the north. In spite of vestry control, the Virginia and Maryland clergy enjoyed remarkable tenure during the eighteenth century, and it was only when Dissenters began to appear in large numbers in the Virginia back country in the 1740's, accompanied by revivalist preachers, that the Church establishment came under serious criticism.

The Anglican Church had a very stormy history in those colonies south of Virginia, as Dissenters had comprised a formidable proportion of the European population since the first settlers had arrived. Religious liberty proclaimed by the proprietors and trustees of the Carolinas and Georgia invited Scotch-Irish Presbyterians and a variety of Protestant sects from Europe. Therefore, when the Church was legally established in South Carolina in 1709, it had considerable support among the wealthy in Charlestown, but stubborn opposition elsewhere among the Dissenters, who numbered only a little less than half of the total population throughout the colonial period. The Church in North Carolina fared even worse where the Anglicans were always a minority. Several royal governors' attempts to establish the Church failed in the local assembly until 1765; yet even that Bill was ignored in most of the parishes which preferred to choose Presbyterian ministers. Georgia, like North Carolina, had a majority of Dissenters. They were guaranteed religious freedom by the charter of 1732. When the colony finally passed under royal government, the shadow of privilege eventually gained for the Church in 1758 was hedged in by so many restrictions that the Dissenters had conceded virtually nothing.

The Society for the Propagation of the Gospel did, however, assist the Church in the Carolinas and Georgia. But there was little encouragement to spend money in provinces where its missionaries were often resented and ignored, when congregations of converts were crying out for assistance in New England and the middle colonies. And even after the Society decided, in 1763, to direct a greater proportion of its funds to the south, only four missionaries were appointed after that date to Georgia (not surprising in a colony where Anglican worship was regularly observed in only three parishes). And one missionary was sent to South Carolina where the Society insisted that the provision made by the assembly to support the Church should be sufficient to maintain the clergy. North Carolina presented a more difficult problem for the Society, because there the population, scattered over vast areas of the inland, was either already lost to dissent, or Anglican in name only. Governor Tryon's efforts finally got a Bill through the local assembly in 1765 to provide a maintenance for the Anglican clergy, while, at the same time, guaranteeing the Bishop of London's authority over the clergy, a concession the North Carolina assembly gave grudgingly. Therefore, those clergy (almost all came from the British Isles) appointed to those provinces after 1765 were allowed a stipend of only £20 Sterling for a two-year period in order not to afford the local vestries any excuse to ignore the ministerial taxes provided by law. Even so, the Society sent only seventeen clergy to North Carolina after 1763, many of them were before long lost to the more secure Chesapeake parishes, or were worn out by the Dissenters' malice, or the unhealthy climate.

It was, therefore, in the north where the Society became most earnestly involved. The Dissenters felt threatened by the northern High Church clergy, craving attention from England's politicians and prelates in their bid to hedge America's potential for social levelling with an Anglican establishment. The Dissenters were not threatened by the contented incumbents of the Chesapeake establishment; nor did they fear the parade of immigrant clergy whose brief careers in the colonies further south left the Church still struggling for survival at the time of the Revolution.

Some of the terms I have used need explanation. The American clergy used the terms "Anglican" and "Episcopalian" almost synonymously when referring to themselves, and a few called themselves "Churchmen." However, there was a tendency, especially among the clergy in Connecticut, to prefer the term "Episcopalian" when they were writing about Church affairs in a strictly local sense. I have used the terms "Tory" and "Whig" to identify individuals' social and political views. I have applied the term "Loyalist" to anyone who remained loyal to the Crown.

This monograph, in its original form, was accepted by the University of Toronto as a thesis for the degree of Doctor of Philosophy in 1977. To complete the research I am deeply indebted to the International Nickel Corporation of Canada, and the Government of the Province of Ontario whose fellowships generously provided me with the financial assistance necessary to undertake this study. I would like to express my gratitude to the Library of Congress, the New York Historical Society, the New York Public Library, the Historical Society of New Jersey, the Historical Society of Pennsylvania, the Massachusetts Historical Society, The Connecticut State Library, the Connecticut Historical Society, the Delaware Historical Society, the Long Island Historical Society and the Church Historical Society in Austin, Texas for allowing me to use their resources. The staff of the State Library of New South Wales helped me in providing access to printed primary sources and secondary publications. I am also very grateful to the parishes of the Protestant Episcopal Church in the United States who permitted me to read their vestry records and other manuscript materials. I would like to express my gratitude to the University of Toronto and the staff of the Robarts Library for their support and assistance. I am very grateful to Professor Arthur Worrall of Colorado State University in Fort Collins who directed my initial interest in the American Loyalists. Professor John Beattie in the History Department of the University of Toronto was always generous with his advice and support. Finally, I must express my gratitude to Professor William H. Nelson of the University of Toronto who gave me assistance and welcome advice during his supervision of the dissertation.

Chapter

1

Missionaries to the Americans

The Church of England was no stranger to seventeenth century Americans. It was legally established in Virginia soon after the first settlement, and by the end of the century it had become the established religion in Maryland's Roman Catholic refuge[1]. Even the settlements south of the Chesapeake had some form of Anglican settlement—though only nominal in many areas—before the colonies separated from Britain. In Virginia and Maryland the Church had generally been part of the colonists' cultural heritage, and except for groups of land-hungry Dissenters who made their way through the back country, it remained an acceptable institution until the mid-eighteenth century. South of the Chesapeake, the Dissenters, who had formed a large proportion of the population since the establishment of the Carolinas and Georgia, resented the taxes the local assemblies imposed on them to support the Anglican Church, which were associated in their minds with the privileged wealthy in the coastal urban centres.

The New England settlers knew the Church of England as a vestige of Roman Catholicism; a tool of the tyrannical Charles 1 and Archbishop Laud from whom they had fled to preserve their Congregationalist form of worship. Presbyterians and Quakers had made their homes in the middle colonies of New York, New Jersey,

---

[1] With the exception of the Separatists in Plymouth Colony, the established churches in New England also regarded themselves as "Church of England" in the seventeenth century. See: Perry Miller, Orthodoxy in Massachusetts, 1630-1650 (New York, 1970), and Edmund S. Morgan, Visible Saints: The History of a Puritan Idea (New York, 1963).

and Pennsylvania, and their dissent from the National Church gave them a common bond with the New Englanders, ever fearful of encroachments upon their religious and political freedom.

When William 111 chartered the Society for the Propagation of the Gospel in Foreign Parts (hereafter called the Society) in 1701 to provide clergy for his subjects in the American colonies who were destitute of religious instruction there were only three Anglican churches north and east of the Delaware River. The first of these was King's Chapel in Boston, built in 1688. Massachusetts Governor Edmund Andros had earlier offended the Congregationalists whom he compelled to share their South Church with the small Anglican congregation in Boston. Now Kings Chapel appeared as a physical reminder, a portent that their cherished independence of England's National Church was under threat. Governor Fletcher had granted the large tract of land on which the New York Anglicans built Trinity Church in 1693. The Anglican beginnings in these two provinces were ominous for both of these churches obtained their land and charters through royal favour. Charles 11's agent Edmund Randolph had intrigued to bring the first Anglican priest over to Boston, and Governor Fletcher had made sure that a bill passed in the New York Assembly to provide support for six Protestant ministers in the city's four counties was interpreted so as to give the Church of England an establishment at the Presbyterians' expense. In Pennsylvania no denomination claimed to be established, therefore, of the three Anglican churches, only Christ Church in Philadelphia was founded in peace with the Dissenters.[2]

The churches in the large towns supplied the needs of the wealthy merchants, royal officials, and others aspiring to recognition in the governor's circle, many of whom had naturally been Churchmen in England. Outside the large towns, however, particularly in the middle colonies, people battling to carve farms out of the wild were too poor to build churches and pay ministers, and for these folk the Society would recruit missionaries in the British Isles, allow them £20 to cover travelling expenses, and

---

[2] Michael G. Hall, <u>Edward Randolph and the American Colonies 1676-1703</u> (New York, 1960), pp.48,114,115; Arthur Lyon Cross, <u>The Anglican Episcopate and the American Colonies</u> (Conn., 1964), p. 34; Carl Brtidenbaugh, <u>Mitre and Sceptre: Translantic Faiths, Ideas, and Politics, 1689-1775</u> (NewYork, 1962), p. 117.

provide a yearly stipend ranging from £30 to £50 sterling. The missionaries took with them a small library of religious books which the Society periodically supplemented with prayer books, hymn books, and booklets – most commonly explaining to the laymen the importance and meaning of the sacraments.

The Society owed its foundations largely to the enthusiasm of Thomas Bray who, after a brief visit to the colonies in 1693 as the Bishop of London's commissary, engaged the interest of the leading Churchmen in England with his accounts of the dire need for clergy and churches in America. With the help of Bishop Henry Compton and the Society for the Propagation of Christian Knowledge, which had been founded a few years earlier to supply Bibles and Anglican literature to the needy in Britain, he brought the matter before William 111 who granted the new Society a charter in June 1701.[3]

From its beginning the Society directed its attention to the English settlers in America who it expected could be brought into the Church of England. The first two missionaries, George Keith and John Talbot, confirmed the reports Bray had brought back to England, and set about the work of converting the colonials with remarkable endeavour. The Quakers, in particular, interested Keith who had earlier forsaken the Presbyterians to become a Teacher among them in England before returning to the orthodox Anglicanism of his forebears.[4]

Apart from providing religious instruction, the Society considered that its missionaries were educators in a broader sense for many settlers, without teachers of any kind, were slipping beyond the pale of English civilization, or, at least, so ran reports from America. The work of the Society's priests, schoolteachers, and catechists was therefore to disseminate English culture and extend the Church among the settlers, thereby maintaining a cultural and political trans-Atlantic community.

There was ample work for the Society in the middle colonies, but when it established missions in New England, the

---

[3] Charles F. Pascoe, ed., Classified Digest of the Records of the Society for the Propagation of the Gospel in Foreign Parts, 1701-1892 (London, 1893), p.7.
[4] William Stevens Perry, The History of the American Episcopal Church, 1587-1883 (Boston, 1885), 2 vols. Vol. 1, The Planting and Growth of the American Colonial Church, 1587-1783, p.206.

Congregationalists naturally resented them, for these colonies were well provided with clergy and schools, and they felt that the Society, which ranked among its members the Archbishops of Canterbury and York, the Bishop of London, and many other Church dignitaries and wealthy laymen, was deliberately using its influential patronage and funds to undermine the Congregationalist Church. The Congregationalists considered themselves to be the established church in Massachusetts and Connecticut and only grudgingly conceded the Anglicans atoleration. But the Society, its missionaries and principal laymen, never accepted this distinction; they considered all of the American colonies to be within the provisions of the Society's charter.[5] The seal the Society adopted depicted, a ship with a minister standing at the prow, open Bible in hand, approaching a welcoming group of people standing on the shore exclaiming "Transiens adjura nos." Thus, when a small group of Anglicans, or Dissenters driven to separation by personal quarrels or theological disputes, requested the Society to "Come over and help us," the Society accepted the opportunity to extend the national church.

And the clergy were quick to single out for cultivation the "honest Proselytes," as Timothy Cutler called them, from the Dissenters attending Church for the novelty, or, like James Wetmore of Rye in New York, to "make a proselite" for the ministry of any promising young graduate. Proselytizing continued throughout the colonial period, and some newly founded congregations, like the one at Taunton, which the Bristol missionary in Rhode Island nurtured in the 1740's, which needed prayer books from the Society in order that they could learn the liturgy. And the Pomfret congregation in Connecticut, as late as 1770, built their church and hired their priest even before they had learned the liturgy. Hence, each new Anglican Church in the northern colonies, especially in

---

[5] The Massachusetts and Connecticut Assemblies' attempts to force Anglicans to pay taxes to support Congregationalist ministers was a constant theme in the correspondence between the missionaries and England. The Society's Secretary, Philip Bearcroft, informed commissary Roger Price in 1742 that the Massachusetts Charter did not permit its Assembly to create an establishment in America; however, he added, neither was the Church of England established in the American colonies. Secretary to Roger Price, Nov. 6, 1742, S.P.G. Correspondence, Series B, vol. X,186a.

New England, held the threat of Episcopal encroachment, and perhaps the eventual destruction of the New England religious system.[6]

The Congregationalist austerity had served the New Englanders well when their success required sacrifice, but by the turn of the eighteenth century several urban centres had grown up in the northern colonies, and the colonial upper class were ready to grasp the cultural wealth and sensual religious appeal of the Church of England. The Church's rich literary heritage and its splendid aesthetic ceremony offered the New England Americans a rational, serene and orderly alternative to their own ascetic culture. Contact with this wealth of Anglican literature shattered the Congregationalist Church in 1722 when five clergymen were converted to the Church and declared their intention of taking Anglican orders. John Dummer, Connecticut's agent in London, had sent Yale College a gift of eight hundred volumes to furnish its wholly inadequate library, among which were the works of Isaac Newton, Robert Boyle, Francis Bacon, and some of the Anglican writers like Bishop Tillotson. This sudden introduction to what Samuel Johnson termed the "new learning" finally led him, with two other scholars, Timothy Cutler, Rector of Yale College, and James Wetmore, into Anglican orders for three new missions the Society created for them. The Connecticut practice of denying church membership to those who could not claim a conversion experience meant that many people were denied baptism, thus opening the way for the Church of England to offer the sacraments to those people denied them by the Congregationalists. From that time the Church increased steadily until the Great Awakening finally cleaved the New England Congregationalists, and shook the Presbyterians in the middle colonies, leaving the Church a very considerable force.[7]

When evangelist George Whitefield stormed the American

---

[6] Timothy Cutler to Secretary, Dec. 30, 1742, S.P.G. Correspondence, Ser. B, X, 15; James Wetmore to Secretary, Dec, 28, 1747, B, XV, 116; Godfrey Malbone to Sec., May 2o, 1772, B, XX111, 435

[7] Thomas Chandler, The Life of Samuel Johnson (New York,. 1805), pp. 5, 10; Richard Warch, School of the Prophets: Yale College 1701-1740, (New Haven and London, 1973), p.103

colonies in 1739 many missionaries were afraid for their congregations, and some were affected by "this enchanting Delusion." Throughout the northern provinces Whitefield and his "Strolling Teachers" pronounced Anglican priests "unconverted" and "leading all under [their] Charge down to Hell." In Lewes, Delaware, William Becket noted that Whitefield had repeatedly preached from a balcony, and some people, including a few Anglicans, set up a sect for him. The missionary at Radnor, Pennsylvania, reported that Whitefield "raised such Confusion" that he "made a very great rent in all ye Congregations belonging to the Church of England." Some of his own congregation not only ran after him, they "adore[d] him as an oracle from heaven." Whitefield was, indeed, "ye immediate dictator of ye Holy Ghost." At Brookhaven, on Long island, Isaac Browne, one of Samuel Johnson's recruits from Yale College, lamented that in spite of all his troubles "Enthusiasm has got a hold." People claimed that "any convert is fit to be a Preacher and has a call from the Holy Ghost," needing no "imposition of Hands or license from any Body." If Theophilus Morris were to complain of anything in Connecticut, he wrote in 1740, it would not be the bad roads, it would be "the wretched fanaticism that runs high in this country, and a body would be apt to think higher than it did in England in Cromwell's time." The upheaval in Charles Brockwell's mission in Salem, Massachusetts, echoed the ugly scenes of the previous century. "Enthusiasm" he wrote "may be as memorable as was 1692 for witchcraft, for ye converted cry out upon ye unregenerate, as ye afflicted did then upon ye poor innocent wretches [that] unjustly suffered." However, Whitefield's antics soon drove them back to Church along with many bewildered Congregationalists. Samuel Johnson, long after, noted that during the Great Awakening "a multitude of people could find no rest for the Sole of their Feet till they retired into the Church as the only Ark of Safety."[8]

Though George Whitefield and his followers took only a few

---

[8] Ebenezer Punderson to Secretary, March 31, 1742, B, X, 39; Wiiliam Becket to Secretary, April 25, 1741, B, 1X, 95; William Currie to Secretary, July 7, 1740, B, V11, part 2, 199; Isaac Browne to Secretary, June 16, 1741, B, 1X, 79; Theophilus Morris to Secretary, September 15, 1740, B, V11, part 2, 53; Charles Brockwell to Secretary, Feb. 18, 1742, B, X, 37; Samuel Johnson to Archbishop, March 20, 1759, Lambeth Palace Library, vol. 1123, part 2, 130

"Giddy-Brained" Episcopalians from the Church, the Great Awakening did split the already uneasy Presbyterians who were preoccupied with internal disputes. The conservatives, largely of Scotch-Irish origin, who became known as the "Old Side" turned upon the "New Sides", those Presbyterians, often of New England stock, who took up Whitefield's denouncement of unregenerate clergy, and insisted upon a confession of spiritual awakening from clergy and laity alike. Similar divisions appeared among the New England Congregationalists where churches divided into "Old Light" and "New Light" factions. In some parishes the revivalist preachers carried almost entire congregations with them, and the undignified wrangling between rival factions left the conservative elements almost nowhere to turn except to the Church of England. The "Old Side" and "New Side" ministers did provide an alternative for them, but nevertheless, the Church of England benefited from the religious confusions.[9]

The Church in Connecticut more than in any of the other colonies benefited from the religious commotions as new congregations mushroomed, but the glowing reports to London from the clergy in the other colonies testified to considerable increases there too. Missionaries moving to more lucrative missions left behind congregations desperate at having their churches "Empty and Unsupplied" as New London's St. James vestry recorded in 1742, especially as many of the "Most cool and & Considering people" were turning to the Church of England. And older established churches embarked upon expensive extensions or more elaborate stone churches to replace temporary buildings, even designing them, as the Perth-Amboy missionary reported from New Jersey, so that they could "lengthen it, as the Congregation increases" which seemed most likely as "most of the Dissenters there, spawn of Tennant and Whitefield" were contributing "their assistance to the work."[10]

---

[9] Edwin Gaustad, The Great Awakening in New England (Gloucester,Mass., 1965), p. 74; Leonard Trinterud, The Forming of the American Tradition. A Re-Examination of Colonial Presbyterianism (Philadelphia, 1949), p.107; Richard Backhouse to Secretary, July 25, 1741 B, 1X, 104.

[10] Vestry Book of St. James Church, New London, April 19, 1742; Samuel Johnson to Secretary, April 6, 1742, B, X, 45; William Skinner to Secretary, Oct. 29, 1744, B, X11, 7.

The Great Awakening worked wonders for the Church at Yale College, too. Over twenty years later the church wardens of the Guilford church in Connecticut were to call Samuel Johnson "A Father and Friend." It was a title well-earned because he became the backbone of the Church in Connecticut, and his influence was felt throughout New England and the middle colonies. From his church at Stratford he guided young students at nearby Yale College, in New Haven, who were preparing for Anglican ordination. Correspondence flowed to the Society naming students, graduates, and Dissenting Teachers who were taking Holy Communion at Johnson's Christ Church in Stratford. The religious hysteria of the Awakening had impressed upon the minds of the Yale students the dangers inherent in a religious system based upon no higher authority than the views of cobblers and ploughmen. They saw in the Church constitution a model of eighteenth century British social and political stability which they thought they might use to counter the extremes that the American provinces faced. The apostolic succession theoretically placed Church government above human interference, and in its constitution Church and State were as weft and warp of fine fabric. .It offered an antidote to the pragmatic experiment in emotional individuality.[11]

The evangelicals, who seceded from Christ Church in Philadelphia to establish St. Paul's Church, were, twenty years later, still enamoured of George Whitefield's style of preaching. They wrote to him in August 1764, to enlist his help in gaining for them a minister like himself. "If he prays before & after Sermon Extempore, & can Preach without Notes it would be the more agreeable." A good voice, and an understanding of oratory would make him very welcome, they explained. The Reverend Walter Chapman of Wiltshire in England, whom Whitefield recommended to them, however, hedged his bets. Though he was used to writing his own sermons, he wrote, he might try to preach extempore. However, he could not promise to measure up to the talented Mr. Whitefield "who has been Thundering & Lightning, awakening enlightening comforting and refreshing, for upwards of 30 years." Twenty years earlier, Commissary Archibald Cummings of Christ Church, from which the St. Paul's enthusiasts had broken away, had held a very

---

[11] Church Wardens of Guilford to Secretary, July 8, 1768, B, XX111, 170.

different view of Whitefield and his kind. After the Christ Church congregation had insisted on Cummings giving the evangelist leave to preach from his pulpit, he declared Whitefield to be "enthusiastically mad."[12]

During the early 1740's many young men entered the Society's service who were to form the backbone of the Church in the northern provinces: Ebenezer Thompson at Scituate, Massachusetts; Hezekiah Watkins who went to New Windsor in New York; William Sturgeon who became the Society's catechist to the Negroes in Philadelphia; William Gibbs, Joseph Lamson, Ebenezer Dibblee, Jeremiah Leaming, and Richard Mansfield were among those who took charge of the various congregations in Connecticut. Several other Yale graduates were preparing for Episcopal ordination (which had to take place in England) during this period but later changed their minds, possibly being put off by the fate that befell John Checkley, son of the missionary at Providence, Rhode Island, who died of smallpox in London in 1744, or Barzillai Dean, who was lost at sea two years later, and Richard Miner who, having survived five months in a French prison, died in England soon after. At the Yale College commencement in September, 1748, the progress made over the previous few years was evident, for the presiding dignitaries included ten Anglican priests who were present to see two other priests, William Sturgeon, and Jeremiah Leaming, graduate M.A., and seven other students, about to take Episcopal ordination, receive their Bachelor degrees.[13]

To hold new congregations together until priests could be provided for them Samuel Johnson introduced a departure in Church procedure by allowing students preparing for ordination to

---

[12] Copy of letter to George Whitefield in New York from wardens and vestry, dated August 16, 1764, in St. Paul's Church vestry minutes, Aug. 6., 1764; Walter Chapman's letter quoted in St. Paul's vestry minutes, March 4, 1767; Archibald Cummings to Secretary, November 14, 1739, B, V11, part 2, 232

[13] Philip Bearcroft to Roger Price, Sept. 27, 1744, B, X111, 19; Philip Bearcroft to Gov. William Shirley, Mar. 25, 1745, B, X111, 62; Samuel Johnson to Secretary, Feb. 12, 1745, B, X111, 101; William Vesey to Secretary, n.d., B, X111, 207; Philip Bearcroft to Richard Caner, June 27, 1745, B, X111, 358; Edward Vaughan to Secretary, Feb. 14, 1744, B, X11, 2; Samuel Johnson to Secretary, Mar. 27, 1747, B, XV, 52; Philip Bearcroft to Samuel Johnson, Dec. 27, 1757, B, XV, 228; Samuel Johnson to Secretary, Feb. 10, 1747, B, X1V, 22; Henry Caner to Secretary, July 12, 1750, B, XV111, 12; Joseph Lamson to Archbishop of Canterbury, n.d., B, XV, 56.

perform as lay readers. Many of the Yale graduates who were later to play a vital role in the Church, such as Thomas Chandler and Samuel Seabury, the younger, gained their initial training in this manner. At Johnson's request the Society assisted the growing Church by appointing the lay readers as its catechists with an annual salary of £10 sterling. When Samuel Seabury, the elder, moved from Connecticut to Long Island, and had his son appointed as catechist to part of his mission, the system of lay readers began to assume a widely accepted place in the American Church. Though this was a departure from customary Church practice the Society further sanctioned Johnson's endeavours in 1742 by resolving to appoint only students preparing for Episcopal ordination as its catechists and school teachers.[14]

Johnson's solution to the lack of ordained priests caused concern among some clergy, in particular those originally from Britain. He explained to the Bishop of London in 1732 that having candidates for ordination read sermons and prayers "omitting everything that is proper to the priest's office" in "Villages & destitute places" was necessitated by American conditions. The Society, he explained, had "never intimated the least disapprobation" of the policy, and had given tacit approval by receiving for ordination candidates who had been trained in this way.[15]

The rapid growth of the Church, however, also contained seeds of discord, for, in Connecticut particularly, Dissenters who were converted to the Church brought with them a fiery, somewhat Puritanical zeal, which set them apart from Episcopalians in the other colonies. More specifically, they resented British clergy who had often been used to performing their parochial duties perfunctorily among indifferent parishioners. The Connecticut clergy could not tolerate the slightest suggestion of laziness or moral laxity among their colleagues. Earlier, Episcopalians had welcomed British clergy the Society had sent over when the Church was generally unknown, unsupported, and often confused with Roman Catholicism. . The developments of the 1740's changed this situation as Dissenting clergy and whole congregations were converted to the

---

[14] Samuel Seabury to Secretary, Sept. 30, 1748, B, XV1, 51; Philip Bearcroft to Roger Price, Nov. 6, 1742, B, X,188.
[15] Samuel Johnson to Bishop of London, June 4, 1732, Vol. 1, 245. Fulham Papers.

Church of England. Connecticut had less experience of British missionaries than the other northern colonies because the Yale defectors of 1722 had provided leadership from the early years of the Church's growth, but in the 1740' congregations were leaderless in spite of the many lay readers, for these, though they could catechise children and converts and read sermons on Sundays, could not perform the full service or administer the sacraments. Thus, at a time when entire congregations were strangers to the Church of England doctrines, they came in contact with British clergy who were strangers by speech and behaviour and lacked New England's puritanical background.

As early as 1743 Samuel Johnson recommended that the Society appoint only local people to missions in Connecticut as they were "generally much more acceptable to the people" than those who came "Strangers to the Conduct of things in these Countries."His fears proved to be well-founded for within a few years several British clergy had met with serious opposition from their Connecticut congregations. Explaining to the Society Theophilus Morris's problems he pointed to the root of the conflict between New England congregations and immigrant clergy. The Church was recruited from Puritan Society, he wrote; consequently it was "surrounded by Venomous enemies;"therefore their ministers had to display the highest moral standards and boundless zeal. While Morris was unsuitable for New England, Johnson suggested, "He might be useful under a regular Establishment ," presumably Virginia or Maryland where the Church was not under constant pressure to prove its worth.[16]

There was a common view in the colonies north of the Delaware that the southern colonies were a suitable dumping ground for unsatisfactory clergy. Samuel Auchmuty, rector of Trinity Church in New York, writing to the Society about James Lyons, who had run into trouble with his congregations in Connecticut and New York, advised that "dispatching him to North Carolina" would be a suitable solution. Samuel Johnson suggested to the Society Virginia or Maryland as a suitable place for Lyons to "begin the World a new," though he doubted he would be useful anywhere. However,

---

[16] Samuel Johnson to Archbishop of Canterbury, May 22. 1743, B, X1, 33; Samuel Johnson to Secretary, Dec. 3, 1743, B, X1, 37

when the Society sounded out the Governor of North Carolina, he refused to accept both James Lyons, and Thomas Brown, who was officiating at Albany in New York. Thomas Bradbury Chandler of Elizabeth Town, New Jersey, returned from Maryland in 1767 pleased with the morals of the people, but the Anglican clergy were "full as bad as has been represented to us, and perhaps worse." Of the forty-five clergy, he could count only five or six of good character.[17]

The Americans certainly had cause to complain. During the 1740's the Society dismissed four clergy and transferred three others accused of misconduct. Three of these were from Ireland, one was a Scot, and two others were almost certainly from the British Isles, while only one was an American. The American was Jonathan Arnold, a former New Haven Congregationalist Teacher, who became the Society's missionary at West Haven and Waterbury in 1736. He moved to the Society's mission on Staten Island early in 1740. However, in 1744, he claimed that because his parishioners had failed to pay their subscriptions, he had been forced into "secular business." Finally, the Secretary of the Society accepted the Staten Island church subscribers' accusations of remissness and dismissed him.[18]

Jonathan Arnold was replaced by Theophilus Morris who had left Ireland in 1740, unable to secure a living. In less than eighteen months, charges of drunkenness led to his removal to New London.

---

[17] Samuel Auchmuty to Secretary, May 5, 1766, B, 11, 17; Samuel Johnson to Secretary, Aug. 5, 1763, Sept. 14, 1764, B, XX111, 185, 187; Samuel Auchmuty to Samuel Johnson, Aug. 7, 1766, p. 9, Hawks Papers, Johnson Mss. (Church Historical Society); Thomas Chandler to Samuel Johnson, June, 9, 1767, Herbert and Carol Schneider, eds., Samuel Johnson, President of King's College. His Career and Writings 4 vols.;(New York, 1929), I, pp. 406-409.

[18] Samuel Johnson to Secretary, April 5, 1740, B, V11, part 2, 30; Jonathan Arnold to Secretary, Dec. 26, 1744, B, X111, 285; Dr. Bearcroft to Samuel Johnson, June 10, 1745, B, X111, 354; Subscribers of Staten Island to Secretary, Nov. 22, 1744, B, X111, 287; Connecticut clergy to Bishop of London, Sept.. 11, 1735, Fulham Papers 1, 263.
19 Bishop of Dublin to Bishop of London, Nov. 19,1739, B, V11, part 1, 273; Thesophilus Morris to Secretary, Dec. 1, 1743, Nov. 21, 1743, B, X1,67, 66; Samuel Johnson to Secretary, Dec. 3, 1743, B, X1, 37; Roger Price to Secretary, Jan. 4, 1743, B, X1, 6; "Affidavits from individuals at Derby that Thesophilus Morris was Drunk" n.d., Testimony from West Haven Church Wardens, Dec. 10, 1743, B X1, 77,79; James McSparren to Secretary, Dec., 1743, B, X1, 21.

This appointment was indeed unfortunate because the congregation there had wanted a New Englander. Very soon Morris was again facing charges of drunkenness. However, while Morris admitted to occasional drinking, that was not the entire story of his troubles, for he, like other immigrant clergy, was simply not used to American conditions. He preached well, Samuel Johnson informed the Society, but the "Suddainness & Impatience of his Temper... & want of making Allowances for the Temper & Prejudices of the Country" aroused his congregation against him. Without a house and glebe at New London, the priest lodged with the local butcher under whose careful eye his " innocent Freedoms were often construed into Crimes, necessary Refreshments into Intemperence" and before long even the butcher lost his business among the Episcopalians. In December, 1743, he took the advice of three of his colleagues and went to one of the Society's missions in Delaware where he died on arrival. James McSparran advised the Society not to replace Morris at New London until that mission should provide a house and glebe for the minister. [19]

The Derby congregation in the West Haven mission gave the same treatment to Morris's successor, James Lyons, a former Presbyterian minister in Pennsylvania before conforming to the Church. They refused to have this "Irish Teague & Forreigner" and declared they would not supply a house and glebe, as the Society insisted, unless they could have a local-born priest. Lyons found the same "national spirit" among recently ordained Ebenezer Thompson and other New England clergy. Lyons' uncultivated manner and shabby dress did little to assauge their bigotry, and, to complicate matters, he refused to have Johnson's theology students reading in his mission, and after only two years in Connnecticut he moved to Long Island.[21]

[This is footnote 20, not 21]

Unfortunately, on Long Island, Lyons could not escape Samuel Johnson, neither could he escape the "Congregational Spirit" where "the Ministers are so dependent upon the People." Within a short while he was criticized for his "thread bare coat" and for officiating

---

20 James Lyons to Secretary, May 8, 1744, May 23, 1744, B, X111, 125, 128; Subscribers of Derby to Secretary, Jan. 24, 1744/5, B, X11, 183; Secretary to Roger Price, [Nov. 6, 1742], B, X, 188.

in Church "in a lay Habit, with a tolerable blew Cloath." All this he blamed on having to support his family solely upon the Society's bounty. Further, he became involved in a dispute with Johnson's nephew, Floyd Smith, over a horse. His acquittal did not remove the taint of being on the wrong side of the influential missionary at Stratford.[21]

Time appears not to have mellowed the New England Episcopalians' parochialism. In 1772, Godfrey Malbone, one of about three Anglicans living in Pomfret, Connecticut, having finally recruited sufficient numbers of disaffected Dissenters to join the Church, found that he had no ordained Anglican clergyman to accept the Society's bounty to minister in Pomfret's recently built church. Henry Caner 1of King's Chapel in Boston recommended Richard Mosely, late chaplain of the man-of-war Salisbury. However, Malbone found that he could not recommend Mosely for a settled mission because he had "met with the Fate, of all Strangers that come among Us, to be censured for a Freedom and Openness which do not exactly correspond with our Manners or the Taste of the Country." Consequently, the Society appointed Mosely to its Litchfield and Cornwall mission, far from Pomfret, where he was rejected in favour of that parish's own choice. Richard Mosely did, however, prove to be suitable at Johnson Town on the Mohawk River in New York where he apparently served with satisfaction until 1774 when ill health forced him to resign.[22]

Three other clergy, Stephen Roe and a man named Blackall, both from Ireland, and William Lindsey from Scotland, had trouble also during the 1740's with the American Episcopalians. Blackall's "Imprudent behaviour" in Pennsylvania drove away part of the Pequea congregation, and the Society dismissed both William Lindsey from the Bristol mission in the same province, and Stephen Roe, bigamist and father of an illegitimate child in Boston, from King's Chapel in Boston. Roe, in particular, upset Roger Price at King's Chapel and the senior clergy in Massachusetts because they claimed that Roe had arrived with a bad character, yet the Society

---

[21] James Lyons to Secretary, Oct. 20, 1761, Oct. 9, 1762, Oct. 8, 1763, Sept. 14, 1764, Oct. 10, 1764, Oct. 17, 1766, B, 111, 196, 200,202, 204, 205.

[22] S.P.G. Journals, X1X, 292, 371, 335, XX, 158.

had allowed him a very generous bounty.[23]

The Massachusetts Church, though not as closely knit a community as that in Connecticut, also learnt in these early years that American clergy were more suitable than immigrants. Alexander Malcom, a Scot, had tried school teaching in Queen Anne County, Maryland, and then New York before taking holy orders. When he resigned the Marblehead mission in 1745, the vestry nominated for ordination and appointment as their minister Peter Bours, a Newport-born Episcopalian and son of a Rhode Island Council member, because, they claimed, some of the Society's British missionaries were "not so well acquainted with the Spirit & Temper" of American congregations. Perhaps Malcom's lack of acquaintance with the local "Spirit & Temper" accounted for his resignation letter stating that he found living with them agreeable "excepting the hardship of spending every year a good deal of money out of my own pocket." He accepted a living in Annapolis, Maryland. Roger Price, when pushing his favourite hobby horse of a mission at Hopkinson near his King's Chapel in Boston, requested that the Society send "a native of Old England." James Lyons maintained, until the Society finally dismissed him in 1767, that his problems stemmed largely from his being a "forreigner" among the American clergy, and most of those immigrant clergy who did remain in New England felt with Lyons "the inexpressible Disadvantage" the "Europeans laboured under."[24]

---

[23] Richard Backhouse to Secretary, May 25, 1743, B, X1, 189; Philip Bearcroft to Richard Locke, April 3, 1746, B, XV, 212; Philip Bearcroft to Robert Jenny, April 8, 1746, B, XV, 212a, Secretary to Governor William Shirley, March 25, 1745, B, X111, 62.

[24] Alexander Malcom to Church Wardens of Marblehead, Oct. 28, 1749, B, XV11, 74; Alexander Malcom to Secretary, Nov. 30, 1749, B, XV11, 77; Wardens and Vestry of Marblehead to Secretary, Dec. 5, 1749, B, XV11, 78; John Usher to Secretary, Feb.12, 1752, B, XX, 25; Alexander Malcom to Secretary, no date, B, V11, part 1,267; Nelson Rightmyer, Maryland's Established Church (Baltimore, 1956), p. 201; Roger Price to Secretary, Jan. 4, 1743, B, X1,6; James Lyons to Secretary, Oct. 8, 1763, B, 111, 202. In his Mitre and Sceptre: Transatlantic Faiths, Ideas, Personalities and Politics 1689-1775 (New York, 1962), pp. 183, 255, Carl Bridenbaugh states that James Lyons' claim that "we Europeans are of the weak side" refers to the Anglican clergy among the New England Dissenters. Lyons was actually referring to the New England-born Anglican clergy's rejection of immigrant Anglican clergy. See James Lyons to Secretary, Oct. 9, 1762, Oct. 8, 1763, Sept. 14, 1764, B, 111, 200, 202, 204. David C. Humphrey, in his From King's College to Columbia 1746-1800 (New York, 1976), p.

The New Englanders certainly had their own view of what should be done in their churches. However, if the immigrant clergy actually spoke as Charles Brockwell wrote to the Bishop of London in 1752, one could hardly blame them for giving voice to their nascent nationalism. Having learned that his hopes of being appointed commissary in New England had been dashed, Charles Brockwell wrote that he had " vanity enough to lay an imaginary claim" to that office as he had "some education in an English University, had been 15 years in this Country" as the Society's first missionary at Salem. Denied the office of commissary, he requested a living in "Dear old England" on the same income as he received in America.[25]

These areas of friction might have been more easily overcome had there been a bishop in America to supervise the clergy. The Society held money in trust donated for the purpose of supporting an American bishop. It had acquired land in Burlington, New Jersey, for a bishop's residence, but the money and land were never used in the colonial period, for, though the American clergy made several requests for bishops during the first half of the eighteenth century, their petitions fell before the English Dissenters' opposition. The Bishop of London's responsibility for the colonial Church – a vague relationship which dated back to William Laud's elevation to the See of London in the early seventeenth century – was to remain ill-defined but tacitly accepted on both sides of the Atlantic until the end of the War for Independence. Three thousand miles weakened the bishop's authority, and, after 1748, the colonies were without even the limited supervision of commissaries.[26]

Bishop Henry Compton instituted the policy of appointing commissaries when he sent James Blair to Virginia and Thomas Bray

---

72, refers to the "coolness mixed with occasional bitterness in the relationship between foreign-born and colonial-born clerics." However, Scots-born, Rhode Island missionary James McSparren, in calling for " a just Ballance between ye Europeans and Americans" was not prompted by his annoyance at Samuel Johnson gaining the ear of the Society's Secretary in making missionary appointments in America. He was referring to Samuel Johnson's young lay readers making alterations in the Church liturgy.

[25] Charles Brockwell to Bishop of London, Sept. 15, 1752, Fulham Papers, V1, 27.
[26] Arthur Lyon Cross, The Anglican Episcopate, pp. 125, 246; S.P.G. Journals, XX, 11, XXIV, 185.

to Maryland in 1695. Dissatisfied with the vague legal relationship between the London diocese and the colonies, Compton had his authority specified in the royal instructions to the colonial governors, a policy which continued until his death in 1723. His successor, Edmund Gibson, obtained a royal commission, which more clearly defined his authority over the colonial Church. Edmund Gibson's successor, Thomas Sherlock, was a keen advocate of an American episcopate, and he adopted a policy which continued until the colonies became independent. He declined to accept a royal commission such as Gibson had accepted, thereby hoping to force the ministry to send bishops to the colonies. Therefore, after Sherlock's elevation to the See of London, no further commissaries were appointed to America, though the traditional relationship between the Bishop of London and the American clergy continued.[27]

Without episcopal supervision, the Church of England clergy, whether missionaries of the Society or independently supported by their parishes, had to rely upon the Bishop of London and the Archbishop of Canterbury for advice and the very limited supervision they could afford. However, all of the Anglican clergy could benefit from the bonds with the English Church that the Society provided. The annual anniversary sermons preached before the Society's members in February at St. Mary-le-Bow Church in London were eagerly awaited in America because they offered the only public indications of the Society's policies. Usually, they were received with great joy and appreciation, though occasionally the sermons displayed a lack of understanding -- even confusion – about the Church in America.

Frequently, the American Dissenters obtained copies of the anniversary sermons before the Anglican clergy and that caused some consternation. The English Dissenter Thomas Hollis was quick to supply copies of the sermons to America, which enabled the Dissenters there to broadcast their opinions of them well before the Anglican clergy were able to respond. King's Chapel Rector Henry Caner was stymied by the Boston Dissenters' comments on the Bishop of Llandaffs' 1768 sermon of which he knew nothing. "The Dissenters have received them from their friends and have made

---

[27] Arthur Lyon Cross, The Anglican Episcopate, pp. 29-34, 55-58, 113-125.

their remarks" he wrote "which the Missionaries for want of seeing them are obliged to be Silent."[28]

The anniversary sermons were a wonderful means of keeping the American clergy in touch with how the bishops thought of the mission to America, but the Abstracts of Proceedings, which were appended to the sermons, were a powerful conveyer of information between England and America and among the clergy in the various American colonies. The Society's Standing Committee received all correspondence from America. The Committee consisted of a small number of the Society's members in Anglican orders and was convened by the Secretary to the Society. He was invariably an eminent Anglican, perhaps an academic, who, once invited to fill that office, resigned his membership of the Society and took a salary for his services. After discussing the correspondence from America, the Standing Committee made recommendations to the Society's general monthly meeting for further consideration.[29]

Because of the time delay in the exchange of correspondence between England and America, the missionaries often received instructions from fellow clergymen in the colonies who had received the sermons and abstracts. John Lyon had left his parish in Taunton, Massachusetts, for Lewes in Delaware when he learned of his appointment to the Society's mission of Gloucester and Waterford in New Jersey. The news reached him from the Rector of King's Chapel in Boston, who had gained the information from the 1769 Abstracts of Proceedings.[30]

The Society's Abstracts served to keep the missionaries in touch with "home", as they often referred to England, and equally important, they supplied information about missionaries in other colonies who distance and inadequate transport might prevent them from knowing. The Abstracts could also be embarrassing to the colonial clergy. During the riots of 1765 over the Stamp Act, clergy who preached submission to Parliament's authority could become targets of Whig abuse when summaries of their letters were included in the Abstracts for all to read. Some clergy requested that

---

[28] Henry Caner to Secretary, May 5, 1768, B, XX11, 122; Thomas Hollis to Jonathan Mayhew, March 4, 1765, Thomas Hollis Papers.
[29] S.P.G. Journals, XIX, 378, 382.
[30] John Lyon to Secretary, Oct. 25, 1769, B, XXI, 170.

their letters at that time, and, again when Independence was declared, not be included in the Abstracts. Writing from Boston in June, 1775, Joshua Weeks explained to the Society the commotions in Marblehead which forced his family to seek refuge with Jacob Bailey on the Kennebec River, and his own flight to Boston. He requested the Society not to quote his letter in the Abstracts, knowing well that he could endanger his friends. The Rector of Trinity Church in New York, marking his letter to the Society in May, 1765, "Private", urged that the name of the Society's corresponding member St. George Talbot of New York "be as little mentioned as possible in the Society's Abstracts" because "his character, I must confess, among us, is really bad" and his name published in the Abstracts would give the Dissenters grist for their mill. Samuel Auchmuty's warning was a little difficult for the Society to observe because Talbot was a great benefactor to numerous churches in Connecticut and New York. St. George's Church in Milford, Connecticut, was named after him, and his estate was willed to the Society on his death.[31]

When submitting their biannual notitia parochialis, missionaries had a printed list of questions to answer. If missionaries were able to answer all the questions, the Society could know the population of their parishes, how many were already baptized, how many had been baptized in the current year, how many were Roman Catholics and how many were "Heathens and Infidels." Some clergy, like John Pierson in Salem, New Jersey, in 1739, could not report with accuracy, because of the twenty five mile extent of his mission. However, missionaries could inform the Society of the number of baptisms, catechumens, and communicants.[32]

A number of missionaries warned the Secretary that some clergy were exaggerating the numbers of communicants in their missions. Philip Reading wrote from Delaware in 1766 that clergy who wrote

---

[31] John Beach to Secretary, April 22, 1766, B, XXIII, 37; Luke Babcock to Secretary, March 22, 1776, B,III, 21; Vestry Minutes of St. Peter's Protestant Episcopal Church, Milford, Connecticut, 1765 and 1770; Samuel Auchmuty to Secretary, May 31, 1765, Jan. 17, 1771, April 25, 1771, B, II, 12, 38, 39; St. George Talbot to Secretary, Sept. 10, 1762, B ,II, 207; Ebenezer Dibblee to Secretary, March 25, 1761, B, XXIII, 93; Joshua Weeks to Secretary, June 2, 1775, B, XXII, 258.

[32] John [Pierson] to Secretary, May 10, 1739, B, VII, part I, 167; "The Printed Notitia Parochialis" follows item VII, part I, 167.

"pompous descriptions of their services" bring "invidious remarks" from the Dissenters. Mather Byles, at Christ Church in Boston, was at pains to state correctly the numbers of his congregations and communicants to avoid giving the Dissenters cause to "raise a violent Clamour." But it appears that clerical errors were made during the process of compiling the Abstracts. William Andrews and Ebenezer Dibblee in Connecticut, and Leonard Cutting on Long Island pointed out errors in the Abstracts which inflated their numbers of communicants. Archbishop Thomas Secker knew well how the Dissenters' minds worked. He urged Samuel Johnson, in March 1763, to inform himself or the Society if any missionaries were exaggerating accounts in their notitia parochialia. Errors of that kind could spur the Dissenters to scorn at a time when the Society was under fire for proselytizing in New England while neglecting the Indians and the needy in the frontier settlements.[33]

The correspondence from America touched upon almost every aspect of colonial life as well as Church affairs. Peter DeLa Roche, missionary to the French and English at Lunenburg, Nova Scotia, needed advice on what to do about a French settler accused of abusing his thirteen year old daughter. The French congregation was divided over the matter and the missionary had no books to help him. Some clergy sought publication details of books they had heard of, others needed advice about how to cope with laymen who, for example, denied the sacrament of baptism to their children. To help its missionaries, the Society provided libraries to each mission, which were placed in the care of the church wardens. The same authors appeared in the missionaries' inventories: Potter, Tillotson, Patrick, Whitby and Blackall, among others. They often requested material on infant baptism, for example, or collections of sermons. William Currie reported that at his mission in Pennsylvania, Richard Allestree's Whole Duty of Man "is now in great Esteem by hundreds of people who knew nothing of it before [George] Whitefield Condemn'd it," and " I have given away all I had by me, and have

---

[33] Philip Reading to Secretary, Sept. 5, 1766, B, XXI, 196; Mather Byles to Secretary, April 14, 1769, B, XXII, 77; Ebenezer Dibblee to Secretary, July 6, 1762, Samuel Andrews to Secretary, July 1, 1767, B, XXIII, 96, 14; Leonard Cutting to Secretary, Dec. 28, 1768, B, II,144; Archbishop to Samuel Johnson, March 30, 1763, Lambeth Palace Papers, vol. 1123, part 3, no. 300.

purchased some at [my] own charge."[34]

Some lonely missionaries needed an encouraging word as they neared retirement. In 1772, Isaac Browne implored the Secretary to write to him once in a while to encourage him in "this wearisome Pilgrimage." The Society's "Bounty and kind support," he wrote, had allowed him to educate his two sons, one for law, one for physic. A few of the immigrant clergy became fascinated by America's wild life, though few went so far as Roger Price who treated the Secretary with a pair of American tortoises, even though it took considerable persuasion to get a ship's captain to take them aboard. The relationship between the Society and its missionaries became very dear, especially when they felt estranged from their Dissenter neighbours in the midst of constant bickering over the Church's presence in New England. The Society's Secretary was a sympathetic friend in whom they could confide their grief. So close was the relationship that when William McGilchrist, the missionary at Salem, Massachusetts, died during the Revolutionary War, in 1780, he bequeathed his American funds and outstanding salary, together with his library, to the Society.[35]

Apart from advice and the Society's annual salary, its gratuities, usually amounting to £20 sterling, which it allowed to missionaries in distressed circumstances, or £10 sterling to cover removal expenses to new missions, were a real blessing which strengthened their ties with England. The Society could not go so far as to comply with the wishes of its missionary John McDowell, at St. Phillip's Parish in North Carolina, whose executors requested that it take his son under its care when he died in 1764. Nor could it comply with a similar request that it provide for the orphans of its missionaries, but it did have a policy of allowing a half year's salary to their widows. Not many clergy were in so fortunate a position as the rectors of Trinity Church in New York whose widows were allowed a pension for life. However, the Society did make a generous annual

---

[34] Peter De La Roche to Secretary, August 26, 1776, Nov. 28, 1771, B, XXV, 207, 174; Wardens and Vestry, St. George's Church, Schenectady, to Secretary, June, 1774, B, III, 14; Solomon Palmer to Secretary, Nov. 1, 1768, B, XXIII, 314; William Currie to Secretary, Sept. 28, 1741, B, IX, 111.

[35] Roger Price to Secretary, Oct. 6, 1749, Secretary to Roger Price, Oct. 5, 1749; B, XVII, 73, 208; Isaac Browne to Secretary, April 6, 1772, B, XXIV, 49; S.P.G. Journals, XXII, General Meeting, Oct. 20, 1780.

contribution to a corporation, founded in the northern provinces, in the 1760's, to support the widows and children of Anglican clergy.[36]

The position of Secretary to the Society naturally incurred heavy responsibilities and was entrusted to eminent clergymen who received a professional salary for their services. Between 1740 and 1785, when the Society's association with the American States came to an end, the position was held by only four people, each one resigning after many years of service, a situation which provided a degree of stability to the missionaries who all felt a strong bond with them. While in London for ordination, it was the Secretary with whom the candidates had the closest contact, and who often provided useful advice about what to expect from the bishops who were to examine them.

The financial cost and danger of the journey to England were prohibitive for some, though for those who were able to go it remained a memorable experience. On February 16, 1760, when the Massachusetts country boy Jacob Bailey, aboard the Hind, neared Spithead, he "could not forbear shedding tears" at the first sight of British shores. The journey had taken five weeks. Eight years later, William Ayers of Philadelphia and William Frazer, who had been in America only three years, spent seven weeks together at sea. Seventeen years earlier, Thomas Bradbury Chandler had to endure a nine week return voyage to Elizabeth Town, New Jersey. Samuel Cooke, who became his neighbour and close friend at the Shrewsbury mission, arrived in New York at the same time as Chandler after eleven weeks at sea. The journey was harrowing and could be frustrating. Scotsman Alexander Murray set out from London on July 2, 1762, to board ship in Portsmouth, from whence he sailed to Halifax, Nova Scotia. He finally reached Philadelphia on December 10, minus some of his belongings stolen by the ship's steward.[37]

---

[36] S.P.G. Journals, XVI, 202; Church Wardens and Vestry, St. Phillip's Parish, North Carolina, to Secretary, April 7, 1760, B, V,68; John McDowall to Secretary, July 3, 1761, B, V, 74; Corporation of Trinity Church Minutes of Vestry, May 27, 1784, May, 1, 1788.(Possession of the rector)

[37] William S. Bartlett, ed., The Frontier Missionary: A Memoir of the Life of the Rev. Jacob Bailey (New York), 1853, p. 57; William Frazer to Secretry, Oct. 20, 1768, B,

The trip "home" was a very costly business, even though successful candidates for ordination received the £20 King's Bounty to defray their expenses. William Clark and John Wiswall paid £80 each to gain ordination. As an added bonus, Clark contracted smallpox in London before returning to a very disappointing clerical career in Dedham, Massachusetts. The cost of ordination was only the beginning of John Wiswall's burdens. When he arrived at his mission in Falmouth, Massachusetts, he kept school, became a proprietor of his church, purchased a pew, and collected £100 sterling from visitors in order to help finish building the church. Agar Treadwell returned to America with Alexander Murray in 1762. He died in Trenton, New Jersey, after only three years as priest. The voyage to England, and the expenses later incurred because of ill health, left his widow poor. Provost William Smith of the College of Philadelphia begged the Society to afford her a gratuity, in addition to the customary six months salary allowed to widows of its missionaries. Similarly, Abigail Bours, the widow of the Marblehead missionary, had to request help from the Society in 1762 because her recently deceased husband "having had the greatest part of [his] Fortune expended on his Education and Voyage to England to receive holy Orders." Nathaniel Evans borrowed £40 sterling to go to England but did not live long enough to repay his debt. Aeneas Ross, after fulfilling the requirements for ordination, and appointed as assistant to his father at Immanuel Church in New Castle, Delaware, had to apply to the Archbishop of Canterbury for his return fare to America in 1741. Few were as fortunate as Joshua Weeks whose costs for ordination were met by St. Michael's Church in Marblehead, Massacusetts, or Ebenezer

---

XXIV, 238; Thomas Chandler to Secretary, Nov. 11, 1751, Samuel Cooke to Secretary, Nov. 27, 1751, B, XIX, 91, 92; Alexander Murray to Secretary, Aug. 6, 1762, April 9, 1763, B, XXI, 98, 100. Alfred Grant's Our American Brethren: A History of Letters in the British Press During the American Revolution, 1775-1781 (North Carolina, 1995), p. 12 provides asummary of the time it took for letters from London to reach American ports between May 1778 and February 1781. Julia M. Flavell's article "Government Interception of Letters from America and the Quest for Colonial Opinion in 1775", William and Mary Quarterly, vol. LVIII, number 2, April, 2001, pp. 403-430, notes that Post Office Packet Boats were quicker than the merchantmen and men-of-war; they could do the trip from America to England in one month.

Kneeland, whose passage to England was paid by the wealthy Boston merchant John Rowe.[38]

Nevertheless, in spite of the difficulties facing candidates for ordination, once in England, they did not find the process very threatening. The Society would not recommend a candidate to the Bishop of London for examination unless he had a parish to return to in America. Since more candidates in England were being ordained than there were vacant livings, the Society was wise, especially as most clergy in the northern provinces were supported in part by its funds. The candidate should normally be twenty four years of age before being ordained, but this requirement was waived for Americans. Because of the cost and travelling involved, Americans were often admitted to deacon and priest orders in the same week; canon law forbade the ordination of a candidate being admitted into both orders on the same day.[39]

Jacob Bailey arrived in England with letters of recommendation from Henry Caner of King's Chapel in Boston. His experience was probably typical of that of other American candidates for ordination in London. He had an introduction to a well-known bookseller who directed him to lodgings used by other Americans in London for ordination. The same day he met Charles Greaton who was seeking ordination for Boston's Christ Church. His parents were comunicants of King's Chapel and, like Bailey, he carried a reference from Henry Caner. The following day they visited Dr. Bearcroft, the Society's Secretary. Later they went to Lambeth Palace to meet Archbishop William Secker. After half an hour of conversation, and after reading the recommendations they had produced, he declared

---

[38] William Clark to Secretary, April 15, 1774, B, XXII, 147; John Wiswall to Secretary, Aug. 11, 1775, B, XXII, 269; William Smith to Secretary, Dec. 13, 1765, B, XXIV, 199; Abigail Bours to Secretary, May 10, 1762, B, XXII, 76; Edward Evans to Secretary, no date, B, XXI, 60; Clifton K. Shipton, Harvard Graduates, (Boston, 1970), XIV; William L. Sasche, The Colonial American in Britain (Connecticut, 1956), p. 74; Aeneas Ross to Archbishop of Canterbury, Jan. 10, 1740, April 2, 1741, B, VII, part 2, 183, 185.

[39] Norman Sykes, Church and State in England in the Eighteenth Century (Connecticut, 1962), p. 110; Arthur Middleton, "The Colonial Virginia Parson," William and Mary Quarterly, XXVI, number 3, pp. 425-440; S.P.G. Journals, XVII,532; Edward Winslow to Secretary, Sept. 4, 1764, B, XXII, 274.

that he had no scruples about admitting them to ordination.[40]

The following day Bailey was examined by the Bishop of London's assistant, Dr. Nicholls, who had him translate part of the Greek New Testament into either Latin or English. He was then asked to translate parts of Grotius' de Veritae into English. Finally, he had to translate the Thirty Nine Articles into Latin and explain their meaning in English. Bailey passed the examination with flying colours. Two days later, the Bishop of Rochester admitted him to deacons orders at Fulham Palace. Two weeks later, the Bishop of Peterborough ordained him priest at St. James' Church. All that now remained was for him to pay the eleven shillings for the cost of his deacons orders, half a guinea for priests orders, half a crown to the man who attended at the alter, and one pound eighteen shillings and six pence for his licence from the Bishop of London. Finally, he had to pay a further one pound eighteen shillings and six pence for the Bishop of London's licence to preach in America.[41]

Soon after that, Jacob Bailey's brush with England's noble society came to an end. From the Society he collected the royal bounty of £19.7.6 that all American clergy received after ordination, and half a year's salary from the Society's banker before returning to New England with James Greaton on a frigate that breezed home in a remarkably short thirty two days. Bailey was heading for his mission at Pownalboro on the Kennebec River, with the Society's annual bounty of £50 sterling per annum, "favourable even beyond [his] most sanguine expectations." Greaton would go to a troubled career at Christ Church in Boston.[42]

Few American candidates for ordination would experience the personally tailored introduction as Jacob Duche. In December, 1762, William Smith, Provost of the College of Philadelphia, was at hand to tutor Duche in the ordination process. When Smith accompanied his fellow Christ Church, Philadelphia, protégé to see the Bishop of London, he was "frightened out of his almost." After that meeting they visited. the Archbishop of Canterbury with whom they dined.

---

[40] William S. Bartlett, The Frontier Missionary, p. 61; Henry Caner to Bishop of London, Oct. 26, 1759, Fulham Papers, XXII, [145], Henry Caner to Secretary, Oct. 28, 1759, B, XXII, 99.
[41] William S. Bartlett, The Frontier Missionary, pp. 61-65
[42] William S. Bartlett, The Frontier Missionary, pp. 66-67.

After dinner, Duché was examined. Then he was summoned to the Archbishop's "Closet, where he gave him [Duché] so grand a lecture on the Ordination Service," as Smith had "never before heard."[43]

Thomas Coombe, another Philadelphian, went to England for ordination in 1768, but he declined to take advantage of the age dispensation, because to do so would disqualify him from accepting a living in England. At that time he was waiting for a call to Christ Church in Philadelphia, which was necessary for him to avoid having to return to England at a later date to obtain a licence from the Bishop of London. American candidates were required to preach in the London churches, but for Coombe, still only in deacons orders, it was an opportunity to prove his worth beyond doubt. He enjoyed enormous popularity as a preacher while basking in the company of Benjamin Franklin and Mrs. Macauley, that "Amazon of Literature." He was in no hurry to return to America, where he would depend on the caprice of lay subscription, when he had the prospects of a secure living in England.[44]

For those clergy in the American provinces who were not missionaries, an annual fee of two guineas allowed them the privilege of a correspondence with the Society's Secretary, one which often proved useful, for most clergy needed the ear of the Bishop of London or the Archbishop at one time or another in settling disputes with the Dissenters, or to obtain charters for new churches. Influential lay persons were also welcomed as corresponding members of the Society. Such persons could offer social prestige and political influence to the Church and the Society. In 1762, George Harrison wrote to Archbishop Secker, whom he had known in England as the Bishop of Oxford, requesting help in obtaining the Society's support for a mission at Flushing and Newtown on Long Island. Colonel Skene of Skenesborough, in New York, appeared before the Society with a recommendation from

---

[43] William Smith to Richard Peters, Dec. 14, 1762, William Smith Papers, II, 105. (Historical Society of Pennsylvania)

[44] Thomas Coombe to William Smith, March 12, 1770, William Smith Papers, I, 70.(Church Historical Society, Texas); Thomas Barton to Secretary, Oct. 18, 1768, B, XXI, 18; Thomas Coombe to his father, Nov. 1, 1769, Oct. 3, 1769, Dec. 6, 1769, June 6, 1770, Oct. 8, 1770, Aug. 29, 1771, Thomas Coombe Papers: Correspondence and Business, 1765-1803. (Historical Society of Pennsylvania)

Governor William Tryon, in May, 1773. He presented the Society with a gift of two hundred acres of land to be used as a glebe for an Anglican minister. He also promised to build a church and a parsonage house. He donated a further gift of one hundred acres of land for the use of the minister and his successors. Among the impressive list of the Society's corresponding members were: Governor John Wentworth of New Hampshire; New York's Governor William Tryon; the governor of Nova Scotia, William Campbell; John Robinson and Joseph Harrison, collectors of customs in Newport and New Haven; the influential New York landowner Colonel Frederick Philips; Enos Alling, whose wealth served the Church well in the colonies, and St. George Talbot of New York, whose fortune went to the Society on his death in 1767.[45]

Apart from their relationship with the Society, the clergy also had other common bonds. Nearly all of the American-born clergy were graduates of one of the four colleges in Boston, New Haven, New York or Philadelphia, and some had been members of the same class. Many, too, were related through marriage, in ceremonies more often than not performed by fellow missionaries. The clergy enjoyed social engagements together as members of the philosophical societies, library companies, and medical associations since many of them were practising physicians.

During the first half of the eighteenth century, the Society relied upon commissaries in Boston, New York and Philadelphia for advice about American affairs, but after Bishop Gibson's commission expired it looked to a number of senior clergymen; consequently, the rectors of the old-established churches in the three principal cities, the missionary Samuel Johnson, the Provost of the College of Philadelphia William Smith became the Society's informants with the Secretary's permission to mark their correspondence "personal" for his attention. These and other leading Churchmen could also enjoy privileges denied to the Dissenters. When Samuel Johnson and Timothy Cutler conformed to

---

[45] S.P.G. Journals, XVI, 177, XIX, 25, XVIII, 483, XVII, 464, XIX, 421; Harry Monroe to Secretary, May, 22, 1767, B, III, 264; St. George Talbot to Secretary, May, 16, 1761; B, II, 206; Ebenezer Punderson to Secretary, March, 26, 1762, B, XXIII, 293; John Breynton to Secretary, Jan. 16, 1769, B, XXV, 135; George Harison to Archbishop, Jan. 2, 1762, Lambeth Palace Library, vol. 1123, part, 3, 244.

the Church of England in 1722, both were awarded the M.A. and Doctor of Divinity degrees by both Oxford and Cambridge Universities. This practice of rewarding Americans who worked for Church and State continued, and, often at the Society's recommendation, or by direct correspondence with the Archbishop of Canterbury or Bishop of London, honorary degrees could be obtained – a mark of scholarship and a sure sign of the coveted status of "gentleman." And for the long serving, lesser lights, such as Hugh Neill in Pennsylvania, a recommendation from the Society's Secretary might persuade the Archbishop to elevate them, also, to the status of gentleman scholar.[46]

This privileged relationship with the Society was a mark of high esteem, for these clergy were unofficially performing some of the duties which belonged to the commissaries, but it did not obviate the serious disability the Church suffered without a resident bishop. A bishop in America would have been able to make immediate decisions about the locations and needs of new missions, and he might have been able to help reconcile warring factions within congregations, which often emerged when deciding upon the choice of a new clergyman. Conflicts arising between missionaries seeking appointment to the same mission could have been resolved quickly instead of the inevitable resort to a protracted correspondence with London where the ultimate authority lay.

The resentment that the Dissenters felt about the rapid growth of the Church during the 1740's was intensified by the Bishop of Oxford, who, in his anniversary sermon before the Society, took advantage of the religious turmoil in the colonies to urge the appointment of a bishop for America. Coming from this apostate from the English Dissenters, Thomas Secker's rallying cry added insult to injury, and it brought upon him a loathing from the Dissenters which only increased with time. This sermon of 1741 was the beginning of Thomas Hollis's "fixt dislike" of that "Leviathan," Secker. In his correspondence from London with the New England

---

[46] Henry to Bishop of London, Nov. 6, 1762, Fulham Papers, VI, 46; Samuel Johnson to Secretary, May 31, 1765, January 21, 1766, B,II, 12, 18; Thomas Bradbury Chandler, The Life of Samuel Johnson. The First President of King's College, New York(New York, 1805), p. 73; William L. Sasche, The Colonial American in Britain (Westport, Conn. 1956), p. 78; Hugh Neill to Secretary, June 8, 1761, B, XXI, 112.

Dissenting clergy, Hollis never doubted that Secker's anniversary lecture was the "root sermon of all misrepresentations, rancour, & baseness" which underlay those that followed from "the Youngling Bishops" at St. Mary-le-Bow.[47]

As Bishop Secker pointed out, after only forty years in existence the Society could claim a remarkable achievement, for the Church of England could boast no less than fifty-five churches built, with many other congregations meeting in private homes. Three churches in Boston were a considerable inroad into the Congregationalist stronghold, and in New England's coastal towns from Portsmouth, New Hampshire, in the north, to Newport, Rhode Island, in the south, ten Anglican churches were served by the Society's missionaries.

There were no cities in Connecticut with the wealth and population of Boston, but there too, eight churches were built in the larger coastal towns, with several small chapels studded among the inland communities. Further south and west, the colonies of New York, New Jersey and Pennsylvania could claim similar achievements. On Long Island there were three churches, and north of Manhattan, churches were established at Rye, New Rochelle and Westchester. Thirty miles north up the Hudson River the church at Newburgh and the neighbouring communities, isolated among the rugged hill country, were served by one of the Society's itinerant missionaries. A further eighty miles separated Newburgh from the Society's most northerly reaches at the garrison church at Albany where the Mohawk River joins the Hudson.

To the west of the Hudson River in New Jersey the Society's missionary at Newark also officiated in the church on Staten Island. From Newark, along the coast to the entrance of the Delaware, and then north along the River to Trenton, the Society supported nine churches, while its aid reached a further ten churches between Philadelphia, and Lewes, situated midway down the Delaware peninsula, and as far inland as Lancaster in Pennsylvania.

The city churches were quite magnificent structures, but some of the rural churches were remarkable, too. In 1740, the Society's

---

[47] Thomas Secker, Anniversary Sermon, Feb, 20, 1741 (London, 1741); Thomas Hollis to Jonathan Mayhew, June 24, 1765, Thomas Hollis to Andrew Eliot, May 25, 1768, Thomas Hollis Papers.

Massachusetts missionary Charles Brockwell claimed that St. Peter's Church in Salem "for its beauty exceeds any in the province." In Derby, Connecticut, there was "a pretty neat church," while at Stratford, the existing church was soon to be replaced by a grander edifice, topped with a stately gold weathercock that would rise six feet above the church spire. The church at Newark in New Jersey could boast a "Stately and magnificent Fabrick of fine hewd Stone & Lime," the most spectacular in the province. And, in 1745, Richard Backhouse could claim that his Marcus Hook congregation had replaced their wooden structure with a bigger one of brick. His Chester church, in Pennsylvania, had built "a Handsome Belfry of Stone" big enough for three bells.[48]

It seemed that everywhere the Dissenters looked in the northern provinces they saw signs of the Church of England's presence, and when the Society opened its mission at New Haven, in 1752, within sight of Yale College, President Clap's toleration of the College's episcopal minority came to an abrupt end. Behind these advances was the Society with its intimate relationship with the prelates, whose political influence could always be called upon to gain favours for the Church. Between 1727 and 1742, the clergy in Massachusetts and Connecticut, with the help of the Society, the Bishop of London, and the Archbishop of Canterbury, waged an intermittent campaign against laws which taxed the Episcopalians for the support of Dissenting Teachers. In 1742, the Dissenters finally conceded victory to the Episcopalians, though several missionaries in the 1760's were still complaining that members of their congregations were being fined for refusing to pay the tax.[49]

With the help of the English prelates, the American clergy made

---

[48] Charles Brockwell to Secretary, Feb. 23, 1739/40, B,VII, part 2,[38]; Theophilus Morris to Secretary, Sept. 15, 1740, B, VII, part 2, 53; Elizabeth P. McCaughey, From Loyalist to Founding Father: The Political Odyssey of William Samuel Johnson (New York, 1980), p. 24; Samuel Johnson to Secretary, Sept. 29, 1744, B, XIII, 100; Edward Vaughan to Secretary, Dec. 17, 1743, B, XI, 165; Richard Backhouse to Secretary, Nov. 15, 1745, B, XII, 56.

[49] Elizabeth P. McCaughey, From Loyalist to Founding Father, p. 20; Philip Bearcroft to Roger Price, Nov. 6, 1742, B, X, 186a, 188; Susan M. Reed, Church and State in Massachusetts (Urbana, Illinois, 1914), chapter V; Connecticut clergy to Secretary, March 29, 1739, B, VII, part I, [42].

several attempts to promote Anglicans to positions in royal government. They habitually looked to London for help in furthering their cause, and support was usually forthcoming. In 1742, the Society's Secretary informed Roger Price, Rector of King's Chapel in Boston, that the recently appointed governor of Massachusetts, William Shirley, was a member of the Church of England and that he had been accepted as a corresponding member of the Society. In 1755, Samuel Johnson and Thomas Chandler joined with the Trinity Church clergy in an address to the Archbishop requesting that all future royal governors be Churchmen, and, in particular, they put forward the name of Colonel John Schuyler, a trusted friend and benefactor of the Church, as the man they wanted to be the next governor of New Jersey.[50]

In November 1765, the Vestry of Trinity Church in New York agreed to address the recently appointed Governor Sir Henry Moore for his protection of their rights and privileges in the interest of "true Religion and virtue." Again, when William Tryon arrived in New York, in 1771, Samuel Auchmuty wrote to the rector of Christ Church, Richard Peters, in Philadelphia, that our new governor "is all that Fame has reported of Him – The Gent – a good man . . . His behaviour at Divine Service is exemplary & truly becoming a Christian." His excellency, he continued, "has not been absent from church one Sunday yet. A glorious example!" And in the following year his excellency lived up to expectations. To St. George's Chapel he donated a "sett of Church furniture, Plate and Books" as a New Year gift, and a piece of plate valued at thirty guineas to Myles Cooper for his recent services in London "in procuring a Remission of the Quit Rents" on land belonging to Trinity Church.[51]

In 1770, an Anglican layman in Pomfret, Connecticut, went even further in search of favour for the Church of England. Godfrey Malbone wrote to the Bishop of Bangor that he was gathering support among the local Congregationalists to establish an Anglican church in that community in order to avoid paying taxes levied

---

[50] Secretary to Roger Price, Nov. 6, 1742, B, X, 186a; Samuel Johnson and Trinity Church clergy to Archbishop of Canterbury, Jan. 29, 1755, B, III, 324.
[51] Trinity Church Vestry Minutes, Nov. 15, 1765, Dec. 29, 1772, (possession of the Rector); Samuel Auchmuty to Richard Peters, Aug.18, 1771, Richard Peters Papers VII, 69 (Historical Society of Pennsylvania).

upon them to build, what they considered to be, an unnecessary new meeting house. His efforts to promote the Church were also spurred by his concern at the political disturbances over imperial taxation, especially in Newport, Rhode Island, which he had recently left for the tranquility of rural Connecticut. In his letter, he urged his old Oxford friend, the Bishop, to ensure that all government officers sent to America be members of the Church of England, and that they attend Church services regularly. Further, he added, all office holders in America should be Anglicans as "a very essential Step" to securing stability in the colonies.[52]

When a member of the New York Council lay dying, in 1768, Samuel Auchmuty, in one of his typical tirades against the Dissenters, urged the Society's Secretary to engage the Archbishop's influence to secure the appointment of an Anglican in his place. "His Grace & Friends of the Church," he wrote, should keep "a watchful Eye least we have another Presbyterian run upon us. The whole Council (except one) belong to the Church. That one came in, in a clandestine manner." These attempts to enlist their English friends' support were accompanied from time to time by requests that the ministry revise the charters of Connecticut and Rhode Island to provide those provinces with governors appointed by the Crown. Samuel Johnson sent such a proposal to Secretary Philip Bearcroft, in 1765, entitled "Proposals Regarding the Government of this [Connecticut] Colony." It recommended that the government of the colony should be passed back to the Crown. A change of that kind would allow the governor a negative vote, thus removing the Council from dependence upon the people.[53]

With the disposal of Crown lands in the hands of the royal governors in New Hampshire and New York, the Church, again, stood at a great advantage over the Dissenters. Governor Benning Wentworth allocated between 200 and 350 acres for the Church in each of 128 townships he had surveyed in the 1740's. When part of

---

[52] Godfrey Malbone's Deposition, Brookline, Sept. 28, 1769, B, XXIII, 429; Godfrey Malbone to John Bishop of Bangor, Feb. 9, 1770, B, XXIII, 432; Godfrey Malbone to Rev. East Apthorp, Croyden, England, Nov. 1, 1769, B, XXIII, 430.

[53] Samuel Auchmuty to Secretary, July 9, 1768, B, II, 29; Samuel Johnson to Philip Bearcroft, April 14, 1751, Herbert and Carol Schneider, eds., Samuel Johnson, President of King's College. His Career and Writings(4 vols.; New York, 1929), I, pp. 145-150.

that land was transferred to the administration of New York, Samuel Auchmuty, writing from Trinity Church, in 1767, in his customary egoistic manner, and almost purring with pride, announced to the Society that, at his personal request, Governor Sir Henry Moore had granted 24,000 acres to Trinity Church, and he had made a similar offer to King's College.[54]

The Ministry Act of 1693 which had given the Church an establishment in the counties of New York City, and the clergy's subsequent attempts to have it extended to other counties, made it almost certain that when the New York Assembly proposed raising funds by lottery for a college in 1746, the hostility between the Anglicans and Presbyterians would boil to the surface. Some Presbyterians, like the lawyer William Livingstone, would have had the college established on a strictly non-secular basis, but when the Assembly appointed a board of trustees to supervise the establishment of the college, the two Dutch Reformed Church members and the lone Presbyterian on the board were outnumbered by six Anglicans, whose influence was increased the following year when Trinity Church donated a block of land for the site of the new college. A college to inculcate Church principles, the clergy claimed, was essential now that the Presbyterian New Sides were establishing a college in New Jersey. The opposition that Livingstone, assisted by John Morin Scott and William Smith, jr., put up to the Anglicans over control of the college brought the close connection between the royal governors, the English prelates and the Society under bitter attack. Samuel Johnson's pleas to the Archbishop for the appointment of a resident bishop at this time were, of course, welcomed, but temporarily shelved. Nevertheless, once again Trinity Church took advantage of its royal patronage and wealth by offering Johnson the presidency of the college, who, being appointed simultaneously as assistant minister at Trinity Church on a purely nominal basis, would initially need no salary from the college funds. This manoeuvre, clearly intended to present their opponents with a fait accompli, finally helped the Anglicans gain a

---

[54] Philip Bearcroft to Governor [Benning] Wentworth, July 10, 1745, B, XIII, 355; Governor John Wentworth to Bishop of London, April 28, 1770, Fulham Papers, VI, 114; Samuel Auchmuty to Secretary, June 12, 1767, B, II, 24; Vestry Minutes of Trinity Church, New York, Feb. 6, 1767, Aug. 7, 1769. (Possession of the Rector)

royal charter for King's College under their control. And more manna fell from heaven in 1759, when Samuel Johnson wrote to "Dear Brother" William Johnson in Middleton, Connecticut, that the Society had donated £500 sterling to the College, and one of its members had bequeathed "a noble Library consisting of 1500 volumes."[55]

In Pennsylvania, where no denomination enjoyed any form of establishment, or official favour from the proprietors, the process of establishing a college lacked the bitterness which prevailed in New York. The College of Philadelphia, which developed from the grammar and charity schools supported by the Presbyterians and Episcopalians, received its charter a year after the New York Anglicans gained the charter for their college. William Smith, an Episcopalian from Scotland, was appointed Provost, with the Presbyterian, Francis Alison, serving as Vice-Provost, under the supervision of a joint Presbyterian-Anglican board of trustees. All was not peace and quiet in the College though, for the need to maintain a balance between the two parties on the faculty and board of trustees was a constant concern, but the ecumenical nature of the College lasted throughout the colonial period. Much of this success was no doubt due to the complicated structure of Pennsylvania politics, where many Anglicans joined with the Quakers to oppose the proprietor's privileges, while some Anglicans, William Smith among them, sided with the Presbyterians to uphold the proprietary government.[56]

William Smith's leadership of the Proprietary Party in Pennsylvania appears to be, at least in part, explained by his close connections with the Proprietor Thomas Penn. As Provost of the College of Philadelphia, Smith received £50 per annum from the Proprietor, who, in 1764, also allowed him a share of the receipts of the Chester County prothonotary office. The Proprietors also recognized the importance of supporting Smith's clerical colleagues.

---

[55] Carl Bridenbaugh, Mitre and Sceptre, pp. 144-145; David C. Humphrey, From King's College to Columbia, chapters 2 and 3; Vestry Minutes of Trinity Church, New York, April 9, May 14, 1754; Samuel Johnson to Mr. William Johnson at Middleton, Aug. 1, 1759. "Johnson Members of the Family" Box 2. (Connecticut Historical Society)

[56] Carl Bridenbaugh, Cities in Revolt: Urban Life in America, 1743-1776, (New York, 1964), p. 178

Thomas Penn went to great lengths to encourage Thomas Barton to give up his idea of seeking a better living in Maryland in 1768. His tireless work for the Church, his interest in assimilating the Germans and Indians made him too valuable an asset to lose. The Society increased his salary to keep him at Lancaster. Whether or not Thomas Penn influenced that decision, he knew of it. Furthermore, he made available the Proprietor's Costenega Manor, near Lancaster, for Barton's personal use. The Anglican church in York was built on land donated by the Proprietors, and St. Peter's Church in Philadelphia was also built, in 1761, on land they had donated. However, the mistrust between the English colonists, Ulstermen, Germans and Scotch-Irish, and the rivalry between the Anglicans and Old Side Presbyterians for religious dominance made life factious and uneasy. Thus, Pennsylvania was set apart from the New England provinces, which were ethnically and in religion far more homogenous. In order to assimilate the large numbers of German immigrants, co-operation between Anglicans, Presbyterians, Quakers and other groups called for toleration and co-operation.[57]

The missionaries in rural Pennsylvania were necessarily caught in the cross-current of political alignments; nevertheless, many of them privately supported the Anti-Proprietary Party. The intricacies of Provost Smith's political manoeuverings made it very difficult for them to feel at ease with him. While he was co-operating with the Presbyterians at the College, and as leader of the Proprietary Party he could also share in the antipathy that the rural clergy frequently expressed towards them. In one of his many, lengthy commentaries to the Society on Pennsylvania affairs, he wrote with satisfaction in 1768, that the Bucks County Anglican congregation, twenty five miles from Philadelphia, were building a church. They were being "greatly encouraged by many Quakers" (the mainstay of the Anti-Proprietary Party) "who at this Day declare themselves highly desirous of seeing the Church flourish, from a Fear of being over-

---

[57] James H. Hutson, Pennsylvania Politics 1746-1770: The Movement for Royal Government and its Consequences (Princeton, New Jersey, 1972), pp. 159-160; William H. Nelson, The American Tory (Boston, 1961), p. 41; Frederick V. Mills, Sr. Bishops By Ballot, p. 64; Vestry Minutes of Christ Church, Philadelphia, Aug. 19, 1761; Thomas Barton to Secretary, Oct. 18, 1768, B, XXI, 18.

run by Presbyterians." The missionaries in Pennsylvania, therefore, were more likely to share an affinity with the clergy to their north than with the clergy in Philadelphia who co-operated with the Presbyterians, and who even seemed to lean towards the Methodists.[58]

Their view of religious dissent, and their smug conviction that with royal patronage behind them they were engaged in a crusade for the National Church in the northern provinces, led many of the Anglican clergy to preach indiscreet sermons on the anniversary of the execution of King Charles I, in which they deplored the horror of regicide, and extolled the virtue of obedience to legitimate rulers. Charles Brockwell, King's Lecturer at King's Chapel in Boston, preached such a sermon and drew upon the Anglicans the wrath of Jonathan Mayhew from Boston's West Church in 1750. His "Discourse Concerning Unlimited Submission and Non-Resistance to Higher Powers" became a powerful missile in the Dissenters' arsenal against Anglican attempts to introduce resident bishops. On Guy Fawkes Day, November 5, 1751,1754, 1758, 1768, 1770, and the anniversary of "King Charles Martyrdom", 1735, 1746, 1747 and 1774, Isaac Browne preached at his missions in Brookhaven, New York, and later at 2Newark and Second River in New Jersey, on Romans 13: 1-2 "be Subject to the higher powers." He deplored that any people should in "a mock Court Arraign, try, and Execute their Father and King and ye Lords annointed." It is no wonder that he should continue with "'tis to be hoped, ye like will never be Again to the end of time," in the troubled times of the late 1760's and early 1770's. And secure behind British lines in New York City, Charles Inglis preached at St. George's and St. Paul's Chapels on January 30, 1780, "being the anniversary of the Martyrdom of King Charles I" a sermon entitled "The duty of Honoring the King." These sermons naturally brought boundless accusations from their enemies that they were teaching absolute submission to tyrannical rulers, and as the Seven Years' War came to an end the Dissenters were certain that the Church would be established in the new acquisitions, and

---

[58] William Smith to Secretary, Oct. 21, 1768, B, XXI, 261

probably in the seaboard colonies, too.[59]

The days following the defeat of General Braddock's expedition in 1756, when Thomas Barton's congregation in Pennsylvania would attend church bearing muskets and vowing they would die "Protestants & Freemen, sooner than live Idolators & Slaves" were soon to end. Four years later he could write to the Society of the "Happy Train of glorious Conquests" that would permit the propagating of the gospel – by which he meant "Anglican" – "far into America." He proposed that "the Lands belonging to the Romish Clergy in Canada" be used to support an Anglican bishop and missionaries in the newly acquired territory. For Alexander Murray, Barton's closest clerical neighbour, the fall of Quebec should lead to "the allotment of Lands towards the Support of Clergy Regularly Ordained in our Church," thus putting an end to the missionaries' dependence on their congregations' financial support. At Albany, New York, the Society's missionary John Ogilvie, who had been chaplain with the Royal American Regiment at Niagara, gave thanks for the victory in Europe and America by land and sea. Preaching at St. George's Chapel in New York in January, 1761, Samuel Auchmuty told his hearers that the day the "Gallic encroachments commenced" in north America was an "Event, by far ye greatest yt ever happened in this American World," because it led to the entire "Conquest of Canada." The Marblehead missionary Peter Bours was overjoyed in July 1761, at the news of the "Subjection of the whole Country of Canada" which would render America "a free and happy People." Unfortunately, Peter Bours died two years later and could not know the precise nature of the freedom and happiness that the French capitulation would bring. The work before the Church would require careful supervision, and a bishop sent to the colonies would certainly have behind him strong ministerial influence. And, in 1769, Samuel Auchmuty made it perfectly clear how he envisaged the power of an American bishop. He would have sufficient "weight & influence

---

[59] Richard Hooker, "The Anglican Church and the American Revolution." Unpublished Ph.D. thesis, Chicago University, 1943, p. 14; Merle Curti, The Roots of American Loyalty (New York, 1968), pp. 10-11; Carl Bridenbaugh, Mitre and Sceptre, pp. 99-100; Isaac Browne, MSS Sermon, Romans, 13: 1-2, (New Jersey Historical Society); Charles Inglis, "The Duty of Honoring the King," (New York, 1780).

with the Governors of the provinces, & his Majesty's Civil officers" to protect Church interests.[60]

The growing population of the Carolinas and Georgia, and the settlements springing up in the western parts of the middle colonies were proper areas for the Society's attention where it could provide religious instruction and schoolteachers for the settlers too financially burdened to provide for themselves. So far, the southern colonies had shared but a fraction of the Society's bounty, for American candidates seeking ordination were invariably determined to return to their homes in the Chesapeake and middle and New England provinces, and British clergymen prepared to emigrate were reluctant to face the hardship of the wilderness parishes offered them outside the established towns. In Pennsylvania, the missionaries were anxious to assimilate the German population. Among the Lutherans, particularly, whose mode of worship was closely akin to that of the Church, the Society's prospects were promising. The Indians, too, within the British colonies, among whom so little had been achieved, and those living in the former French possessions who had fallen under the influence of the Roman Catholic missionaries, as well as the Negroes, offered ample work for the Society which was bound to win approval from its benefactors in England.

Trinity Church had opened a school for the parish poor and Negroes in New York, not long after its foundation, which the Society assisted by providing a salary for one of the ministers to catechize the Negroes. By the middle of the century, Trinity parish had built a separate school to accommodate thirty Negro children under the supervision of a teacher and the Society's catechist. The Society extended this scheme to Philadelphia in the 1740's when it appointed William Sturgeon as its catechist to the Negroes at Christ Church.[61]

---

[60] Thomas Barton to Secretary, Nov. 8, 1756, Dec. 6, 1760, Nov. 16, 1764, B, XXI, 1, 8, 14; Alexander Murray to Secretary, Jan. 25, 1764, B, XXI, 101; John Ogilvie to Secretary, Feb. 1, 1760, B, II,105; Samuel Auchmuty, MSS Sermon, Deut., 11: 12; Peter Bours to Secretary, July 20, 1760, B, XXII, 74; Samuel Auchmuty to Secretary, July 22, 1769, B, II, 33.
[61] Samuel Auchmuty to Secretary, March 30, 1748, May 2, 1761, B, XV, 81, II, 2; John Ross to Secretary, July 2, 1762, July 6, 1763, B, XXI, 219, 222; William Sturgeon to

Many of the Society's missionaries undertook the work of catechizing Negroes in their parishes, and in some missions the Society's schoolteachers taught reading and writing to Negro children. The Society's work among the Negroes, however, was limited since most of them were on the plantations in the South where it supported few missionaries until the mid-1760's, and even then it assisted only the colonies south of the Chesapeake. Furthermore, the Society's influence among the Negroes, even in the northern colonies, depended upon their owners' willingness to allow instruction to them.[62]

The American Indians had a much greater appeal to the Society because of the strategic role they played in the struggle against the French. The Iroquois, whom the British Crown declared to be British subjects in 1756, and their allies, whose lands stretched across central New York from the Hudson River west to Lake Erie, were of vital importance to British military strategy. With a system of alliances, the British hoped to unite the Iroquois and the Albany fur traders in order to remove the influence of the French. However, the Mohawks proved to be the most receptive to British offers of alliance against the French encroachments upon their lands.[63]

In accordance with King William III's instructions, the first of a long line of the Society's missionaries arrived at Albany in 1704 to minister to the Europeans, who were mostly of Dutch descent, and the Mohawks. Many of the missionaries worked very hard to reach the Indians, hoping that by Christianizing them they would attach them more closely to Britain and its national church, but their hunting expeditions, which the missionaries could not join, and the drunken bouts, encouraged by the Albany profiteers, negated much of the missionaries' work. Henry Barclay, like his father Thomas, whom he followed to the Albany mission, reached the Dutch settlers

---

Secretary, Nov. 20, 1763, B, XXI, 281; Vestry Minutes of Christ Church, Philadelphia, June 8, 1762, March 30, 1763 April 28, 1763.
[62] The Society's lecturers at St. Mary-le-Bow Church did not begin to criticize the Southern planters for neglecting their Negroes' religious education until the 1760's, when opponents of the Church were insisting that the Society had been chartered for that purpose. Furthermore, the condition of the Negroes in the South provided the lecturers with an excellent opportunity to point out the apparent duplicity with which some Americans were proclaiming their love of "liberty."
[63] Michael Kammen, Colonial New York: A History (New York, 1975), pp. 115, 319.

through his command of their language, and he eventually became so proficient in the Mohawk dialect that he was able to preach to them in their own language, and publish a Mohawk edition of the Book of Common Prayer. When Barclay left the Albany mission in 1746 to become rector of Trinity Church in New York, John Ogilvie replaced him. Ogilvie, a native of New York and a Yale graduate, had been studying for ordination with Samuel Johnson at Stratford, Connecticut, while gaining practical experience as a lay reader. His command of the Dutch language made him particularly well suited for the Albany mission. However, when he left Albany in 1759, to join a regiment bound for Canada, the work of preaching to the Indians along the Mohawk River came to a halt until the 1760's, when the war against the French and the subsequent Indian uprisings along the frontier of the English colonies were brought to an end. Nevertheless, John Ogilvie's claim that the Mohawks and most of the Six Nations Iroquois went with the expedition to Canada, where he officiated to the Mohawks and the Oneidas, stands as a testimony to his effectiveness.[64]

However, in the 1760's, there was a "handsome Stone" church "with a steeple and Chancel" built at Fort Hunter on the Mohawk River. Sir William Johnson, the British High Commissioner for Indian Affairs in the northern colonies, had assisted by providing "a Neat Organ" which cost him £100 sterling. He could also claim another church built at nearby Conajaharie. He also headed a small group of subscribers in the building of St. George's Church at Schenectady.[65]

William Smith in Philadelphia and Thomas Barton in Lancaster, Pennsylvania, were among several Anglican clergy who were anxious to support Sir William Johnson in providing priests and teachers for the Indians. Thomas Barton made a number of visits to

---

[64] John Wolfe Lydekker, The Faithful Mohawks (Cambridge, 1938), chapter 2, The First Decade (1704-1713); Henry Barclay to Secretary, Oct. 15, 1740, B, VII, part 2, 141; John Ogilvie to Secretary, Feb. 1, 1760, B, II, 105; Samuel Johnson to Secretary, Christmas, 1747, B, XV, 28; Henry Barclay to Secretary, Nov. 7, 1748, B, XVI, 55.

[65] Henry Barclay to Secretary, April 26, 1742, B, X, 111; Willis T. Hanson, A History of St. George's Church in the City of Schenectady (Schenectady, 1919), vol. I, pp. 33, 40; Sir William Johnson to Thomas Barton, Dec. 2, 1766. Peter Force Papers, Series 8D, Sir William Johnson Papers, 1755-1774 (Library of Congress); Sir William Johnson to Secretary, Dec. 3, 1773, B, II, 94

Sir William Johnson with whom he developed a close friendship. In April 1767, he enlisted a waggon-maker, a carpenter and joiner and several other tradesmen to join Sir William in establishing his new town at Johnson Hall. He informed Sir William, on another occasion, of the superior results the German farmers in Pennsylvania achieved with their agricultural methods compared to the inferior methods used and results achieved by the Dutch farmers he had observed in the Mohawk Valley. Glass-making and chinaware in Pennsylvania were as good as could be made in England, he wrote, and to prove his point he sent Sir William a piece of glass together with written instructions on how to raise silk worms, another of Pennsylvania's achievements.[66]

However, most dear to the heart of this frontier missionary was pacification of the Indians. He had one Indian boy at his home learning arithmetic and writing, with plans to take in about twelve more boys. In November 1766, he forwarded to the Society his plan for establishing schools for the Indians. Barton envisaged schools for Indian boys would be opened on the Mohawk River, at Fort Pitt and the back parts of South Carolina. Each school would accommodate ten boys, and he costed the project in detail. He wrote, we "must extend the light of knowledge to . . . conciliate them to us." Using the language of the day, he wrote, they see us as intruders on their "Rights and Property." Financial support would come from the Pennsylvania Assembly and a royal grant of land, he hoped.[67]

Unfortunately, he informed the Society, because of the "Poverty of the Times" and an increasing family, he would have to seek a living in Maryland. Here was a man of action with sound ideas. The Society resolved to open a school for ten Indian boys under the supervision of Sir William Johnson, costing £150 sterling per annum. The Society also resolved to increase Barton's salary by £10 sterling per annum "if that may be ye Means of prevailing upon him to continue in their Service." To give him further encouragement, the Proprietor allowed Barton the use of his Costenego Manor, near

---

[66] Thomas Barton to Sir William Johnson, April 12, 1767, July 8, 1771, Peter Force Papers, Series 8D, Sir William Johnson Papers, 1755-1774.

[67] Thomas Barton to Sir William Johnson, July 22, 1767, Peter Force Papers, Series 8D, Sir William Johnson Papers, 1755-1774; Thomas Barton to Secretary, Nov. 10, 1766, B, XXI, 17.

Lancaster. Such generosity allowed Thomas Barton to remain in Lancaster.[68]

A similar scheme to reach the Indians was developed among the clergy at Trinity Church in New York, in 1771. Samuel Auchmuty, Myles Cooper and Charles Inglis, with Sir William Johnson's support, planned to establish a college in the Mohawk Valley for Indian youths, who could later be trained at King's College for the ministry. When Myles Cooper sailed for England, in 1771, with addresses from the New York and New Jersey clergy on the subject of an American episcopate and requests for a charter to establish King's College as the nucleus of an American university, he also carried a proposal to establish the college they were planning. The scheme would require financial backing from the British government and that probably explains why the proposal failed at that time.[69]

Meanwhile, Sir William Johnson found the man he was looking for. In May 1770, Thomas Barton and William Smith recommended John Stuart to the Society for ordination. Stuart had already visited Sir William Johnson and he was eager to undertake work with the Mohawk Indians. He was the son of a magistrate in Philadelphia and a graduate of the College of Philadelphia. Charles Inglis wrote from Trinity Church in New York that he was six feet four inches tall, "of a robust Constitution, a good scholar, & of unblemished Character." His stature impressed many, and his subsequent career at Fort Hunter certainly proved him to be a man of character. After the War for Independence, his scholarship was affirmed conclusively in Ontario where he translated St. Matthew's Gospel into the Mohawk language for his former congregation.[70]

---

[68] S.P.G. Journals, XVII, 281, 286; Thomas Barton to Secretary, Oct. 18, 1768, B, XXI, 18; Thomas Barton to Richard Peters, Aug. 24, 1768, VI, p. 62, Richard Peters Papers. (Historical Society of Pennsylvania)

[69] David C. Humphrey, From King's College to Columbia, 1746-1780, pp. 144-149.

[70] Thomas Barton to Secretary, May 16, 1770, B, XXI, 22; William Smith to Secretary, May 26, 1770, B, XXI, 266; Sir William Johnson to Richard Peters, William Smith and Thomas Barton, April 16, 1770, B, II, 91; Richard Peters to Sir William Johnson, March 31, 1770, Peter Force Papers, Series 8D, Sir William Johnson Papers, 1755-1774; Charles Inglis to Samuel Johnson, Dec. 22, 1770, Hawks Papers, Johnson MSS, No. 42. (Church Historical Society, Austin, Texas); S.P.G. Journals, XXV, 24.

*Portrait of John Stuart.
(Courtesy of Library & Archives Canada/ C-011057).*

For a little while Sir William Johnson's dream of bringing Christianity to the Iroquois Indians looked like becoming a reality. In addition to "little" John, as Samuel Auchmuty called him, William Smith and Sir William Johnson had Jacob Hall, soon to graduate from the College of Philadelphia, in mind as teacher and catechist for the Conajaharie Village. As for Schenectady, they planned to send William Andrews, who had recently arrived from Ireland. Andrews' relatives in Schenectady, as well as his stated intention to learn the Mohawk language, were enough to attract Sir William Johnson's attention. In December 1770, he was ordained for the Schenectady mission. However, by late 1773, he found the situation too great a financial burden, and, with the help of Sir William Johnson, he moved to a parish in Virginia.[71]

Nevertheless, John Stuart remained as the mainstay of Sir William Johnson's long-cherished dream of binding the Iroquois to Britain. In August 1770, the Society appointed Jacob Hall as catechist and teacher at Conajaharie where he could learn the Mohawk language. However, by mid-1771, he had changed his mind. Therefore, the burden fell upon John Stuart at Fort Hunter, and John Doty, a graduate of King's College, who officiated at Schenectady from 1774 until 1777, when he was forced to seek safety in Canada.[72]

The Society also worked earnestly to win the Nova Scotia Indians away from the Roman Catholic teachings of the French. In Thomas Wood they found the man who, like Henry Barclay in New York, would devote himself to learning the local Indian language. In less than three years after leaving his mission among the Mohawk Indians, Henry Barclay was to recommend for ordination this

---

[71] Samuel Auchmuty to Richard Peters, Aug. 18, 1771, Richard Peters Papers, VII, 69 (Historical Society of Pennsylvania); William Smith to Secretary, May 26, 1770, B, XXI, 266; William Andrews to Secretary, Dec. 26, 1770, June 24, 1771, B, III, 4, 6; Thomas Barton to Sir William Johnson, Nov. 6, 1769, Samuel Auchmuty to Sir William Johnson, Nov., 14, 1769, Peter Force Papers, Sir William Johnson Papers; Sir William Johnson to Secretary, Dec. [6], 1769, B, II, 90; William Andrews to Secretary, Nov. 25, 1773, B, III, 11; William Smith to Sir William Johnson, March 31, 1770, Peter Force Papers, Sir William Johnson Papers.

[72] S.P.G. Journals, XVIII, 393; Thomas Barton to Sir William Johnson, July 8, 1771, Peter Force Papers, Sir William Johnson Papers, 1755—1774; Church Wardens and Vestry of St. George's Church, Schenectady to Secretary, Dec. 10, 1773, B, III, 12; S.P.G. Journals, XX, 84, XXI, 343.

scholarly man who would eventually take up the challenge.[73]

Thomas Wood had practised as a surgeon in America for some years and also with Governor William Shirley's regiment before being ordained priest. In 1749 he took the Society's mission at New Brunswick and Elizabeth Town in New Jersey. Two years later he decided to go to Nova Scotia, where his knowledge of French could be put to good use. In 1762, when the Vicar General of Quebec, Monsignor Maillard, was buried at St. Paul's Anglican Church in Halifax, Nova Scotia, Thomas Wood delivered the sermon in French. Monsignor Maillard's services to the Nova Scotia Indians had been appreciated sufficiently to gain him a salary from the British government. Probably his example inspired Thomas Wood to work with the Indians, because in September 1763, St. Paul's Church in Halifax granted him leave for five years to go to Annapolis Royal in order to begin learning the Micmac language. Using Maillard's papers, Wood translated the Book of Common Prayer into the Indian language with corresponding English and French versions. In July 1766, he sent the first pages of his English-Micmac grammar to England, and the following year he wrote to the Society that he had preached to the Indians in their own language at St. Paul's Church in Halifax.[74]

The Church of England was making some progress in the 1750's among the Pennsylvania German Lutherans and Calvinists who, without institutions for training their own ministers, depended upon Europe to supply their need. Congregations, which could not engage misters, lost some of their members to the Church, or, in some cases, they invited the local Anglican priest to officiate for them in their own churches. Many of the younger generation, like the New York Dutch earlier in the century, were breaking away from their parents' language and traditions, and found the Church a convenient alternative. The German congregation in Reading

---

[73] S.P.G. Journals, XVI, 169; Henry Barclay to Secretary, May 12, 1749, B, XVII, 101.
[74] Secretary Philip Bearcroft to Wardens and Vestry, Elizabeth Town, Oct. 3, 1749, B XVII, 203a;Thomas Wood to Secretary, Nov. 9, 1751, B, XIX, 94; Governor Belcher to Secretary, Feb. 3, 1763, Thomas Wood to Secretary, Oct. 27, 1762, B, XXV,21, 24; St. Paul's Church, Halifax, copy of vestry minute, Sept. 11, 1763, Lt. Governor Wilmot to Secretary, Oct. 1, 1763, B, XXV, 33, 34; Thomas Wood to Secretary, Oct. 14, 1763, July 30, 1764, April 1, 1765, July 27, 1766; Lt. Governor Franklin to Secretary, Dec. 29, 1766, B, XXV, 37,51,63,85,103.

shocked the Society's fiery Scottish missionary with their organ and violins at their services, but his neighbour at Lancaster, Thomas Barton, a much more tolerant man, and more experienced in the variety of modes of worship the colonies presented, thought that an organ might be just the little incentive needed to bring the Germans into the Church.[75]

A number of incentives were tried to tempt the Germans into the Church of England, and when the German congregation in Philadelphia was making enquiries among the Philadelphia clergy about uniting with the Church, a number of ministers were prepared to convert, but the need to go to England for Anglican ordination deterred all but one, Paulus Bryzelius, who finally went to the Society's German and French mission at Lunenburg in Nova Scotia. The intensification of Pennsylvania's political disputes set the religious denominations against one another in their bid for the Germans' support and the plans to unite the two Churches came to an end along with the scheme to establish English schools for the children of German settlers.[76]

By the middle of the eighteenth century the presence of so many non-English speaking Germans on the western extremes of European settlement was causing alarm. William Smith was afraid that the younger generation of Germans born in Pennsylvania, whose ambition was to own large farms, not having experienced conditions in Europe, and not understanding the difference between the British and French political systems, might be won over by French offers of land in the Ohio Valley. As early as 1753 he had written to the Archbishop of Canterbury about assimilating the German immigrants. He had recruited the help of the Presbyterian Minister Samuel Chandler, in London, who shared his concern. Smith's many contacts in England and his endless energy eventually brought about positive results.[77]

In March 1754, William Smith returned to America from his

---

[75] Alexander Murray to Secretary, March 26, 1772, Thomas Barton to Secretary, Dec. 6, 1760, B, XXI, 108, 8.

[76] William Smith to Bishop of London, Dec. 18, 1766, Fulham Papers, VIII, 30

[77] William Smith to Samuel Chandler, May 30, 1754, William Smith Papers, VI, (Historical Society of Pennsylvania); "Remarks by his Grace of Canterbury, on a paper sent him by Mr. Smith . . . " Samuel Chandler to William Smith, Jan. 28, 1755, William Smith Papers, I, 5, 9 (Church Historical Society, Texas).

fund-raising tour on behalf of the College of Philadelphia, carrying a letter from Samuel Chandler addressed to James Hamilton, Lieutenant Governor of Pennsylvania, and other dignitaries. The letter announced that a Society established in England had appointed them to oversee a scheme to provide teachers and ministers for the Pennsylvania Germans. The Society, of which Samuel Chandler was Secretary, consisted of an impressive list of people including aldermen of the City of London and headed by the Earl of Shaftesbury. The Society could also claim the King and Prince of Wales among its patrons.[78]

A Committee of Trustees, with William Smith acting as Secretary, met at William Allen's house in Germantown, in August 1754. It appointed persons from among the German Calvinists, Lutherans and English protestant denominations to establish schools and to appoint teachers for the towns where German people were most numerous. The German Lutheran leader Henry Mühlenberg gave whole-hearted support to the scheme. He won over Lutherans and Calvinists in several parishes, including New Hanover in Philadelphia County, which offered the Trustees the use of its school buildings.[79]

The scheme soon ran into trouble when the publisher of a widely circulated German language newspaper, Christopher Sauer, opposed it. Even before the Philadelphia Trustees' first meeting, Henry Mühlenberg wrote to Benjamin Franklin that Sauer had "made haste to ferment against the scheme." Sauer, a German Dunker living in Germantown, was, according to Mühlenberg, opposed to the orthodox clergy, and in his articles claimed that German farmers would finally have to pay for the schools, possibly forcing them to sells their farms. He claimed that the German schools were tools of oppression that would leave the German settlers servants of the Proprietors. It is quite likely that William Smith's involvement in the scheme augured the spectre of the increasing influence of the Anglican Church in Pennsylvania.[80]

---

[78] "Copy of a letter dated March 15, 1754, to James Hamilton ...", William Smith Papers, VI (Historical Society of Pennsylvania).
[79] "Minutes of a meeting of Trustees at William Allen's house, German-Town, August, 10, 1754", William Smith Papers, VI (Historical Society of Pennsylvania).
[80] "Minutes of a Meeting of Trustees ... August 10, 1754, William Smith Papers, VI. (Historical Society of Pennsylvania)

Both Mühlenberg and Benjamin Franklin attempted to counter Sauer with an opposition printing press, but they were unable to obtain the services of a German printer. Therefore, that "Incendiary Sauer," as Samuel Chandler called him, continued with his propaganda. And he succeeded in bringing the scheme to an end. In April 1764, Samuel Chandler wrote to Richard Peters that the German schools were finished.[81]

The possibilities that lay before the Church in the northern colonies at the end of the Seven Years War were certainly considerable, but the Church suffered from a very serious deficiency, one which was inherent in its expansion from the beginning. It could not thrive without help from Britain, and the privileged position in which the English connection placed the American Church was bound to stigmatize Anglicans with the odour of Old-World privilege which was gradually becoming anathema to the main stream of American thought. Furthermore, the large numbers of clergy and laity recruited from the Dissenters in the formative years needed episcopal supervision to ensure their proper assimilation into the colonial Church of England. Some of the clergy were beginning to ask themselves precisely what was the character of the Church after seventy years existence in the northern provinces.

---

[81] Samuel Chandler to William Smith, Jan. 28, 1755, William Smith Papers I, 9 (Church Historical Society, Texas); Samuel Chandler to Richard Peters, April 12, 1764, William Smith Papers, I, 42. (Church Historical Society, Texas); Arthur M. Schlesinger, Prelude to Independence: The Newspaper War on Britain 1764-1776 (New York, 1965), p. 286; John A. Neuenschwander, The Middle Colonies and the Coming of the American Revolution (New York, 1973), pp. 17-19.

CHAPTER

II

The Americanization of the Church

When Thomas Secker lauded the Society's achievements from the pulpit of St. Mary-le-Bow, in 1741, few Americans could have predicted the amazing growth the Church was to make in the northern colonies during the twenty five years that were to follow. In order to meet the needs of its increasing following, Trinity Church, the majestic reminder of England's National Church in New York City, opened St. George's Chapel in May 1752, blessed with a donation of £10 sterling from the Archbishop of Canterbury. Fourteen years later, the New York Anglican community was treated to a band performance, at the request of Governor Sir Henry Moore, to celebrate the dedication of St. Paul's Chapel.[1]

The Christ Church congregation in Philadelphia was also increasing and St. Peter's Church was opened in 1761, built on land donated by the Penn family, for the prosperous and affluent who were turning to the Anglican Church as a more suitable expression of their new-found genteel status. The following year, William McClennachan led a faction to found a third church, St. Paul's, to cater for the demands of the Evangelicals of Christ Church and St. Peter's Church. The church wardens and vestry wrote to the Bishop of London, in June 1764, that their new church was "a large Commodious Church, the largest in this City or Province."[2]

---

[1] Vestry Minutes of Trinity Church, May 20, 1752, July 10, 1752, Oct 29, 1766, Nov. 4, 1766; Samuel Auchmuty to Samuel Johnson, Nov. [-] 1766, Schneider's Johnson, I, 381-383.
[2] Christ Church Vestry Minutes, Aug. 19, 1761 (possession of the Rector); St. Paul's Minutes of Vestry, 1762-1774, Aug. 19, 1762, June 21, 1762, (Historical Society of Pennsylvania).

West of Philadelphia, Lancaster's Anglican congregation was able to exchange the Court House, which had served as its meeting place, for a stone church, in 1752. A public lottery, authorized by the General Assembly of Pennsylvania enabled the congregations of Reading and York to begin building their churches--the land at York was the gift of the proprietors. The Anglican congregations in Huntingdon, in York County, and Carlisle, also benefited from the same lottery which allowed them to complete, or repair, their church buildings.[3]

In New Jersey, a small stone chapel had housed the Anglican congregation of Amwell, about fifteen miles north of Trenton, since 1751. South of New Brunswick, the Society established a new mission at Spotswood and Freehold, in 1765, where churches already existed. By 1744, the congregations of New Brunswick, and nearby Piscataway, had built a second church, this one of stone and lime. While a church had been built at Shrewsbury, as early as 1715, the Middletown community of that mission began building its own church in 1744. The Anglicans at Trenton began building St. Michael's Church in 1748, to be completed in 1753. By the late 1760's, the Anglican Church was making headway in Sussex County, which the Society's Elizabeth Town missionary Thomas Bradbury Chandler considered to be frontier, and undoubtedly "within the original Intention" of the Society's charter. While the Anglican families in Sussex County were following Chandler's advice about how to elect church wardens and vestrymen, he had Uzal Ogden, the son of a New Jersey Anglican family, appointed as the Society's catechist, and settled at Newtown, where Christ Church was to be built.[4]

---

[3] Vestry Book of St.James Church, Lancaster, entry 1751; George Craig to Secretary, June 16, 1752, B, XX, 124; Alexander Murray to Secretary, June 12, 1765, XXI, 102; William C. Carter and Adam J. Glossbrenner, History of York County, 1729-1834 (Harrisburg, 1930), pp. 29-33.

[4] William Frazer to Secretary, Oct. 20, 1768, B, XXIV, 238; William Ayers to Secretary, Sept. 30, 1771, B, XXIV, [8]; Bruce E. Steiner, Samuel Seabury, pp. 62-63; S.P.G. Journals, XVI, General Meeting, July 19, 1765; William Skinner to Secretary, [1742], Oct. 29, 1744, B, X, 109, XII, 7; Alfred Stubbs, A Record of Christ Church, New Brunswick (New York, 1850), p. 5; John Miln to Secretary, June 10, 1744, B, XII, 23; John O. Raum, History of the City of Trenton, New Jersey (Trenton, 1871), p. 108; Thomas Chandler to Secretary, Jan. 5, 1770, June 24, 1771, B, XXIV, 97, 99; Thomas Chandler to Bishop of London, no date, Fulham Papers, XXII, [268a];

In the province of New York, John Beardsley was visiting the Anglicans at Poughkeepsie and nearby Fishkill, in the mid 1760's, from his mission in Connecticut. His visits led to churches being opened there in 1769 and 1774. Further south, John Ogilvie, assistant minister at Trinity Church, in New York City, officiated at the opening of St. Peter's Church in Peekskill, on August 9, 1767.[5]

In Connecticut, the Anglicans at Stratford were able to complete Christ Church in 1744. They were assisted in their work by friends in New York, Boston, and, in particular, by a Stratford merchant, William Beach, brother of the missionary at Newtown and Reading. According to Samuel Johnson, it was "a very neat building for this country" and a rival to the "several larger and more magnificent in Boston, New York and Rhode Island," in that it was "more truly English than they generally are." Away from the coast, the Church continued its inroads into areas formerly the preserve of the Congregationalists. A congregation at Milford opened their church, in 1770, which they named "St. George's," after their wealthy New York benefactor, St. George Talbot. He also extended his assistance to Christ Church in Stamford. To his gift of twenty two acres of land to that church he added a bell, a tankard and a silver salver, in 1765. At his request, the Stamford missionary Ebenezer Dibblee travelled to Danbury to officiate at the opening of the church there, in 1765. The occasion was a double blessing because it was Dibblee's place of birth, and many of those in attendance had withdrawn from the Congregationalist Church from which he had defected in 1747.[6]

In the 1760's, in spite of the economic difficulties brought about by the resistance to Imperial taxation, new churches were being built at Sharon and Pomfret. Roger Viets, the missionary at Symsbury, claimed that the church under construction at Great Barrington was "by far the most beautiful and expensive Building in the Country." Other parishes, such as, Stratford, New Milford and Ripton, were

---

Edward A. Webb, ed., The Historical Directory of Sussex County, New Jersey (no place, 1872), p. 46

[5] Vestry Minutes of Christ Church, Poughkeepsie, Oct. 26, 1766 (possession of the Rector); Wardens and Vestry of St. Peter's Church, Peak's Kill, to Secretary, Oct. 15, 1770, B, III, 2.

[6] St. Peter's Protestant Episcopal Church Records, 1764-1869 (formerly St. George's Church), Entries 1765, 1770; Ebenezer Dibblee to Secretary, April 8, 1765, Oct. 28,1765, B, XXIII, 102, 103; Samuel Johnson to Secretary, Sept. 29, 1744, B, XIII, 100

either replacing old structures, or extending their churches to accommodate their growing congregations.[7]

In Boston, King's Chapel began preparations for a grander structure in 1742. Governor William Shirley laid the foundation stone in April 1749, and the congregation began services there five years later, even though it was not yet finished. It was designed to be as impressive as any in London, however, without its majestic spire it took on a somewhat military appearance. A local Dissenting minister, Mather Byles, who would later join the Anglican Church, remarked that "he had often heard of the Canons of the Church, but never had seen the Port-holes before."[8]

By that time three Anglican churches in Boston had become the centre of a cluster of churches in the small towns situated around. Most threatening to the Dissenters was Christ Church in Cambridge. It was within sight of Harvard College, and certainly in breach of the Society's mission which was to provide clergy to colonists without religious instruction. Also close to Boston was the church at Dedham, which was opened in April 1764. In 1768, the Society declared Dedham and Stoughton to be a mission, specifically to secure land bequeathed to the Church by a member of the Dedham congregation. Further afield, and more in keeping with the Society's charter, were the missions established on what the Society termed the "Eastern Frontiers" of New England. Jacob Bailey arrived at Pownal Borough on the Kennebec River in Maine, in 1761, to minister to a population of many origins. Among his following were migrants indebted to sea captains for their passages from Germany. To add to his difficulties, the previous itinerant missionary, William McClennachan, had absconded with the Society's library to begin his enchantment of the evangelical faction of Christ Church in Philadelphia. A further attempt at fulfilling the Society's mandate to minister to those without religious instruction led to the

---

[7] Roger Viets to Secretary, March 14, 1764, B, XXIII, 370; Thomas Davies to Secretary, June 25, 1765, B, XXIII, 86; Christopher Newton to Secretary, Jan. 3, 1766, B, XXIII, 289; Brooklyn ,Trinity Church Records, 1771-1866 (formerly Trinity Church, Pomfret), vol. I, page 1.

[8] Roger Price to Secretary, May 3, 1742, B, X, 2; Charles Brockwell to Bishop of London,, Dec. 16, 1754, Fulham Papers, VI, 33; F.W.P. Greenwood, A History of King's Chapel in Boston (Boston, 1833), p. 122; Carl Bridenbaugh, Cities in Revolt: Urban Life in America, 1743-1776 (New York, 1955), p. 21

appointment of Ranna Cossit to Clermont and Haverhill in New Hampshire, in 1773.[9]

Significantly, these rapid increases had been gained at the expence of the Dissenters, and by 1760 the Episcopalians who had been converted from the Congregationalists and Presbyterians formed an overwhelming majority of the Church population. Between 1760 and 1783, when the British-American connection was formerly ended, ninety two of the one hundred and thirty one priests who served in the colonies north of the Delaware River to Nova Scotia were American-born. All of the twenty two American-born Connecticut clergy had been recruited from the Congregationalists, and eight of those had been Congregationalist Teachers. Half of the twenty two Massachusetts and New Hampshire clergy who were converts from the Congregationalists had come from the Congregationalist ministry. That so many clergy were converts is a very important reflection upon New England's social and cultural development, but, while defection from the Dissenters was not so obvious in the middle colonies, the Church there, too, had an important appeal. Four New York clergy had been recruited from the Congregationalists and four from the Presbyterians. In New Jersey, four of the eleven American-born clergy had been Congregationalists and 4 had been Presbyterians. Pennsylvania and Delaware, while relying more upon British immigrants to supply the ministry than the provinces to the north, nevertheless, had among their twenty two clergy, seven American-born, of whom three had been Dissenting Teachers. The scattered population in the infant province of Nova Scotia was in no position to supply its own needs, and only one of its eight clergymen was of colonial origin.

Even clergy recruited from the British Isles were not necessarily representative of the Anglican Church, for seven of those who ministered in the northern colonies in the 1760's and 1770's had been Teachers in the Scottish or Irish Presbyterian Church, and,

---

[9] East Apthorp to Secretary, Sept. 29, 1762, B, XXII, 5; Carl Bridenbaugh, Cities in Revolt, p. 25; Ebenezer Miller to Secretary, April 13, 1761, B, XXII, 191; S.P.G. Journals, XVIII, 77, XIX, 354, 399, XX, 169; Edward Winslow to Secretary, Jan.1, 1765 B. XXII, 275; Jacob Bailey to Secretary, June 20, 1767, March 26, 1761, June 27, 1768, B, XXII, 61, 59, 63.

judging by their reaction to American society and to their congregations, it appears that they, like the New England Congregationalists who joined the Church, had been looking for a more structured religion which would inculcate standards of behaviour that might bring stability to a volatile society.

William Currie had left his Scottish home in the 1730's to become a tutor in Virginia before deciding upon the ministry as a career. However, the Presbyterian ministry, to which he was naturally inclined, proved unsatisfactory, for the deference he had known in Scotland was not part of the American Presbyterian character, and eventually he turned to the Church of England. Typical of the British converts from the Dissenters was Colin Campbell of Burlington in New Jersey. Lamenting the flood of itinerant preachers in the colonies in the mid-1760's, he recalled that as a youth in Scotland he had seen such "Soul saving Ministers" and "idle Drones" who had sent him in search "after a rational Religion" which would bring "peace harmony & order" out of "confusion." Harry Munro, having seen America as a Presbyterian, discovered that, if he were to remain in America, the Church of England would be more suitable to his social outlook. John Bradstreet, church warden at St. Peter's Church, Albany, and a corresponding member of the Society, requested the Society, in 1769, for a missionary with "Fashion and weight with Abilities and Character" to serve this rapidly growing town on the Hudson River route to Canada, and he finally got the man he wanted. Munro was "by birth and education a gentleman," as he later described himself to the Commissioners to hear Loyalist Claims in London, who had gone to America "not as an adventurer nor as a missionary of any society but as a gentleman and clergyman already provided for in his own country having purchased a chaplaincy of a Regiment in his Majesty's service."[10]

Alexander Murray gave no reason for his conversion to the Church, but he bristled with indignation at the Pennsylvanians' lack of respect for clergy of all denominations. Behind the vitriolic

---

[10] Henry Pleasants, The History of Old St. David's Church at Radnor (Philadelphia, 1915), p. 99; Harold Donaldson Eberlein and Cortlandt Van Dyke Hubbard, The Church of Saint Peter in the Great Valley, 1700-1940 (Richmond, Virginia, 1944), pp. 36-37; Colin Campbell to Secretary, July 30, 1764, B, XXIV, no number; John Bradstreet to Secretary, July 2, 1769, B, III, 106; Memorial of Harry Munro, Commissioners for Loyalist Claims, XXXXV, 51.

invective he levelled at the Dissenters in every letter he wrote to the Society was his disgust at the Americans' inability to accept British social stratification. Presbyterians, Lutherans, and Calvinists alike made his blood boil by insisting upon the right to "Hire a Minister generally no longer than a year" which rendered "his office as Contemptible as Poor."[11]

Many of the American-born clergy, especially New Englanders, could understand people like Murray and Campbell, for they had turned to the Church to escape the upheavals of the Great Awakening which had asserted individual opinion above clerical authority, emotion above reason. One of the early converts from the Dissenters' ranks in Connecticut, John Beach, journeyed from his Reading mission to the western towns of New Milford and New Fairfield, in 1750, to be convinced anew of his earlier conviction of the dignity of Anglican worship. The people there were being transformed into "extravagant Enthusiasts" by a "Mechanic" whose " Screaming and hallowing" was audible a mile away. Another convert from the Dissenting Teachers, Isaac Browne, viewing the havoc Whitefield's spawn had created in his normally peaceful Brookhaven on Long Island, pointed the direction that individualism based upon nothing more than emotion would lead his countrymen. First "4 or 5 Common Ploughmen" came to plague Brookhaven, followed by "a poor illiterate Weaver" and finally a carpenter and "an ignorant School master," who claimed that "any convert is fit to be a preacher and has a call from the holy Ghost" without "the imposition of Hands or licence from any Body." Browne considered this departure from ecclesiastical authority a direct threat to "Church and State" since few of those strolling preachers ever bothered to pray for the Royal Family.[12]

It is significant, therefore, that nearly every Connecticut and several Massachusetts clergymen who were converted from the Congregationalist Church gave as their major reason their dissatisfaction with Presbyterian ordination. In 1754, Samuel Johnson explained in a letter to Yale College President Thomas Clap that he had earlier conformed to the Church as "the only stable

---

[11] Alexander Murray to Secretary, March 26, 1772, B, XXI, 108.
[12] John Beach to Secretary, April 9, 1750, B, XVIII, 28; Isaac Browne to Secretary, June 16, 1741, B, IX, 79.

bulwark against . . . rigid Calvinism, Antinomianism, enthusiasm, divisions, and separations . . . so rife and rampant among us." The Church and its "articles, liturgy, and homilies" provided an "ark of safety" and "the golden means" amidst confusion. Two years earlier he had defended the Church against critics who claimed that it was prospering in New England by courtesy of the Society's money. He had no doubt that those ministers conforming to the Church did so because they, like himself, were persuaded of the right of episcopacy and liturgy. Those Dissenting Teachers and students converting to the Church of England usually came in contact with a neighbouring missionary, or with the zealous Samuel Johnson. Solomon Palmer, upset by Connecticut's religious upheaval, approached Johnson who lent him the works of Richard Hooker and John Potter. Palmer had been a Congregationalist Teacher at Cornwall, Litchfield county, for over 10 years when he left for episcopal ordination, in 1754, bearing a letter from Samuel Johnson explaining that he had for 3 or 4 years "been under considerable Anxiety of Mind, on Account of the dubiousness of the validity of His Ordination, and the Lawfulness of extempore Prayer." As often happened when Dissenting Teachers converted, they brought part of their congregations with them, and Palmer was able to return to Litchfield County as the Society's itinerant missionary among members of his former congregation, who, like himself, had been "put upon enquiring for more rational grounds of Religion." Similarly, Ebenezer Punderson had conformed in 1733, and with the prospect of his Connecticut congregation joining the Church, the Society obligingly appointed him their itinerant missionary.[13]

Fourteen years later, Mather Byles, the great grandson of the New England divine Increase Mather and nephew of Massachusetts governor Jonathan Belcher, left the Congregationalist Church in New London for Christ Church in Boston. He had refused to tolerate the noisy disturbances of a sect of Baptists known as Rogerines, as

---

[13] Samuel Johnson to Thomas Clap, Feb. 5, 1754, Samuel Johnson to Dr. Douglass, Jan. 15, 1752, Schneider's Johnson, I, pp. 176-180, 156-158; Joint letter from Connecticut clergy to Bishop of London, no date, New York and Connecticut clergy joint letter to Bishop of London, July 2, 1754, Fulham Papers, XXI, 52; Samuel Johnson, James Wetmore, Isaac Browne, Henry Caner to Bishop of London, March 14, 1733/1734, Fulham Papers, I, 259.

strident in their defiance of Congregational authority as they were determined to stop him from preaching. Their "clamorous Testimony against Idolatrous Worship" might have taken a heavier toll had not some members of his congregation supported him when he had them jailed. However, others of his congregation disapproved of his stern defence of his authority, and no doubt his preaching submission to Parliament during the Stamp Act disturbances put him at odds with many of his parishioners.[14]

Byles was socially at home in New London; among his friends was Matthew Graves, the Anglican missionary at St. James Church, and collector of customs Duncan Stewart, one of his "intimate Friends, and generous a Benefactor." He had been thinking of joining the Anglican Church for some years and, according to Matthew Graves, he became "convinced that Episcopacy opens ye regular Door into the Vineyard and Fold of Christ." When he was invited to go to Christ Church in Boston, Daniel and William Hubbard of Boston paid for his passage to England, and the Governor of Massachusetts, customs commissioners John Temple and Charles Paxton, with a number of wealthy Bostonians, subscribed to pay for his additional expenses. He sailed for England on May 14 1768, with a letter of recommendation from the New London collector of customs Joseph Harrison. Mather Byles, he wrote, was the only "dissenting Minister" he had heard of "who had the Courage and Resolution" to oppose the tumult over the Stamp Act. He concluded that "Honours of Oxford, or Cambridge" would be a suitable reward. Such a scion of New England's eminent Puritan theologians was indeed a coup for the Church; Byles returned to Boston with an annual salary of £40 sterling from the Society and an Oxford D.D. The Society further showed its gratitude to Byles by allowing him two gratuity payments of £10 each when his Christ Church subscribers failed to provide the full amount of

---

[14] Clifford K. Shipton, Sibley's Harvard Graduates: Biographical Sketches of those who attended Harvard College, (Boston, 1970), XIII, 1751-1755, Mather Byles; Arthur J. Worrall, Quakers in the Colonial Northeast (Hanover, New Hampshire, 1980), p. 115; Mather Byles to Mary Byles, June 26, 1764, (Folder 1753-83), Mather Byles to Katy Byles, Dec. 8, 1765, vol. I, Byles Family Papers ; Joseph Harrison to Bishop of London, May 12, 1768, Fulham Papers, VI, 66; Mather Byles to [Mather Byles, Sr.], Feb. 8, 1762, (MSS Connecticut Historical Society); Matthew Graves to Bishop of London, April 19, 1768, Fulham Papers, XXI,179.

the £100 they had promised.[15]

Of all the New Englanders disaffected from the Puritan culture Nathaniel Prince was the most explicit when considering his motives for joining the Church. Coming from a talented family—his brother was Thomas Prince the Puritan historian—he excelled at mathematics which he taught at Harvard College for fifteen years before resigning to become a Dissenting Teacher in Stratford, where Samuel Johnson was ever alert for a worthy apostate. His conversion to Anglicanism followed within two years. In 1745 he explained to the secretary of the Society that during the "Times of Desolation," when Whitefield brought "Chaos and disorderly opinions" to New England, he saw that "the Creeds, the lord's Prayer and the Commandments being constantly repeated" every Sunday were the social ballast that held the members of the Church of England firm in their faith.[16]

Samuel Johnson's recommendation for ordination, together with the probability that Prince's congregation would follow him into the Church, brought an enthusiastic response from the Society. However, letters from Charles Brockwell in Salem and Roger Price, Rector of King's Chapel in Boston, casting doubt on Prince's moral character dampened Secretary Bearcroft's initial enthusiasm. He urged Samuel Johnson that, considering the Society's dismissal of another recently converted Congregationalist Teacher, Jonathan Arnold, he should be absolutely certain about Prince's suitability. Johnson's advice prevailed, but the Society was apparently determined to play safe. At the cost of forfeiting Prince's Stratford

---

[15] Mather to Polly Byles, Feb. 18, 1768, "List of subscribers for Mather Byles going to England for holy orders," May 4, 1768, Byles Family Papers (Folder 1753-1783); The Holyoke Diaries, 1709-1856, Edward Holyoke, May 14, 1768 (Salem. Mass., 1921), p. 30; Joseph Harrison to Bishop of London, May 12, 1768, Fulham Papers, VI, 66. In public, Byles was no doubt urging toleration of Parliament's legislation, but to his sisters he wrote "It greatly rejoyces my heart . . . to have such certain information that the Stamp Act is repealed. See Mather Byles to Polly and Katy Byles, June 2, 1766, Byles Family Papers, vol. I; Mather Byles to Secretary , April 20, 1770, Oct. 19, 1770, April 29, 1772, Oct. 21, 1772, B, XXII, 79, 80, 84, 85.

[16] Samuel Johnson to Secretary, Jan. 10, 1744, B, XI, 38; Secretary to Samuel Johnson, May 30, 1744, B, XIII, 29; Samuel Johnson to Secretary, Feb. 12, 1745, B, XIII, 101; Charles Brockwell to Secretary, July 28, 1744, B, XIII, 118; Nathaniel Prince to Secretary, Aug. 29, 1745, B, XIII, 105; Roger Price to Secretary, Nov. 14, 1746, B, XIV, 7.

followers, he was sent to The Moskito Shore, on the Bay of Honduras, where he died within two years.[17]

As Congregationalists turned to the Church they joined others in pressing upon their superiors in England their belief that the Church in America was important to colonial dependence upon Britain, and its corollary that Congregationalism would replace the monarchy with a republic. To remarks about dissatisfaction with Presbyterian ordination, the senior clergy added their own comment that the candidates going to England for ordination were loyal to the British constitution: the phrase "well attached to the Constitution both in Church and State" became a fairly standard formula and integral part of all recommendations from the northern provinces.[18]

The dignitaries attending the General Court, and the clergy, teachers and students associated with Yale College made New Haven an expensive place to live; consequently the Episcopalians had difficulty retaining a minister with acknowledged ability until the Society settled a £40 annual bounty upon the parish, in 1767, when Bela Hubbard moved there. Nevertheless, for forty years Samuel Johnson's influence from his church in Stratford, ten miles away, had been profound. But Harvard had no Johnson, and none of its graduates who turned to the Church ministry displayed the unswerving determination that characterized the Yale converts. Several of its graduates, however, after searching for Congregationalist pulpits, did eventually find their way into the Church, for in Boston and the prospering coastal towns of Massachusetts and Rhode Island, the Church of England had outgrown its minority role and now offered a respectable career to Harvard graduates seeking security and social prestige.[19]

Jacob Bailey spent five years teaching school and preaching in Massachusetts and New Hampshire before choosing the Church. His dislike of the religious bigotry he experienced as a youth in rural Massachusetts later became a conviction that New England's

---

[17] Secretary To Samuel Johnson, June 10, 1745, B, XIII, 354; Secretary to Nathaniel Prince, June 30, 1746, B, XV, 205; Nathaniel Prince to Secretary, Jan. 20, 1748, B, XVI, 158; Henry Caner to Secretary, Jan. 31, 1750, B, XVIII, 13.

[18] Representative of this standard phrase are: Connecticut clergy to Bishop of London, Sept. 13, 1753, Boston clergy to Bishop of London, Dec. 12, 1754, Fulham Papers, XXI, 56, 60; Joshua Bloomer to Secretary, May 7, 1772, B, III, 125.

[19] Bela Hubbard to Secretary, Sept. 15, 1767, May 4, 1768, B, XXIII, 168, 169.

religion had become an empty hypocritical ritual, and not aesthetically pleasing either. While touring Connecticut during his student days at Harvard he had been concerned at the way the Congregationalists vied with one another in extempore prayer as though they were mere contestants in a festival of piety.[20]

Not all of the Massachusetts converts to the Church ministry were as dissatisfied with the New England religious system as Bailey. His brother-in-law, Joshua Weeks, who became minister at the Marblehead church, had grown up among his father's sophisticated circle of friends. His Harvard thesis that "sunspots have their origin in the eruptions of burning mountains" reflected the scientific bent of his father, who was a physician, and his decision to take the gown combined his desire for polite company and social prestige with his inclination towards rational learning.[21]

The recruits from the middle colonies reflected a wider range of religious affiliation and professional experience. Hence, they usually lacked the bunker mentality that characterized so many of the converts from the Congregationalist Church. Jonathan Odell, Joshua Bloomer and Luke Babcock represent a spectrum of liberal views that set them apart from some of their New England colleagues.

Jonanthan Odell was a native of Newark, New Jersey, a descendant of the founding generation of Massachusetts province, and son of the daughter of Jonathan Dickinson, first president of the College of New Jersey. After graduating from that College, in 1756, he taught at the College's grammar school before studying medicine and joining the British army. In 1764, he went to England, recommended by Benjamin Franklin, where he supported himself by teaching at a London school while preparing for Anglican ordination. His subsequent career as the Society's missionary at Burlington, in New Jersey, and his friendly relations with the Quakers there, suggests that the Church offered him a liberal alternative to the Dissenting Churches surrounding him.[22]

---

[20] William S. Bartlett, ed, The Frontier Missionary, pp. 3, 26, 37-39, 40-43, 50-51.

[21] B. Wentworth to Secretary, Nov. 14, 1762, William Hooper, John Troutbeck and William McGilchrist to Secretary, Nov. 6, 1762, B, XXII, 262, 301; Sibley's Harvard Graduates, XIV.

[22] S.P.G. Journals, XVII, 182; Moses Coit Tyler, The Literary History of the American Revolution (New York, 2nd printing, 1963), II, pp. 99-100; James

In 1768, Samuel Johnson, who had retired from the presidency of King's College to return to his church in Stratford, continued to prepare promising young men for ordination, and on whose behalf he used his considerable prestige to secure the Society's support. He wrote to the Society in 1770 that he had a design "of holding here [Stratford] a Little Academy or a Resort for young Students of Divinity, to prepare them for Holy Orders." He taught his students Latin Greek, Hebrew and divinity, after which he procured for them an M.A. degree from King's College, if they had no graduated elsewhere. The Society assisted his scheme by directing to his church in Stratford libraries bequeathed by American and English well-wishers. To keep congregations together which had no minister, and to gain practical experience and financial support for his students, Johnson had them assist as lay readers. When he informed the Society about his school, he had four young men nearing completion of their studies, one of whom was Samuel Tingley from New York. After his ordination he became Thomas Chandler's curate at St. John's Church in Elizabeth Town, New Jersey, before being invited to Lewes in Delaware where the Society later appointed him its missionary.[23]

Another of Johnson's students, a man with a similar background to Jonathan Odell, was Joshua Bloomer. Samuel Johnson described him as an "amiable and studious Lad, and, designed for the pulpit." A native of New York, presumably of Anglican background, he graduated from King's College where he caught Samuel Johnson's attention. However, before taking holy order, Bloomer served as a major with the army during the French and Indian Wars, which gave him, like Odell, a far broader experience than many of his colleagues.[24]

Coming from a similarly chequered background as Odell and

McLachlan, Princetonians 1748-1768: A Bibliographical Dictionary (New Jersey, 1976), pp. 109-110; Jonathan Odell to Secretary, July 5, 1768, B, XXIV, 133;
[23] Samuel Johnson to Secretary, June 11, 1770, B, XXIII, 203; Thomas Chandler, John Beach, John Preston to Bishop of London, Jan.,15, 1773, Thomas Chandler to Bishop of London, Jan. 16, 1773, Fulham Papers, XXII, [278], 279; S.P.G. Journals, XX, 194; Samuel Tingley to Secretary, Nov. 9, 1774, B, XXI, 183; Vestry Minutes of St. Peter's Church (formerly St. George's Church), Milford, Connecticut, Vol I,, Entry 1771.
[24] Myles Cooper and Samuel Auchmuty to Secretary, Nov. 28, 1768, B, III, 121; Samuel Johnson to Secretary, Nov. 7, 1768, B, XXII, 198.

Bloomer, Luke Babcock returned from ordination in England in 1770 to minister at Colonel Philipse' Manor in New York. His father, Joshua, had practised medicine in Westerly, Rhode Island, where Luke was born in 1738. After graduating from Yale College he became postmaster in New Haven where he owned a shop. He continued his studies in medicine and theology in England before presenting himself to the Society for ordination. The Connecticut clergy recommended him as having "a great proficiency in the Liberal arts and sciences, especially in medical science and theology."[25]

Abraham Beach, like Jonathan Odell and Joshua Bloomer, served with the military during the French and Indian Wars, and like Luke Babcock, became a shopkeeper. At Hartford, Connecticut, in addition to keeping shop, he was collector of taxes. Several years after graduating from Yale College he became, like his father, a Church communicant. Again Samuel Johnson at Stratford had a hand in guiding this young Yale man into the Church. In 1767, after studying Anglican theology with his uncle John Beach, the Newtown missionary, and Samuel Johnson, he returned from England to become missionary at New Brunswick, New Jersey.[26]

Another Yale victory for the Church was Ephraim Avery. The year he graduated from Yale College, in 1761, he was the Society's teacher at Second River, a clear indication that he was being groomed for the Church ministry. Like so many Yale graduates, he found the Church a more congenial culture than the Congregationalist meeting house where his father was minister in Pomfret, Connecticut.[27]

---

[25] Franklin Bowditch Dexter, Biographical Sketches of the Graduates of Yale College (6 vols; New York, 1885-1912), II, 362; Bela Hubbard to Secretary, Sept. 18, 1769, B, XXIII, 173; Samuel Johnson to Secretary, Sept. 20, 1769, B, XXIII, 200; Abraham Jarvis and Connecticut clergy to Secretary and Bishop of London, Sept. 14, 1769, B, XXIII, 423, Fulham Papers XXI, 89; S.P.G. Journals, XIX, 160.

[26] Franklin Bowditch Dexter, Biographical Sketches of the Graduates of Yale College, II, 446; William Buell Sprague, Annals of the American Pulpit (9 vols; New York, 1857-1869), V, 255; Church Wardens and Vestry, New Brunswick, New Jersey, to Secretary, Nov. 18, 1766, Abraham Beach to Secretary, Jan. 13, 1768, B, XXIV, 298, 299; Samuel Johnson to Secretary, July 5, 1766, B, XXIII, 193.

[27] Franklin Bowditch Dexter, Biographical Sketches of the Graduates of Yale College, II; Jeremiah Leaming to Secretary, Jan. 2, 1765, B, XXIII, 244; Samuel Auchmuty to Secretary, Sept. 10, 1764, B, II, 8

The American-born who became clergymen in the middle colonies differed from the Connecticut, and some of the Massachusetts clergy in that they chose the positive aspects of the Church of England without declaring themselves enemies to their former religion. While religious tolerance in the middle colonies allowed them to regard the Church as a social ballast, it did not represent to them the only alternative to religious and political anarchy.

Regardless of their origins, the clergy in the northern provinces did look to the Church as an escape from American excesses. It offered a dignified, structured alternative to the Presbyterian and Congregationalist systems which they thought placed more authority with the individual than was wise. The colonial Anglican clergy, like the clergy of other denominations, were trying to define their status as gentlemen of learning with an income to match. Alexander Murray made the point clearly in a letter to the Society in 1764, when he wrote that dependence upon pitiful subscriptions must reduce the missionaries to the status of "Fools & Slaves of a Few," resulting in "Poverty & Contempt" which "no Man of Letters or common Abilities" will accept. With this idea in mind, the Connecticut Congregationalist minister Noah Welles lampooned the Anglican clergy in a pamphlet he published anonymously, in 1762, entitled "The Real Advantages . . . By Conforming to the Church of England." He explained that the Church was for polite gentlemen on the road to high office. Welles' claim was not completely untrue. Nevertheless, in spite of the Society's financial support, some Anglican clergy looked to the provinces south of the Delaware where they would not be dependent on their parishioners for support. Because the Society's missionary, John Beach, at Reading in Connecticut, was named in Welles' pamphlet, Samuel Johnson, who was unaware that the anonymous author was ministering very near to his Stratford parish, was eager to have John Beach reply to it. Johnson's son, William Samuel, had reminded his father a little while earlier that the financial difficulties of the Anglican clergy were real; nevertheless, the dissenting clergy laboured under the same disadvantage. Therefore, it was time, he wrote, "to stimulate and awake the slumbering genius of our clergy" to demonstrate that they are inferior to none in literary abilities.[28]

Many of the Anglican clergy objected to being hirelings of their congregations, and the Church, with the Society's financing rescued them from total dependence upon their congregations, and their ordination vows committed them to obey a superior above the laity. Regardless of what happened between priest and people, the Bishop of London or the Archbishop of Canterbury was the ultimate authority. The Dissenting Teachers in the middle colonies were completely at their congregations' mercy for financial support, and, like the Anglican clergy, they had trouble keeping their parishioners to their promises, a common failing, but one which could be disastrous. But the Society's financial assistance decreased the missionaries' dependence, and to improve their lot it had introduced a rule in 1742 requiring each mission to provide a house and glebe for the missionary's personal use.

The Society's Scottish-born missionary James McSparran, at St. Peter's Church in Narragansett, Rhode Island, had been concerned about the direction the American Church was taking when he wrote to the Society, probably in 1742, recommending that before the Society appointed a missionary in America, the congregation should provide a house and a glebe for the minister. The idea appealed to Roger Price at King's Chapel in Boston, who wrote to the Society in support of McSparran's scheme. The failure of congregations meeting their monetary obligations, he wrote, "generally occasions quarrels between Minister and People," and McSparran's scheme would "prevent a dependency of the Clergy upon the People, which is a great obstruction to the progress of the Church here." This scheme might be the means of the Church in the northern colonies one day being "settled upon a Foundation that may be perpetual." The Society adopted McSparran's plan, and many missions endeavoured assiduously to meet their obligations. The mission at Rye, in New York, for example, provided very good facilities, however, some congregations, like St. James in New London,

---

[28] Alexander Murray to Secretary, Jan. 25, 1764, B, XXI, 101; [Noah Welles], The Real Advantages . . . By Conforming to the Church of England (no place, 1762); Samuel Johnson to Archbishop, Jan. 6, 1763, Lambeth Palace Library, vol. 1123, part 3, 289; William Samuel Johnson to Samuel Johnson, Dec. 31, 1762, Schneider's Johnson, I, 329-330.

Connecticut, were reluctant to comply with even this reasonable request. The failure of some congregations to provide the required house and glebe, and to honour their subscription bonds continued throughout their association with the Society. In 1768, the Society's general meeting declared its unwillingness to appoint a missionary to Jamaica on Long Island, following Samuel Seabury's removal to Westchester, New York, because of that mission's failure to meet its monetary obligations. The Newtown congregation of that mission was described as "remarkably obstinate" in their failure to provide support and housing, being "determined to make the Minister's Situation precarious and dependent."[29]

Even after the Society had implemented its new rule, missionaries lamented that so much power remained with the laity, but, because of the peculiar circumstances of the American Church, they could do nothing about it. From the outset a new congregation petitioning the Society for assistance had to guarantee to provide the clergyman with a salary, which, added to the Society's stipend, usually amounted to £80 sterling annually. Arranging subscriptions to pay the priest, build the church and parsonage, and purchase a glebe had to be left with the laity, thus the formation of a new mission placed the priest at the mercy of his parish.

In the 1760's nearly all congregations petitioning the Society for assistance requested a priest in one of the other missions, or a lay reader, to be appointed their missionary. And to this right of invitation the American vestry added the authority to dismiss a minister, to collect subscriptions, and the responsibility for church maintenance, which meant that the vestry controlled almost every aspect of the Church. Yet while all missionaries objected to the difficulties the system presented, none would have interfered with the congregations' right to call ministers. Even Thomas Chandler, one of the most ardent supporters of an American bishop, would not interfere with the congregations' right to choose their own ministers. In October 1767, he wrote to the Bishop of London to introduce his pamphlet "An Appeal to the Public in Behalf of the Church of

---

[29] Roger Price to Secretary, May 3, 1742, B, X, 2; James McSparran to Secretary, May 19, 1744, B, XIII, 75; Matthew Graves to Secretary, Sept. 7, 1748, B, XVI, 23; S.P.G. Journals, XVIII, 66; Secretary Philip Bearcroft to Roger Price, Nov. 6, 1742, B, X, 186a; Roger Price to Secretary, May 5, 1743, B, XI, 1.

England in America," intended to defend the right of Anglicans to have an American resident bishop. Commenting on the state of the Church in Maryland, from whence he had recently returned, he wrote that the churches were built and endowed at the parishioners' expence "yet the Proprietor claims the sole right of Patronage, and causes induction to be made without any regard to the opinion of the parishioners."[30]

Thomas Coombe, while enjoying immense popularity as a preacher in London, summed up the difference between the Church in England and America in a letter to his father in 1770. In America "a Clergyman receives a Salary for the Duty which he performs" but in England "Livings are freehold Estates, and the Incumbents of such have the Privilege of supplying their churches by Curates, and residing themselves at a Distance." Even worse he continued, "A great Man therefore who gives a Clergyman a Living" considers him "ever after as his Dependent, I almost said, his Slave."[31]

The right of congregations to choose their own ministers was further complicated by the absence of a system of promoting missionaries who possessed outstanding talent. Naturally, clergy strove to find recognition by looking to missions which offered greater and more certain financial support. Some clergy were attracted to missions in larger and more culturally diverse towns. The only way most clergy could increase their income, apart from their customary medical practices, was to move to a parish which received greater support from the Society, since dependence upon their congregations' subscriptions could place them in financial difficulty. Thus, parishes, which should have supported their own clergy with minimal support from England, tended to lose their ministers to poorer parishes which received greater assistance from the Society. In 1745, commissary Roger Price, rector of King's Chapel in Boston, advised the Society that the practice of missionaries moving from one mission to another, even to other provinces, had a negative effect. He suggested, instead, that deserving clergy should be given a higher bounty in the mission they were currently serving. That would bind the missionary and

---

[30] Thomas Chandler to Bishop of London, Oct. 21, 1767, Fulham Papers, VI, 164.
[31] Thomas Coombe to his father, June 6, 1770, Thomas Coombe Papers, Correpondence and Business, 1765-1803.

his congregation together. Nevertheless, the problem persisted through the colonial period.[32]

The church wardens and vestry of the New Brunswick mission in New Jersey wrote, in 1763, that Robert McKean was the third missionary the Society "have been pleased to remove from us . . . it would more effectually answer their Pious Design . . . to appoint one for a longer duration." When Leonard Cutting arrived to replace McKean (he would stay only two years before moving to the Hempstead mission on Long Island) the church wardens and vestry complained that their church "appeared rather as a Door opened for the reception & Transition of Missionaries to other Livings . . . so short has been the stay, so Sudden the Change, that many who joined with us, being yet wavering& unfixed, left us & United with Different Societies."[33]

A similar succession of missionaries followed at Gloucester and Waterford in the same province. Certainly, missionaries' accounts indicate that the number of professing Anglicans were very few, however, David Griffith's rapid departure from Gloucester in 1771 angered William Smith and the Philadelphia clergy. Griffith wrote to the Society that because the salary was insufficient, he would leave "immediately' for New York. According to Smith, he said "he only accepted of [the] Gloucester Mission by way of Title, to get ordained by; but not to stay with them."[34]

Francis Hopkinson, poet, musician, artist, and later, politician, travelled with William White to England in 1770 for Anglican ordination. They were both graduates of the College of Philadelphia, with the New Jersey missionary and poet Nathaniel Evans and Thomas Coombe. White returned to Philadelphia as assistant minister at Christ Church with Thomas Coombe. But the Society declined to appoint Hopkinson to Bristol, Bucks County near Philadelphia because the congregation had yet to provide the required house and glebe. Two years later William Smith again recommended Hopkinson for the Bristol congregation. Again the

---

[32] Roger Price to Secretary, Nov. 30, 1745, B, XIII, 74.
[33] Church Wardens and Vestry of New Brunswick to Secretary, [Oct. 24, 1763], Oct. 9, 1764, B, XXIV, 263, 268.
[34] David Griffith to Secretary, New York, Feb. 7, 1771, B, XXIV, 129; William Smith to Secretary, Jan. 14, 1771, B, XXI, 268.

Society declined for the same reason. However, the Society's Secretary, Dr. Hind, wrote to Smith privately that, apart from the Bucks County congregation failing to meet the housing requirements, if Hopkinson were appointed to Bucks County, he would be "a mere Bird of Passage; his Object being a Church in Philadelphia." Besides, the Secretary wrote, he also appeared to expect everything to be done at his demand. (Francis Hopkinson, apart from being very talented, was also cousin of Dr. Johnson, Bishop of Worcester.)[35]

The Society did, however, receive heartening news from Ebenezer Dibblee in Stamford, in November 1760. The death of James Wetmore from smallpox had created a vacancy which that mission offered to Ebenezer Dibblee. Rye was one of the New York parishes where the Church was nominally established by law, and it attracted the attention of missionaries looking for an improvement in their financial circumstances. Dibblee wrote that "the straitness of my family circumstances would have induced me . . to accept." However, the difficulties his removal would have caused his Connecticut parish "and to avoid the Reproach that we seek not the Churchs[sic] good, but our own, influenced me wholly to decline their Invitation." The Society had recently increased his salary to £50 per annum, probably as a mark of its appreciation for his work and because of his financial need.[36]

However, the clergy would not introduce any kind of taxation for their support, preferring instead an income completely independent of the laity, from rents collected from land granted to the Church by the Crown. Thus, the American clergy brought into the Church of England American principles which made them display an ambiguity both to the institution and to American society. Popular control prevented the Church from performing its traditional Old

---

[35] William Smith to Secretary, [Oct., 1770], B, XXI, 267; Samuel Magaw to Secretary, Oct. 14, 1770, B, XXI, 153; Minutes of Vestry, Christ Church, Philadelphia, June 19, 1772, Nov. 16, 1772, Nov. 23, 1772, Nov, 30, 1772; S.P.G. Journals, XIX, 325, XX, 194; R. Hind to William Smith, Aug. 29, 1774, William Smith Papers, II, 4, (Church historical Society); Kenneth Silverman, A Cultural History of the American Revolution (New York, 1976), pp. 58-59; Moses Coit Tyler, The Literary History of the American Revolution 1763-1783, I, pp. 164-167.
[36] Ebenezer Dubblee to Secretary, Nov. 25, 1760, Samuel Johnson to Secretary, Nov. 25, 1760, XXIII, 92, II, 76.

World role. The clergy were unable to assume what they believed to be their rightful authority; they had to obey their congregations' dictates, frequently paying themselves at the same time. Writing from his Oxford mission, near Philadelphia, in 1763, Hugh Neill declared that "This is no Country [for] a missionary to make his fortune, when the only way for him to increase his congregation, is to give up all pretentions to their subscriptions, and to let them know that he preaches freely among them as the Apostles did, without fee or reward."[37]

Hezekiah Watkins found out the difficulty of keeping people to their subscription promises when he re-opened the New Windsor mission in New York. Not only had that mission been closed some years earlier because of its failure to pay its share of the missionary's salary, by 1759 Watkins claimed he had received no more that £15 currency per year. Furthermore, because he had never been officially inducted into the church and glebe, the trustees had pocketed the glebe rent. After Samuel Johnson at King's College and the Rector of Trinity Church, Henry Barclay, in New York, had used their influence with the governor to have him officially inducted, he received only half of the glebe rent. The trustees were mostly dissenters with little sympathy for the Anglican priest. "To Go, or not to Go has been the point" he complained to the Society, having almost ruined his constitution by "Extraordinary Riding and Fatigues," travelling over 2000 miles annually for 15 years.[38]

Outside the major cities, Presbyterian ministers also had trouble collecting subscriptions and pew rents. Some churches hired collectors on a commission basis. However, even the suggestion that an Anglican clergyman might take defaulting subscribers to court could be disastrous, as Jacob Bailey discovered when his dissenter enemies on the Kennebec River spread such a rumour among his parishioners. To bring them back to church, he had to make a public declaration waiving all debts.[39]

William Clarke in Dedham and Stoughton, Massachusetts, was

---

[37] Hugh Neill to Secretary, May 2, 1763, B, XXI, 117.
[38] Hezekiah Watkins to Secretary, June 29, 1759, June 24, 1761, May 13, 1762, Oct. 30, 1764, B, III, 299, 301, 303, 305, 308.
[39] Leonard J. Trinterud, The Forming of an American Tradition (Philadelphia, 1949), p. 204; Jacob Bailey to Secretary, June 27, 1768, B, XXII, 63.

faced with a similar problem. His Stoughton congregation had "defected," he wrote in 1773, and all he could recover of his dues were small sums assessed by law in the Congregationalist parishes. He could recover no more without a "Tedious process at Law" which would "Greatly Hinder, if not finally obstruct" his usefulness. He continued that his Dedham congregation were "prospering & Growing" in spite of the Church's unpopularity. Clarke was singled out for ill-treatment two years later by the Sons of Liberty, and probably his comment regarding '"Disloyalty & Disobedience to Government" reflects the disharmony between him and some members of his congregations.[40]

At Groton and Norwich, in Connecticut, John Beardsley had praise for a few members of his Groton congregation, but he wrote more positively about his congregation at Norwich. However, even though he had provided a house at his own expence, and he had enclosed the glebe of 14 acres given to the mission by the former missionary, Ebenezer Punderson, he could not convince many of his subscribers to pay what they had promised. He informed the Society that his ultimate avenue, after persuasion had failed, would be to "employ A Legal Collector, which gives me no Small Concern . . . as it will tend to prevent the growth of the Church." The Society had appointed him to that mission in August 1761; three years later, lack of financial support caused him to contemplate leaving, in order to avoid bringing "both me and my profession into contempt." At Christmas, 1766, he moved to Poughkeepsie, in Dutchess County, New York, where he had been ministering occasionally since his arrival in Groton. His final letter from Groton, in October 1766, suggested to the Society that some of his congregation were not pulling their weight. According to the Connecticut Grand List for taxation purposes, his subscribers in Groton were assessed on average at £50 each, while those professing to be of the Church of England, but who were not subscribers, were valued at about £60 each. His Norwich subscribers, while not as wealthy, were assessed on average about £33 each, and his non-subscribing professed Anglicans averaged about £56 each. .[41]

---

[40] William Clarke to Secretary, Oct. 26, 1773, XXII, 144
[41] John Beardsley to Secretary, Sept. 26, 1764, Oct. 4, 1766, B, XXIII, 54, 62, Feb. 26, 1767, III, 24; S.P.G. Journals, XV, 117,125.

When subscribers did pay, they often did so in "Produce of any Kind and [at] their own Price," as Leonard Cutting found at New Brunswick, New Jersey. Thomas Thompson at Chester, Pennsylvania, lost several of his congregation to the Quakers because "of their owning much Property and because of their influence in government," and by their "careful promoting of each other & worldly Interest." He was disillusioned with their being more concerned with wealth and political influence than with the gospel. They value a missionary, he declared, only for "the annuity he has to spend and their share of it." By "annuity" he meant the Society's bounty.[42]

As a member of the Episcopal Church in Scotland, George Craig went to Philadelphia in the early 1740's, where his uncle, Archibald Cummings, had been rector of Christ Church, and then the Bishop of London's commissary. George Craig returned to England in 1750 for ordination. The Society appointed him to the Lancaster mission, but before long he was at odds with his vestry, and in 1758 he moved to Chester, where he complained that, though the mission was opened in 1701, and in spite of the Society's requirement since 1742 that missions provide a house and glebe, there was still no provision made. After two years in Chester he had received no subscriptions, nor did they provide "so much as a Stable for their Missionary's Horse."[43]

Undoubtedly there were congregations which, because of poverty, could not support their own ministers, and missionaries were usually understanding. Son of a Pennsylvania Dissenting minister William Thompson took Anglican orders to become itinerant missionary in York and Cumberland Counties, in Pennsylvania. He took up his position there in May, 1760. Two years later his congregation had fallen far short of the subscription promised to him. The glebe was uncultivated, therefore it brought

---

[42] Leonard Cutting to Secretary, Nov. 26, 1765, B, XXIV, 295; Thomas Thompson to Secretary, May 16, 1752, B, XX, 116.

[43] Robert Jenny to Secretary, April 10 1745, B, XII, 37; S. Nicholls to Bishop of London, Aug. 27, 1750, Fulham Papers, XXIII, 169; George Craig to Secretary, July 17, 1760, B, XXI, 46. The Record Book of St. Paul's Church, Chester, Pennsylvania, entry for Oct. 6, 1753, noted a letter from the Society stating that if the vestry did not repair the church and provide a house for the missionary, the Society would withdraw its support.

him no relief. In order to supplement his income, he requested the Society's permission to minister as chaplain to the army on the frontier, a request the Society declined. His congregations were suffering hard times during the Indian uprising of 1763; Thompson was forced to evacuate from his mission, together with 750 families. The vestry of Christ Church in Philadelphia supplied money, food, clothing and medical supplies to his parish, as well as to families of the non-Anglican communities. At Thompson's request, Christ Church also supplied "two chests of Arms; half a barrel of Powder, 400 [pounds] of lead, and 200 [pounds] of swan shot and 1000 flints," for families wishing to return to their farms. Thompson had a large family, and, according to William Smith, having "grown very bulky & Corpulent," and being no longer able "to endure the vast Fatigues" of his mission, he removed to Trenton, New Jersey, in June, 1769.[44]

Many a missionary wished to be as independent as John Preston at Perth-Amboy. Fifty years old, healthy and "a man of letters," according to his church wardens, John Preston was chaplain to the 26th regiment stationed in New Jersey from July, 1767, until it left in 1777. He was serving at the same time as the Society's missionary, receiving the missionary's salary in addition to his chaplain's pay. Writing to the Society in October, 1769, in a style that is remarkable for its directness and lack of deference, he informed them that he had "declined accepting the gratuity" from his congregation because he did not choose "to lye under pecuniary obligations to any of them." He considered the American missions to be of no greater value than that of the salary from England and the rent of the lands annexed to them, and he would never ask any of his parishioners for a farthing of what they had subscribed. He was actually receiving the subscriptions from the Perth-Amboy congregation which were collected by the church wardens; he was referring to the Woodbridge congregation which never offered to pay him, nor did they pay his predecessors. He was a man of independent means.

---

[44] Thomas Barton to Secretary, May 8, 1760, July 31, 1760, B, XXI, 5,6; William Thompson to Secretary, Nov. 13, 1765, Aug. 20, 1766, Oct. 2, 1764, B, XXI, 294, 295, [291]; S. P.G. Journals, XV, 267; Vestry Minutes of Christ Church, Philadelphia, Aug. 10,1763, Sept. 7, 1763; William Smith to Secretary, Oct. 22, 1768 B, XXI, 261; William Thompson to Secretary, June 26, 1769, B, XXIV, 175.

However, the Society, knowing well the problems facing its missionaries, requested that he not refuse the subscriptions because that could "be an injury to his Successor and to the Mission."[45]

This dependence on subscriptions not only placed the missionary under economic hardship, congregations consisting of so many recruited from the Dissenters with their independent tradition often rendered his efforts at reconciling factions within his congregation useless. James Lyons referred to the factious members of his Brookhaven mission on Long Island as "Churchmen in words, but Congregationalists in Discipline." Leonard Cutting found a similar problem with the Piscataway congregation in his New Brunswick mission in New Jersey. Dissenters who had joined the Church, divided into two parties over a land dispute. The warring factions demanded that Cutting take sides. When he refused to deny communion to a member of the minority party, the others retaliated, some leaving the Church, others giving up their pews declaring they would not renew their subscriptions the following year.[46]

The position seemed hopeless, especially as some clergy feared that the Society understood little about America. Hezekiah Watkins, in describing the difficulties of bringing in subscriptions in his New York mission, where true Churchmen were few, commented that "People in This Country, are so very apt to make such Loud Clamours when they are sued for what they had promised to pay a minister." He continued "It is not Easey for the Good People in England where Things Relating to This Subject are well Regulated by Good Laws, to conceive the Difficulties which attends a missionary" in the colonies. This lack of first-hand acquaintance with conditions in America was also a concern to the Chester missionary George Craig. In 1760, reciting once again his litany of complaints about the state of the Church in Pennsylvania, he called for the appointment of bishops. Without their help the Church "will ever be a jumble of confusion," he wrote. Support for missionaries urging vestries to provide houses and glebes, or to meet monetary

---

[45] S.P.G. Journals, XVIII, 89, 317; John Preston to Secretary, Oct. 10, 1769, March 19, 1771, B, XXIV, 279, 281; Church Wardens and Vestry of Perth-Amboy to Secretary, June 16, 1769, B, XXIV, 278.

[46] James Lyons to Secretary, Oct. 8, 1763, B, III, 202; Leonard Cutting to Secretary, Nov. 26, 1765, B, XXIV, 295.

obligations was, for him, essential to obviate the missionaries' becoming an "Object of ... Contempt, and his Doctrine too." Like so many other Anglican clergy, he stressed the need for bishops to confirm and to reinforce the sponsors' obligations at christening as essential if the Church were to retain its distinction from the dissenting sectaries. He shared the view of other Anglican clergy in the northern provinces that the close of the war with France was an opportune time to remedy the situation. However, anticipating the failure of such an appointment, he urged as an alternative the appointment of some "discreet person or persons" to visit the missions to allow the Society a better understanding of the situation facing the clergy. And following the disturbances over the Stamp Act, James Scovil at Westbury, Connecticut, urged the appointment of resident bishops "to ordain, govern and confirm, those of our Communion." He reminded the Secretary that "They who live in England, where the Church is rather Triumphant, can have but a faint Idea of its truly Militant State here in New England."[47]

"The Good People in England" were clearly not completely familiar with the geographical details of their American missions. Englishman Matthew Graves arrived in New London, Connecticut, in 1747, to find that his "expectations" of his new mission were not the deliberate consequence of his church wardens' misrepresentations. It was, Samuel Johnson explained, "a misunderstanding by the [Society's] Secretary's not distinguishing between or not considering the distance between New London and Hebron which was annexed to it." The Hebron Anglican community had a glebe of eighty acres "which the Society must apprehend as belonging to or being near New London." A distance of about twenty miles meant that the New London missionary could "never be the better for it." Samuel Johnson, always the father and confidant of new recruits and new arrivals, explained to the "stunned" Englishman that coming from England where the Church "is established and uppermost and flourishing" to America where the Church is in a "militant depressed state" and "scattered about in little parcels and among enemies, and without ministers" needed

---

[47] Hezekiah Watkins to Secretary, May 13, 1762, B, III, 303; George Craig to Secretary, July 17, 1760, B, XXI, 46; James Scovil to Secretary, July 6, 1767, B, XXIII, 343.

careful study and understanding. The Connecticut people possess "a spirit of liberty [that] beats high in their veins, beyond what Europe ever knew," he explained[48]

The task facing the Society's Secretary was enormous. He had to deal with volumes of correspondence each month from missionaries on the coast of Africa, in The West Indies, Central America and most of the American colonies from Georgia in the south to Newfoundland in the north. He had to read patiently pleas from many priests from the various colonies for the appointment of American bishops, to which he could offer no more than his sympathy. Then, there were senior clergy whose letters often appeared to question the Society's understanding of American affairs. One such letter came from Samuel Auchmuty on January 30, 1770, in which he urged action regarding Governor of New York Henry Moore's offer of land, and Sir William Johnson's need for a missionary on the Mohawk River. Dr. Burton's reply appeared to Auchmuty to be reproachful, so he defused his feelings in a letter to Richard Peters in Philadelphia. "The Truth of the matter is" he wrote "we are blessed . . . with an old lazy Secretary, who has neither leisure nor Inclination to put the best foot forward, and with a board of Bishops and Laity who neither care what becomes of the American Church, or the American clergy." Auchmuty was simply being his pompous self. However, his comments that followed do get to the heart of what concerned many American priests. He continued "I most sincerely wish that the Society would procure an able clergyman from America to act as their Secretary. They would then do business as it ought to be done."[49]

Similar references to English Church leaders' lack of knowledge of the American provinces came from William Sturgeon, a minister at Philadelphia's Christ Church, and his political ally, John Hughes, in 1765. Hoping to gain support from the Society and the British ministry, they were suggesting that islands along the coast of New Jersey, whose legal ownership, they claimed, lay with the King,

---

[48] Matthew Graves to Samuel Johnson, June 18, 1748, Samuel Johnson to Matthew Graves, June 27, 1748, Schneider's Johnson, I, pp. 131-134.
[49] Samuel Auchmuty to Richard Peters, Sept. 2, 1771, Wallace Papers, IV, 25 (Historical Society of Pennsylvania); Samuel Auchmuty to Secretary, Jan. 30, 1771, Aug. 16, 1771, B, II, 35, 37.

should be given to the care of the colony of New Jersey. The proceeds derived from the administration of the land could be used to support the Society's missions. "We are better Acquainted" they wrote "with some Advantages that may be had in this Great new World [than] Gentlemen in Great Britain with Ten Times our Abilities who are altogether Unacquainted with every part of the Country and the Particular Modes of Settlement."[50]

For an American like Thomas Coombe who had the advantage of understanding the Church on both sides of the Atlantic, the problems facing a clergyman in America were very clear. He was brought up in Philadelphia's Christ Church, and left for England in 1769, planning to return in the Society's service. But having had considerable success in London as a very popular preacher in Deacon's orders, he began to cast his eyes upon one of the more secure livings in the large American cities. Among the offers made to him was a call on subscription to the prestigious Trinity Church in New York, and the suggestion that he might be called to Trinity Church in Boston. Yet he knew that even those wealthy appointments were precarious, and he had "spent some anxious days, and sleepless nights" over the prospect of depending "upon the caprice of a Congregation" in America. "I well remember" he wrote to his father from London, in 1771, "the fare old Dr. Jenny met from his congregation who considered their paying him his salary during his sickness and decline, as a very vigorous effort of charity on their part. And the same I suppose will always be the case, when a Clergyman's support arises from subscription - -subscription the most unworthy of all supports."[51]

William Clarke of Dedham, Massachusetts, was in England for ordination at about the same time as Thomas Coombe. He found out very soon after returning from England what Thomas Coombe and many others discovered. Clarke's ordination had cost him £80 sterling, including a bout of London's smallpox, only to return to continual confrontation from his mission, especially the Stoughton

---

[50] William Sturgeon and John Hughes to Secretary, March 23, 1765, B, XXI, 283.
[51] Thomas Coombe to his father, Oct. 3, 1769, Aug. 29, 1771, Thomas Coombe Papers: Correspondence and Business, 1765-1803; Vestry Minutes of Trinity Church, New York, Nov. 9, 1773; Anne Rowe Cunningham, ed., <u>Letters and Diary of John Rowe Boston Merchant 1759-1779</u> (Boston, 1903), p. 238.

congregation. The lesson was clear to him, in 1774, when he wrote to the Society that "a young man must have much Courage and resolution who Enters on a new Mission in this Country."[52]

Many missionaries longed for the day when the British ministry would allocate land in America to maintain the Church, a subject continually discussed in the correspondence between America and London. The idea held great appeal for Samuel Peters, who, in one of his numerous, lengthy letters to the Society ferociously denouncing the pinch-penny attitude of his Connecticut congregation, claimed that only then "peace might prevail between Priest & People, which is a rare thing in America unless the Priest will pay himself and be very grateful to his Hearers besides."[53]

Isaac Browne made his feelings about subscriptions clear when he wrote from New Jersey in April, 1768. He was referring, in particular, to the newspaper and pamphlet controversy provoked by Thomas Chandler's writings promoting the appointment of an American bishop. "The Church of England in this part of the World" he wrote "is truly Militant, and the clergy are more so than the other Members of the Church." There is no provision in many of the provinces for the clergy's support, he explained, other than voluntary contributions "or obligations by Note or Bond, all of which are a perfect cheat in too many Instances, and meer Impositions on the Society and their clergy." To make them good, the clergy have no option other than to go to law and destroy the Congregation and earn a bad name for himself. Members of the Society in London knew of these problems facing their missionaries. Bishop of London Thomas Sherlock refused to appoint Samuel Fayerweather to Taunton, Massachusetts, in 1756, because "his bond from Taunton people was good for nothing." He added that he had known "instances of it from other places and Taunton . . . never intended to pay what they had promised him."[54]

During the years of the War for Independence refugee clergy in London worked hard on behalf of the Church in America. The Brookhaven parish, on Long Island, where James Lyons struggled

---

[52] William Clarke to Secretary, April 15, 1774, B, XXII, 147.
[53] Samuel Peters to Secretary, June 26, 1771, B, XXIII, 333.
[54] Isaac Browne to Secretary, [April 6, 1768], B, XXIV, 40; William Johnson to Samuel Johnson, Jan. 10, 1756, Schneider's Johnson, I, pp. 232-235

for twenty two years before being dismissed, in 1767, recruited the assistance of clergy in New York and London to gain the Society's financial support. The Society had not supported a minister at Brookhaven since Lyons' dismissal. In 1781, the Brookhaven congregation requested help for Thomas Lambert Moore who had departed for London, without invitation, seeking ordination. Thomas Bradbury Chandler, writing to the Bishop of London from Cowes, on the Isle of Wight, stated that Moore's character was very good and his bond "is good as an American Title can be, from a part of the country where the Church is not established." The request from Brookhaven was unlikely to succeed in such troubled times, and when the Society's English benefactors were reluctant to subscribe to help Americans in revolt. Furthermore, several of the Brookhaven subscribers were Presbyterians, and the Huntingdon church (which had formerly been part of that mission) seemed to be "almost destitute of real professors" of the Church of England.[55]

Perhaps the interest being shown in the Church on Long Island, in such a bleak political climate, encouraged the Society to look with favour upon the application. Perhaps the Islip community's support for the Brookhaven petition kindled warmer feelings in London. Islip had never had a settled minister of any denomination. However, they had built a church, which they had called "Charlotte" after the Queen, as an expression of their loyalty to Britain. The Reverend Mr. Morice, the Society's Secretary, wrote to the Bishop of London that Moore was related to "Dr. More formerly Minister of St. Botolph Aldergate." Thomas Lambert Moore also had the support of émigrés Jonathan Boucher, a vocal Maryland Loyalist, who frequently attended the Society's monthly meetings at St. Mary-le-Bow Church, and New Yorker John Vardill, famed "spy" and friend of the ministry. The Society did support Moore's ordination for Brookhaven, adding a gratuity of £20.[56]

The uncertainty of income from subscriptions led several

---

[55] Thomas Chandler to Bishop of London, Aug. 8, 1781, Fulham Papers, XXII, [310]; Subscibers of Caroline Church, Suffolk County, New York, April 17, 1781, Church Wardens and Vestry of Caroline Church, April 20, 1781, Fulham Papers XXII, 299, 301.

[56] S.P.G. Journals, XXII, 430; Subscribers of Islip, Suffolk County, May 1, 1781, Fulham Papers, XXII,305; Dr. Morice to Bishop of London, July 27, 1781, Fulham Papers, XXII, 309; Loyalist Claims, Memorial of John Vardill of New York, XLII.

clergymen (Ebenezer Dibblee, Solomon Palmer, John Beardsley and Isaac Browne, to mention a few) to cast envious eyes upon the four New York parishes, though the security of that establishment was more imagined than real. In May, 1760, James Wetmore died in his New York mission. His son, Timothy, read services at the church to hold the congregation together. He was concerned about the difficulties clergy faced in the New York parishes, where the Church was legally established, when he wrote to the Society in 1761. In the Rye parish, the vestry called the priest, who was then inducted by the governor. However, the vestry was comprised, not only of Anglicans, but of all the sects in the parish. A dominant vestryman, who was allegedly indifferent to religion, and son of a former Society missionary (probably John Thomas of Hempstead, Long Island, 1704-1724) was the dominant influence with a number of vestrymen who were neither Anglican no communicants. Wetmore explained that they controlled the church affairs and decided who should be priest. Therefore, the establishment was no more than a chimera. John Milner left the legally established Westchester parish, in 1765, for a parish in Virginia "where the Church is established in reality" he wrote "and some certain provisions made for the clergy." After fourteen years in Delaware and Pennsylvania, Hugh Neill left the Society's service to take a parish in Maryland. He informed the Society, in 1766, that Governor Sharpe had inducted him into St. Paul's Parish in Queen Anne County, worth £300 sterling per annum. Now, having acquired "a considerable Landed Estate" he felt free from financial insecurity and the bickering among the Philadelphia clergy and laity. Financial insecurity caused a steady flow of clergy from the northern provinces to Virginia and Maryland where "a man may live comfortably . . . & lay something against a rainy Day," as Thomas Coombe once commented.[57]

No less than ten missionaries left the Society's service for parishes in Maryland and Virginia between 1760 and 1775. Some arrived in the South only after a strenuous odyssey, like John Lyon, who gave up hope after five years dependence on a Massachusetts congregation, stayed but a few days at Gloucester and Waterford in

---

[57] Timothy Cutler to Secretary, May 6, 1761, John Milner to Secretary, [Feb. 3], 1768, B, III, 215, 291; Hugh Neill to Secretary, June 9, 1767, B, XXI, 127; Thomas Coombe Jr. to Thomas Coombe Sr., Dec. 6, 1769, Thomas Coombe Papers.

New Jersey, to which the Society had appointed him, before moving on to the unhealthy mission in Lewes, Delaware. Within one year, he lost his wife and only child, and he was so weakened that he finally retired to a Virginia parish. In 1770, William Clark looked north from his Massachusetts mission. Having braved, what he considered to be the ingratitude of his contentious congregations at Dedham and Stoughton, he concluded that the Imperial disputes were exacerbating a situation already too difficult. He therefore requested that the Society allow him to accept a call to the Anglican congregation at Granville, in Nova Scotia, to whom he had ministered when both they and he had been Congregationalists in Massachusetts. In Nova Scotia, the Church enjoyed government favour, and appeared not to suffer the persecution it experienced in New England. However, the Society remembered well that its reason for opening the Dedham mission was to secure land bequeathed to the Church by one its members there, and advised Clark to stay where he was. The provision of an establishment would remove the most important problem but still leave others.[58]

The Society held the right to present clergy but it never questioned a congregation's claim to choose its own minister. Nevertheless, the Rye and Perth-Amboy congregations were not alone in rejecting their missionaries after they had left the choice with the Society. On guard against any invasion of their rights, the Trenton mission refused to apply for a charter from the governor of New Jersey because that would have given him the right of presentation. The church wardens pointed out to the Society in 1765 "We by no means chuse to accept of One under these Circumstances, For as by the Society's Bounty & Generosity the Church is Supported, We wou'd chuse the Presentation to continue in them 'till that Ceases, and then to be vested in the Congregation." A charter was necessary to allow the church to conduct such business as buying land and accepting legacies. Therefore, the

---

[58] John Lyon to Secretary, Oct. 25, 1769, Jan. 10, 1770, Nov. 22, 1773, B, XXI, 170, 171, 181; William Clark to Secretary, April 23, 1770, Oct. 1, 1770, Jan.16, 1771, B, XXII, 140, 141, 142; Chief Justice Belcher's Minutes of Nova Scotia Corresponding Society, Sept. 25, 1771, Oct. 22, 1771, B, XXV, 172, 173; S.P.G. Journals, XVIII, 466. Hugh Neill, David Griffith, Andrew Morton, William Andrews, Thomas Brown, John Milner, Ichabod Camp, William Thompson and John Andrews moved from missions in the northern provinces to parishes in Virginia and Maryland.

church wardens requested that the Society intervene on their behalf to help them obtain a charter of incorporation to allow them to avoid the governor's involvement. It appears that modification to a charter was possible because, in about 1762, Christ Church in New Brunswick, New Jersey, obtained a charter which specifically gave the presentation of clergy to the Society, and it stated that should the Society fail to nominate a minister, the right of presentation rested with the church wardens and vestry. The church wardens and vestry of St. James Church in New London, Connecticut, set Matthew Graves to thinking about a move to South Carolina, where the Church was legally established, when they informed him that the rector had no function other than reading prayers and sermons. They claimed that neither the Bishop of London nor the Society had any authority over them.[59]

Even Trinity Church in New York, which, along with the other wealthy churches in the big cities, always enjoyed the right to appoint their own rectors and assistant ministers, could cross swords with the Society. Although Trinity Church supported its rector, the Society had for many years helped finance Trinity Church's catechist to the Negroes. In 1747, the Society's catechist, Richard Charlton, who also served as assistant minister to the rector, left Trinity Church for the Society's mission on Staten Island. According to the Governor of New York, he was upset at being overlooked as successor when William Vesey died in July, 1746. Trinity Church chose as their new rector Henry Barclay, the Society's missionary to the Mohawks. The Society had suggested that Trinity Church should look for a suitable replacement for Charlton, but then appointed the recently ordained Bostonian, and Harvard graduate Samuel Auchmuty. The vestry formed a committee which wrote to the Society that the appointment was acceptable except for "one Materiall Qualification . . . the Strength and Clearness of his Voice; Our Church being by all Accounts one of the Largest in America, So that few Gents are perfectly heard in it,

---

[59] Samuel Johnson to Secretary, April 10, 1763, B, XXIII, 184; Church Wardens and Vestry of Perth-Amboy to Secretary, Nov. 15, 1768, B, XXIV, 276; Church Wardens of Trenton, New Jersey, to Secretary, Oct. 6, 1765, B, XXIV, 198; Christ Church, New Brunswick, charter of incorporation, B, XXIV, 256; Robert McKean to Secretary, Oct. 5, 176[2], B, XXIV, 257; Matthew Graves to Secretary, Sept. 2, 1752, B, XX, 35.

We Should therefore have Wished to have been favoured with the Liberty of Making Our Own Choice" and should Auchmuty not meet their requirements, he should leave "and the Honorable Board will Indulge us in the Choice of Another." The Reverend Auchmuty did qualify and the vestry raised a subscription for his support.[60]

When Samuel Johnson left Stratford to become the first president of King's College, in 1754, he wanted John Beach to replace him, but the Reading missionary, originally himself a Congregationalist, knew too well how such an arrangement would upset that congregation's notions of liberty. The Society gave Isaac Browne at Newark, New Jersey, permission to move to Perth-Amboy, but that mission refused to accept him because they had not given him "a call." In fact, they said he was too old, frequently ill, and they considered his practising medicine an obstacle to his ministerial duties. The Oxford mission, near Philadelphia, refused to accept a missionary who was not of their calling. "Such is the Notion" William Smith commented "which their neighbourhood to Philadelphia helps to confirm them in." When Charles Inglis left his Dover mission in Delaware for New York's Trinity Church, in 1766, the Dover congregation rejected the Society's appointee, choosing instead, Samuel Magaw who they described as having been "a Preacher much deservedly Esteemed among the Dissenters of the Presbyterian Denomination." Inglis was concerned about the reaction of the Dover Anglicans to the Society's proposal to assign the Duck Creek part of the Dover mission elsewhere. In his letter to the Secretary he quoted from Charles Ridgely, a member of the Dover congregation, who had written that should the people of the mission think the Society were acting arbitrarily, the union would be dissolved "unless our People are treated with more Respect." Charles Ridgely insisted that the Dover congregation were not averse to American bishops, indeed they understood how necessary bishops were to the American Church. Ridgely's strong views on the Society's "arbitrary" resolutions were more likely a reflection of the laity's view of Parliament's arbitrarily imposing taxes upon the colonies. The Society took heed of the Dover mission's warnings and

---

[60] Henry Barclay to Secretary, Dec. 2, 1746, B, XIV, 95; Governor of New York to Secretary, Dec. 20, 1746, B, XIV, 92; Vestry Minutes of Trinity Church, Nov. 24, 1747, March 8, 1748.

decided to leave matters as they were.[61]

Immigrant clergy, however, often lacked the wisdom of Americans like John Beach, and their failure to understand the independent spirit of American congregations sometimes drove a wedge between minister and people. George Craig offended his congregation in his first year at Lancaster by refusing to choose his senior warden, according to local custom, from the elected vestry, insisting instead, to choose his warden from the congregation at large; consequently, for the four years he remained there, the vestry retaliated by arrogating and sharing the wardens' work among themselves. The Graves brothers also had trouble with their congregations. The Rhode Islanders challenged John Graves' right to appoint a warden. The Society resolved that he should "not relinquish his right of nominating one of the Church Wardens." His brother Matthew, however, met total sovereignty of the people in New London, Connecticut.[62]

Tensions within the Church had many causes. Missions which failed to provide parsonages denied, in many cases, the clergyman's right to privacy. William Gibbs, in 1752, had to live in a room in his church warden's house in Simsbury, Connecticut. Situations like that led to many a clergyman's downfall. In New Jersey, Andrew Morton's innocent interest in the daughter of the vestryman he lodged with developed into sinister scandal as the stories proliferated among the church gossips. This kind of problem could be corrected, but innovations that converted clergy and laity brought into the Church might remain undetected, and added to environmental attrition, could spell disaster. Not long after his arrival in New London, in 1748, Matthew Graves summarised the situation that many immigrant clergy had found. "I cannot from their Behaviour in church conclude that ever they had an Orthodox Minister among them" he wrote. "As my manner of performing

---

[61] John Beach to Samuel Johnson, Nov. 9, 1753, "Johnson Members of the Family, Johnson 2" (Connecticut Historical Society); Isaac Browne to Secretary, Sept. 1, 1768, Oct. 6, 1768, B, XXIV, 41, 42; William Smith to Secretary, May 6, 1768, B, XXI, 259; Charles Inglis to Secretary, Dec. 1, 1766, B, XXI, 150.

[62] Vestry Book of St. James Church, Lancaster, 1744-1846 (possession of the Rector); S.P.G. Journals, XIX, 180; Matthew Graves to Secretary, Sept.2, 1752, XX, 35.

seems strange to them, so does their Religious Deportment to me."[63]

The environment alone upset any idea of transplanting the Church as it funtioned in England. Arthur Browne at Portsmouth, writing his half-yearly notitia parochialis in 1741, had difficulty estimating the number of Church people in his mission because his was the only Anglican church in New Hampshire, and therefore he concluded that "the province at large" was his parish. Theophilus Morris found his Connecticut mission "large enough for a Diocese," but it was small compared with Bailey's on the Kennebec River covering 6000 square miles, having neither church nor parsonage. Bailey's support came almost entirely from the Society because many of his parishioners were German migrants heavily in debt to pay for their passages to America.[64]

Primitive conditions often forced missionaries to depart from the proper decorum that the Anglican service demanded. When Peter De La Roche arrived at Lunenburg, Nova Scotia , as missionary to the French and English, in 1771, he found the church had no communion plate except a small pewter chalice belonging to his colleague, Paulus Bryzelius. Before Bryzelius' arrival at Lunenburg, the previous missionary, Robert Vincent, had used "glasses or a mug," and "as the Communicants are numerous" De La Roche explained "the Alter like a Tavern table is covered with bottles of Wine on a Communion Day, & offers to a beholder who has seen the Sacrament of the Lord's Supper celebrated with even only Decency, the most shocking Spectacle."[65]

Moses Badger, the first itinerant missionary in New Hampshire, without even a solitary church, wrote to the Society that he was neglecting to administer the Communion as he could not perform it "with decency in private houses." The Secretary, flooded with missionaries' complaints that their congregations were refusing the

---

[63] William Gibbs to Secretary, June 23, 1752, B, XX, 43; Andrew Morton to Secretary, Sept. 30, 1762, B, XXIV, 206; New Jersey clergy certificates in behalf of Andrew Morton, Oct. 1, 1762, B, XXIV, 207; John Grandin to Robert McKean, Sept. 19, 1763, B, XXIV, 218; New Jersey clergy to Secretary, Oct. 19, 1763, B, XXIV, 219; Matthew Graves to Secretary, Sept. 7, 1748, XVI, 23.

[64] Arthur Browne to Secretary, Sept. 28, 1741, B, IX, 27; Theophilus Morris to Secretary, Sept. 15, 1740, B, VII, part 2, 53; Jacob Bailey to Secretary, March 26, 1761, June 27, 1768, B, XXII, 59, 63.

[65] Peter De La Roche to Secretary, Oct. 5, 1771, B, XXV, 168.

sacraments, thought it better that Badger should perform it in private houses even if it meant doing it "with less solemnity than could be wished."[66]

The severe North American winter affected English immigrants more than the Americans, and De La Roche urged his vestry to provide a vestryroom and a stove, not only for himself and Bryzelius, who had to stay at the church all day on Sundays in order to preach to the English, French and German speaking people, but also to encourage them to attend. Philip Reading had suffered a frost-bitten leg when travelling to one of his churches in Delaware at Christmas, in 1755, in temperatures so cold that "the bread provided for the celebration of the Lord's Supper became frozen on the table before the Sacrament could be administered." No wonder that Samuel Johnson should have to admit to the Society that the extreme cold compelled some missionaries to omit parts of the Church service.[67]

New arrivals, especially in Pennsylvania and Nova Scotia, were often appalled at what they saw. When Peter De La Roche arrived at Lunenburg, Nova Scotia, in September, 1777, he found "the Spiritual field [to be] like the natural, wild, stoney and overrun with weeds." The congregations were, in general, bound to the Church only by pecuniary interest. In 1775, he was convinced that "Christianity is in America a Specter void of all substance." He was probably referring to the "great numbers of New England people" in Nova Scotia "who may be reasonably enough suspected of disaffection" to Britain. However, not all New Englanders in Nova Scotia were so disappointing. The former New England congregation settled at Granville, probably because they had no Congregationalist minister, attended the Anglican church where they listened to the Society's missionary, Thomas Wood, whose preaching removed their "former prejudices." They became so much at home with their new mode of worship that they invited their former Congregationalist Teacher, William Clark, who had become the Society's missionary at Dedham

---

[66] S.P.G. Journals, XVIII, 37.
[67] Peter De La Roche to Secretary, Oct. 5, 1771, B, XXV, 168; Philip Reading to Secretary, March 15, 1775, B, XXI, 210; Samuel Johnson to Secretary, [1750], B, XVIII, 60.

in Massachusetts, to become their priest.[68]

Sixty miles away at Windsor, Nova Scotia, William Ellis met a common problem. A multiplicity of denominations, none by itself able to support a minister, had subscribed to build the church and pay the missionary's salary. Eventually, when a Presbyterian minister arrived, part of the congregation seceded, claiming sole ownership of the church building. The building used at Windsor as a church, Ellis found, had been built by general subscription, some saying for a schoolroom, some saying for a courthouse; it was actually used as a schoolhouse, courthouse, a Dissenting meeting house, and "occasionally for a tipling house, on which occasions the most indecent scenes" were enacted.[69]

Even the clergy in the older settled provinces where they had to care for four or more separate congregations had difficulty fostering polite manners, for how could a clergyman "kept constantly upon the Wing," enquired James Scovil from Connecticut, "promote the important Cause of God & the Church as a more Constant Residence could do so?" Ebenezer Punderson wrote to the Society, in September 1749, about a tour he had recently made. His exertions appear to have been commonplace in his mission in Connecticut and elsewhere. On Monday, April 1, 1749, he rode from Groton to Middleton, where he preached. The following day he rode six miles to Durham with Ichabod Camp, who was at that time one of Samuel Johnson's readers at Middleton, preparing for Anglican ordination. On Wednesday, Punderson preached at Cohabit, before riding a further eight miles to Guilford. On Thursday he returned to Cohabit, Friday he returned to Middleton. Saturday he rode to Norwich, where he preached the following day before returning to Groton. He probably performed some of his services in private homes, because there were no churches in some of the places he visited. It was a marathon performance from a devoted minister.[70]

Missionaries' efforts to convince congregations of the need to observe the sacraments often resulted in compromise. John Pugh of

---

[68] Peter De La Roche to Secretary, Nov. 28, 1771, Aug. 15, 1775, Oct. 4, 1775, B, XXV, 174, 195, 196; Special Meeting of the Nova Scotia Committee of Correspondence, Oct. 22, 1771, B, XXV, 173.
[69] William Ellis to Secretary, Sept. 14, 1776, B, XXV, 208.
[70] James Scovil to Secretary, July 8, 1766, B, XXIII, 342; Ebenezer Punderson to Secretary, Sept. 25, 1749, B, XVII, 65.

Delaware felt obliged, in 1740, to dispose with sureties at baptism "rather than let them carry their children else where," and George Craig still found twenty years later in Pennsylvania that "the Sponsors are become as Things Obsolete." In 1760, Ebenezer Dibblee at Stamford, Connecticut, informed the Society that he could not persuade his people to appoint guardians and to stand as sureties for children at the time of baptism. Samuel Johnson admitted to the Bishop of London in 1732 that some priests added the words "if there be opportunity" following the exhortation to godfathers, after baptism, to bring the child to the bishop for conformation. The slight amendment was required to avoid the Dissenters' scornful criticism that the nearest bishop was not "within 1000 Leagues of us."[71]

John Langman felt compelled to baptise children in their parents' homes when they refused to take them to church. The Society, far from failing to understand his problems, put the Newfoundland missionary at ease. But two over-zealous Rhode Island Baptist converts brought Samuel Fayerweather rebuke from London when he baptised them after they had renounced their former immersion and insisted upon "truly Christian baptism" in the Church of England. Joseph Bennett tried to encourage his people in Nova Scotia to have their children baptised, but hostility to the sign of the cross needed more than remittance of fees, and it was a problem that clergymen experienced in several provinces. William Ellis wrote to the Society from Nova Scotia for advice about omitting it, especially as the Quaker and Baptist converts ridiculed it. The rector of St. Paul's in Halifax had asked the same question when he visited England, in 1772, but the Society's Secretary had frowned upon any alterations or omissions.[72]

Similarly, fear and ignorance of the Holy Communion puzzled missionaries who tried to maintain strict adherence to Church rites. Both Isaac Browne at Brookhaven, on Long Island, in 1743, and his successor, James Lyons, found their efforts unrewarded, while John Checkley, at Providence, Rhode Island, marvelled at the objections

---

[71] John Pugh to Secretary, Nov. 17, 1740, B, IX, 103; George Craig to Secretary July 17, 1760, B, XXI, 46; S.P.G. Journals, XIV, General Meeting, July 18, 1760; Samuel Johnson to Bishop of London, June 4, 1732, Fulham Papers, I, 245.
[72] S.P.G. Journals, XX, 52, XV, 304; Joseph Bennett to Secretary, July 28, 1763, B, XXV, 30; William Ellis to Secretary, Sept. 14, 1776, B, XXV, 208.

people raised to the sacraments, and declared those "dragged up in Schism" were worse than those brought up with no religion at all. The Connecticut Anglicans baffled Roger Viets and John Tyler when they informed them that if they had true faith they would be saved without the sacraments, and without true faith they would perish anyhow.[73]

Once inside the Church of England, the congregations had to be taught the Church service. De La Roche found that the German school teacher at Lunenburg, Nova Scotia, was also clerk to the English congregation, but as he could not speak English he was "useless beyond saying Amen," so the missionary employed an artillery soldier stationed there. Hardly anybody at Windsor, fifty miles away, would even take the trouble to make any response at all. The Society informed Matthew Graves, in 1765, that he could make the responses in the liturgy himself since his Dissenting hearers in the outlying areas were unable.[74]

Converts came to the Church well equipped with Bibles, but the constant requests to the Society for Prayer Books signifies well enough the difficulties the missionaries faced in teaching their congregations the Anglican service. Theophilus Morris found that nearly all the New London homes possessed Bibles but there was hardly a Prayer Book to be found. The Taunton community in Rhode Island invited John Usher to open their recently built church in 1741. He promised to visit them frequently from his Bristol mission, however, he needed the Society's help to provide Prayer Books so that the congregation could learn the liturgy. When Godfrey Malbone began to organise an Anglican church at Pomfret, in November 1769, he had to be catechist and lay reader in his own house, because the "future Congregation were as ignorant of the Service as so many Iroquois, not above two or three of them having ever Seen a Common Prayer-Book until" he had gone to live there three years earlier. Of course, the Society sent some psalm books to his assistance, but Malbone decided to exchange them for some

---

[73] Isaac Browne to Secretary, no date, B, XI, 140; James Lyons to Secretary, March 25, 1748, B, XVI, 42; James Wetmore to Secretary, March 25, 1748, XVI, 43; John Checkley to Secretary, May I, 1750, B, XVIII, 23; Roger Viets to Secretary, June 25, 1764, B, XXIII, 371; John Tyler to Secretary, Jan. 9, 1770, B, XXIII, 361.
[74] Peter De La Roche to Secretary, Oct. 5, 1771, B, XXV, 168; William Ellis to Secretary, Sept. 14, 1776, B, XXV, 208; S.P.G. Journals, XVI, 375.

religious tracts since the former Congregationalists were already very fond of psalm singing, but were extremely deficient in their understanding of the sacraments.[75]

Clergy anxious to remove Dissenters' objections to the Church sometimes found themselves in danger of departing from the Anglican service. The novelty of seeing an Anglican priest in town for the first time could prompt Dissenters to invite the newcomer to preach at the local meeting house. Aeneas Ross noted that two churches in the outlying parts of his mission were often crowded with Dissenters impressed with the novelty of the Anglican service. Some clergy no doubt adhered to the liturgy, but others appear to have modified it to avoid offending their audiences and losing a valuable opportunity to make converts. John Stuart was the first Anglican priest the Mohawk Indians had seen at Fort Hunter for several years, and he was not there long before the local Dutch Calvinists invited him to perform for them. He explained the meaning of the more objectionable Anglican tenets to them, and, by what he called "moderation," he dispelled much of their prejudice so far that ten or twelve of them proposed joining the Church. Probably Stuart had managed to avoid controversy by concentrating on what the Calvinists and Anglicans had in common, but other missionaries possibly went further in the Dissenting way.[76]

With so many requests for advice about the need for compromise with the Dissenters, and with several clergy preaching to the Dissenters in their meeting houses in the 1760's, the Society began to scrutinize its missionaries' correspondence more closely than before. The Secretary was anxious that Agur Treadwell was "using the Church service and no other" when he preached at the Maidenhead meeting house in 1763. Concern about him no doubt arose from his trespassing into the parish of Samuel Seabury, Jr. on Long Island a year earlier. Alexander Murray, only recently converted from the Presbyterians in Scotland, received the same caution the following year, and news of the Society's apprehensions probably prompted

---

[75] Theophilus Morris to Secretary, Sept. 15, 1740, B, VII, part 2, 53; Godfrey Malbone to Secretary, May 20, 1772, B, XXIII, 435; John Usher to Secretary, Oct. 6, 1741, B, X, 27.

[76] John Stuart to Richard Peters, March 19, 1771, Richard Peters Papers, VII, 33; Aeneas Ross to Secretary, Oct. 11, 1762, B, XXI, 220.

Murray's neighbour, Thomas Barton in Lancaster, Pennsylvania, to explain to the Society that he had adhered strictly to the Church liturgy when opening a new German Lutheran church in his mission.[77]

The Society had cause for concern at certain of its missionaries' behaviour, at a time when others were dwelling in their correspondence upon Dissenter hostility. Joshua Weeks wrote, shortly after taking charge of the Marblehead mission in 1763, an almost unbelievable account of harmony between Anglicans and Dissenters there. Not only did large numbers of Dissenters attend the service, but two of their Teachers with "fair open minds" always attended during the week, and generally joined in the prayers "reading them devoutly & attentively." He went even so far as to draw the Secretary's attention to the distinction between enthusiasts and Marblehead's "regular dissenters (pardon the expression) in the congregational way." The road to harmony lay in his faith in "Christian piety & moderation," but he added "I still adhere strictly & conscientiously to the Directions of our Lyturgy; while I carefully shun those matters that gender to Strife."[78]

The Society praised Weeks' achievement, but probably thought more carefully about his relations with the Dissenters when a few months after his first burst of praise for them he admitted that during the one and a half years before his arrival, when his congregation had been without a clergyman, they had lost some of their affection for the Church and had adopted "more favourable sentiments of the dissenting way of worship." As though not quite sure of himself he hastened to add that he had "often exhorted them to stedfastness" and had given them "no opportunity of straying from the service of the established Church" through his own neglect.[79]

Pressure upon the two ministers to the Germans was greater. Paulus Bryzelius had been an itinerant German Lutheran minister in New Jersey for five years, becoming missionary to the Germans at

---

[77] S.P.G.Journals, XVI, 32, 132; Samuel Seabury to Secretary, March 26, 1763, B, II, 161; Thomas Barton to Secretary, Nov. 10, 1766, B, XXI, 17.
[78] Joshua Wingate Weeks to Secretary, Aug. 13, 1764, June 21, 1768, June 27, 1765, B, XXII, 244, 247, 251.
[79] Jushua Wingate Weeks to Secretary, Dec. 24, 1764, B, XXII, 245.

Lunenburg in 1767. Traugott Frederick Illing had lived sixteen years in London before his ordination, in 1772, to minister to the Germans in Thomas Barton's mission in Lancaster county. Both of these clergymen had been appointed because they could preach in German and English, thus assisting in the long cherished plan of assimilating the German settlers. The Lunenburg Germans in Nova Scotia were so overwhelmed at hearing the service in their mother tongue that "most of the people were shedding tears--the breast work of the upper Galleries were in danger to break down on Account of so many people" crowding into the church. Bryzelius, however, performed the service in his own way, and no doubt, without Common Prayer Books in German, he felt obliged to make parts of the service more like the service his elderly members were used to. The Nova Scotia Corresponding Society, consisting of the governor and other royal officials, to whom the Society had delegated some of its supervisory functions, met in Halifax, in October 1769, and warned him not to depart from the Church liturgy, insisting that there was no need for him to use the Lutheran mode at all. When De La Roche arrived there to assist him, in late 1771, he reported that he had "been obliged to set many things to rights in the manner of celebrating divine worship according to the forms & rules prescribed."[80]

Three scattered congregations, having neither Prayer Books nor knowledge of the liturgy, made Traugott Frederick Illing's work even more difficult. Thomas Barton introduced the itinerant to one of his vestrymen, Colonel James Burd, who took him to the German Lutherans at Middleton, where there was a church, an organ, but no minister. The prospect of having a clergyman encouraged them to join the Church, but how to wean them from their former mode of worship was a question that soon sent Illing along the same slippery path as Bryzelius, and in less than a year he informed the Bishop of London that he would be obliged to "indulge them a little in their

---

[80] Undated, unsigned letter to Bishop of London, Fulham Papers, XXII, 257; Thomas Barton to James Burd, Jan. 2, 1773, Shippen Papers, VII; Unsigned letter to Sebastian Zouberbuhler, June 9, 1767, B, XXV, 109; Minute of the Quarterly Meeting, Nova Scotia Corresponding Society, Oct. 6, 1769, B, XXV, 143; Peter De La Roche to Secretary, Nov. 28, 1771, B, XXV, 174.

own Way."[81]

It was perfectly natural for clergy in these conditions to depart from the Church service, but the Society and some of its missionaries were concerned. Some of the older clergy in America felt that the rapid departure for England for ordination hardly gave newly converted candidates time to become familiar with Church lore. Samuel Auchmuty, giving his opinion of Alexander Murray who was showing interest in a scheme to further the Society's work among the Mohawk Indians, commented that though he had never met Murray, his name suggested that "he must have been bred a Dissenter, and therefore can know but little of church matters." Dr. Bearcroft, the Society's Secretary, expressed concern to William Samuel Johnson, who was visiting London in 1756, about the "hasty recommendations of young gentlemen for orders, from America, and their being sent many times very raw without first obtaining leave to come." Dr. Bearcroft's comment was made during a discussion with William Samuel Johnson about the Rhode Island missionary James McSparran's views of balancing native born American clergy and British clergy, and the embarrassing appointment of John Fowle as missionary to Norwalk, Connecticut. In 1751, the Boston clergy Timothy Cutler, Henry Caner and Charles Brockwell had recommended for ordination the former Dissenting Teacher John Fowle, who had conformed to the Church only six months earlier. The Society appointed him to the Connecticut mission only to dismiss him from its service four years later. When Jeremiah Leaming replaced Fowle, in 1762, he found that he had sold the Society's library and had used the proceeds for his own use.[82]

The English and the American views of what was right for the Church in the American colonies were not always in perfect alignment. The annual convention of New York and New Jersey

---

[81] James Burd to Edward Shippen, April 1, 1773, Balch Papers, II, 17; Frederick Illing to Bishop of London, Oct. 6, 1773, Fulham Papers, VIII, 52.

[82] Samuel Auchmuty to Sir William Johnson, Jan. 13, 1768, Peter Force Papers, Series 8D, Sir William Johnson Papers, 1755-1774; William Samuel Johnson to Samuel Johnson, Jan. 10, 1756, Schneider's Johnson, I, pp. 232-235; John Fowle to Secretary, Sept. 25, 1753, B, XX, 39; S.P.G.Journals,XV, 275; Timothy Cutler, Henry Caner, Charles Brockwell to Secretary, Nov. 1, 1751, B, XIX, 32; Jeremiah Leaming to Secretary, March 25, 1762, B, XXIII, 238.

clergy informed the Society, in 1767, that William Frazer and William Ayers would leave for England for ordination, even though they did not have the Society's approval. Although these two recruits were most likely familiar with Church lore, the convention was pre-empting the Society's right of inviting candidates for ordination, because of the desperate need to supply missions in America. John Ross, member of Christ Church in Philadelphia and one time vestryman, in his privileged role of corresponding member of the Society, wrote to the Secretary, in 1771, requesting a missionary for Trinity Church in Oxford, a few miles north of Philadelphia. However, Ross wanted "an affable Kind, & Courteous English Clergyman" because most candidates sent for ordination from Pennsylvania "are generally Young Presbyterians, who cannot be Supposed will make much Efforts for the Advancement" of the Church. The New Side Presbyterians in Pennsylvania taunted the Old Sides with their claims that converts to the Church were from the Old Side because of their reluctance to make public confessions of the work of grace in their souls. One such convert who proved John Ross wrong was Samuel Magaw of New Castle, Delaware. In 1755, he was studying in the first class at the College of Philadelphia. William Smith was preparing him to be a schoolteacher. Even though the Philadelphia Presbyterians licensed him to teach, he finally left for England in 1766 seeking Anglican ordination. The churchwardens and vestry of Dover, Delaware, recommended him, claiming he was "a Preacher much & deservedly Esteemed" among the Presbyterians. The Society's Secretary Dr. Burton wrote to William Smith, in 1767, that Magaw was "superior to any one, whom the Society hath given a mission to in my time." And when Samuel Magaw and fellow graduate of the College of Philadelphia, John Andrews, appeared for examination before the Bishop of London, Proprietor Thomas Penn wrote that the chaplain had "never examined candidates for orders better qualified," especially Magaw.[83]

---

[83] John Ross to [Secretary], July 6, 1771, B, XXI, 239; Leonard J. Trinterud, The Forming of the American Tradition, pp. 154, 159; Robert McKean and Charles Inglis to Bishop of London, Oct. 2, 1767, Fulham Papers, XXIII, 196; Clergy of Pennsylvania to Bishop of London, no date, Fulham Papers, XXIII, 199; Thomas Penn to William Smith, Feb. 28, 1755, William Smith Papers, II, 4 (Historical Society of Pennsylvania); Wardens and congregation of Dover to Secretary, Nov. 6, 1766, B,

John Lyon in Taunton, Massachusetts, found "many Difficulties attend the Sacred Office of Ministers of the Gospel." In particular, he lamented, was "the Want of A Bishop," since he scarcely knew how to admit people to the communion, "there having been different Methods Used in this Country." Clergy who were certain of correct procedures were confused by laymen who each had his own interpretation of Church law. Theophilus Morris was so dismayed at his Connecticut Anglicans who were "the most versed in casuistry of any people" he had ever met that he was compelled to silence them with Archbishop John Potter's treatise on Church government.[84]

In 1752, Englishman Charles Brockwell at King's Chapel in Boston was becoming concerned about another matter regarding converts to the Church. Edward Bass "late a dissenting teacher, but now a proselyte to ye Church" was assisting the aging Matthias Plant at Newbury Port in Massachusetts. When Bass appeared before the Massachusetts clergy to gain their recommendation to seek ordination, Brockwell and Timothy Cutler of Christ Church, Boston, "strenuously opposed & utterly forbade" his reading the service and sermons in Plant's church. They were further incensed that Plant, during his illness, should have loaned the lay reader his gown because "such proceedings may conduce to the contempt of Religion, and the Ministry." American candidates for the Church ministry had been a cause of concern to the foreign clergy quite early because of what the crusty Rhode Island missionary James McSparran feared to be a departure from Church practices resulting from the influx of clergy and laity from the Dissenting churches. To prevent American clergy from departing from the Church rituals and doctrines, he urged "a just Ballance between ye Europeans and Americans," a proposal very much to the liking of Englishman Matthew Graves in Connecticut and Roger Price at King's Chapel in Boston. Samuel Johnson had earlier pleaded with Matthew Graves to bear with the American departure from the English tradition of

---

XXI, 149; Dr. Burton to William Smith, June 1, 1767, William Smith Papers, I, 55 (Church Historical Society); Thomas Penn to William Smith, March 17, 1767, William Smith Papers, II, 51 (Historical Society of Pennsylvania); William Buell Sprague, Annals of the American Pulpit, V, p.246.

[84] John Lyon to Secretary, no date, B, XXII, 172; Theophilus Morris to Secretary, Sept. 15, 1740, B, VII, part 2, 53.

admitting readers "which the present condition makes it necessary in many places at a distance from ministers." He begged Graves "not to discourage" the young reader at Hebron. Indeed, he urged Graves to meet the reader to offer him guidance. McSparran was concerned enough about the American Anglicans' drift from the mother Church to make a will bequeathing land for building a church and graveyard in his parish. In addition, he donated his farm as a house for an American bishop provided that the first three bishops be born and educated in Great Britain or Ireland.[85]

In particular, McSparran had been watching Samuel Johnson's young lay readers, and in 1748 he wrote to the Society complaining that they were making innovations in the Church service. He felt so strongly about the matter that he preached a sermon from Hebrews 5:4 "The sacred dignity of the Christian Priesthood Vindicated" in August 1751, regarding the dangers that lay readers presented to the Church. He wrote to a clerical friend in Ireland in that year that "the native novanglian clergy of our church, against the opinion of European missionaries, have introduced a custom of young scholars going about and reading prayers, etc., when there are vacancies, on purpose that they may step in them when they get orders." McSparran's concern, while causing concern in England, was one which would continue in the American Church. In 1767, the New York clergy convention brought to heel one of the lay readers in Philadelphia who was reading prayers and sermons of his own composition. The Society's Secretary Philip Bearcroft took McSparran's complaint seriously. He wrote strong warning letters to Roger Price at King's Chapel and to Samuel Johnson at Stratford. To his informer he wrote "be pleased to inform them, & let it be publicly known, that whoever in the Society's service shall designedly omitt, or alter any one word of the Book of Common Prayer, or add any thing to it in their reading that part of the Public Worship will be dismis'd from the service of the Society upon proof

---

[85] James McSparran to Secretary, May 19, 1744, B, XIII. 75; Abstracts of Proceedings appended to sermon preached by Bishop of St. David's before the Society, Feb. 23, 1759; James McSparran to Archbishop, Oct. 18, 1742, James McSparran to Secretary, Sept. 30, 1742, B, X, 12, 13; Charles Brockwell to Bishop of London, Jan. 21, 1752, Fulham Papers, VI, 17; Matthew Graves to Samuel Johnson, June 18, 1748, Samuel Johnson to Matthew Graves, June 27, 1748, Schneider's Johnson, I, pp. 131-134

of such an heinous misdemeanor."[86]

Dr. Bearcroft's letter to James McSparran was also marked "Extract," indicating that it should be included in the Abstract of Proceedings to be appended to the Anniversary Sermon to be preached the following February, for all missionaries to read. Samuel Johnson replied that he had enquired into the matter but only one missionary had sometimes added two or three words in one of the prayers, following "a great Example he heard in London." He added "perhaps the first lesson, or some of the latter part of the Litany may have been omitted on some cold Day," but nothing else. Dr. Bearcroft assured Johnson that the changes mentioned were in order, however, he wanted to give "a Caution to young readers for the future."[87]

The missionaries took heed of the warning, but a few years later when one of Connecticut's oldest and most respected missionaries proclaimed a departure from Church doctrine it became evident that the American Church was heading for more serious problems. John Beach maintained in his sermon A Modest Enquiry into the State of the Dead . . . that the dead were judged immediately, the deserving received their celestial bodies, and proceeded instantly to Heaven. He recognised that his discourse would meet with opposition from among his colleagues, but he did not expect that the Congregationalists' Fairfield County Western District Association would report it to the Society. A committee the Society had appointed to examine the sermon submitted its report in July, 1757, judging it contrary to the Scriptures and to Church doctrine, and requested the Connecticut clergy to discuss and examine the matter. The following October they convened at Stamford to hear the Long

---

[86] James McSparran to Secretary, May 19, 1744, B, XIII, 75; Philip Bearcroft to James McSparran, Oct. 4, 1749, XVII, 205; Matthew Graves to Bishop of London, July 20, 1750, Fulham Papers, I, 288; Philip Bearcroft to Roger Price, Oct. 5, 1749, B, XVII, 208; Samuel Johnson to Secretary, no date, B, XVIII, 60; Philip Bearcroft to Samuel Johnson, Oct. 21, 1750, B, XVIII, 212; Henry Wilder Foote, Annals of King's Chapel (2 vols.; Boston, 1896), II, p.3; Walter Herbert Stowe, "The Seabury Minutes of the New York Clergy Conventions of 1766 and 1767," Historical Magazine of the Protestant Episcopal Church, X,(1941), 158.

[87] Samuel Johnson to Secretary, no date, B, XVIII, 60; Secretary to Samuel Johnson, Oct. 21, 1750, B, XVIII, 212.

Island missionary, Samuel Seabury, junior, refute Beach's sermon.[88]

The matter blew over, but early in 1760, when another spate of religious controversy broke out in Connecticut, claiming some Anglicans among its victims, Samuel Johnson "put Mr. Beach on preaching" a refutation before the clergy convention at New Haven, which the King's College president "thought might be some atonement" for his earlier errors. Beach also took the opportunity, perhaps on Johnson' advice, to re-assert the validity of some of the Church doctrines, including the Trinity, and the eternity of future punishment, which both Anglicans and Dissenters were questioning. Complete with a preface he had written himself, Johnson sent a copy to England as evidence of Church unity.[89]

Samuel Johnson's gesture to trans-Atlantic unity coincided with the first real opportunity the American Church had to place itself upon a firmer foundation. The French departure from the continent offered the Anglicans a unique opportunity to secure priestly dignity, lay subordination, and ecclesiastical propriety; with the assistance of their friends in Britain it was time to settle America's future within the Empire. Everywhere in the colonies there was an air of expectancy, for everyone was sure that the peace would usher in changes in the colonial administration. Many Anglicans hoped the reorganization would remove the democratic charters of Connecticut and Rhode Island, and provide royal land grants for a Church established in the territory recently acquired from the French, and possibly in the old seaboard colonies, too. The long-awaited appointment of an American bishop would finally bring order into the Church; lay casuistry would be spiked; some of the old world authority restored to the clergy; the almost imperceptible innovations in Church polity, and the drift into ecumenism, which appeared to be gaining ground in Philadelphia, might be arrested. However, these plans depended upon the Dissenters being prepared

---

[88] John Beach, A Modest Enquiry into the Stat of the Dead . . . , (New London, 1755); S.P.G. Journals, XIV, March 21, 1760; Report of the Committee to Examine Mr. Beach's Book Read in the Society, Jan. 21, 1757, Lambeth Palace Library, vol. 1123, part 2, 1755-1760, 107; S.P.G. Journals, XIV, Meeting March 21, 1760, XV, Meeting Nov. 21, 1760

[89] Edward Winslow to Secretary, July 14, 1760, B, XXII, 271; John Beach to Secretary, April 22, 1760, B, XXIII, 28; Samuel Johnson to Secretary, Nov, 25, 1760, B, II, 76.

to allow royal favour to the Anglicans. Should trans-Atlantic Dissent prevail in England, then the American Church might be forced to shift for itself for the time being in order to preserve its distinctiveness among the other Protestant denominations.

CHAPTER

III

The Search for Unity

The American clergy's requests for resident bishops were as urgent and prolific after the fall of Quebec as were their claims that the Church was Britain's only hope of stemming the colonies' drift into republicanism. The prelates accepted their advice, but they could only recommend patience while the ministry formulated its plans for over-hauling the administration of the colonies. It was natural for the Americans to fulminate against what they mistook to be British indifference to the colonial Church when they lived in the midst of religious antagonism debated in language echoing the religious-political conflict which had consumed England only a century earlier. They were also concerned that the swell of independence in the American colonies was more than the political manifestation of religious dissent, for it was evident among the Anglicans, too.

Presentiments among the clergy found expression in the Connecticut missionary Edward Winslow's suggestion that the clergy, while pouring out their thanks in church for the elimination of the French threat, should also "impress upon the Minds of the people . . . a suitable Sense of that Duty, Loyalty and Affection" due to the mother country. He detected a stirring in the colonies now that the way to the west was finally opened, and with his colleagues he foresaw that the developments during the next decade or so would determine what kind of American society would triumph: one which would give full reign to the excessive levelling of unbridled individualism, or one in which the individual would take his place in a traditionally structured corporate state.[1]

Three years later, Henry Caner wrote from King's Chapel in Boston to Archbishop Thomas Secker, attempting to explain the recent publication of the Congregationalist minister Ezra Stiles' pamphlet "A Discourse on the Christian Union." Stiles' intention was to "invite all Parties and Sects in the Country to unite against the Church of England." The only reason Caner could give for "this sudden outburst of bitterness" was that at the end of the war between Britain and France the land acquired by the British Crown "will either greatly establish the Church of England, or the dissenting interest in this part of the World." The Dissenters on both sides of the Atlantic were determined "to secure the Event in their favor." The Church, Caner lamented, was handicapped in this contest. "We are a Rope of Sand—There is no Union, no Authority among us; We cannot even summon a Convention for united Counsel and Advice."[2]

If the Anglicans were to grasp the opportunity that now lay before them, the appointment of a resident bishop with sufficient influence with the royal governors to gain favour for the Church would be necessary. Failing that, for the time being at least, there must be unity among the clergy and laity; their conduct must be directed by a common policy; yet the variety of attitudes among the clergy towards the Church, and the subtle changes the environment and recruits from the Dissenters were introducing into the polity and doctrine presented a very serious problem. From Delaware Charles Inglis pointed with some concern to the Parson's Cause which had recently demonstrated a barely concealed lay hostility to the Virginia Church establishment. In Philadelphia, former Society missionary and spurious physician, William McClennaghan, was charming a Christ Church faction at the State House with his Methodist preaching. Such internal weaknesses were very serious at a time when only perfect unity could allow the Church to command the westward expansion that was bound to come. [3]

---

[1] Edward Winslow to Secretary, Jan. 2, 1760, S.P.G. Correspondence, Series B, XXII, 270.
[2] Henry Caner to Archbishop, Jan. 7, 1763, Lambeth Palace Library, vol. 1123, part 3, 290.
[3] Charles Inglis to Secretary Sept. 26, 1760, B, XXI, 140; William Smith to Archbishop, May 1, 1760, Lambeth Palace Library, vol. 1123, part 2, 189.

Many of the clergy realized that leadership must come from an American bishop; yet few ever stated precisely why a resident bishop was so essential. The clergy wrote to England about it; they discussed the subject among themselves; from the pulpit they taught their congregations about the Biblical authority of the episcopate. Samuel Auchmuty preached what he described as his "first Sermon after [his] Induction to the Rectory" of the prestigious Trinity Church in New York, in September 1764, on the authority of bishops and the ordained priesthood, who were not "at Liberty to preach their own darling Opinions, or curious Speculations." Among the Dissenters they endeavoured to foster sympathy for their scheme. Nevertheless, the advocates of American bishops rarely examined their claims beyond the obvious: that a bishop would remove the need for candidates to go to England for ordination, and that he would exercise administrative and supervisory authority over the clergy and laity Indeed, it was quite possible that a majority of clergy did not fully understand what lay behind their talk of American bishops until the Imperial crisis in the mid-1770's finally compelled them to scrutinize their socio-political philosophies more closely. But at least one clergyman had seen through the problem that faced the Church in America, much earlier.[4]

During his student days at Yale College, Thomas Chandler had gained a reputation for being intelligent and perceptive, qualities that brought him to the attention of Samuel Johnson. When he finally broke with the Congregationalists, the year after his graduation, his enthusiasm for the Church became almost fanatical. The Congregationalist minister and scholar, Ezra Stiles, remarked many years later that Chandler had been an avid reader while at College, mostly in History and the Classics, and later he became more widely read in Ecclesiastical History than any of the American Episcopal clergy of his day, an achievement which did not prevent him from becoming "acrimonious, bitter, and uncharitable to all Xtian Sects but his own." Like many others of his generation who were descended from the New England Puritans, he was disgusted by the religious chaos which the frantic strollers left in their wake, and in turn he went to the opposite extreme in his pursuit of a

---

[4] Samuel Auchmuty, MSS sermon, Cor. 2:4--5. (Possession of the Rector, Trinity Church)

hierarchical, structured society. His capacity for missionary work became apparent as soon as he began ministering at St. John's Church in Elizabeth Town, New Jersey, in 1752, for his proselytizing the Dissenters very quickly brought upon him the local Congregationalist minister's wrath.[5]

Nine years later during a lull in the wrangling between Anglicans and Dissenters, Chandler noted that "those disputes have for some time subsided and Charity, candor and moderation seem to have been studied, or at least affected on both sides." The Dissenters, he continued, think "there is no material difference between ye Church and themselves," and the Anglicans appear to hold the same view. Should such harmony continue, he warned, "in time we may come to think that ye unity of Christ's body is a chimerical doctrine--that Schism is an Ecclesiastical Scarecrow--and that Episcopal is no better than ye leathern mitten ordination; or in other words, that ye authority derived from Christ, is no better than that which is given by ye mob." Chandler's thoughts were, in fact, echoing those expressed by the Society's missionary, Arthur Browne, at Portsmouth, New Hampshire, in 1738, just before the Great Awakening. He wrote "a false Notion of Moderation and Charity is diffused thro' the People in Order to defeat the Growth of our Church." The Dissenting Teachers, he continued, were claiming that there was little or no difference between the fundamental teachings of the Church and Meeting House. Next, Chandler turned to the clergy, and in reflecting upon the matter, he began to realize how insidious the problem really was. "I hope the Clergy do not countenance these notions" he remarked, "but if they are suffered to prevail amongst our people, ye Clergy must in some measure be accountable for it."[6]

For the following three years he was still pondering over what to do about ecumenism that could sap the Church's strength and destroy its socio-political usefulness in America. The general harmony had become part of the Dissenters' "secret arts"--one of

---

[5] Ezra Stiles' Diary, III, 398; Thomas Chandler to Secretary, Dec. 10, 1754, Jan. 5, 1762, July 5, 1764, B, XXIV, 76, 79, 84.

[6] Thomas Chandler to Secretary, April 6, 1761, B, XXIV, 78; Arthur Browne to Robert Thomlinson, May 8, 1738, quoted in Gerald G. Goodwin, "The Anglican Reaction to the Great Awakening," Historical Magazine of the Protestant Episcopal Church, XXXV (Dec., 1966), p. 351.

which was their occasional attendance at Church services--which they were using "to undermine ye principles of ye Church amidst ye fairest professions of Friendship." The problem appeared to be widespread and deep-rooted. Samuel Seabury, in New York, gave a similar warning when he was shocked by news of the death of two young Americans off the coast of Delaware, returning from ordination in England, in 1766. "This whole continent" he wrote "will be overrun with Infidelity and Deism, methodism and New Light, with every Species and with every Degree of Scepticism and Enthusiasm; and without a Bishop upon the Spot, I fear it will be impossible to keep the Church herself pure and undefiled."[7]

To prevent "this Evil" Chandler had written to the Society in, July 1762, that it would be helpful "to circulate some Tract upon ye Nature & Constitution of ye Christian Church ye Necessity of Authority derived from Christ in ye Ministers of it." Two years later he offended his Elizabeth Town congregation when he refused his pulpit to the Methodist George Whitefield who had recently been welcomed by the Anglican churches in Philadelphia. The popularity of Whitefield's style, the "Zeal and Piety" of the Elizabeth Town Dissenting Teacher and the resulting "sudden and instantaneous conversions" were likely to sway "ye weaker part of [his] congregation," he feared. "If ye clergy say a word" he wrote "even to their own people concerning ye unity of Christ's body, ye nature of schism or ye necessity of authority derived from Christ in ye Ministers of his religion" they are stigmatized and persecuted. If they remain silent "our people grow indifferent and in time may think it immaterial whether they are in communion with ye Church or join with a conventicle." He regretted the lack of a "Bishop in these parts to whom [he] could apply for advice and direction." In the meantime, he hoped, "ye Clergy will continue in the regular discharge of their duty."[8]

This fading of the distinction between the Anglican and Dissenting cultures was not restricted to Chandler's world. In Nova Scotia, in the 1760's, an Irish immigrant and missionary of the Society, Joseph Bennett, reported that he and the local Dissenting

---

[7] Thomas Chandler to Secretary, July 5, 1762, B, XXIV, 80; Samuel Seabury to Secretary, April 17, 1766, B, II, 169.
[8] Thomas Chandler to Secretary, July 5, 1762, July 5, 1764, B, XXIV, 80, 84.

Teacher were good friends. He reported that the people thought the difference between the Church of England and the Independents was "insignificant." Bennett's Dissenting Teacher was John Eagleson, who had left Scotland for Nova Scotia, where his popularity among his parishioners was such that Chief Justice Belcher and John Breynton, rector of St. Paul's Church in Halifax, advised him to go to England "immediately" in H.M. Ship Mermaid to gain Anglican ordination. John Breynton wrote that Eagleson preached a "Well connected Sensible Catholic Discourse, delivered extempore without Hesitation or Repetition" and that people of "all sorts" subscribed to keep him at Windsor. Closer to Chandler's mission, Isaac Browne was preaching a sermon in June 1767, at Trinity Church in Newark, New Jersey, from John 13:35 "By this shall all men know that you are my disciples . . . love one another." Regretting the enmity between the Christian denominations, he asked "is it not common notwithstanding upon the Account of some small Differences in opinion, some trifling Modes or Ceremonies, religiously to hate and revile each other."[9]

Eventually, Chandler brought together in a pamphlet called <u>An Appeal to the Public in Behalf of the Church of England</u> in America the arguments in favour of resident bishops which the clergy had been using for decades. The argument which had been most consistently urged upon the public since the beginning of the century was the hardship candidates for the ministry were forced to bear in financing the expensive and dangerous voyage to England for ordination. No one could deny that it was a good reason, but Chandler's claim that this imposition was a major obstacle to Church growth was not quite true, though neither he nor any of the American Anglicans appear to have seen the flaw in this argument. The major obstacle to founding new missions was the lack of money, or more important, the reluctance of some parishes to support their own clergy as long as there was a chance of obtaining English money. Between 1763, when the Society decided to stop financing new missions in New England in order to appease the Dissenters,

---

[9] S.P.G. Journals, XV, 136; Joseph Bennett to Secretary, Feb. 21, 1767, B, XXV, 106; William Franklin to Secretary, Oct. 22, 1767, B, XXV, 118; John Breynton to Secretary, Oct. 23, 1767, B, XXV, 121; MSS Sermon, Isaac Browne, John 13:35, June 1767, and on many other occasions. (possession of the rector)

and 1775, there were far more candidates willing to risk the dangers of the voyage to England than the Society could finance. Nine candidates from the northern provinces offered to go for ordination, but were unable because there were no congregations in those provinces able to support ministers without the Society's assistance, while a few other candidates found employment in the south. Samuel Frinck, and Samuel Peters' nephew, John Peters, for example, requested the Society for permission to go to London for ordination in 1763, but Frinck was sent to Georgia instead of his native Rutland in New England, and Peters declined a similar offer of a mission in North Carolina, turning instead to law.[10]

The Dissenters often accused the Anglican clergy of conforming to the Church for material benefits, and in some cases they were right, but a resident bishop would have satisfied the clergy's pleas for episcopal supervision which, in turn, would have helped rid the Church of clergy who might have been motivated merely by the Society's assistance. But still another argument remained in the Anglicans' repertoire. Without bishops in America, the colonial Church was deprived of the sacraments of ordination and confirmation. They were quite right to make this claim, but they were only hinting at an extremely important problem, for many of

---

[10] The candidates offering themselves for ordination were: Samuel Frinck, John Peters, Asa Belew, Ephraim Lewis, Joseph Hutchins, Francis Hopkinson, Ebenezer Kneeland, John Montgomery, and a German Lutheran named Kuhn. See S.P.G. Journals XVI, 80, 383, 213, 12; XVIII, 69, 428; XIX, 325, 19; XX, 194; Samuel Peters to Secretary, Jan. 1, 1770, B, XXIII, 330; William Smith to Secretary, Feb. 22, 1769 and Oct. 22, 1768, B, XXI, 261, 262. Of the six country clergy who began their careers independently of the Society's financial assistance between 1760 and 1775 only Abraham Jarvis and John Marshall in Connecticut, and James Sayre in New York managed to live on their congregations' support. But Sayre only arrived at his Fredericksburg parish in December, 1774, and therefore can hardly be considered as having succeeded. Bela Hubbard in Connecticut, John Lyon in Massachusetts, and John Doty in New York each found that they could not continue independently of the Society's aid, and eventually moved to vacant missions. The year after Chandler published his Appeal the Society's anniversary lecturer, the Bishop of Lincoln, referring to Chandler's claim that large numbers of American congregations were without ministers (which, incidentally, was very misleading) unwittingly confuted part of Chandler's argument with his comment that "this want is not easy to be supplied in the present state of things; for the Missions appointed . . . must be proportional to the state of our charity." Sermon before the Society, February 19, 1768.

the laity were reluctant enough to accept baptism or communion, and with the sacraments of confirmation and ordination denied them, the Anglican path was indeed slippery, especially when Anglican priests like George Whitefield broke in upon the scheme.

Whitefield had received much support from Anglicans in America, causing disturbances among many congregations, even Chandler', as well as widening the gulf between the Philadelphia clergy and those to the north. In Philadelphia, St. Paul's Church, from its foundation in 1760, had been at odds with the Bishop of London as well as with the other Anglican clergy in the middle and New England colonies. The disagreement was basically because of an erroneous view the wardens and vestry of St. Paul's Church held that receiving a licence from the Bishop of London would interfere with their right to appoint their own minister. However, initially, they ran foul of the English Church hierarchy when they appointed William McClennaghan as their founding minister.

Irish Presbyterian William McClennaghan served a number of parishes in America before turning to the Church of England and taking orders in 1755. He became the Society's missionary at Pownalborough on the Kennebec River. In 1759, he left with the Society's library and eventually arrived in Philadelphia where he became very popular among some of the Christ Church congregation who persuaded the aging and ill Rector Robert Jenny to give him the pulpit. His flamboyant, extempore sermons lasting one and a half hours offended William Smith of the College of Philadelphia and William Sturgeon, assistant minister and catechist to the Negroes at Christ Church, as well as most of the missionaries in the middle colonies. Further, McClenneghan had deserted the Society's mission in New England, he had divided the Christ Church congregation and he was preaching without a licence from the Bishop of London. The Philadelphia clergy claimed that McClenneghan was accusing the Anglican clergy of preaching false doctrines and that Sturgeon's catechumens were being taught untruths.[11]

---

[11] William Smith to Archbishop, Oct. 21, 1759, Robert Jenny, William Sturgeon, Jacob Duché, Philip Reading, Hugh Neill, Charles Inglis, William Smith to Archbishop, Oct. 21, 1759, Lambeth Palace Library, Vol. 1123, part 2, [153, 154]; William Sturgeon to Secretary, Aug. 21, 1761, B, XXI, 277.

When Robert Jenny finally refused McClennaghan his pulpit at Christ Church, a faction of that congregation seceded. According to William Smith and William Sturgeon they were led by corresponding member of the Society John Ross, who was a member of the Christ Church vestry from 1763 through 1768 and warden of the secessionist St. Paul's Church in 1763. While the "methodists" were waiting to move into their new place of worship, McClennaghan charmed them in Philadelphia's Assembly House. Services probably moved to St. Paul's Church at the end of 1761 or early 1762. On April 12, 1762, wardens and vestry were elected and a week later McClennaghan attended what was probably the first formal vestry meeting. They resolved to help pay his debts which William Smith informed the Archbishop of Canterbury he had incurred in Boston before arriving in Philadelphia. The Bishop of London refused to license this man who had dismissed himself from the Society's service, had insinuated himself into Christ Church, thereby causing a schism in what had been a united community. Eventually, he became distasteful to his new flock and left for a Maryland parish, stating ill health as his reason. In spite of financial help from St. Paul's Church, he left still in debt.[12]

Between 1765, when McClennaghan left Philadelphia, and 1768, St. Paul's congregation threw themselves upon their idol George Whitefield to find them a minister. Finally Whitefield sent them William Stringer, who presented his credentials to the vestry on August 30, 1768. He had been ordained by "Erasmus Bishop of Arcadia in the Island of Crete." He did not have a licence from the Bishop of London. According to Bishop of London Richard Terrick he was one of John Wesley's lay preachers, and that very soon became clear in Philadelphia. William Smith informed the Bishop of London that Stringer was "very much in the Whitefieldian Strain" with his extempore sermons, and his "Scheme of an angry Predestination & Election." Smith was afraid that the notions at St. Paul's were likely to infect other clergy and congregations.

---

[12] William Smith to Secretary, Aug. 26, 1760, William Sturgeon to Secretary, July 2, 1760, Nov. 20, 1763, B, XXI, 248, 276, 281; William Smith to Archbishop, July 1, 1760, Lambeth Palace Library, vol. 1123, part 2, 189; St. Paul's Church Minutes of Vestry, June 21, 1762, Oct. 11, 1762, Jan. 21, 1764, July 22, 1765, Sept. 9, 1765, Oct. 11, 1765, July 5, 1766; Hugh Neill to Secretary, Dec. 14, 1765, B, XXI, 124.

Commenting upon the general state of the Church in the northern colonies, he noted that "the true manner & Decorum of the Church, seems too much departing from here, & to read the Liturgy, whatever else be added to it, or however little our Canons etc be regarded, is thought sufficient to denominate a Man a Churchman. Shall we never have a Bishop to regulate these Excesses?" he asked. St. Paul's Church vestry had informed Archbishop Secker, in November 1766, that they had built the church and therefore had "the Onely Right of Choosing and Presenting a Minister for it." A little while later they had also made it clear that they were independent of the jurisdiction of the Bishop of London. St. Paul's congregation were most of all concerned that their priest should be personally present at their church and that he and they be satisfied with each other before applying to the Bishop of London for a licence.[13]

In a letter dated April 9, 1767, the Bishop of London explained to the wardens and vestry of St. Paul's Church the position of the Church of England. The Anglican Church does not want to encourage "what seem'd to us to affect an Independency in the Church and throw off the AUTHORITY, which other Congregations of the Established Religion have allways SUBMITTED to." Of greater concern to the Bishop of London was St. Paul's Church "making Application to Mr. Whitefield, an irregular unlicens'd preacher" to recommend a minister for their church "which professes to be regular." The Bishop was anxious to allay any fears that St. Paul's Church might have about their right to elect their own minister. He simply wanted to explain that a minister must appear before the Bishop of London with acceptable testimonials in order to be licenced. He continued "you can't charge me with any Intentions of depriving you of the privilege of choosing your own Minister, or of Claiming the Appointment to myself such an Intention or such a Claim have never been in my thoughts." In order to help St.Paul's Church he offered to licence any clergyman already in America who could present his credentials to "Dr. Smith, Mr. Peters [of

---

[13] Richard Peters to Bishop of London, Aug. 30, 1768, William Smith to Bishop of London, Oct. 22, 1768, Fulham Papers, VIII, 36, 40; Thomas Coombe to Father, Dec. 6, 1769, Nov. 1, 1769, Jan. 3, 1770, Thomas Coombe Papers; Vestry Minutes of St. Paul's Church, Nov. 11, 1766, Feb. 20, 1767, March 4, 1767, Aug 30, 1768.

Philadelphia] or any other licenced Minister of the Established Church." St. Paul's Church vestry decided to accept the.Bishop's explanation and wrote to him, in November 1772, that they wished to be part of the Church of England and requested that William Stringer be ordained and licenced for their church.[14]

On March 12, 1773, the Bishop of London wrote to the St.Paul's Church vestry that, in spite of the irregularities in their proceedings, and, because the New York, New Jersey and Pennsylvania clergy had been active on their behalf, he would do whatever he could to accommodate the American Anglican congregations. His requiring that ministers in America be properly accredited and licenced was motivated solely by the necessity to "Preserve and Maintain the true Interests of Religion." With the fears of St. Paul's Church for their independence finally allayed, William Stringer sailed for England and returned regularly ordained with the Bishop of London's licence. The St. Paul's Church vestry's claim that they wished to be part of the Church of England when they requested ordination and licence for their minister, in November 1772, could be cynically interpreted as an act of expediency. Five months after the vestry accepted Stringer's credentials from England, it resolved to apply to the Governor of Pennsylvania for a charter for their church, only possible if they were in favour with the English Church hierarchy. With rare prescience the vestry then wrote to the Bishop of London that their "union and Mutual Correspondence . . . will last as long as the Church of England Shall Exist in America."[15]

During the search to find a minister suitable to their liking, the church wardens of St. Paul's Church wrote a letter to the clergy of New York and New Jersey requesting their help in obtaining the Bishop of London's understanding concerning their reticence in applying for his licence. The clergy in convention at King's College, New York, in April 1767, replied and their letter to the wardens was

---

[14] St. Paul's Church Minutes of Vestry, May 20, 1767, Nov. 2, Nov. 9, Nov. 30, Dec. 4, 1772. On November 2, 1775, when Richard Peters resigned as rector of Christ Church, Philadelphia, he handed to the vestry a letter from the Bishop of London, Edmund Gibson, dated October 19, 1738, in which he wrote "I do not remember that I have ever given occasion either by word or writing to suspect that I pretend to any more right than that of Licensing the Person who is to be your Minister." Christ Church Vestry Minutes, Nov. 2, 1775.

[15] St. Paul's Church Minutes of Vestry, April 29, 1773, May 4, 1773, Oct. 18, 1773.

read and recorded in the St. Paul's Church vestry minutes. The clergy in convention were sympathetic about the plight of St. Paul's Church and stated that they had already heard that a minister was soon to arrive in Philadelphia from London, in which case he would carry the Bishop of London's licence. Therefore, their problems would be at an end. They also placed the concerns of the St. Paul's Church congregation in a broader perspective. They wrote that they were "very sensible of the unhappy State of the Church of England, not only in your Province, but every where throughout the Continent; which we are convinced must still continue in some Measure to be the Case till the Introduction of Bishops & a regular Discipline."[16]

The claim commonly made by clergy calling for resident bishops in America that they were necessary for disciplinary purposes was not referring to discipline of the clergy or the laity. They were hinting at another concern. In their pronouncements they claimed that bishops' disciplinary powers would bring order to reprobate clergy and laity, and they were referring to the northern more specifically than the southern colonies. In fact, when Samuel Johnson convened the ten Connecticut clergy at Stratford, in October 1766, having emphatically stated their commitment to the appointment of American bishops, they referred to those clergy in the southern provinces who were averse to having bishops among them. Their aversion to bishops, the clergy wrote, "is the Strongest reason for sending them Bishops." Without episcopal supervision, religion was "sinking to the lowest ebb." Too many clergy in the southern provinces, they wrote, consider the Church as "a Trade or means of getting a livelihood; & many of the Laity of course, consider it only as a meer craft." Two days after the clergy in convention wrote their letter to the Bishop of London, Samuel Johnson wrote to Archbishop Secker that to the south where the Church was established, the clergy were "lukewarm" about the episcopate, some were often negligent and some were bad.[17]

---

[16] St.Paul's Church Minutes of Vestry, May 20, 1767; Walter Herbert Stowe, "The Seabury Minutes of the New York Clergy Convention of 1766 and 1767," April 9, 1767, p. 151.

[17] Samuel Johnson, Samuel Auchmuty, John Beach, Joseph Lamson, Jeremiah Leaming, Roger Viets, Bela Hubbard, Solomon Palmer, Christopher Newton, James Scovil, Samuel Andrews, John Beardsley to Bishop of London, October 8, 1766,

But even to hint that clerical remissness was a problem in the northern provinces in the 1760's was misleading because that was no longer a problem, though it had been in the 1740's. As American clergy had replaced those from the British Isles the problem of dissolute clergy had become a thing of the past in the northern provinces. It appears that only John Milner was properly charged in the northern provinces with immorality, after 1760. He was New York born and a graduate of the 1758 class of the College of New Jersey. He was ordained in 1761 for the Society's mission at Westchester. By 1765, because of accusations of totally unacceptable behaviour made about him to the Society, he left for a parish in Virginia. Testimony against his character came from diverse sources that might have been incorrect. However, he was again forced to resign from his parish, in 1770, again charged with similar conduct to that which had been laid against him in New York. Whether or not he was really guilty of the charges of gross misconduct made against him in Westchester and Newport parish in Virginia is uncertain, but he did not tell all he knew to the commissioners to hear Loyalist claims in London, in 1786. He claimed that he was forced to leave his Westchester parish because of the "warm part he had taken in support" of the Stamp Act. He stated that he remained in his Newport parish until 1770 when he was forced to leave because of his support of Parliament's further attempts to tax the American colonies. When hostilities broke out, in 1775, he claimed that he returned to New York, where he remained until 1782, when he left for England. The commissioners to hear Loyalist claims were rarely fooled. However, Milner appears to have been the rare exception. They declared him to have been of "great merit," and he was awarded an annual pension of £60 dating from January 5, 1786.[18]

Fulham Papers I, 308; Samuel Johnson to Secretary, Nov. 12, 1766, B, XXIII, 194; Samuel Johnson to Archbishop, Oct. 10, 1766, Hawks Papers, Johnson MSS, [55].
[18] S.P.G. Journals, XIV, April 18, 1760, XV, 65; Samuel Auchmuty to Secretary, Sept. 25, 1765
B, II, 13; Samuel Johnson to Secretary, July 15, 1765, B, XXIII, 190; Wardens and Vestry of Westchester to Secretary, Oct. 28, 1765, B, III, 288; John Milner to Secretary, Sept. 10, 1765, B, III, 286; Loyalist Claims, vol VIII, "Fresh Claims," Item 56, John Milner's deposition, July 11, 1786. There is an outline of John Milner's career in James McLachlan's Princetonians, 1748-1768, A Biographical Dictionary

By the word "discipline" the American Anglicans meant "strict adherence to Church practice" since so many converts to the Church were refusing to accept the sacraments. However, to admit that would have laid them open to the Dissenters' scorn. When they spoke of the need for resident bishops and a complete Church government they wanted to demonstrate to everyone that there was a fundamental difference between the Church of England and the other Protestant denominations.

When the Anglican clergy spoke of the need for lay discipline they were again unable to state exactly what they meant. Clergy dependent upon subscriptions were at the mercy of their vestries, a situation that was a constant source of trouble in most parishes. The appointment of resident bishops was intimately connected in the minds of many clergy with royal land grants, or, an establishment such as the four New York counties theoretically enjoyed, which would be accompanied with increased powers for the colonial governors. Only this solution would give the clergy what they wanted from the Church of England: independence of the people's dictates, and freedom to serve as clergy in a Church ruled from above, not from below.[19]

The political motives that lay behind the clergy's demands for American bishops, however, would have to be concealed until such time that the ministry in London was prepared to announce its plans for the re-organization of colonial administration. Nevertheless, the clergy who were zealous for the American episcopate were at least partly aware of the internal dangers to the Church, hence their concern. Many of the other clergy were either unaware of the dangers that faced them, or they were prepared to accept the changes that were taking place. Furthermore, many of

---

(Princeton U.P., 1976), pp. 237-238. However, he has Milner dying by April, 1772, which is at least twenty four years before he lodged his claim with the Loyalist Commission in London.

[19] The establishment in the four New York counties was legally precarious since a ruling in chancery declared that the Church could not be properly established in New York without a bishop to "collate" ministers to their parishes. See: Rev. Joshua Bloomer versus Robert Hinchman and Philip Edsall, March 5, 1772 in Duane Papers (New York Historical Society.)

those clergy who appeared to be less enthusiastic about the episcopate were of a generation who had entered the Church while relations between the Dissenters and Anglicans were less acerbic. They were unable to rise to the heights of zealous defence of the Church so characteristic of Thomas Chandler, Samuel Johnson, Samuel Seabury, Samuel Auchmuty and other clergy of their mind. When the Connecticut Dissenting Minister Noah Welles published his "Real Advantages . . . By Conforming to the Church of England," in 1762, in which he lampooned the clergy of the Church of England as being attracted by its wealth and genteel, polite society, tempers flared among the Connecticut clergy. Samuel Johnson's son, William Samuel, asked the Newtown missionary to write a reply to this "vile Ill Natur'd Pamphlet." He singled out Beach as the best man to reply because "sorry I am to say it, there does not appear that Genious & Ability for the Defence of the Church in the younger clergy." Though the younger clergy were very worthy, he continued, "Illy I fear in this respect will they be able to Copy the fair Example which their predecessors who have laid the foundation of this Church in this Country." And when Samuel Johnson needed someone to defend the Connecticut Church, in 1766, he turned to the New Jersey priest, Thomas Chandler, to defend that "Ecclesiatical Flanders" rather than to the clergy nearer to hand. When the American episcopate became the centre of public debate in the late 1760's, Andrew Elliot wrote from his New North Church in Boston to Thomas Hollis in London that "the Episcopalian controversy makes but little noise in our province, indeed if we write we are not likely to have any antagonists among us worthy of notice. Our missionaries are not able to make any tolerable figure."[20]

However, there were missionaries in Connecticut of the younger generation who were concerned about the episcopacy. The Norwich missionary, John Tyler, wrote to the Society, in 1772, about his concerns for the Church both in the American colonies and in England. He referred to "the Petition to Parliament for the repeal of

---

[20] William Samuel Johnson to John Beach, Jan. 4, 1763, William Samuel Johnson Correspondence, 1744 – 1771; Andrew Elliot to Thomas Hollis, Jan. 29, 1769, Thomas Hollis Papers; Thomas Chandler to Samuel Johnson, Feb. 5, 1766, Early Letters by Samuel Johnson, Thomas Chandler, John Hobart, 1754 – 1830. (Transcripts Connecticut State Library)

the 39 Articles of Religion." This petition, commonly referred to as the "Feathers Tavern" petition, convinced John Tyler that it was part of a "formidable Plan concerted, by which Deists, Arrians and all Nonconformists, except Quakers, act jointly to overturn the ecclesiastical Establishment of the Nation." This plan, he wrote, has been adopted by "synods of dissenting Teachers who, for some years past, have frequently met together almost from one end of british Amerca to the other." The purpose of the plan was designed to place every sect on an equal footing. "The Truth is" he wrote "the Establishment of the Church of England is an insurmountable Obstacle" to the non-conformists."[21]

John Tyler had graduated from Yale College in 1765. He left the Congregationalist Church and studied theology with Samuel Johnson at Stratford where he also performed as lay reader in his mentor's absence. After being ordained in 1768, he returned to Norwich where he faced the familiar struggle of convincing his congregation of the need to accept baptism and communion. Like many other Anglican clergy and laymen in New England he suffered under laws requiring Anglicans to pay taxes for the support of Dissenting Teachers. In October 1771, he wrote to the Society asking "Must the national Church be forever persecuted and trodden under Foot in New England?" He was writing during the disturbances between the American colonies and Britain over taxation. He expressed relief, in October 1770, that "a general Importation of british Goods [had] taken Place in America." He wrote to the Society at that time that the improved relations with England had reduced "the Murmurs against Government" and, consequently, relations between the Church and the Dissenters had become less acrimonious. He claimed in 1771 that the Anglicans in Connecticut, as far as he could know, were friends to "King and Parliament to which, they think, every Part of the british Empire ought to be subject and are universally zealous for an Episcopate."[22]

No doubt Tyler's claim that the laity's "universally zealous" support for American bishops was in his mind more than in the minds of the laity. However, he was in accord with the zealous

---

[21] John Tyler to Secretary, May 5, 1772, B, XXII 233.
[22] Samuel Johnson to secretary, May 9, 1768, B XXIII, 197; John Tyler to Secretary, Dec. 26, 1770, Oct. 9, 1771, B, XXIII, 363, 364.

warriors for an episcopate within the orbit of Trinity Church in New York. No doubt they could understand Tyler's concern that the Dissenters were out to whittle away those tenets of Anglicanism to the point where the Church of England would never be the dominant, sober, rational religion holding fast a colonial society within a hierarchical British imperial framework. They were also afraid that the younger generation of missionaries could lose sight of the need to combat creeping ecumenism.

The opportunity to voice their concerns came in 1773. John Sayre was a New York born missionary in Ulster County in New York. In 1769, one year after the Society had appointed him their missionary, it decided that his application for an increase in salary was far too early and the Secretary advised him that "when his usefulness shall more fully appear, and it shall be known" the request would be given further consideration. His opportunity to prove himself came in May 1773, when the senior clergy chose him to preach before the convention of New York-New Jersey clergy in Trinity Church, on May 19, 1773.[23]

Although his sermon was directed at the broader issue of Church reform which Francis Blackburn's pamphlet "The Confessional" had raised, and which the subsequent "Feathers Tavern" petition attempted to accomplish in England in 1772, the reference to American affairs is clear. He chose as his text Thessalonians I, chapter 5, verses 12 and 13 ". . . know them which labour among you, and who are over you in the Lord, and admonish you: and esteem them very highly in love for their work's sake. And be at peace among yourselves." He warned the clergy to guard against those who "will not endure sound doctrine," and called upon them to preserve the Church "from declension." "Let all her Ministers be very watchful," he obliquely hinted to the Philadelphia clergy, that the Church which has withstood so much persecution should "have her hedges undermined by false brethren." He pointed to the spectre of subscription and vestry control that haunted many of the clergy by reminding the laity that they owed their ministers maintenance, obedience, respect and reverence, in that order. He warned the clergy not to be "deluded by designing men, into an opinion that every pragmatical youth hath more knowledge than

---

[23] S.P.G. Journals, XVIII, 226.

the most reverent and learned divine." Hinting that the lack of bishops in America was hastening the Anglican descent into dissent he reminded his listeners that "in this new world, we behold the Church in an unparalleled situation, like a system without a centre" whose clergy "like comets" make "a short visit to the sun, perform a sudden revolution and disappear so soon, and travel to such a distance, that they can scarcely be said to move within the sphere of its attraction."[24]

A few years earlier a country clergyman mused upon a similar theme:

How happy is the parson's lot?
Forgetting Bishops, as by them forgot;
Tranquil of Spirit, with an easy mind,
To all his vestry's votes he sits resigned:
Of manners gentle, and of temper even,
He jogs his flocks, with easy pace, to heaven.[25]

Nathaniel Evans was the Society's missionary in New Jersey for barely two years before his untimely death at the age of twenty five in 1767. He was one of William Smith's elite group at the College of Philadelphia which included the artist Benjamin West, poet-musician Francis Hopkinson and fellow poet Thomas Godfrey. He understood well that left long enough to fend for themselves in America, with each successive request for help from England turned down, the Anglican clergy might indeed resign themselves to their lot. Forgetting bishops and acquiescing in government by convention would bring the clergy into line with so many of the laity in the northern colonies who Samuel Tingley at Lewes in Delaware described as "Churchmen by profession, but Presbyterian by Trade," or as James Lyons at Brookhaven on Long Island would have it, "Churchmen in words, but Congregationalists in Discipline."[26]

---

[24] John Sayre, A Sermon Preached before the Convention of Clergy . . ., May 19, 1773 (New York, 1773), pp. 13, 14, 17, 25.

[25] "Poems on Several Occasions with Some Other Compositions by Nathaniel Evans."(Philadelphia, 1772) Quoted in Thomas Firth Jones, A Pair of Lawn Sleeves(Philadelphia, 1972), p.28

[26] Kenneth Silverman, A Cultural History of the American Revolution, (New York, 1976), p. 58; Samuel Tingley to Secretary, March 5, 1782, B, XXI, 186; James Lyons to Secretary, Oct. 8, 1763, Oct. 17, 1766, B, III, 202, 209.

Given time, the clergy might even embrace their independence from the parent Church, eventually to echo the view of Jonathan Boucher and many other clergy in Virginia and Maryland where, for the time being, they felt secure in their legal establishment. Jonathan Boucher left England in 1759 to become a tutor in Virginia. He returned to England three years later to receive Anglican ordination for a snug living in St. Mary's parish in Caroline County. He wrote to his former teacher in England, John James, rector of Saint Bees Church in Cumberland, in 1767, that the Virginia clergy "are much less under ye Controll of dogmatis'g Superiors here than you are; and amongst other acceptable Effects of such Inatten'n in our Govern'rs, let Me whisper in y'r Ear that I have hitherto escap'd Notice & Censure, tho' I have not above two or three Times in ye 5 years I have been an officiat'g Mini'r here, read ye Athanasian Creed . . . I do not think my Pride w'd suffer Me now to act in a subordinate Capacity to any Man whatever."[27]

The concerns John Sayre expressed were also in the minds of some influential people in England. When Willard Wheeler was in England for ordination, in 1767, he met Bishop Secker who informed him that the Ministry was averse to sending bishops to America when the colonies were on the eve of rebellion and independence. He said that requiring American clergy to go to England for ordination was a means of binding the colonies to England. The Proprietor of Pennsylvania, Thomas Penn, told Richard Peters, Rector of Christ Church in Philadelphia, in the same year, that requiring candidates for the Anglican ministry to present themselves in England for ordination "keeps up some sort of dependence on the mother country." When William Walter went to England for ordination, in 1763, he received a rather choleric reception from Bishop of London Richard Osbaldeston. "You are like the rest always in great haste to give people Trouble out of Season" he said "and when you have got your twenty pounds [the Society's allowance to American ordinands] we never hear any more of you." When William Walter returned to Trinity Church in Boston he wrote to Bishop Osbaldeston's successor, Richard Terrick, to

---

[27] "Letters of Rev. Jonathan Boucher" Maryland Historical Magazine, VII, Number 4 (Dec. 1912), pp. 352-353.

show that he was sensitive to the bishop's rebuke.[28]

John Sayre's language and the sentiments expressed by Thomas Penn and the English prelates resonate comments that the famous English Dr. Johnson wrote in the same year that Sayre preached before the New York-New Jersey clergy. Dr. Johnson had been touring the western Scottish islands when he observed that the attraction of the American frontier to discontented Scottish highlanders was a threat to the survival of British culture. Scottish highlanders migrating to America, he wrote, will be lost to the British nation "For a nation scattered in the boundless regions of America resembles rays diverging from a focus. All the rays remain but the heat is gone. Their power consisted in their concentration. When they are dispersed, they have no effect."[29]

Considering the attitude of friends at "home", and with the clergy and laity in the Church apparently sliding into what appeared to be amorphous religious ecumenical oblivion, the future of the Church of England in America was uncertain. Unless an American bishop were appointed soon, disaster loomed. The clergy's concern increased as successive ministries in London failed to respond to their requests. The indifference with which the English ministers and prelates appeared to view their plight served to strengthen a nascent nationalism among the Anglican clergy in America who gradually began to seek alternative ways by which they could provide their Church with leadership. There was one organisation, however, which they could make use of to enforce discipline and defend Church practices in the colonies.

Annual conventions of clergy brought together missionaries in each province, and formed the basis of a nascent inter-colonial union. They had their origins in those which the Bishop of London's commissaries had periodically called, but since Bishop Gibson's death in 1748 there had been no commissaries. However, with the death of Commissary William Vesey, first Rector of Trinity Church, New York, in July 1746, senior missionary James Wetmore used the

---

[28] Clifford K. Shipton, Harvard Graduates, XIII, "Willard Wheeler"; Frederick V. Mills, Sr., Bishops by Ballot: An Eighteenth Century Revolution (New York, 1978), p.63; William Walter to Bishop of London, Sept. 10, 1764, Fulham Papers, VI, 52.
[29] Bernard Bailyn, "The Challenge of Modern Historiography," The American Historical Review, Vol. 87, No. 1 (Feb., 1982), p.15.

Society's directive that missionaries "preserve a Christian agreement and Union with one another" as his authority to call the New York clergy to a convention in September, 1746. Even while Commissary Roger Price was still officially the only clergyman in New England who could legally convene the clergy, Samuel Johnson was holding informal conventions following the Yale College commencements at which he relayed the Bishop of London's instructions to the other missionaries, and had them add their signatures to testimonials for candidates going to England for ordination.[30]

Thomas Chandler and Robert McKean in the neighbouring parish of Perth-Amboy took a lead from Samuel Johnson to initiate conventions of the New Jersey and New York clergy in June 1758. The occasion of their meeting was the preferment of Thomas Secker to the See of Canterbury. Thomas Secker was the darling of the Anglican clergy in the northern provinces and in their congratulatory letter to him the clergy made their wishes for an American bishop very clear. The clergy were anxious to concert themselves in readiness for the inevitable increase in hostility from the Dissenters that was bound to follow as the war with France was concluded. And northern New Jersey, settling fast, opened up opportunities for the Church to move in ahead of their opponents, with the Society's funds. They were also determined that Church leadership should not slip into the hands of grasping Governor Bernard, who had only recently arrived from England, and knew little about American affairs.[31]

The following October, the Connecticut clergy followed the New York-New Jersey example in formalizing the conventions Samuel Johnson had initiated. The letter to Archbishop Secker, signed by eight of the Connecticut missionaries, was carried to England by James Scovil, on his way to receive ordination for the Waterbury mission. They took the opportunity of congratulating Thomas Secker on his preferment to urge the appointment of a bishop for America. Within two years the Pennsylvania and Massachusetts

---

[30] James Wetmore to Secretary, Sept. 18, 1764, B, XIV, 111; Samuel Johnson to Bishop of London, Sept. 17, 1750, Fulham Papers, I, 289; Vestry Minutes of Trinity Church, New York, July, 10, 1746.
[31] Address of the New York and New Jersey clergy to Archbishop Secker, June 22, 1758, Lambeth Palace Library, vol. 1123, part 2, [120].

clergy had begun holding conventions. The entire contingent of Massachusetts clergy, together with those from Rhode Island, wrote to the Bishop of London, on January 1, 1761, from their voluntary meeting to pledge their loyalty on the accession of King George III. They expressed their "Zeal" for "a Bishop to reside among" them in order to alleviate the difficulties forced upon them by "great Distance" from England which they must "for ever labour under, till the Favour" of a resident bishop should be granted. In the early 1760's these conventions did little to create a union between the various provinces because they were conducted almost entirely on a provincial basis, restricting their work to interviewing candidates seeking recommendations for ordination, arranging for the clergy to officiate at the vacant missions, advising the Society about congregations needing its support.[32]

Both Samuel Johnson and Henry Caner had been urging the Society for many years to do something about providing the American clergy with some form of leadership until bishops could be appointed. Henry Caner presented his thoughts on the subject in December 1760. He wrote to the Society that for thirty years he had been acquainted with the missions in the "Northern District of America." He believed that "most of the Defects which have happen'd among the Society's Missions, have been owing to the want of a proper Authority." A resident bishop was an "Expedience too remote to be thought of," however, the Church had neither a "Commissary or the least Shadow of Authority among us." He recommended that an "Arch Deacon, Commissary or other Officer properly authorized" might help settle disputes "not only between the Clergy and their People, but among the Clergy themselves." He suggested the Society might appoint "a Clergyman of Prudence and Experience as an Inspector or Visitor of the Missionaries and Churches" who might help remedy the "sundry Improprieties and Misaffections now subsisting among the Churches in New

---

[32] William Smith to Archbishop, July 1, 1760, Lambeth Palace Library, vol. 1123, part 2, 189; Massachusetts and Rhode Island clergy to Bishop of London, Jan. 26, 1761, Fulham Papers, VI, 44; Connecticut clergy to Archbishop, Oct. 5, 1758, Lambeth Palace Library, vol. 1123, part 2, 122; James Scovil to Secretary, June 28, 1763, B, XXIII, 339; Edmund and Helen Morgan, The Stamp Act Crisis: Prologue to Revolution (Collier Books, New York, 1967), p. 21.

England."[33]

However, it was William Smith who finally came up with a scheme to regulate the Church, which he placed before the Society early in 1764 when he was in London. A graduate of the University of Aberdeen,[34] Smith had risen soon after his arrival in America from private tutor to Provost of the College of Philadelphia. He was a very talented man and a respected mathematician. In 1762, at the request of the Pennsylvania Proprietor and Lord Baltimore, the Proprietor of Maryland, he had been involved in evaluating a "New Instrument" made specially for the purpose "by Sisson to run the long-disputed west line between Pennsylvania & Maryland." Smith did not gain the position of surveyor for himself, it was given to Mason and Dixon, surveyors brought in from England for that purpose. However, that disappointment led to a chance meeting with David Rittenhouse. Lancaster missionary Thomas Barton, brother-in-law of Rittenhouse, did the introductions and soon Smith was on his way to posthumous glory. He recognized the importance of the orrery that Rittenhouse was building, and he had the College of Philadelphia award the brilliant clockmaker-scientist a master's degree. In 1769, with David Rittenhouse's assistance, Smith was able to be part of a scientific observation of the transit of Venus between the Sun and the Earth that would not be possible again until 1874. Smith's calculations in 1769 have been shown to be only one-tenth of one percent different from calculations made by scientists two hundred years later using radar.[35]

William Smith was a consummate diplomat with a love of intrigue. He managed to remain on amicable terms with the Presbyterians who comprised most of the faculty of the College, while at the same time, with the help of the College Trustees, the majority of whom were Anglican, he managed to ensure that the

---

[33] Henry Caner to Secretary, Dec. 8, 1760, B, XXII, 101,102.
[34] While William Smith is generally credited with being a graduate from the University of Aberdeen, one of his biographers, Thomas Firth Jones, claims that though he stayed four years at that university, he did not gain a degree. See: A Pair of Lawn Sleeves: A Biography of William Smith (1727-1803) (Philadelphia, 1972), pp. 2-3.
[35] William Smith to Thomas Penn, Oct. 22, 1760, William Smith Papers, II, 18 (Historical Society of Pennsylvania); William Smith to Secretary, March 11, 1762, B, XXI, 250; Thomas Firth Jones, A Pair of Lawn Sleeves, pp. 85-94.

Church service was used at the official College functions. He defended the proprietor's interests against the Quakers and their allies in the Pennsylvania Assembly, a policy which placed him at odds with many of the Church of England laity and rural clergy. His intimacy with the Penn family in England, and his success in directing young Presbyterian College students into the Church ministry gained many considerations for the Church in Pennsylvania, as well as the respect of the English prelates.[36]

Smith had gone to England in 1762 to raise money for the College of Philadelphia, and during the two years he was there he concluded that while the ministry was so unsettled, the appointment of American bishops was for the time being out of the question. Commissaries for America were unlikely because the Bishop of London was old, reportedly lacked zeal, and had declined taking out a commission to govern the colonial Church. In any case, Smith learned in 1763, if and when America got a bishop, the mitre would go to an Englishman, of the Canterbury diocese, as some of the legacies for that purpose stipulated.[37]

Hence, William Smith's proposals went before the Society's general meeting on March 16, 1764, and he was invited to join a committee with the two archbishops, the Bishops of London, Durham and Winchester to examine them. His proposals were accepted three weeks later. The Corresponding Society was just what the provinces needed, and probably better than any other examination of the American Church in the northern provinces, Smith's scheme analyzed the basic problems it faced. In fact, because it was not for outside reading, Smith was able to state precisely what the Church's problems were. Because of the recent territorial gains, and the predicted natural population increase (and he could honestly have added, because of the Dissenters' inflexible attitude towards Anglican encroachment in New England during the previous two years) it would be imperative that the Society be advised more accurately than before of the needs of the colonial Church. He continued with a discussion of the basic problems

---

[36] Thomas Penn to William Smith, Feb. 15, 1756, May 26, 1758, William Smith Papers, II, 7, 12. (Historical Society of Pennsylvania)
[37] William Smith to Richard Peters, Dec. 14, 1762, April 24, 1763, William Smith Papers, II, 105, 122. (Historical Society of Pennsylvania)

needing attention. Some congregations which could maintain their clergy would not do so while English funds were available to them, and those that did deserve the Society's assistance often fell short of meeting the subscriptions they had promised. Furthermore, as the deeds to the Church property were often held in the names of one or two individuals, disputes within the parish sometimes resulted in one party claiming sole ownership of the church, calling in a Dissenting Teacher to replace the missionary. This point had greater credence because only a year earlier a faction in Andrew Morton's New Jersey congregation had locked him out of the church and evicted him from the parsonage. Many of these difficulties, Smith concluded, could be obviated by the appointment of some of the colonial clergy as the Society's agents, who, together with the missionaries and lay Corresponding Members, would form a Corresponding Society to make decisions affecting local matters. Perhaps with knowledge of a letter five clergy from Pennsylvania and Colin Campbell of New Jersey had written to the Bishop of London, in February 1763, requesting that Smith be appointed commissary when that time should come, and certainly with an eye to his own future, Smith proposed that the agents "ought to be the same as the Bishop's commissary, when any is appointed." There would be three agents, one in each of the three zones: Massachusetts, New Hampshire, Rhode Island; New York and Connecticut; New Jersey and Pennsylvania. They would take charge of the deeds of Church property which would be held in the Society's name, and they would visit the missions triennially to settle any disputes between priest and congregation. Apart from providing for better supervision of the missions, the scheme would unite the laity with the clergy in decision making, very important if they were to be encouraged to assume complete financial responsibility for their churches.[38]

The Society's general meeting approved the scheme on April 13, 1764, a few days before Smith sailed for America. The Society's committee which examined Smith's scheme approved of all of his proposals, but stated that it was not yet prepared to name the

---

[38] Andrew Morton to Secretary, Sept. 30, 1762, Aug. 8, 1763, New Jersey clergy to Secretary, Oct. 1, 1762, B, XXIV, 206, 207, 217; S.P.G. Journals, XVI, 116, 117; Pennsylvania clergy to Bishop of London, Feb. 3, 1763, Fulham Papers, VIII, 5.

persons in America who would be appointed its agents. Although the Corresponding Society's resolves would need the Society's approval, the committee recommended that the provincial governors should also be involved in the proposed scheme. Their influence would be useful to the American Church; they could also serve as a restraining force should the experiment lead the colonial Church into too great a degree of independence. The committee also afforded the agents powers that would later cause serious concern among the missionaries. They were empowered to enquire into the missionaries' "behaviour, morals, and diligence in Duty." Smith placed his scheme before the clergy convention at Perth-Amboy the following September. All of the nine New Jersey clergy were there, with four from New York, and Hugh Neill from Pennsylvania. They gave it a very cool reception. They probably knew of, or could guess, Smith's suggestion to the Bishop of London that if he were later to appoint commissaries, the agents would be well suited for the office. The clergy in convention regarded the whole scheme as an attempt to appease the English and American Dissenters' opposition to an American bishop at the expence of the Church. Confident that they would be appointed agents, Auchmuty and Smith were eager to see the scheme adopted, but the New York missionaries were determined not to have the arrogant Auchmuty rule them from Trinity Church, and Thomas Chandler and Robert McKean led the New Jersey missionaries' opposition to any attempts to place them under Smith's supervision. Hugh Neill informed the Society one month later that Smith and Auchmuty were anxious to have the scheme accepted without alteration because "they were in hopes of being Agents themselves," which the other clergy were "unanimously against." They were also suspicious of Smith's friendly relations with the Presbyterians at the College of Philadelphia, and the reputed Methodism of the Philadelphia clergy and laity.[39]

Divisions among the Pennsylvania clergy had erupted into the open in 1762 before Smith left for England. Charles Inglis, Jacob

---

[39] S.P.G. Journals, XVI, 133, 223; Thomas Penn to Trustees of the College of Philadelphia, April 12, 1764, William Smith Papers, II, 33,(Historical Society of Pennsylvania); Convention of clergy, Perth-Amboy, to Bishop of London, Sept. 20,1764, Fulham Papers, VIII, 10; Hugh Neill to Secretary, Oct. 18, 1764, B, XXI, 121.

Duché and Philip Reading had objected to a proposal put forward by four other clergy to authorize Smith to place their request for an America bishop before the Archbishop and the king. Several clergy in Pennsylvania and the other colonies objected to Smith's influence with the bishops and the Pennsylvania proprietors. Hugh Neill wrote to the Secretary that the powers that would accrue to agents in Smith's scheme could damage a missionary's reputation, especially if the agent were "deeply immers'd in politicks, and the Missionary boggles [at] following him thro' all the doublings and windings of State affairs." William Sturgeon, assistant minister at Christ Church, another casualty before Smith's political and religious scheming, grouped Smith among those "Restless Ambitious Spirits Dabbling in Politicks, and Religion at the same Time, and thereby Endeavouring to cover, under the last, the low, Dirty part Views of the first."[40]

In 1762, Reading, Duché and Inglis were concerned that Smith might misrepresent them in England as being Methodists. William Smith was contemptuous of the Whitefieldians in Philadelphia. However, Samuel Auchmuty, writing a letter to the Society's Secretary, in April 1765, marked "Private" --- an indulgence allowed to a small number of senior American clergy --- remarked "with pain" that Inglis' "adopting the principles & Cant of the Methodists" had won him a position as assistant minister at Trinity Church. This stigma of "Wesleyism" or "Methodism" also gave the Delaware missionary, Philip Reading, reason to be wary of William Smith. Reading had accepted an invitation from the "Methodists" at St. Paul's Church to preach during William McClennaghan's absences. Jacob Duché had less to fear because, like Smith, he possessed a somewhat chameleon persona. To some he was another "Methodist"; to others he was, according to Smith, "that shining youth"; to John Ross, the pillar of St. Paul's "Methodists", he was an "Ingenious, Agreeable Young Gentleman, the delight of all who knew him, And promising to be the most Agreeable Preacher in America." However, in 1763, Oxford missionary Hugh Neill was not far from the commotions Whitefield had brought upon the Philadelphia clergy and laity who "received him with open Arms,

---

[40] Hugh Neill to Secretary, Oct. 18, 1764, William Sturgeon and John Hughes to Secretary, March 23, 1765, B, XXI, 121, 283.

and still continue to follow him from the Church, to the Meeting House, and from thence to the Church again, with a greater degree of veneration . . . than if his Grace of Canterbury was to condescend to pay them a visit." He described Jacob Duché as a true follower of the revivalist. According to Neill, when the Trinity Church "methodists" in New York invited Duché to be their minister, he sent them Charles Inglis from Dover, Delaware, "a Gentleman who had been approved of by Mr. Whitefield in his public Sermons." Perhaps Duché's eloquence and melodious voice in the pulpit account for much of his popularity, but his alleged affinity with the Methodists gave strength to the general belief that Philadelphia was Weslyan.[41]

When Smith returned to America in the spring of 1764 he had lost his earlier following. Hugh Neill, and the New Jersey clergy, Richard Charlton, Colin Campbell, Andrew Morton, Samuel Cooke and Robert McKean, who had earlier supported his leadership, had never expected to be placed under his supervision as agent within the framework of the Corresponding Society they met at Perth-Amboy. Robert McKean's support for Smith, when he visited England, in February 1762, was designed to secure a bishop or "Till the happy event be brought about, Commissary, or Superintendents, with proper powers." They now joined with the six New York-New Jersey clergy present at Perth-Amboy to oppose the scheme. Only Samuel Auchmuty wanted to accept Smith's scheme in its original form, but after the convention had finished amending the plan to establish a Corresponding Society, much of its usefulness was destroyed.[42]

The alterations they made to the scheme made it clear that they were unhappy with the idea of accepting agents shorn of commissarial dignity who would hold far greater powers over the clergy than anyone in America had previously held. The agents,

---

[41] Samuel Auchmuty to Secretary, undated letter marked "Private," apparently dispatched with his letter to the Secretary, April 13, 1765, B, II, 9; Vestry Minutes of St. Paul's Church, Nov. 15, 1762; William Smith to Secretary, Aug. 26, 1760, B, XXI, 248; John Ross to Secretary, July 2, 1762, B, XXI, 219; Hugh Neill to Secretary, Oct. 17, 1763, Oct. 18, 1764, B, XXI, 119, 121.

[42] Robert McKean to William Smith, in London, April 28, 1762, B, XXIV, 259; Hugh Neill to William Smith, May 20, 1762, William Smith Papers, I, 36 (Church Historical Society)

who could be none other than Smith and Auchmuty, would have so much authority over the missionaries, most of whom were aware of the influence they wielded in London. They were uneasy about article four of Smith's proposals. The agents' commission to visit missions to ascertain whether vestries were meeting their obligations to maintain church buildings, glebes and subscriptions to their ministers was no threat, indeed, that could be beneficial. However, they did object to the proposal that the agents should examine "all Disputes likely to arise in this [meeting monetary obligations to clergy and maintaining buildings] or any other score." The phrase "any other score" represented the Society's recommendation that agents enquire into the missionaries' "behavior, morals, and diligence in Duty." Even if those words were not expressly written in the copy of Smith's scheme placed before the Perth-Amboy convention, in September 1764, the clergy were suspicious. Their letter to the Society, dated September 20, 1764, requested removal of the phrase "any other score" because the agents might construe it to mean that they could meddle in matters that did not concern them. The clergy also objected to so much authority being given to the Society's lay members. Therefore, they proposed that any new members admitted should be approved at a general meeting of the Corresponding Society with a quorum of eleven members, six of whom should be clergy. The clergy's objections were strong enough to have the Society postpone discussion of the proposed changes.[43]

A week before the Perth-Amboy convention met, Samuel Johnson convened the Connecticut clergy at New Haven. They used the occasion to congratulate Richard Terrick on his preferment to the See of London. They dwelt upon the vastly extended territories under the king's sovereignty since the conclusion of the recent wars. However, the thrust of their message was that they hoped that "at this important Conjuncture, that it is reserved for one of the Glories of your Lordship's Episcopate, that these Countries may be provided for with Bishops." The Connecticut clergy did not have the opportunity to discuss Smith's scheme, though Samuel Johnson had given his approval to it while the Perth-Amboy convention was in progress. Nevertheless, it is extremely unlikely that the Connecticut

---

[43] S.P.G. Journals, XVI, 223.

clergy would have accepted Auchmuty's leadership. Johnson's support for the appointment of American agents was not to be misconstrued as support for an increase in Smith's influence in the American Church. When Smith left for England on his fund raising tour in 1762, Johnson wrote to Archbishop Secker that "a certain gentleman gone to England from America this winter, whose ambition is" to be made the first bishop in America if peace is declared would be "very disgustful" to the generality of the Church here, "nor can it be imagined that any one from America would be acceptable.".[44]

While Smith was in England the disagreements among the Pennsylvania clergy were further aggravated, and this probably explains why his scheme received so little support from there. Hugh Neill, who had been Smith's strongest supporter eighteen months earlier, openly opposed the plan for a Corresponding Society. In Smith's absence, George Whitefield had visited Philadelphia, and to Neill's disgust, he had preached from the Christ Church pulpit, gaining a sufficient number of supporters to establish a church within the Oxford mission, only nine miles from Neill's own Trinity Church. The Rector of Philadelphia's Christ Church, Richard Peters, described his assistant as "the best Preacher I ever heard." And Duché used his talents to recruit support for the break-away congregation at Oxford, which John Ross, Christ Church vestryman and leading benefactor of St. Paul's Church, was helping to finance. When Smith returned to America, however, he remained a consumate diplomat in his dealings with the "methodists" at St. Paul's Church and with the Presbyterians at the College. To make matters worse, the murder of a number of Indians at Lancaster heightened the tension between the Anglican-Quaker faction which was endeavouring to have Pennsylvania's proprietary government replaced by a royal governor, and the Presbyterians who were supporting the Proprietor to prevent any closer relations with the Crown. Smith's alliance with the Presbyterian party, and his preference for peace with the "methodists" sent Neill to Perth-

---

[44] Samuel Johnson to Archbishop, Sept. 20, 1764, April 10, 1762, Schneider's Johnson, I, pp. 347, 316-321; Samuel Johnson for the Connecticut clergy to Bishop of London, Sept. 14, 1764, Fulham Papers, I, 296.

Amboy to quash his plan to assume greater powers in the Church.[45]

Another of Smith's former allies had turned against him by 1764. His habit of mixing politics with religion had made his friendship with the rector of Christ Church, Robert Jenny, and his assistant, William Sturgeon, rather tenuous. In 1761, Sturgeon fell into disfavour with the Bishop of London for performing a marriage ceremony without first obtaining the required licence, a circumstance John Ross used to cause trouble for Sturgeon who had been instrumental in closing Christ Church to McClennaghan. Ross, who sat on both Christ Church and St. Paul's vestries, complained to the Society that Sturgeon had been neglecting his work as catechist to the Negroes, and though he appears not to have been guilty of the charges Ross laid against him, he could only gain a nominal vindication from the Christ Church vestry. In April 1761, the Society's Secretary, Dr. Bearcroft, wrote to William Smith "the Caution concerning Mr. Ross, I shall remember, and in truth he had very little, if any, influence with me before." Nevertheless, John Ross's influence carried sufficient weight to gain for him a partial victory. The Society ruled that while Sturgeon had cleared himself of total neglect of his duty as catechist, his "attention to it has been very Superficial, and unequal to the nature of that Duty." His employment as the Society's catechist with an annual allowance of £50 sterling was brought to an end. The vestry of Christ Church had deducted the Society's allowance from Sturgeon's annual £200 salary as their minister. Sturgeon had earlier informed the Society that Christ Church had agreed to pay him the £200 should the Society withdraw its support. However, the absence of entry in the vestry minutes that Sturgeon's salary was restored to £200 probably expresses their lack of affection for him. A month after the Perth-Amboy convention, Sturgeon replied to the Christ Church vestry's request that he make up his mind about his earlier statement that he did not intend to stay with them. Apart from poor health, he wrote, "some hard Usage" he had received from the vestry had caused him to consider resigning. He finally resigned two years later, but not until his relations with the vestry had become acrimonious and untenable. Sturgeon was therefore friendless when Smith returned to America to resume his intimacy with the Christ Church vestry,

---

[45] Hugh Neill to Secretary, Oct. 18, 1764, Oct. 17, 1763, B, XXI, 119, 121.

the Presbyterians and "Methodists. A year before his resignation, Sturgeon had joined forces with two Christ Church members, John Hughes and Benjamin Franklin, in offering assistance to the Society on behalf of the Anti-Proprietary Party. Franklin used his influence with the Bishop of London to secure ordination for his political allies, and Smith hit back by successfully obstructing Sturgeon's attempts to regain the Society's patronage.[46]

Significantly, none of the other Pennsylvania clergy went to the Perth-Amboy convention. Thomas Barton liked the Presbyterians and Methodists even less than Neill. Writing to Sir William Johnson in 1770, he wished Whitefield "would settle among the Senecas." He was less acerbic in his denunciation of the Philadelphia clergy's infatuation with Whitefield only because he was further from them. His disgust at the Lancaster murders brought from him a pamphlet denouncing the Quakers' refusal to police the European frontier settlements. Barton privately favoured the Anti-Proprietary Party, but his close friendship with Smith and the many benefits he received from the proprietor, Thomas Penn, forced him to remain silent. And, in his view, since the German Lutherans were proposing to join the Church of England, and the Quakers were politically allied with the Church, the time was ripe to appoint an American bishop. Barton wrote to the Society in November 1764, that "The Establishment in America has long been talk'd of, and long expected [and] this could never in any former Time, be introduced with more Success than at Present." Smith's scheme would have brought his hopes to an end.[47]

From Perth-Amboy the Society received the American judgement

---

[46] Robert Jenny to Archbishop, Nov. 29, 1758, Lambeth Palace Library, vol 1123, part 2, [123]; William Sturgeon to Secretary, July 2, 1760, B, XXI, 276; John Ross to Secretary, July 2, 1762, B, XXI, 219; Secretary Philip Bearcroft to William Smith, April 20, 1761, William Smith Papers, I, 32 (Church Historical Society); William Sturgeon to Secretary, Nov. 20, 1763, B, XXI, 281; S.P.G. Journals, XV, 399; William Sturgeon to Secretary, [Nov. 15, 1762], B, XXI, 278; William Sturgeon and John Hughes to Secretary, March 23, 1765, B, XXI, 283; William Sturgeon to Secretary, March 25, 1765, B, XXI, 284; William Smith to Secretary, March 3, 1766, Sept. 1, 1767, B, XXI, 254, 258; Vestry Minutes of Christ Church, Philadelphia, March 30, 1763, April 28, 1763, Oct. 30, 1764, Oct. 17, 1763, Nov. 19, 1764, Jan. 21, 1766, Feb. 17, 1766, July 28, 1766, July 31, 1766.
[47] [Thomas Barton] The Conduct of the Paxron-Men, Impartially Presented ... (Philadelphia, 1764); Thomas Barton to Secretary, Nov. 16, 1764, B, XXI, 14.

on the proposed Corresponding Society. To make their wishes perfectly clear, they used the occasion of Richard Terrick's preferment to the See of London to combine their congratulations with a plea for an American bishop. William Smith wrote privately to the Bishop of London announcing that the clergy "who are all my most particular friends, have signified to the Society their Approbation of the present Plan for Corresponding Societies, and their earnest wish that I might undertake the Agency for Pennsylvania & New Jersey." He made no reference to the heated debate that his scheme had raised, but the convention's modifications to the scheme would alone have given the Society ample evidence that the clergy were unhappy. Hugh Neill, anxious that the Society should understand, wrote a very detailed account of the Perth-Amboy proceedings, pointing out the dangers that would face missionaries who might differ with Smith and his associates over politics. Neill had good cause for alarm as he imagined himself sharing the fate of Sturgeon who had retired to his farm in the Oxford mission. His letter laid the whole business of the Corresponding Society aside temporarily. Daniel Burton, the Society's Secretary, wrote to Smith, in September 1765, that nothing had been done about the Corresponding Society since Smith left England. The scheme was "suspended last winter, as there was good Assurance given by the Ministry" that the appointment of two bishops for America was likely. However "by the change of Hands, That matter is at present over." With the postponement of Smith's scheme it sank even further from view as hostility from New York and New Jersey increased.[48]

With the Corresponding Society scheme laid aside for the time being the New York and New Jersey clergy set about tightening up their organisation to show that their conventions were a more suitable temporary alternative to agents or commissaries until bishops could be appointed. Encouraging news arrived from Boston

---

[48] William Smith, Richard Charlton, Isaac Browne, Colin Campbell, Samuel Auchmuty, Hugh Neill, Samuel Cooke, Samuel Seabury, Thomas Chandler, Robert McKean, John Milner, Andrew Morton, Agur Treadwell, Leonard Cutting to Bishop of London, Sept. 20, 1764, Fulham Papers, VIII, 10; Willima Smith to Bishop of London, Sept. 26, 1764, Fulham Papers, VIII, 12; Hugh Neill to Secretary, Oct. 18, 1764, B, XXI, 121; Daniel Burton to William Smith, Sept. 20, 1765, Hawks MSS, William Smith Papers, I, 9. (Church Historical Society)

the following summer when the Massachusetts clergy showed signs of joining their New York colleagues in convention. Timothy Cutler, Rector of Christ Church, in Boston, died while the city was in uproar over the Stamp Act, and after his funeral the clergy gathered at Henry Caner's house. Probably prompted by Auchmuty who was visiting Boston at the time, they decided that a union such as the other clergy had formed would be necessary to sustain themselves against persecution that would surely follow if they were to continue preaching submission to Parliament. William McGilchrist was there from his mission in Salem. It was quite an occasion, fourteen clergy attended "and made something of an Appearance for this country, when we walk'd together in our Gowns and cassocks." Henry Caner, as secretary and moderator, gave a discourse in King's Chapel, before getting down to business. After dinner they were joined by Governor.Bernard. Henry Caner had written privately, in November 1762, to congratulate Richard Terrick on his preferment to the See of London. He stated that he would gladly unite with the New England clergy but he had no authority to convene them. He wrote "it is hoped your Lordship will either appoint a Commissary or some Person properly qualified to become the Center of Union among the clergy here." Perhaps, with the death of the Rector of Christ Church in 1765, Henry Caner could see his way clear to achieving a position of leadership in New England to counter what appeared to be the growing influence of the Church leaders in Philadelphia and New York..[49]

Now that the Massachusetts clergy were finally convinced of the need for unity, the clergy at Trinity Church in New York set about formalizing their conventions and forming a basis for a more general union among the clergy. On May 21, 1766, fourteen clergy attended the first New York convention at Samuel Auchmuty's house. The eight New York clergy were present with six from New Jersey. Samuel Johnson and Abraham Jarvis were present to represent Connecticut. After hearing Auchmuty preach in Trinity Church, they set to business. The New York clergy had held conventions for several years with their New Jersey colleagues, but

---

[49] Henry Caner to Secretary, Aug. 22, 1765, XXII, 112; Henry Caner to Bishop of London, Sept. 10, 1765, Nov. 6, 1762, Fulham Papers, VI, 54, 46; William McGilchrist to Secretary, June 27, 1766, B, XXII, 180.

on the morning of the 21st they formalised their proceedings for the future. Johnson presided as they established the rules for the presidency, agreed upon a quorum, allowed full voting privileges for clergy attending from other provinces. But most significant of all, they ruled that the conventions be responsible for examining all future candidates seeking ordination, approving all missionaries' requests for removal to other missions, and examining requests from new congregations seeking the Society's assistance. These measures were designed to make the establishment of the Corresponding Societies unnecessary, but what they needed was some form of official recognition in America to sanction the independent direction they were taking.[50]

Sir Henry Moore had only recently arrived to take up his appointment as governor of the province, and so they now set about winning his support. The address they finally agreed upon began by congratulating him on his appointment and then followed an account of their leaderless plight that had compelled them to resort to the measures they had adopted in convention. The governor declined to receive their deputation, no doubt feeling that while it was personally desirable and expected of him as the agent of the Crown to assist the clergy, he could not become party to what looked like unilateral action without instruction from the prelates at home.[51]

The clergy, not the least set back by the governor's rebuff, sent off their letter to the Society outlining the decisions they had reached in convention, convinced that their show of initiative in the face of ministerial indecision would gain approval. Before their letter reached England they received news from the Archbishop of Canterbury that the political climate in the colonies, and the hostility from the English Dissenters, had made it impossible to appoint bishops for America. "The Dissenters in America are so closely connected with those in England" Archbishop Secker had written to "Good Dr. Johnson" in September, 1758, that then, and in the years to follow, proselytizing in New England could threaten the Society's fund raising in England. The only alternative now would be to

---

[50] "The Seabury Minutes of the New York Clergy Conventions of 1766 and 1767," Historical Magazine of the Protestant Epscopal Church, X (1941), pp. 132-143.
[51] "Seabury Minutes," pp. 136, 138, 140.

implement the scheme for Corresponding Societies. The Archbishop had already begun to urge the Bishop of London to take out a commission in order to appoint commissaries who would take the place of the agents Smith had proposed.[52]

The New York-New Jersey clergy, convinced that Secker's decision would delay indefinitely the appointment of bishops to the disadvantage of the American Church in the long run, sent Charles Inglis off to Philadelphia to gain the support of the clergy there for the proposals the New York clergy were preparing to submit to their brethren scheduled to meet at Shrewsbury in October, 1766. But after two hours discussion with the Rector of Christ Church, Richard Peters, he found him "well affected to the cause" but "diffident and adverse" to pushing the American episcopate. The New York and New Jersey clergy met at Shrewsbury, New Jersey, with Jeremiah Leaming and Abraham Jarvis representing Connecticut. William Sturgeon and Richard Peters were the representatives from Pennsylvania (Smith was attending the College Commencement in Philadelphia.) Hugh Neill, was also there, though he had moved to Maryland one month earlier. Samuel Auchmuty, suspecting what Thomas Chandler and his friends had planned to do at the convention, stayed away. Instead, he sent letters he had received from the Archbishop requesting the American clergy to let the matter of the American episcopate rest until a more suitable climate prevailed. The convention elected Thomas chandler its president, with Myles Cooper and Samuel Cooke a committee to draft a letter to the Bishop of London. The sentiments it contained proved too strong to gain the support of the two Pennsylvania representatives, though the New York, New Jersey and Connecticut clergy all concurred. The letter criticized the Archbishop's plan to appoint commissaries who had in the past proved inadequate in their supervisory role, and who were also inferior to a "public Declaration of the Convention" which could be far more effective in supervising Church affairs than any commissary. They wanted

---

[52] Archbishop to William Smith, Aug. 2, 1766, William Smith Papers, I, 51 (Church Historical Society); Thomas Secker to "Good Dr. Johnson," Sept. 27, 1758, William Smith Papers, I, 25 (Church Historical Society); S.P.G. Journals, XVII, 110; Archbishop to Samuel Johnson, March 30, 1763, Lambeth Palace Library, vol 1123, part 3, 300.

"Unalienable Episcopal Power, and not Commissariat Power." To appoint commissaries, apart from admitting defeat to the Dissenters, would be (as Chandler wanted to write) "instead of a fish they give us a serpent," meaning the appointment of Auchmuty and Smith as commissaries instead of "Bishop Johnson," as Chandler would have had it.[53]

In the meantime the convention set about another scheme which would unite the clergy more tightly under convention control, and thus obviate the need for commissaries. The scheme was a corporation to provide financial assistance for widows and orphans of clergy. Myles Cooper and Charles Inglis were appointed to begin a correspondence with Sir William Johnson whose influence with the British ministry might lead to a land grant to finance the corporation.[54]

Both William Smith and Richard Peters had wide experience in Pennsylvania politics, they understood the need to avoid allowing the bishops controversy to upset the harmony among the various religious and cultural groups in that province. Richard Peters' experience as Secretary to the Governor, and his collaboration with the Presbyterians as a trustee of the College of Philadelphia had taught him the meaning of restraint. When he attempted to moderate the proceedings at the Shrewsbury convention he found them "full of a kind of resentment" about their failure to gain an episcopate for America. Myles Cooper, Inglis and Ogilvie (Auchmuty's two assistants), Chandler, Seabury, Cooke and McKean, in particular, seemed quite incapable of listening to any alternatives to their plans. When Smith and Auchmuty heard of the convention's presumptuous resolutions they reacted with far more hostility than the amiable Richard Peters. Smith, referring to St. Paul's Church congregation, which was at that time contesting the Bishop of London's right to license clergy for America, pointed out to Richard Terrick that their seeking "an independent Church of

---

[53] Thomas Chandler to Samuel Johnson, Jan. 19, 1767, Schneider's Johnson, I, 391; Charles Inglis to Samuel Johnson, May, 28, 1766, Schneider's Johnson, I, 363; "Seabury Minutes," p. 157; Thomas Chandler, Samuel Cooke, Myles Cooper to Bishop of London, Oct. 10, 1766, quoted in Samuel A. Clark, The Episcopal Church in the American Colonies: The History of St. John's Church, Elizabeth Town, pp. 118-128.
[54] "Seabury Minutes," p. 144 – 145.

England" in America was a "Notion [which] gains too much ground here" among the missionaries who were setting up "a kind of Synodical or Presbyterian, or Self-delegated Government by Conventions." Particularly galling to Provost Smith was the arrogance of the "Missionaries . . . and Servants of the Society" in convention who "had put one of their own Number [Chandler] in the chair, while a Member of the Society and Clergyman of Respect [Richard Peters] was present." Samuel Auchmuty met with Samuel Johnson's son before he boarded ship in New York bound for London to persuade him to "make some Apology for the warm proceedings" of the clergy, and gave him a letter for the Society's Secretary urging him to give a "check to their Career" before they begin "to Rule the Society & their Superiors" in America. Placing himself squarely with Smith in the business of commissaries and the Corresponding Society he argued that he knew of no better plan, until bishops could be appointed, than to establish commissaries as the Society's agents in the Corresponding Society, for until "some Subordination should take place . . . Independency and Confusion will ensue," especially as in the conventions "every little Missionary has as much, & in general more to say, than even the members of the Society abroad." The egalitarian spirit of the clergy in convention was particularly threatening to the Rector of Trinity Church. Auchmuty had written to Samuel Johnson that "my two Assistants [are] fond of power, equally intoxicated" as Myles Cooper who was "as warm, & as wrong as the next."[55]

While the Shrewsbury convention was in progress Auchmuty was at Stratford where Samuel Johnson was presiding over a convention of the ten Connecticut clergy. The letter they sent to the Bishop of London totally ignored the prelate's decision to implement the Corresponding Society in America, concentrating instead upon their dire need of episcopal guidance. Auchmuty was content that at least they had not directly raised their objections to the Corresponding Society, but he did not know that Johnson and

---

[55] William Smith to Bishop of London, Nov. 13, 1766, Richard Peters to Bishop of London, Nov. 14, 1766, Fulham Papers, VIII, 25, 27; Fragment of a letter from Samuel Auchmuty to Samuel Johnson, no date, and Jan. 3, 1767, Hawks MSS, Samuel Johnson Papers, [64], 10. (Church Historical Society); Samuel Auchmuty to Secretary, Dec. 20, 1766, B, II, 22.

Chandler had planned beforehand what the Shrewsbury convention would do; nor did he know that Samuel Johnson's son would leave for England carrying a letter to the Archbishop stating what had been omitted from the Stratford convention's letter to the Bishop of London. As the ministry was "so inattentive, & I doubt utterly averse" to helping the American Church, Samuel Johnson wrote, the American clergy must give up hope. Particularly biting was the fact that while he was writing, the Dissenters were holding a synod not far from Thomas Chandler's parsonage in Elizabeth Town to organise opposition to the American episcopate. In this letter Johnson, even more bluntly than in the letter from Shrewsbury, pointed to the direction some of the clergy were heading. If the ministry would not heed their pleas, he urged, then the Archbishop and bishops should take matters into their own hands and consecrate bishops for America, for bishops should not be "treated as meer Creatures of State."[56]

Apart from the Pennsylvania representatives, the clergy at Shrewsbury had supported the convention's resolutions. Of the New York clergy, only James Lyons and Harry Munro were absent. The Society's letter dismissing Lyons from the Brookhaven mission was on its way when the convention met, and a three-cornered struggle between Munro, his patron, Colonel Fredrick Philips, and the congregation at Philipsburg Manor had occupied Munro's attention during his first year in Anglican orders. New Jersey missionary Isaac Browne, had not attended the Shrewsbury convention, but he had expressed strong support for the American episcopate. However the Stamp Act had compromised him. By preaching obedience to legal government and toleration of the unfair legislation he had drawn mockery from a number of his congregation who rallied to David Griffith, a New York physician. Griffith was challenging Browne's monopoly of the medical practice in the Newark-Second River mission, and during 1766 he was seeking Anglican ordination for part of that mission. By October 1766, it is quite possible that Browne was beginning to share

---

[56] Samuel Johnson, Samuel Auchmuty and the ten Connecticut clergy to Bishop of London, Oct. 8, 1766, Fulham Papers, I, 308; Samuel Johnson to Secretary, Nov. 12, 1766, B, XXIII, 194; Samuel Johnson to Archbishop, Oct. 10, 1766, Hawks MSS, Samuel Johnson Papers, no number. (Church Historical Society)

Auchmuty's suspicion of the conventions. Apart from a natural inclination to avoid contention, he was unhappy with the leading conventioner, Myles Cooper, who was encouraging Griffith's intrusion into his mission. Of the Connecticut clergy, only Matthew Graves appears to have been indifferent to the convention's proceedings. He never got along with the local clergy who he considered too democratic and innovative with their love for conventions and lay readers. In Pennsylvania, Thomas Barton, secure from the Philadelphia clergy's influence, and too much a frontier missionary to ignore the importance of bringing order to the west, supported the action taken at the Shrewsbury convention. When he sent his half-yearly report to the Society in November, 1766, he had recently returned from a tour of New Jersey and New York, and though he had not been present at the convention, he gave whole-hearted support to its resolutions.[57]

As soon as the clergy had concluded their work at Shrewsbury, the committee chosen to compose the letters to England set to work. Within a few days Chandler had the most urgent letter off to the Bishop of London, before leaving for Philadelphia where he called on the "American Colossus" Provost Smith, who wanted to know the reason for the northern missionaries' hostility towards him. Smith attempted to exculpate himself from Chandler's accusation that he was deliberately throwing cold water on the scheme to obtain bishops so that he could gain commissary powers over the missionaries, but Chandler returned to Elizabeth Town convinced that the Provost was a doubtful Anglican.[58]

When the clergy next convened, following the King's College commencement in May 1767, Chandler was in Maryland. He had gone there with a view to accepting the offer of a lucrative parish, while at the same time sounding out some of the local clergy about the proposed American episcopate. Samuel Auchmuty, fearing that the clergy would bring to New York the egalitarian ideas they had aired at Shrewsbury, urged the Philadelphia clergy to help him

---

[57] S.P.G. Journals, XVII, 139; New York clergy to Secretary, March 19, 1767, B, III, 263; Thomas Chandler to Secretary, Dec. 4, 1767, XXIV, 93; Isaac Browne to Secretary, June 12, 1769, B, XXIV, 43; Thomas Chandler to Samuel Johnson, Sept. 9, 1768, Schneider's Johnson, I, 446; Thomas Barton to Secretary, Nov. 10, 1766, B, XXI, 17; Isaac Browne to Secretary, April 6, 1767, B, XXIV, 35.

[58] Thomas Chandler to Samuel Johnson, Oct. 19, 1766, Schneider's Johnson, I, 369.

subdue the missionary upstarts. In particular, he wanted Richard Peters or William Smith to attend "for I fear the same Spirit will prevail that appeared at the last Jersey one: however I shall give myself very little trouble about it. Lords all, & Masters all, I find will not do, either in church or state." It was difficult for Samuel Auchmuty to accept the missionaries' challenge to his authority, especially as some, like Chandler and Inglis, were his intellectual superiors. He considered that his family background elevated him above most of his Anglican colleagues. His father was a judge with the Admiralty Court in Boston, his uncle was the Dean of Armagh in Ireland, and his own cultivated manner and marriage into one of New York's wealthiest families fitted him well for the prestigious Trinity Church rectory. He had begun his career in the ministry as the Society's catechist to the Negroes and assistant to Henry Barclay at Trinity Church. While he satisfied the Society of his diligence as catechist, his real interest lay with the polite society at Trinity Church. His sermons, some of which have survived, are largely concerned with social manners; they lack the intellectual acuity seen in those of Samuel Provost who was his assistant at Trinity Church in the late 1760's. His valuable property in the city and his large two-stored house with its extensive library and well-stocked wine cellar were matched by an arrogant and condescending manner which offended many of the poorer members at Trinity Church and its two chapels as well as many of the country clergy. His personal pride was so hurt in 1767 when a number of condemned criminals were too "stupidly ignorant," or more likely, disinclined to listen to his pompous preaching, that he had their execution delayed to allow him more time to bring them to repentance.[59]

Had Samuel Auchmuty been aware of the discussions at Trinity Church, before his appointment as catechist and assistant minister to Rector Henry Barclay in 1748, he might have been offended, though probably not less confident of his abilities. When William Vesey died in 1746, the Trinity Church vestry called Henry Barclay from

---

[59] Samuel Auchmuty to Richard Peters, May 11, 1767, Richard Peters Papers, VI, p. 49 (Historical Society of Pennsylvania); Samuel Auchmuty to Samuel Johnson, Feb. 14, 1767, No. 11 Hawks MSS, Johnson Papers (Church Historical Society); Memorial of Robert Nicholls Auchmuty on behalf of his mother Mary Auchmuty, Loyalist Claims, XXXXV, 171; Samuel Auchmuty, MSS Sermon, 2 Cor. 4:5 (Possession of Rector, Trinity Church, New York)

the Mohawk mission to succeed him. The governor of New York would have preferred Barclay to stay with the Mohawk Indians at a time when the Indians friendly to the French were menacing Albany. However, in spite of petitions from the Mohawks who were upset at losing Barclay, the governor informed the Society that he was "imprudent and impolitick" enough to induct him as the new rector of Trinity Church. Consequently, Richard Charlton, who had aspirations of succeeding Vesey, resigned as catechist and assistant minister at Trinity Church to take the Society's mission on Staten Island. The vestry requested Samuel Johnson at Stratford to suggest a suitable replacement. However, the Society had decided upon Auchmuty for the position. The Trinity Church vestry replied that the Society's appointee might not meet the requirements of their church. "The Strength and Clearness of his Voice; Our Church being by all Accounts one of the Largest in America, So that few Gents are perfectly heard in it, We would therefore have Wished to have been favoured with the Liberty of Making Our Own Choice." They continued that if the Society's candidate did not measure up to their standards, he might have to go. They wrote that they expected "the Honourable Board will Indulge us in the Choice of Another." Presumably, Samuel Auchmuty's appearance, family pedigree and voice pleased the genteel Trinity Church society. He was appointed catechist and assistant minister in March 1748.[60]

None of the Philadelphia clergy went to Auchmuty's aid in May 1767. Nevertheless he soon found an ally in the Connecticut representative Jeremiah Leaming. Immediately the convention commenced business Auchmuty began to read the missionaries a lesson in subordination to their superiors, which they silenced with a resolution forbidding any member to speak twice on the same subject, or to leave the meeting without the presiding minister's consent.[61]

Having failed once more to bring the convention to heel, the Rector of Trinity Church chose to oppose the missionaries over James Lyons' request that the convention attempt to persuade the

---

[60] Trinity Church vestry minutes, Nov. 24, 1747, March, 8 1748 (possession of the Rector); Governor of New York to Secretary, Dec. 20, 1746, B, XIV, 92; Henry Barclay to Secretary, Dec. 2, 1746, B, XIV, 95.
[61] "Seabury Minutes," p. 156.

Society to reconsider its recent decision to dismiss him. When he had replaced Isaac Browne at Brookhaven on Long Island, many of the recent converts from the Congregationalists left the Church preferring Browne's evangelical style of preaching. To make matters worse, Lyons became involved in a legal dispute with his church warden, Samuel Johnson's stepson, William Nicholls. As the Society was refusing to finance any new missions in New England, Samuel Johnson and several other New Englanders were determined to secure Brookhaven for a recent Yale graduate waiting to take the gown. In 1764, Samuel Johnson, with the support of his Connecticut colleagues Jeremiah Leaming and Ebenezer Dibblee, had been anxious to have Ebenezer Kneeland, a native of Hebron, Connecticut, and future husband of Johnson's eldest granddaughter, appointed to Brookhaven "if Mr. Lyons would make way for him." The Society had agreed to Kneeland's ordination when "Lyons has relinquished that Mission and is provided for." However, James Lyons stayed on and the Connecticut clergy lost their candidate to the 59th Regiment stationed at Louisburg. Most of the clergy at the convention agreed that the Brookhaven missionary lacked zeal, but felt some compassion for the aging man, whose major fault lay in his being a catholic-spirited European among puritanical American nationalists. Only a few months earlier Auchmuty had begged the Society to give the "poor wretch" Lyons a mission in the southern colonies. But now, together with Jeremiah Leaming, he had his negative vote placed on the convention's minutes, which he followed up with a letter to the Society urging that Lyons' dismissal would make the missionaries more careful in the future.[62]

The American clergy's correspondence to London betrayed their bickering and jostling for power, but reports from Smith and Auchmuty that the missionaries were bent upon wresting control of

---

[62] Ebenezer Dibblee and Jeremiah Leaming to Secretary, Aug. 12, 1764, B, XXIII, 208; Samuel Johnson to Secretary, Aug. 13, 1764, XXIII, 186; Samuel Peters to Secretary, Aug. [1764], B, XXIII, 321; Schneider's Johnson, I, The Autobiography, p. 49, Samuel Johnson to William Samuel Johnson, May 25, 1769, Feb. 24, 1770, pp. 454-455, 465-466; S.P.G. Journals, XVI, 7, 383; Governor Wilmot to Lords of Trade, May 6, 1766, B, XXV, 79; "Seabury Minutes" pp. 158-159; James Lyons to Secretary, Sept. 14, 1764, B, III, 204; Samuel Auchmuty to Secretary, May I, 1767, March 29, 1766, B, II, 23, 15; Samuel Auchmuty to Samuel Johnson, May 25, 1767, Hawks MSS, Samuel Johnson Papers, 12.

American Church affairs from London brought a sharp rebuke from Richard Terrick. When Thomas Chandler read the Bishop of London's letter he invited William Smith to join with the clergy at Elizabeth Town in October to help remove the misunderstandings. Both Smith and Auchmuty were careful to avoid the convention, so did Samuel Seabury, and Richard Charlton who was supposed to preside.[63]

When the clergy met at Chandler's home, on October 7, 1767, the first item for consideration was Terrick's reply to their Shrewsbury addresses, in which he had expressed concern about the Presbyterian nature of their conventions. Making it quite clear that they knew the identity of the Bishop's informer, they replied that their views were "as far from Congregationalism, Presbyterianism, or Independency, as those of our Accuser, whoever he may be, nor have we a better Opinion of than he, of Synods that are formed upon such Principles." They went on to deny any attempt in their conventions to enforce clerical conformity. They insisted that as the American Church had "no Ecclesiastical Superior . . . within the Distance of a Thousand Leagues" leadership should pass to those with superior abilities properly exercised through conventions, and warned that any individual who claimed that lead because of the "conceit of the Superiority of his own Abilities" would naturally meet opposition.[64]

It seemed that unity was to remain a chimera within the American Church. The New York-New Jersey clergy would not allow the Church to be controlled from Philadelphia; the clergy from Delaware to Massachusetts would not accept the authority of Samuel Auchmuty and William Smith as commissaries; the clergy in New England were apprehensive of the militants centred around Trinity Church in New York who appeared too forward in their correspondence with their superiors in England. The clergy in Maryland and Virginia, secure in their livings, would have no truck with the Northerners' conventions and their plans to bring episcopal inquisitors to America. Further south, the clergy often stayed only

---

[63] Thomas Chandler to William Smith, Sept. 5, 1767, Oct. 17, 1767, William Smith Papers, I, 56, 57, (Church Historical Society).
[64] Thomas Chandler and Myles Cooper to Bishop of London, Dec. 5, 1767, Fulham Papers, VI, 168.

long enough to be convinced of the futility of attempting to secure their salaries from Presbyterian-controlled vestries which, in many cases, refused to collect ministerial taxes provided by law. These clergymen were scarcely likely to become united through conventions with the clergy to the north who they would most likely never meet. In spite of their efforts, Johnson, Chandler, and their followers could not claim any real co-ordination among the clergy in convention by 1767, and Chandler found himself grasping at almost any opportunity to create a unified policy.

His final opportunity came in October 1768, when William Smith attended the convention of clergy at New Brunswick, New Jersey. Nineteen clergy were present. Eight came from New Jersey; seven from New York; three from Pennsylvania and Roger Viets represented Connecticut. Smith had an opportunity of uniting the clergy in a very personal way from the Delaware to Massachusetts in a scheme that would appeal to all of the Anglican clergy. He presented his draft constitution of a corporation that had been approved in principle at Shrewsbury eighteen months earlier. At that time the convention had appointed Smith and three other clergymen to prepare a constitution for the "Corporation for the Relief of Widows and Children in the Communion of the Church of England in America." However, the burden had fallen on Smith who had originally suggested the idea after observing a similar corporation the Philadelphia Presbyterians had established. To Chandler and some of his colleagues the scheme smacked of Smith's earlier attempt to allow the laity a voice in Church councils. Nevertheless, Chandler saw in the scheme an excellent opportunity to commit the Society to place American Church property at the Corporation's disposal. Therefore, as president of the New Brunswick convention, he used his influence to insert two additional clauses into the constitution. Article five provided that the Society should deduct £3 per annum from each missionary's salary which would then be made available to the Corporation's fund. Article six provided that the Society should contribute to the Corporation £3 per annum for each vacant mission. The proceeds from glebes belonging to vacant missions would also be deposited into the

Corporation's fund.[65]

Chandler was convinced that Smith was determined to take every opportunity to hinder the New York-New Jersey clergy's attempts to avoid his commanding influence. Chandler complained to the Society, in 1770, that letters directed to New York via Smith in Philadelphia were being unnecessarily delayed. The Society's letters to New York "when directed to Dr. Smith's Care, are frequently twice as long in coming from England." Smith, he wrote, was frequently away from home "and seems always very forgetful of such a trifling matter as the forwarding of letters or Parcels." Chandler insisted that the clergy, apart from Smith, were unanimously in favour of the alterations, but at least Myles Cooper was beginning to suspect him of pushing too hard and too far. Cooper wrote to Smith that he doubted if he would attend any more Corporation meetings since he "saw so much partiality at the last in New Jersey" that he was sick of the matter. "You cannot but recollect" he continued "what prevarications & mean unmanly Subterfuges were made use of even before your Eyes, & yet his word is to be credited . . . when all ye words of ye best Laymen in the country were decreed to be Trifles not worth regarding."[66]

The scheme did finally succeed, though without articles five and six. The Society guaranteed to pay £60 each year into the Corporation's funds, and the clergy were left to take care of all other arrangements. But, while it brought a promise of a grant of land from the governor of New Jersey, Sir William Franklin, it did not bring about the union desired. The Corporation could have become a focal point, a common meeting ground, since it was to provide

---

[65] William Smith to Thomas Penn, [Jan. 4, 1769], William Smith Papers, II, 70 (Historical Society of Pennsylvania); Convention of Clergy at New Brunswick to Secretary, Oct. 12, 1768, B, XXIV, 315, 316.

[66] Thomas Chandler to Secretary, July 5, 1770, B, XXIV, 98; Myles Cooper to William Smith, April 10, 1769, William Smith Papers I, 62 (Church Historical Society). The New England clergy were not part of the original scheme, and later attempts to include them met with very little success. Two Connecticut clergymen, Kneeland and Leaming, finally joined, but, according to Charles Inglis, it would have required "a little volume" to explain the other clergies' objections to be being absorbed into a broader union with the middle colonies. See: William Smith to Thomas Penn, [Jan. 4, 1769], William Smith Papers, II,, 70 (Historical Society of Pennsylvania); Charles Inglis to Samuel Johnson, Oct. 10, 1770, Hawks MSS, Samuel Johnson Papers, 39 (Church Historical Society).

against exigencies which faced all of them, but the clergy could not divorce even this basic concern from their personal concepts of the social-political function they intended the Church to provide in America.[67]

Without episcopal supervision the Church appeared to be heading for dire straits. The drift into dissent, manifest in the breakaway St. Paul's Church in Philadelphia, seemed likely to worsen, particularly as most of the clergy shared with the Dissenters the same indignation about Parliament's attempts to tax the colonies. The understanding between Dissenters and Anglicans in political affairs was beginning to extend to religion, too. The constant bickering among the Anglican clergy so thoroughly sickened Philip Reading that he declared that he would not attend any further conventions, preferring instead to remain in his Delaware parish, secure from their "systems of divinity and politics." Philip Reading was the son of Oxford University's Sion College librarian. He had been educated at Winchester School and University College, Oxford. He went to Pennsylvania in the early 1740's where he became a tutor in Philadelphia. In 1745, he returned to England seeking ordination for the Delaware mission of Apoquiniminck. From 1746 until his death in 1777, his commitment to that sprawling mission gained him acceptance in that community, and high esteem with the Society. His active participation in Delaware with the opponents of the Stamp Act probably set him to thinking about ecumenism in broader terms, and his subsequent study of the seventeenth century writers Hugo Grotius and Samuel Pufendorf suggested to him that the religious hair-splitting between Anglicans and Dissenters had no real basis. Perhaps his experience of preaching in the open air in the remote parts of his mission, where no churches were built, led him closer still to the Methodists he had associated with at the rebel St. Paul's Church in Philadelphia a few years earlier.[68]

---

[67] Secretary Dr. Burton to William Smith, May 20, 1769, William Smith Papers I, 63 (Church Historical Society); S.P.G. Journals, XVIII,86, 140; Myles Cooper to Sir William Johnson, Nov. 27, 1766, Peter Force Papers, Series 8D, Sir William Johnson Papers; Richard Peters to [Secretary], Nov. 8, 1769, B, XXI, 133.

[68] Philip Reading to Secretary, no date, B, XII, 75; Robert Jenny to Secretary, Nov. 14, 174[5], B, XII, 39; George Ross to Secretary, Nov. 23, 1745, B, XII, 43; Thomas Barton to Secretary, New York, Jan. 8, 1779, B, XXI, 36; Philip Reading to Richard

The northern clergy realized that the problem most basic to the future of the Church was the lack of a resident bishop. By 1766, the Anglicans in all of the northern provinces had begun to hold conventions, but differences over ecumenism continued to divide the clergy, as did their views on how best to secure the episcopate for America. Naturally, personality conflicts thrived in a situation where talented men strove for recognition in an institution which, because it failed to provide a hierarchy of professional appointments, could not offer promotion.

The conventions had proved useful in a limited way. They had mediated in disputes between clergy and their congregations, they had provided a systematic avenue of communication between the laity and the Society, and by examining candidates and supervising their preparation for ordination they had kept the Church free from the accusations which some of their southern brethren had brought upon the Church there. The New York-New Jersey conventions, in particular, had been alert to any irregularities appearing in the conduct of the clergy. They had prevented the appointment of clergy of unsound reputation to their parishes, and they had conscientiously enquired into reports of clerical neglect of duty or misconduct. But the conventions could only make recommendations; they could not direct the Church. The frustration the clergy felt at having to advise the Society and prelates, and then wait for months on end for a reply was a heavy burden for them to bear. The future of the Church would therefore rest with the Anglicans' efforts to gain a resident bishop. However, such an achievement would be difficult considering the innate hostility the Dissenters felt for the Church at the end of the Seven Years' War when everyone was alert to reports of plans afoot in London to reorganise the administration of the colonies.[69]

Peters, Sept. 23, 1771, Richard Peters Papers, VII, 79, (Historical Society of Pennsylvania); Philip Reading to Secretary, Sept. 5, 1766, Oct. 3, 1772, B, XXI, 196, 206; Minutes of St. Paul's Church, Philadelphia, Nov. 15, 1762.

[69] When George Spencer went to London, recommended by Benjamin Franklin in 1766, he was ordained and given the Society's mission at Spotswood in New Jersey. The New York-New Jersey convention learned of the appointment, and knowing his true reputation, had the Society revoke his appointment. They inserted an advertisement in the New York Journal to inform the public that they had not been responsible for recommending Spencer to the Bishop of London. The conventions

kept a close watch on candidates preparing for ordination, and occasionally had to reprimand them for departing from accepted Church practice. William Ayers, for example, was ordered to desist from reading prayers and sermons of his own composition in the New Jersey churches without authorization from the clergy. "Seabury Minutes," pp. 148-149, 150-151, 158.

CHAPTER

IV

Bishops for the Americans

Thomas Secker's elevation to the See of Canterbury, in 1758, was the occasion for rejoicing among the Anglicans in the northern colonies, for in him they knew they had a zealous leader for their cause, and like most of themselves, he was an apostate. Nearly twenty years of corresponding with Samuel Johnson had taught Archbishop Secker how difficult it was for the Church to function properly without episcopal supervison. He shared the American High Churchman's view that the influence of the Church of England was vital to the continuation of the colonies' dependence upon Britain, and he soon let it be known that he was about to introduce changes in the administration of the Church.

He had been upset to hear about John Beach's sermon on the "State of the Dead," and he was far from convinced that the rot had not set in deeper, but to compound matters, news was reaching England of William McClennaghan's Methodist preaching among the Anglicans at Christ Church in Philadelphia. Declension within the Church was to be taken seriously, but yet another problem was asserting itself. The recent influx of New England Dissenters into the Church had raised a clamour among their English co-religionists about the Society's concentration in New England, the success of which had been reflected in the very poor response to the Society's recent collection throughout the Kingdom. Worse still, there was even the possibility that the Society might lose its charter if the feeble numbers that constituted some of the New England missions were publicized in England.[1]

While he had no intention of giving up his design to bring the American Dissenters into the Church, he saw the need for the Society to move with greater caution than before. He informed Samuel Johnson that it would be necessary to stop opening new missions in the areas already served by Congregationalist and Presbyterian ministers unless sufficiently large numbers requested help. The Society would have to devote more assistance to the work of Christianizing the American Indians, work which the Dissenters insisted was the original purpose for chartering the Society. Further, so that he could be better prepared to anticipate the Dissenters' opposition, he requested that Johnson send him any information that he could gather about the American Dissenters' plans, any complaints they might make about the Society's activities, together with any publications hostile to the Church and the Anglican responses. He enlisted Johnson's assistance in finding out exactly who the American Dissenters were corresponding with in England so that he could be prepared for them, too. Such was Secker's plan to prepare the ground for the eventual appointment of American bishops, a prospect he declared he would never abandon as long as he should live.[2]

Secker's elevation to Lambeth Palace was soon followed by the accession to the throne of George III and the promotion of Richard Osbaldeston to the diocese of London. The young king's interest in the progress of the colonial Church portended well for the advocates of the American episcopate, and Bishop Osbaldeston was anxious to have the traditional relationship between his diocese and the American colonies ended once and for all. But until the war could be brought to a formal conclusion, and until the ministry was ready to announce its plans for the colonies, it would be necessary to proceed cautiously in New England.[3]

The English Church could make large sums of money available to

---

[1] Archbishop to Samuel Johnson, Sept. 27, 1758, William Smith Papers I, 25 (Church Historical Society).
[2] Archbishop to Samuel Johnson, Sept. 27, 1758, William Smith Papers, I, 25 (Church Historical Society); Archbishop to Samuel Johnson, March 30, 1763, Lambeth Palace Library, vol. 1123, part 3, 300.
[3] Archbishop to Samuel Johnson, March 30, 1763, Lambeth Palace Library, vol. 1123, part 3, 300.

the Americans, and while the policy of secrecy Secker had adopted was very wise, maintaining secrecy would be extremely difficult as the money was provided by the Society. Therefore, it would be essential to exercise caution in bringing proposals before the Society's monthly meetings because they were open to all members, who were invited to attend through advertisements in the London newspapers. Consequently, the American Dissenters were always able to learn from England what the Society had resolved, often before the missionaries. The Dissenters on both sides of the Atlantic knew almost instinctively that the impending peace would intensify the campaign to send bishops to America, and every ear was strained to glean each scrap of information on the subject.

The Boston Dissenters set to work in 1762 to steal a march on the Anglicans when they had the General Court pass a bill which would have incorporated a Society for Propagating Christian Knowledge among the Indians of North America. Henry Caner, himself a convert from the Connecticut Congregationalists, sent a copy of the bill to Secker, pointing out that the ulterior motive was to turn the American Indians away from the Church of England, and so draw attention to the Society's use of its funds for missionary work among the Dissenters rather than among the Indians - - unwelcome publicity which might even terminate the Society's existence. Not one of the proposed Corporation's officers or members, Secker wrote to the Bishop of London (who was taking the waters at Bath) belonged to the Church, though there were many Dissenting ministers, including that "joub mouthed Bespatterer of our church & our Missionaries," Jonathan Mayhew. While the Society could not openly oppose the bill. The Archbishop alerted the Bishop of London, whose office allowed him to meet with the Lords of Trade, to look out for its appearance. In the meantime Secker and his American correspondents would search for possible objections to its receiving royal assent.[4]

The proposed Corporation was particularly threatening because, in spite of Secker's decision to direct Society funds away from New

---

[4] Henry Caner to Archbishop, Aug. 9, 1762, Archbishop to Bishop of London, Oct. 5, 1762, Archbishop to Henry Caner, Oct. 6, 1762, William Smith to Archbishop, Nov. 22, 1760, Henry Caner to Archbishop, Dec. 23, 1762, Lambeth Palace Library, vol. 1123, part 3, 269, 276, 277, 282, 288.

England, the first new mission to be established after he had disclosed his policy to Johnson, in September 1758, was on the doorstep of Harvard College. Charles Brockwell had been trying to get a church built in Cambridge for several years, and finally, when the Society appointed the son of a wealthy King's Chapel parishioner, East Apthorp, as their missionary, a handful of wealthy Anglicans began to build. Thomas Secker had expected this mission to "furnish a Handle for more than ordinary Clamour." Therefore, he met with his fellow bishops to discuss the matter privately before making it public. He made no reference to the danger of arousing the Dissenters' resentment when he brought the matter before the general meeting of the Society which passed it unanimously. Apthorp's "Abilities, Temper and Discretion," the Archbishop hoped, would put the Dissenters at ease, but the new Anglican church, within sight of the College, loomed even more portentous when the "discreet" missionary erected a "handsome House" nearby, one rather more befitting an archbishop than a missionary to the Americans. The Cambridge congregation, which Apthorp admitted was not numerous and was supported by an impressive list of six "very rich" and twelve other wealthy and influential families, presented the Dissenters a perfect example with which to expose the Society's misapplication of its funds.[5]

The creation of a new mission at Cambridge served to substantiate a public warning that had already been proclaimed in America about the Anglicans' plans. The warning had come from Ezra Stiles in a sermon he had read in Rhode Island to a small group of ministers not long after the fall of Quebec. A year later he published this Discourse on the Christian Union, in which he urged the Congregationalist churches, so badly divided after the Great Awakening, to unite with all Protestant churches in their commonly-held beliefs. The natural growth of the Congregationalist church, he stated, during the century to come would overwhelm all other denominations in the westward expansion. Beneath his

---

[5] William McGilchrist to Secretary, July 27, 1761, B, XXII, 177; William Agar to Secretary, no date, B, XXII, 2; East Apthorp to Secretary, Sept. 29, 1762, B, XXII, 5; Archbishop to Henry Caner, July 19, 1759, Archbishop to Samuel Johnson, July 19, 1759, Lambeth Palace Library, vol. 1123, part 2, 144, 145 Henry Wilder Foote, Annals of King's Chapel (Boston, 1896), II, p.177.

moderate tone, however, was a warning to the Dissenters. They must make up their minds that they would win the contest to defend individual against authorised interpretation, the democratic church against hierarchical rule. Anglicans from Delaware to New Hampshire could see that the Church of England's strength in New England was the real reason for Stile's sermon and the heated controversy that was to follow. The message was certainly not lost on Henry Caner who promptly sent it off to the Archbishop of Canterbury with a note that it was intended "to invite all Parties and Sects in the Country to unite against the Church of England." The reason for this outburst, Caner wrote, was the Dissenters' fear that land, ceded to the British Crown at the end of the War, would be used to further the interests of the Church of England in America. "So remarkable a Crisis, it is natural to imagine will fall under such Regulations, as will either greatly establish the Church of England, or the dissenting interest in this part of the World." Archbishop Secker, too, found that Stiles had "entered into a great deal of curious matter, both ecclesiastical & political," though it was far less threatening than another pamphlet which had already reached the Archbishop and was causing him some concern.[6]

This pamphlet, The Real Advantages . . . by Conforming to the Church of England, threw the American clergy into a panic. Thomas Secker thought the author must have been Jonathan Mayhew, but in fact was Noah Welles, a minister at Stamford pretending to be an apostate Anglican priest. He was ridiculing the ostentation and snobbery of the Church, whose clergy were bought with the Society's "silver and gold." Secker was particularly upset over the accusation because only a year earlier the Litchfield missionary, Solomon Palmer, had written a long, detailed letter to the Society charging that it was maintaining clergy whose congregations could easily provide for their priests. Palmer singled out John Beach's mission for special comment which, "being rich and numerous," could well do without the Society's money. He also claimed that the "Rhoad Island Mission" had no need of the Society's assistance. Palmer was almost certainly referring to Trinity Church in Newport.

---

[6] Ezra Stiles, <u>A Discourse on the Christian Union</u> (Boston, 1761); Henry Caner to Archbishop, Jan. 7, 1763, Archbishop to Henry Caner, March 20, 1763, Lambeth Palace Library, vol. 1123, part 3, 290, [301?].

When their missionary, Marmaduke Browne, died in 1771, Samuel Auchmuty claimed that the Newport mission could independently support one, if not two, ministers. The Society's funds, he advised, could be of more use elsewhere. Solomon Palmer also named the Middleton-Wallingford, the Stratford and Derby missions in Connecticut, as well as his own Litchfield mission, as being able to support their own clergy. These missions, and others, he claimed, were communities whose "Ability is greater than their Liberality."[7]

The Dissenters had added insult to injury by making sure that the pamphlet would reach London before the missionaries could get a glimpse of it. When Samuel Johnson obtained a copy he asked John Beach to reply to it. Beach had a special reason for accepting the assignment for in his pamphlet Welles taunted his Anglican with the remark that had he taken Presbyterian ordination he would have had to teach Calvinist "monkish holiness as Br. B-- is said to have done, while he was among the presbyterians." Mr. B --lost no time in enlisting the help of Samuel Johnson's lawyer son in answering this "vile Ill Natured Pamphlet" who immediately set about providing Beach with a list of salaries paid to Dissenting Teachers in the large Connecticut towns. In May 1763, Beach's reply was inserted in the press, but by that time Samuel Johnson was already hunting around for someone to quiet that "rough, ludicrous, audacious & malicious . . . enemy . . . to the Trinity, to Royalty & Episcopacy," Jonathan Mayhew.[8]

The death of the Braintree missionary, Ebenezer Miller, in February that year, provided an opportunity for the Dissenters to focus their hostility and resentment towards the Society. Just ten days after his death there appeared in the Boston Gazette "an anonymous gross insult" to Miller and the Cambridge mission which the naïve East Apthorp thought fit to answer in a pamphlet entitled Considerations on the Institution and Conduct of the Society for the Propagation of the Gospel in Foreign Parts. In this

---

[7] Noah Welles, The real Advantages . . . by Conforming to the Church of England (1762), p. 34; Archbishop to Henry Caner, Oct. 6, 1762, Lambeth Palace Library, vol. 1123, part 3, 277; Solomon Palmer to Secretary, March 2, 1761, B, XXIII, 300; Samuel Auchmuty to Secretary, April 25, 1771, B, II, 39.

[8] William Samuel Johnson to John Beach, Jan. 4, 1763, William Samuel Johnson Correspondence, 1744-1771 (Connecticut Historical Society); Samuel Johnson to Secretary, May 10, 1763, B, XXII, 170.

piece, dedicated to Archbishop Secker, and following the more recent line of argument taken in the Society's anniversary sermons, he dismissed the anonymous author's claim that the Society had been chartered to work among the American Indians. He insisted, instead, that even if Mayhew's claims were true it would have been useless going to the Indians when the English settlers they came in contact with needed moral reformations so badly. Nothing of what Mayhew wrote was new, but the Dissenters were upset by the patronizing style in which this Cambridge University educated, Bostonian insinuated that the Society had helped lift New Englanders from their Calvinistic savagery to Anglican refinement.9

Apthorp's twenty three pages of Considerations soon fell before the one hundred seventy six pages of Mayhew's Observations on the Charter and Conduct of the Society for the Propagatrion of the Gospel in Foreign Parts. Without denying the Society's right to send missionaries to those colonies in need of its assistance, Mayhew accused the Society of long harbouring a desire to destroy and root out all the New England churches as part of "their grand design of episcopizing . . . all New England, as well as the other colonies." As though deliberately timed to add further grist to Mayhew's mill, news arrived from his English correspondent, Thomas Hollis, while the Observations were being printed, that "the Archbishop & pious Society" had successfully opposed the bill to incorporate the Society for Propagating Christian Knowledge among the Indians of North America.10

Before the American clergy could send copies of the Apthorp-Mayhew pamphlets to England, Thomas Hollis, with a rare sense of humour, had the Society's printer, A.Miller, print the Observations, with Apthorp's pamphlet appended, a copy of which Secker found lying open in the New York Coffee House in London. It seemed that the Dissenters had read Secker's mind, because just as he had decided to direct the Society's energies away from New England,

---

[9] William McGilchrist to Secretary, June 27, 1763, B, XXII, 178; East Apthorp, Considerations on the Institution and Conduct of the Society for the Propagation of the Gospel in Foreign Parts (Boston, 1763), p.17.

[10] Jonathan Mayhew, Obervations on the Charter and Conduct of the Society for the Propagation of the Gospel in Foreign Parts (Boston, 1763), p. 107; Jonanthan Mayhew to Thomas Hollis, April 27, 1763, Thomas Hollis Papers; Samuel Johnson to Secretary, May 10, 1763, B, XXII, 170.

the New Englanders had brought the whole question of the Society's function into public debate. This last contribution from Mayhew, Secker confided to Samuel Johnson, would make it much more difficult to secure the appointment of an American bishop.[11]

East Apthorp had not expected to be so badly mauled, and utterly refused to engage in any further controversy with Mayhew, partly because he agreed with his adversary's claim that the Society was misapplying its funds at Cambridge. He had informed the Society's Secretary six months before Mayhew's pamphlet appeared that the congregation at Cambridge was very small. Nothing Johnson could do would bring him back into the fray. Besides, he wrote to Johnson, his parish did not want him to engage in any further controversy, and as the Dissenters had objected to the Society supporting the Cambridge mission "their opinion has weight enough with me, to make me uneasy."[12]

East Apthorp, in spite of his Considerations, did not harbour any personal grudge against the Boston Dissenters. A year after his publication he wrote to the Society on behalf of Harvard College, whose library had been totally destroyed by fire. He requested the Society's "assistance, as they have done formally, by a present of Books." At its general meeting in July 1764, the Society read Apthorp's letter, postponed its decision to the following meeting, and, presumably let the matter rest. Perhaps the experience of public debate convinced Apthorp it was time to bow out. In January 1764, he wrote to the Society that for "Domestic" reasons and for the settlement of his "private fortune" he planned to go to England in the near future. At midday on September 10, 1764, he set sail for England with Captain Jarvis. A month later, Jonathan Mayhew was pleased to write to Thomas Hollis that with Apthorp's sudden departure for England, the Cambridge church was closed and the Anglicans, in general, were attending the Congregationalist church there. Thomas Hollis replied to Mayhew that "the Fathers of New England should crown with oak Leaves the Man, who, by his sole

---

[11] Thomas Hollis to Jonathan Mayhew, Dec. 6, 1763, Thomas Hollis Papers; Archbishop to Henry Caner, Sept. 15, 1763, Lambeth Palace Library, vol. 1123, part 3, 319.
[12] East Apthorp to [Samuel Johnson], July 22, 1763, Hawks Papers, Johnson MSS, number 4 (Church Historical Society).

judgement & energy hath forced" that departure. The American defence now fell to Henry Caner at King's Chapel whose efforts only stirred Mayhew into further debate. Finally, the Society decided to defend itself, paid for one hundred copies of Secker's personal reply to the Bostonian and sent them off to America hoping to have heard the last of the matter.[13]

Secker's pamphlet was the last serious defence against Mayhew, and he soon called upon Dr. Samuel Chandler, a respected English Dissenter, to persuade Mayhew to let the matter rest. While the Archbishop and William Smith, then in London on business for the College of Philadelphia, were trying to convince Samuel Chandler that the limitations that would be imposed on an American bishop would protect American Dissenters' rights, Samuel Chandler was writing to the generous-minded Rector of Christ Church in Philadelphia, Richard Peters, for his opinion of the worth of Secker's promises. Chandler was convinced of Secker's sincerity, though Mayhew never was. However, the controversy had done two things. The Society's activities had been brought before the public, and in the debate it had come off second best. Most important, the Dissenters had shown how far they would go to keep bishops out of America. The Society now determined to steer clear of New England's troubled waters. When the New England town of Rutland sent Samuel Frinck for ordination, in 1763, he returned as missionary to Georgia. Three years later, the Society clarified its mission more precisely: it would "provide Missions where no establishment is provided, or where the Provision for Ministers is mean." The Apthorp-Mayhew controversy slowed down the Society's encroachment in New England until the War between Britain and the American colonies brought the Church of England's growth to a complete halt. The lesson was not lost on the Dissenters. Thomas Hollis had informed Mayhew of the Society's decision to divert its efforts away from New England and they knew what to do

---

[13] East Apthorp to Secretary, March 12, 1764, B, XXII, 9; S.P.G. Journals, XVI,148; East Apthorp to Secretary, Jan. 9, 1764, B, XXII, 8; Anne Rowe Cunningham, ed., Letters and Diary of John Rowe Boston Merchant 1759-1762 (Boston, 1903), p. 61; Jonathan Mayhew to Thomas Hollis, Oct. 17, 1764, Thomas Hollis to Jonathan Mayhew, March 4, 1765, Thomas Hollis Papers; Thomas Bradbury Chandler, The Life of Samuel Johnson, D.D., the First President of King's College, New-York (New York, 1805), p. 195.

if future efforts were made to introduce bishops into America. Furthermore, the dispute had produced divisions within the Anglican congregations in some of the New England towns and at Woodbridge in New Jersey where some of the laity possibly took seriously Mayhew's warnings of the civil powers that would shroud the American episcopate.[14]

Many clergy felt the same way as Edward Winslow, who was quite sincere, when he wrote, in July 1763, that "there has been not the least particular Cause to provoke" such a "malignant Spirit of Opposition" among the Dissenters. The Anglicans' assumption that as members of the National Church they were the only truly loyal subjects of the Crown led them to view the Dissenters as second class subjects who had no right to object to any privileges the Church might enjoy. Winslow continued, in his letter of July 1763, that the "indecent reflections upon the Venerable Society & the general Constitution of the Church" were occasioned by the growth of the Church and the "Accession of Territory on this Continent. The Dissenters are from hence jealous, the Church may meet with some further Encouragement, & perhaps enjoy those essential Parts of Her Worship & Discipline which we have hitherto been destitute of." When the Society extended its assistance to Hebron in Connecticut, Samuel Peters wrote that the Dissenters were "very Spightfull at my comeing home" after he had forsaken them for the Church of England. Yet he could not concede that they had the right to be upset at his arrival during the heated debate over the Society's presence in New England.[15]

The Anglicans' refusal to allow the Dissenters equality with themselves, however, did not prevent them from understanding the significance of the hostility since the fall of Quebec. Henry Caner, referring to Stiles' Christian Union observed that they were convinced that the lands recently taken from the French would be

---

[14] Abraham Jarvis to Samuel Johnson, July 30, 1764, Hawks Papers, Johnson MSS, No. 50 (Church Historical Society); Richard Peters to Archbishop, Oct. 17, 1763, William Stevens Perry, <u>The History of the American Episcopal Church 1587-1883</u>, II, p. 391; Thomas Hollis to Jonathan Mayhew, March 4, 1765, Thomas Hollis Papers; Ebenezer Dibblee to Secretary, Sept. 29, 1763, March 26, 1764, B, XXIII, 99, 100; James Parker, Woodbridge, New Jersey to Secretary, Sept. 22, 1764, B, XXIV, 313.
[15] Samuel Peters to Secretary, April 13, 1762, B, XXIII, 319; Edward Winslow to Secretary, July I, 1763, XXIII, 403.

organised with an Anglican establishment which they were determined to prevent at all costs. The Dissenters were quite right in their assessment of the situation, and the Anglican clergy in the northern colonies grew impatient with the successive British ministries which seemed to listen more to the English Dissenters than to the Churchmen. Even when tempers were frayed during the controversy with Mayhew, Samuel Johnson wanted to send representatives to urge the ministry to create royal governments in Connecticut and Rhode Island, and proceed with an ecclesiastical settlement for the northern colonies.[16]

On October 5, 1765, a recent recruit to the Philadelphia Shippen legal firm, Jasper Yeates, wrote excitedly to his brother of the arrival in Philadelphia of the stamped paper that was to be the means of raising a revenue in the American colonies. The news "put the city in a Ferment" and the bells of Christ Church and the other churches "rang muffled." He continued that John Hughes, who had been appointed Distributor of Stamps by George Grenville, the architect of the Stamp Tax, had been forced to give up his office and "the Scene is now changed:- The Bells ring a Note widely different from their former one."[17]

For the Anglican clergy, the Stamp Act was a true crisis: it was the first test they faced that added political to their already existing ecclesiastical differences with the Dissenters. From Waterbury, Connecticut, James Scovil wrote that the clergy have for long been reproached "with the hated Name of Jacobites, Persons disaffected to the present Royal Family of blessed Memory, but when the Stamp Act brought our Loyalty to the Test, I thank God the Scale turned, greatly, in our Favour." The missionary at Stamford, Ebenezer Dibblee, regretted the "general discontent and disturbance in this and ye other Provinces." In spite of the troubles, he claimed that his parish was increasing. He found it "Incredible that an Internal Tax upon the Subjects of these Provinces should be the foundation of all those Publick Disturbances." Nevertheless, the Stamp Act and the subsequent political opposition to Parliament, aggravated by

---

[16] Henry Caner to Archbishop, Jan. 7, 1763, Samuel Johnson to Archbishop, Dec. 20, 1763, Lambeth Palace Library, vol. 1123, part 3, 290, 336.
[17] Jasper Yeates to John Yeates, Oct. 16, 1764, Oct. 5, 1765, Simon Gratz Collection, Case 2, Box 13 (Historical Society of Pennsylvania).

Chandler's ill-timed pamphlets in support of an American episcopate, convinced Dibblee that the mid-1760's was "a Critical day in the Provinces of America." In 1768, the Simsbury missionary in Connecticut, Roger Viets, wrote to the Society that the "late Regulations of the Government on your Side of the Water" have induced the Dissenters to "look on us Missionaries and our Parishioners, as too much connected with Europe." In October 1765, John Beach warned his Newtown parishioners in Connecticut not to have "any Concern in ye Seditious Tumults." He claimed that he could "not discover ye least inclination towards such Rebellious Conduct in any of the Church people here." Six months later, he wrote to the Society that his congregation was peaceable and growing. His success with his congregation had brought upon him the wrath of "a lawless Sort of men who stile themselves ye Sons of Liberty." He observed that where the Society's missions existed in Connecticut "and Church People abound, there the inhabitants are vastly more peaceable and ready to yield obedience to the Government of England." However, where there was no mission and "few or no Church People, there they are Continually Cabaling, and declare they will spill Ye last drop of Blood rather than Submit to ye late act of Parliament." There can be little wonder that Beach should beg the Society not to quote his letter in the Abstracts of Proceedings which were appended to the Society's annual Anniversary Sermons "lest it Should expose me to ye Rage and Violence of ye Mobb."[18]

The Stamp Act and subsequent legislation to raise taxes in America resulted in similar consequences and responses from Anglican clergy throughout the provinces north of the Delaware. At Rye, New York, Ephraim Avery reported that his people "esteem the Act rather oppressive; but to resist to higher Powers in a rebellious Manner" was unthinkable. Andrew Morton wrote from Amwell in New Jersey, "the Stamp Duty is look'd upon among us as an intolerable Burthen, and meets with great Opposition." He feared

---

[18] Richard James Hooker, "The Anglican Church and the American Revolution," p. 36, Unpublished Ph.D. Thesis, University of Chicago, 1943; James Scovil to Secretary, July 6, 1767, B, XXIII, 343; Ebenezer Dibblee to Secretary, Oct. 28, 1765, March 25, 1766, April 6, 1768, B, XXIII, 103, 104, 108; Roger Viets to Secretary, June 25, 1768, B, XXIII, 380; John Beach to Secretary, Oct. 2, 1765, April 22, 1766, B, XXIII, 36, 37.

for the future. In Delaware, Philip Reading was embarrassed by the "situation into which the Colonies have been brought . . . by the regulations that were attempted to be imposed upon them. In these difficulties as a member of this Community" he wrote "I am necessarily involved." Although he had declared his "utter abhorrence of every opposition to the high powers" he had given his support to colonial resistance.[19]

William Agar, the missionary at Cambridge, Massachusetts, from whence East Apthorp had retreated to England, found the congregation of a "very capricious temper, and this Stamp Act, has made it Dangerous to preach Loyalty and Subjection." Nearby Braintree missionary Edward Winslow regretted the "many Disorders which have of late happen'd in this province, and the neighbouring colonies, on the Occasion of the Stamp Duties." He urged his congregation to patience and toleration until "our Superiors . . . alleviate or remove any Burthen which may appear to be beyond our Strength to bear." While being opposed to the unfair Stamp Duty, Mather Byles could still find humour in the heated hostilities in Boston. He wrote to his sister Mary that his wife had begun weaning his son "Walter who resents it much, as an Infringement upon Liberty, Property, and the Rights of Magna Carta.[20]

For many Anglican clergy, the Society's decision not to open any more missions in New England in order to appease the Dissenters' clamour in the press was painful enough. However, the Anglican laity's reputed rejection of the colonial extra-legal opposition to the Stamp Act and the clergies' preaching of toleration should have brought them some recognition from England. Instead, their loyalty during the Stamp act crisis gave James Scovil "real grief and concern, to find the Venerable Society declining to open any more Missions in New England." Ebenezer Dibblee at Stamford could not understand why, in spite of the Church's loyalty, the authorities in England could not be made "sensible of the importance and

---

[19] Ephraim Avery to Secretary, March 25, 1766, B, III, 231; Andrew Morton to Secretary, Sept. 26, 1765, B, XXIV, 231; Philip Reading to Secretary, Sept. 5, 1766, B, XXI, 196.

[20] William Agar to Secretary, May 1, 1766, B, XXII,1; Edward Winslow to Secretary, Jan. 8, 1766, B, XXII. 277; Mather Byles to his sister Mary Byles, May 7, 1766, Byles Family Papers, 1753-1865 (Massachusetts Historical Society).

necessity of setting up an Episcopate in America." Further, "to find the Venerable Board so reluctant to establish any more new Missions in and about New England, in consequence of the late Clamours" was quite incomprehensible. Nevertheless, all Americans were united in news of the official repeal of the objectionable Stamp Act. Dibblee wrote "our Churches have Rid out the Late Storm and tempest, and something of Calm Ensues the happy Repeal of the Stamp Act." From Boston, Mather Byles could write to his sisters in 1766, "it greatly rejoyces my heart after so long a silence on your part, to have such certain information that the Stamp Act is repealed."[21]

Samuel Andrews was concerned that the "dutiful Behaviour" of his congregation "in the late Times of General Confusion and Disorder" might leave them at a disadvantage, following the repeal of the Stamp Act. The Dissenters, he wrote, see that they "having Nothing to fear from your side the Water" and Churchmen "must have a melancholy Prospect before them unless powerfully supported from Home" with the establishment of an American Episcopate. Even before fears such as those Andrews expressed had reached England, the Society's Secretary, Daniel Burton, had written to Thomas Chandler that he feared Parliament's repeal of the "offensive Act" might be construed "into timidity . . . weakness and irresolution of our councils." The American clergy "who have shown themselves such steady friends to our government" he wrote "must be very uncomfortable," though he saw no hope of bishops being sent to America for the time being. In 1770, during the period of non-importation of British goods, Joshua Weeks wrote the Society a lesson on the violence in Massachusetts. "You may depend on it as a certain fact, that all our Confusions have arisen from the sudden repeal of the stamp-act. Half the country were then sumitting [sic] to it. The utmost the wisest & best men among us expected was a repeal of the obnoxious parts only." But the repeal of the whole act served to feed the opposition in their determination to Parliament's further acts. "If Parliament will not maintain it's own right & authority," he warned, "why should we expose ourselves to every

---

[21] James Scovil to Secretary, July 16, 1767, B, XXIII, 343, Ebenezer Dibblee to Secretary, Oct. 8, 1767, Oct. 7, 1766, B, XXIII, 107,105; Mather Byles to Polly and Katy Byles, June 2, 1766, Byles Family Papers, I.

kind of infamy & violence for them."[22]

Even before the summer riots, the Connecticut clergy had held their annual convention at Hebron, in June 1765. Samuel Johnson was unable to attend because of the distance and the poor state of the roads. Nevertheless, thirteen clergy, with Jeremiah Leaming as Clerk of Convention, wrote addresses to the Bishop of London and the Archbishop of Canterbury, together with a copy for the King, should the Bishop of London see fit to present it. They requested the appointment of one or more bishops for the colonies to perform the necessary functions. Perhaps with prescience, they added that such an appointment might "very much conduce to the Promotion of Loyalty . . . [and] the advantage of the Church of England in particular."[23]

A month later, Samuel Johnson wrote to the Bishop of London to endorse the proceedings of the convention, and to emphasize the danger and cost of going to England for ordination. He also took the opportunity to thank Richard Terrick for his "excellent sermon before the Society" as Bishop of Peterborough in February of the previous year. In his sermon, Richard Terrick demoted the Indians to "a remote intention of the Charter of the Society." Indeed, with the recent acquisition of vast territories from France, he claimed, the spread of Christianity was far too great a task for the Society. The spread of Christian culture was a "National concern," the execution of which "would be an Event, which would shine in the Annals of History." Such an event could only be accomplished by providing "a more regular exercise of Discipline for the Administration of those offices of our Church" which would come with the appointment of "a Superior Order in the Ministry."[24]

Two months later, in September 1765, James Scovil, Thomas Davies, Samuel Andrews, Bela Hubbard and Abraham Jarvis

---

[22] Samuel Andrews to Secretary, June 25, 1766, B, XXIII, 12; Joshua Weeks to Secretary, April 12, 1770, XXII, 253; Dr. Burton to Thomas Chandler, May 26, 1766, quoted in letter from Thomas Chandler to Samuel Johnson, Sept. 5, 1766, Schneider's Johnson, I, pp. 366-369.

[23] Convention of Connecticut clergy to Bishop of London, June 5, 1765, Fulham Papers, I, 298, 300.

[24] Samuel Johnson to Bishop of London, July 15, 1765, Schneider's Johnson, I, p. 352; Richard Terrick, S.P.G. Anniversary Sermon, Feb. 17, 1764.(Library of Congress).

"accidentally convened" in Connecticut to assure the Society that the Church of England in general, and their own parishes in particular, disapprove of the tumults in Connecticut. They continued that they "warn [their] Hearers . . . of the unreasonableness, and wickedness of their taking the least part in the Tumults or opposition to his Majesty's Acts." These were sentiments that Bela Hubbard reiterated in his letter to the Society in 1767. Perhaps the accidental convention was designed to assist Bela Hubbard and Abraham Jarvis, victims of the Society's decision not to open new missions in New England. Davies was missionary at New Milford from 1762 until he died in 1766. James Scovil was stationed at the Watertown and Westbury mission from 1758 until he departed for the province of New Brunswick in 1786. Abraham Jarvis and Bela Hubbard went together to England, in 1763, for ordination, Jarvis for Middletown, Hubbard for Guilford. Their vestries hoped their parishes would become the Society's missions. The two men were ordained, but without the Society's financial support. Bela Hubbard and other clergy frequently requested that the Society appoint Guilford as a mission. He even suggested to the Society that if an American bishop were appointed, he might "be provided for" in his parish. However, apart from a £10 sterling gratuity, Hubbard was forced to rely upon his congregation for support. Samuel Johnson, whose niece Hubbard had married, pleaded his case, and he took the vacant New Haven mission in 1767. Abraham Jarvis remained at Middletown, in spite of his pleas and those of the Connecticut clergy in convention for the Society's support. His parish was better able to support its minister than that at Guilford. In March 1762, the vestry had offered him £66 currency, to be supplemented by the Society's £20 sterling. However, if the Society should give more than that amount, it would be deducted from the amount they had pledged. They paid his ordination expenses, and moreover, they were able to maintain him through the Revolutionary War years.[25]

---

[25] James Scovil, Thomas Davies, Samuel Andrews, Bela Hubbard, Abraham Jarvis to Secretary, Sept. 15, 1765, B, XXIII, 417; Samuel Andrews to Secretary, Aug. 20, 1763, Abraham Jarvis to Secretary, Jan. 1, 1765, Nov. 21, 1767, Bela Hubbard to Secretary, Jan. 30, 1767, Sept. 15, 1767, Secretary of Connecticut Convention Jeremiah Leaming to Secretary, Sept. 26, 1773, B, XXIII, 6, 181, 182a, 183, 167, 168; S.P.G. Journals, XV, 392; Samuel Johnson to Archbishop, Oct. 20, 1763, Lambeth

Soon after that accidental convention, Jeremiah Leaming, who had played a prominent role at the clergy convention the previous June, wrote to the Society that there had been a "most Rebellous [sic] Outrage, committed on Account of the Stamp Act: while those Towns where the Church has got Footing, have calmly Submitted to the Civil Authority." Jonathan Mayhew's preaching of sedition was behind the disturbances, according to Leaming. Mayhew, he wrote, "has abused the Church with Impunity, and perhaps he thinks he may escape in abusing the State also. I fear he will do much mischief if he is not curbed in Season." No doubt those disturbances prompted Leaming to bring to conclusion and publish, in 1766, his "Defence of the Episcopal Government of the Church" which the convention of clergy had requested he undertake in June.[26]

When the New York-New Jersey clergy met the following October 1765, the riots gave them an excuse to substitute the Connecticut clergies' requests with what almost amounted to a demand for more forceful action on behalf of the American Church. A month before the convention met, Samuel Johnson had learnt that the English Dissenters and the opposition in the colonies to the Stamp Act had persuaded the bishops to put aside their plans to urge the ministry to send bishops to America. On October 2, thirteen clergy from New York and New Jersey convened at Perth-Amboy. Following Samuel Johnson's diplomatic approach of the previous July, they singled out Richard Terrick, and to him they wrote "you have been pleased publickly to declare your Sentiments on the Subject and your Wishes in our Favour in your most excellent anniversary Sermon." To him the clergy sent their addresses for presentation to the King, the Society, the two archbishops, and the two universities. Hinting at Terrick's sermon and the colonial riots, they explained that they had never expected "a more favourable time" for setting Church affairs right. They reviewed the attempts to obtain an American bishop from the beginning of the century. They claimed that as the National Church they were entitled to bishops

---

Palace Library, vol. 1123, part 3, [326?]; Samuel Johnson to Secretary, Nov. 12, 1766, B, XXIII, 194.

[26] Jeremiah Leaming to Secretary, Sept. 30, 1765, March 25, 1766, B, XXIII, 246, 247; Jeremiah Leaming, "A Defence of Episcopal Government of the Church: containing remarks on two late, noted sermons on Presbyterian Ordination" (New York, 1766).

with both civil and ecclesiastical powers. However, in order to obviate the Dissenters' opposition, they were prepared to accept the appointment of bishops with purely ecclesiastical authority. They then proceeded to caution that while it had been important to give attention to the American Church at the beginning of the century it was now absolutely essential if the colonies were to remain in the Empire. They drew a parallel between the political and religious strife of the seventeenth century and the current American disturbances. They suggested that if England allowed the Dissenters to dictate colonial affairs, then "the Time is not far distant, when they will be able, not only to prevent our having Bishops in America, but once more to exterminate Episcopacy throughout the Kingdom and subvert the Church, in which Case the State must again Shift for itself as well as it can." They were suggesting that the American Church might have to follow a more independent path if it were to survive.[27]

At this time the militant clergy in New York and New Jersey were really seeking a bishop with authority to influence political decisions and to enlist the royal governors' patronage for the Church. But they understood that if they were ever to have a bishop at all he would have to be introduced into America with very modest powers. The New York-New Jersey convention's letters to England had emphasized the purely ecclesiastical nature of the bishops they were requesting. They would have no jurisdiction over non-Anglicans, and they would have no political influence in America, whatsoever. Nevertheless, Samuel Auchmuty explained to Samuel Johnson a few months after the convention that he found the moderate Dissenters had no objections to bishops with the limited authority the Anglican clergy were publicly claiming, though such "Pretty Dogs" had no right to interfere in Church matters anyhow. "Their impudence" he wrote "is beyond all bounds." If the clergy had been honest they would have admitted in their addresses to England that many of the American Church laity were also opposed to bishops coming to their country. The Dissenters had got hold of a

---

[27] Samuel Johnson to Bishop of London, Sept. 5, 1765, Schneider's Johnson, I, p. 354; Richard Terrick, Anniversary Sermon, Feb. 17, 1764; New York and New Jersey clergy to Secretary, Oct. 3, 1765, B, XXIV, 314; New York and New Jersey clergy to Bishop of London, Oct. 2, 1765, Fulham Papers, VI, 156.

"spurious Copy of one of our Addresses," Auchmuty wrote, and were very unhappy that the clergy were pushing for the appointment of an American bishop. He continued "They have stir'd up my Congregation, but . . . upon talking with the better sort of them, they begin to be convinced of the Necessity & Utility of having a Bishop."[28]

Six months later, on April 8, 1766, a bizarre tragedy presented an opportunity for the clergy to dramatize their requests for American bishops. With night coming on, and a storm raging, a ship struck Hereford Bar, about twelve miles north of Cape May, in its approach to Delaware Bay. In the confusion, the long boat was lowered without oars, leaving the captain, twenty-three passengers and crewmen aboard to perish. Among those lost were Samuel Giles and Hugh Wilson, two recently ordained Anglican priests, and William Smith's young brother, James, no more than sixteen years old.[29]

All that was saved of Hugh Wilson's and Samuel Giles' belongings were "a gown and Cassock, a very few Books that floated on shore but all ruined [by] the Water, and Mr. Giles Letter of orders." The loss of two clergymen while braving the "Terrors of a Voyage 3000 Miles, together with the Fear of Small-Pox and many other Dangers and Expenses," as Connecticut missionary Roger Viets styled it, was an opportunity too good to miss. As soon as the news reached New York, Samuel Seabury, Samuel Auchmuty and Charles Inglis wrote individually to the Society stressing the disadvantages the lack of resident bishops forced the American Church to endure. On April 17 Seabury informed the Society that "not more that 4 out of 5 who have gone from the northern colonies, have returned." The following evening, Samuel Auchmuty learned of the tragedy and wrote "in great haste" that he had just broken the dreadful news to Samuel Giles' wife, who, with a four-year-old child, was left widowed and in debt. He urged the Society to gain the King's support, and he confided to Samuel Johnson "This recent loss of two worthy clergymen would afford them a sufficient excuse

---

[28] Samuel Auchmuty to Samuel Johnson, April 30, 1766, Hawks Papers, Samuel Johnson MSS, 8.
[29] Hugh Neill to Secretary, May 19, 1766, B, XXI, 125; William Smith to Secretary, March 3, 1766, B, XXI, 254; Thomas Firth Jones, A Pair of Lawn Sleeves: A Biography of William Smith (1727-1803) (Philadelphia, 1972), p.67.

for such an Application." Charles Inglis wrote to the Society, on the same day as Samuel Auchmuty, in a more threatening tone. "I pray God the Government may not have cause to repent, when it is too late, their omission of what would be so great a means of securing the affections and dependence of the Colonies and firmly uniting them to the mother country."[30]

The grief American families and friends felt at the loss was compounded by the financial burden they had to bear. Samuel Auchmuty and his assistant at Trinity Church John Ogilvie had lent Samuel Giles the money to go to England, and Trinity Church raised a sum of money to help his widow. The Oxford missionary Hugh Neill had paid for his nephew Hugh Wilson's education, he had also paid the £100 to send him to England. The Dissenters, Neill wrote, "can send out an Innumerable Tribe of [Teachers] of all sorts, without any Expences," yet the Church must suffer for want of ordination in America. With its customary generosity, the Society allowed Giles' widow a gratuity of £20 sterling, and it reimbursed two other people who had also supported him. Hugh Neill also received a £10 sterling gratuity to help offset his losses.[31]

Following the letters from New York, further reminders of the loss of the two clergy and the need for the appointment of bishops reached the Society from Long Island, Pennsylvania and Connecticut. Leonard Cutting, who was the missionary at New Brunswick, New Jersey, had a particular interest in both Giles and Wilson. He had tutored Samuel Giles in Latin and Greek at King's College in New York. He accepted a call to St. George's Church at Hempstead on Long Island, in July 1765. He had found difficulty in collecting subscriptions, and living in the military barracks in New Brunswick with his family made him "liable to be incommoded by every Party of Soldiers" passing through, and he would be forced to "immediately quit should any be quartered there." The church

---

[30] Hugh Neill to Secretary, May 19, 1766, B, XXI, 125; Roger Viets to Secretary, Nov. 25, 1766, B, XXIII, [373]; Samuel Seabury to Secretary, April 17, 1766, Samuel Auchmuty to Secretary, April 19, 1766, Charles Inglis to Secretary, April 19, 1766, B, II, 169, 16, 57; Samuel Auchmuty to Samuel Johnson, April 30, 1766, Hawks Papers, Samuel Johnson MSS, 8.

[31] Samuel Auchmuty to Secretary, April 19, 1766, May 5, 1766, B, II, 16, 17; Hugh Neill to Secretary, May 19, 1766, June 9, 1767, B, XXI, 125, 127; S.P.G. Journals, XVII, 86.

wardens and vestry of that church, therefore requested the Society to appoint Hugh Wilson to their mission on his return from England. When Cutting heard of the tragedy - - the Society's letter appointing him to Hempstead was lost with Wilson- - he added his lament at the "Danger & Expence that Attend the Voyage Home" to those reaching the Society.[32]

Hugh Wilson had left America with recommendations from Charles Inglis, who was then missionary at Dover, Delaware, and the Lancaster missionary Thomas Barton with whom he had been studying Divinity. When Barton heard of Wilson's death, he wrote to the Society that in Pennsylvania, three missions and twelve churches were vacant. He also listed several churches in New Jersey, New York and Delaware that were without clergy. Without bishops, the Church of England, he lamented "sits like a distressed mourning Child that has lost a tender Parent." From New Jersey, Isaac Browne, a missionary of thirty three years service, himself a lone survivor of the voyage to England in 1733, wrote of the persecution the Church suffered for want of an American episcopate. In Connecticut, Samuel Andrews and James Scovil took the opportunity of linking the sea disaster with the lawful behaviour of their congregations during the recent disturbances over the Stamp Act. Samuel Johnson joined with them in stressing the absolute necessity of strengthening the Church whose principles fostered loyalty and obedience to Parliament.[33]

On May 21, 1766, six weeks after the loss of Giles and Wilson, all of the nine New York clergy convened at Samuel Auchmuty's house, in New York City, with Samuel Cooke, Thomas chandler and Robert McKean of New Jersey, Samuel Johnson and Abraham Jarvis

---

[32] Leonard Cutting to Secretary, Aug. 19, 1766, B, II, 140, July 11, 1765, B, XXIV, 292, July 26, 1766, B, XXIV, 296; Church Wardens and Vestry, Christ Church, New Brunswick to Secretary, July 26, 1765, B, XXIV, 293; Samuel Johnson to Secretary, April 15, 1765, B, XXIII, 189.

[33] Thomas Barton to Secretary, Aug. 8, 1765, Nov. 10, 1765, B, XXI, 15, 17; Hugh Neill to Secretary, Oct. 18, 1764, B, XXI, 121; Charles Inglis to Secretary, July 2, 1765, B, XXI, 147; Isaac Browne to William Smith, July 28, 1766, Hawks Papers, William Smith MSS, I, 8; Samuel Andrews to Secretary, June 25, 1766, James Scovil to Secretary, July 8, 1766, Samuel Johnson to Secretary, July 5, 1766, B, XXIII, 12, 342, 193; Samuel Johnson to Archbishop, May 2, 1766, Schneider's Johnson, I, pp. 360-361.

from Connecticut. Their purpose was to add the convention's formal support to the clergy's letters to England about the sea disaster. Before they proceeded to that business, they sought to take advantage of their privileged status as priests of the National Church. Their address to Sir Henry Moore began with congratulations on his appointment as Governor of New York. They then explained that the duty of the Church "to inculcate the great Principles of Loyalty & Submission to Government" was hindered "as it still continues in an imperfect State" for want of resident bishops. However, even though the Rector of Trinity Church, himself, waited upon their patron, he declined to receive their address, probably not because of his busy schedule, as he claimed, but rather because he was reluctant to become involved in matters that were the concern of the prelates in England. Thereupon, the convention unanimously resolved "to give themselves no further trouble about presenting it."[34]

The convention proceeded to examine the address that John Ogilvie and Samuel Seabury had prepared. It contained the arguments that the clergy conventions pursued until 1775, arguments that persistently found their way into the individual clergy's correspondence to London. They were a restatement of arguments contained in Samuel Seabury's letter to the Society of April 17. Lamenting the loss of the two recently-ordained missionaries, the letter referred the Society to an "exact Calculation made not many years ago, that not less than one out of Five who have gone home for holy orders from the Northern Colonies, have perished in the attempt, Ten having miscarried out of Fifty one."[35]

Samuel Johnson had introduced that calculation when he was defending his lay readers, in 1750, against Rhode Island missionary James McSparran's claims that they were altering the Church liturgy. At that time, he wrote to the Society that of twenty-five candidates sent to England for ordination, five had died. Two years later, in a letter referring to the death of Jonathan Colton, who had returned to America in Anglican orders, only to die of smallpox a week later, he wrote that "of 29 who have gone for Orders, 6 have

---

[34] Seabury "Minutes," pp. 138-140.
[35] New York Clergy Convention to Secretary, May 22, 1766, B, III, 330; Seabury "Minutes," pp. 136.

lost their lives, which is more than one to five." Fourteen years later, when he learned of the loss of Giles and Wilson, Samuel Johnson wrote to Archbishop Secker "these two make up ten valuable lives that have now been lost for want of ordaining powers here, out of the 51 (nigh one in five) that have gone for orders from hence within the compass of my knowledge in little more than 40 years; which is a much greater loss to the Church here in proportion than she suffered in the times of popish persecution in England!" However, while the New York convention claimed this situation to be "an incalculable argument for the necessity of American Bishops" it was not a true statistical representation of American losses while seeking ordination in England. Apart from the deaths of Giles and Wilson, Samuel Johnson's son, William, died of smallpox in London in 1756. The son of the Bristol, Rhode Island, missionary, John Usher, according to the Society's 1758 Abstracts of Proceedings, died of smallpox, in France, though no date for his death was given. Dying of smallpox in London, or dying in a French prison was tragic, but they were risks anyone crossing the Atlantic for any reason had to take. In 1759, Samuel Peters survived smallpox in London and returned to his home in Hebron, Connecticut. William Clark also recovered from smallpox in England ten years later, to become missionary in Massachusetts. Joseph Lamson accompanied Richard Miner to England in 1744. Both were taken prisoner and held in Spain before being imprisoned in France. Lamson finally returned to Connecticut; Miner died in Salisbury, England.[36]

The death of Giles and Wilson, within reach of the New Jersey shore, was indeed a drama of such huge dimensions that it tore into the consciousness of Anglican and Dissenter, alike. Nevertheless, the sea claimed the lives of only two missionaries to the Americans after 1750. From 1766, when Samuel Johnson's statistics became part of the Anglican clergy's litany of arguments in favour of an American episcopate, they remained among the most emotively charged pleas for their cause. They could now claim the role of a beleaguered

---

[36] Samuel Johnson to Secretary, [1750], B, XVIII, 60; Samuel Johnson to J. Berriman, Oct. 30, 1752, Schneider's Johnson, I p. 159; Samuel Johnson to Archbishop Secker, May 2, 1766, Schneider's Johnson, I, pp. 360-361; Abstracts of Proceedings for 1758, appended to Sermon before the Society in Feb. 1759; Willliam Clark to Secretary, April 15, 1774, B, XXII, 147; Timothy Cutler to Secretary, June 7, 1744, B, XIII, 87; Petition of Joseph Lamson to Archbishop, [no date], B, XV, 56.

minority, deprived of their basic rights.

In 1771, when Thomas Chandler was preparing his "Address from the Clergy of New York and New Jersey to the Episcopalians in Virginia . . . " he wrote to Samuel Johnson that he could remember the names of only eight of the ten candidates for ordination who lost their lives: Browne, Miner, Dean, Colton, Johnson, Usher, Giles and Wilson. He could have included John Checkley, intended for Newark, New Jersey, who died of smallpox in London in 1744. Moreover, the Newark missionary, Isaac Browne, claimed in 1748 and 1766 that he was "only one of three brothers who survived that undertaking" of the sea voyage to England in the early 1730's. If Isaac Browne meant "siblings," Chandler could have added a second "Browne" to make up the total of ten lives lost. Isaac Browne was the third son of David Browne of West Haven, Connecticut.[37]

All of the clergy attending the New York convention signed the addresses it collectively approved. However, not all were completely at ease with the militant language that marked the addresses to England from this convention and that held at Perth-Amboy of the previous year. The clergy in Philadelphia, and others elsewhere, were searching for an accommodation with the Dissenters. Samuel Auchmuty was uneasy about control passing from Trinity Church to the clergy in convention. Especially threatening was Thomas Chandler, whose energy and intellect earned him Samuel Johnson's confidence.

The day before the clergy convened in New York, ten clergy met at Wallingford, Connecticut, where they recommended Abraham Beach to the Society for ordination. Presumably, the deaths of Giles and Wilson were discussed, but they made no reference to the matter in their letter. Samuel Johnson and Abraham Jarvis were attending the New York convention, perhaps Johnson's absence accounted for their silence. Nevertheless, Samuel Andrews and James Scovil, who were present at Wallingford, did write to the

---

[37] Thomas Chandler to Samuel Johnson, Oct. 26, 1771, Schneider's Johnson, I, pp. 482-483; Isaac Browne to Secretary, March 25, 1748, Oct. 6, 1761, B, XVI, 74, XXIV, 23; Isaac Browne to William Smith, July 28, 1766, Hawks Papers, William Smith MSS, I, 8; Franklin Bowditch Dexter, Graduates of Yale College, I, 380; Edward Vaughan to Secretary, Feb. 14, 1744/5, B, XII, 2.

Society stressing the loyalty of their congregations, and urging the appointment of resident bishops in order to avoid the "Numerous Lives unfortunately lost" in seeking ordination.[38]

In Massachusetts, Henry Caner convened the clergy at his house, early in June. The fourteen clergymen "made something of an Appearance" in their "Gowns & Cassocks" as they filed into King's Chapel to hear Caner's sermon, followed by dinner attended by Governor Bernard. The convention that followed produced no response similar to that of their colleagues in New York. In Pennsylvania, the Stamp Act had further aggravated the internal political disputes, and when William Smith heard of his younger brother's death with Giles, he lamented the loss to the Society but declined to follow the New York convention's example of capitalizing on the incident.[39]

These petitions to England, however, were to be of no avail because the decision whether or not to appoint a bishop for the colonies was ultimately determined not by the American clergy's show of determination, but by the political unrest in America, and the resolute opposition demonstrated by the English Dissenters. While the colonies "were on Fire about the Stamp Act," Archbishop Secker informed William Smith, he had not thought it worthwhile to present their petitions to the King, and subsequent changes in the ministry and continued political unrest in America once again brought about the American clergy's efforts to nothing.[40]

To add insult to injury, accompanying the Archbishop's letter to William Smith was a copy of a sermon the Bishop of Gloucester, William Warburton, had read before the Society's anniversary meeting in February. Bishop Warburton's scathing attack on the institution of slavery in the American colonies was a reminder to the American "petty tyrants over human freedom" of their hypocritical assertion of their own liberties. The Anglican clergy in the northern

---

[38] Connecticut clergy to Secretary, May 20, 1766, B, XXIV, 297; Samuel Andrews to Secretary, June 25, 1766, B, XXIII, 12; James Scovil to Secretary, July 8, 1766, B, XXIII, 342.

[39] William McGilchrist to Secretary, June 27, 1766, B, XXII, 180; John Lyon to Secretary, July 3, 1766, B, XXII, 173; William Smith to Secretary, [May] 3, 1766, B, XXI, 254.

[40] Archbishop to William Smith, Aug. 2, 1766, William Smith Papers, I, 51 (Church Historical Society).

colonies, reading his sermon, though they might well have sympathized with his sentiments, were angered by his lack of understanding of the religious and political conflict many of them were waging against the Dissenters. The Bishop declared that while he knew little of the Society's foundation, he presumed the "peculiar objects of its exhalted Charity were the barbarous Americans." However, because of poverty that afflicted those Englishmen who left "the <u>Old World</u> to enjoy… <u>the free worship of God according to his own conscience</u>," the Society diverted its assistance to them. Nevertheless, those Presbyterians of New England who are "the Established Church" have objected to the Society's help. Therefore, he continued, the Society should leave them be, and get on with its original purpose of Christianizing the Indians. To rub salt into wounds already inflicted, he added that the important mission to the Indians had been hindered not merely by the rapacious pursuits of the colonists, but by the quality of the Society's missionaries. [41]

This sermon enraged many of the Anglican clergy. Thomas Chandler wrote to Samuel Johnson that the Bishop of Gloucester "has established Presbyterianism in New England & demolished all your missions, with one stroke. I think it is rather hard upon you, at these years, to be obliged to decamp, and enter upon a mission to the Chickasaws or Cherokees." The Bishop, he added, was guilty of "so gross ignorance" of the primary design of the Society. When the Rev. Andrew Eliot of the North Church in Boston read the sermon, he wrote to Thomas Hollis "it seems according to Dr. Warburton we now need Missions to convert us not from heathenism but from infidelity." Not only were the American clergy angered by the Bishop's ignorance, they, and their English colleagues, were embarrassed. The following year, Thomas Hollis wrote to Andrew Eliot that he wanted to send him a copy of the 1767 Anniversary Sermon "but could not procure it, the Propagators being become unusually shye to whom they distribute copies of it." Fortunately, for the American Anglican clergy, there was one English prelate who could be relied on to correct Warburton's errors, and to Robert Lowth, Bishop of Oxford, Chandler sent his "spirited letter." [42]

---

[41] William Warburton, Bishop of Glocester, Anniversary Sermon, Feb. 21, 1766.
[42] Thomas Chandler to Samuel Johnson, Oct. 19, 1766, Transcripts of Early Letters by Samuel Johnson, Thomas Chandler, John Hobart, 1754-1830 (Connecticut State

Occasionally the American clergy expressed dismay at the decisions arising from the Society's monthly meetings. And the absence of a consistent message being delivered through the anniversary sermons further confounded the clergy's efforts to fortify the Church's position in the middle and New England provinces. Only two years after Bishop Warburton had sown his seeds of doubt about the Society's mission, the anniversary lecturer, the Bishop of Lincoln, John Green, further confused the issue. While defending the presence of the missionaries among the colonists, and giving support to the appointment of an American bishop, he denied that slavery was "expressly forbidden" in the gospels or apostolic writings.[43]

Samuel Johnson convened the Connecticut clergy at Stratford on October 8, 1766, to consider the fate of their addresses to the Bishop of London and Archbishop Secker of June the previous year. Eleven clergy attended with Samuel Auchmuty from New York. They expressed their regret that their requests for bishops were followed immediately by the Stamp Act riots. Nevertheless, bearing in mind the respect for royal authority their parishioners had shown during the disturbances, they repeated their plea that bishops be sent "at least to some of these colonies (for we do not expect one here in New England)." Introducing another string to their bow, they referred to the clergy in some of the colonies where the church was established, who neglected their duty, too many of whom consider the Church as "a Trade or means of getting a livelihood." They concluded that was the "Strongest reason for sending them Bishops."[44]

The following month, Samuel Johnson wrote to the Society his own account of the Stratford convention. Reciting once again the perils facing candidates for ordination, he wrote about poverty that prevented many potential candidates from seeking ordination. He suggested that the Society might allow £20 or £30 to defray their expenses until they could be ordained in America. It appears that

---

Library, and also quoted in Schneider's Johnson, I, pp. 369-371); Andrew Eliot to Thomas Hollis, Jan. 7, 1767, Thomas Hollis to Andrew Eliot, May 11, 1767, Thomas Hollis Papers (Massachusetts Historical Society); Samuel Auchmuty to Samuel Johnson, [no date], Hawks Papers, Samuel Johnson MSS, [64].

[43] John Green, Bishop of Lincoln, Anniversary Sermon, Feb. 19, 1768.

[44] Connecticut clergy to Bishop of London, Oct. 8, 1766, Fulham Papers, I, 308.

neither he nor the other clergy would accept the wisdom of the Society's decision not to open any more new missions in New England.[45]

A week before the Stratford convention, the New York-New Jersey clergy convened at Shrewsbury on October 1, 1766. They were determined to find a way to quash the action being taken to introduce the corresponding societies and commissaries into the colonies. They considered how to proceed in their design to obtain the episcopate. They discussed the Philadelphia clergy's indifference to resident bishops, and the lack of zeal among the Massachusetts clergy and some of the Connecticut clergy. They finally concluded that the main stumbling block was not the divisions among the northern clergy, but the indifference, if not hostility, among the clergy in the southern colonies. To remedy this shortcoming, the convention appointed Myles Cooper to visit Annapolis to promote their scheme among the Maryland clergy. To prepare the ground for Cooper's visit, Samuel Johnson wrote to John Camm at the College of Virginia to gain his help in influencing the Virginia clergy, and if possible, to kindle some interest in the provinces to the south. The following June, Myles Cooper and Robert McKean, missionary at Perth-Amboy in New Jersey, set out with the New York convention's letter of recommendation to the Governor of Maryland. Myles Cooper was an excellent choice as representative to the southern provinces. An Oxford graduate and President of King's College, his well-known wit and taste for good wine, made him convivial company for the southern clergy who would be more at home with him than with the often humourless, narrow-minded New Englanders. Chandler had already corresponded with Dr. Gregory Sharpe, master of the temple, hoping that he would be able to influence his brother, the Governor of Maryland. However, Cooper and McKean might just as well have turned around and headed back north with Chandler, who they met at New Castle, Delaware.[46]

The Maryland parish of Coventry - - valued at £300 per annum - -

---

[45] Samuel to Secretary, Nov. 12, 1766, B, XXIII, 194.
[46] Samuel Johnson to John Camm, April 10, 1767, Thomas Chandler to Samuel Johnson, March 31, 1767, Schneider's Johnson, pp. 398-399, 395-397; "Seabury Minutes," p. 159.

had invited Chandler to be their priest, and with heavy family responsibilities, he had decided to consider their offer. When he arrived there, at the end of May, he found that the clergy were as disreputable as the northern clergy believed. Furthermore, they were very much against an American episcopate, and so much averse to having their vacant pulpits filled by northern clergy that some of the clergy and laity, with the Presbyterians' help, persuaded Governor Sharpe to refuse him the parish. The Governor was polite, but when Chandler broached the matter of American bishops, he became too busy with "the provincial acts, the public bans, Balls, Assemblies, and the devil knows what." But Chandler was concerned that the large number of clergy to the south, who were opposed to American bishops, might also have large numbers of contacts in England, and that explains his cautious letter to the Society informing the Secretary that he had refused the Maryland parish at his vestry's request, and for what he called "other reasons."[47]

Chandler's experience in Maryland convinced him that the northern clergy would have to go it alone in pursuit of the episcopate, and when he returned to New Jersey he began to work on the pamphlet that the Shrewsbury convention had commissioned him to write the previous year. He finally presented his piece, An Appeal to the Pulblic in Behalf of the Church of England in America, to the convention of clergy which was conveniently meeting in his own home in Elizabeth Town on October 7, 1767. For a number of years Samuel Johnson and Chandler had been discussing the idea of writing a pamphlet to educate the public about the Church of England in America. Even before his visit to Maryland, Chandler had become "convinced of the necessity of writing" to explain to "the Dissenters and some of the Church people, and perhaps (horresco referens) some of our clergy" the nature of the episcopate. Charles Inglis had raised the matter at one of the earlier conventions and now the work fell to the most able, but there were other reasons why Chandler shouldered so much of the burden. Following the Shrewsbury convention the clergy had time to reflect upon the wisdom of bringing the American episcopate into debate while the

---

[47] Thomas Chandler to Samuel Johnson, June 9, 1767, Schneider's Johnson, I, pp. 406-409; Thomas Chandler to Secretary, Oct. 12, 1767, B, XXIV, 91.

political climate was still uncertain on both sides of the Atlantic. Richard Charlton and Samuel Seabury for the time being lost the enthusiasm that had marked them a year earlier, and it is likely that they felt that Chandler was becoming too much of an agitator. When he had finished the first draft of his Appeal in May 1767, he sent it to Westchester for Seabury's comment, where it lay until Chandler finally recovered it. It was, he wrote to Johnson, Seabury's "want of Seizure & Inclination, & not his want of Abilities" that kept him from the fray.[48]

Chandler had judged Seabury correctly, for his worth as a writer on behalf of the Church was well known. Seabury had known Chandler at Yale, and soon after his ordination he took upon himself the considerable work of defending the Church against the "Watchtower," a series of essays appearing in Samuel Parker's New York Mercury, largely the work of the Presbyterian lawyer William Livingston, attacking the Anglicans' efforts to obtain a charter for King's College. He was a big, robust man who could talk to academics and farmers alike, and in his writings he could lampoon his opponents with language which even made the acerbic Chandler wince. Seabury would have preferred to keep the American episcopate out of public debate for, as he later remarked, arguing with Whigs and Dissenters "was like suing a Beggar, or Shearing a Hog, or fighting a Skunk."[49]

The copy of the Appeal that Seabury received in May 1767 made it clear that Chandler had given up the original purpose for writing the pamphlet, and was now bent upon raising a storm. Beginning with an obsequious dedication to Archbishop Secker, whose name only had to be mentioned in New England to make the Dissenters seethe with indignation, Chandler's pamphlet was as much designed to convince the English prelates and ministry of the need to send bishops to America as to incite the American Dissenters to drastic action.[50] In a very thinly veiled threat to the English ministry

---

[48] Thomas Chandler to Samuel Johnson, Sept. 3, 1767, Hawks Papers, Samuel Johnson MSS, 27; Thomas Chandler to Samuel Johnson, Sept. 5, 1766, Schneider's Johnson, I, pp. 366-369.

[49] Thomas Chandler to Samuel Johnson, April 21, 17[69], Number 28, Hawks Papers, Johnson MSS.

[50] In a letter to the Bishop of London accompanying a copy of his pamphlet, Chandler frankly stated that his purpose was to engage "some Person at Home,

of possible future developments in the American Church he insisted that commissaries could serve no useful purpose in America, and that in the absence of bishops the clergy had been forced to supervise the Church through conventions where the clergy met on "Terms of Equality," a situation "unknown to the constitution of the Church of England."[51]

Chandler made a great deal of the hardships candidates for the ministry had to bear in seeking ordination in London. But any sympathy he might have gained from the Dissenters soon turned to hostility with his repeated insinuations that they were less loyal to the Crown than members of the Church. He reminded the Dissenters, and incidentally he hinted to the English ministry of the direction the American Church might be heading with their conventions, that "anyone who prefers parity and a popular government in the Church will more easily be led to approve of a Similar form of Government in the State." His attempts to place the American Church on the side of American liberty by praising the ministry's repeal of the Stamp Act was not likely to convince his readers, who would soon learn that, one month before his Appeal was published, Parliament was hatching another tax upon the colonies in the form of the Townshend Act--"An Imposition on America . . . as Dangerous as the Stamp Act"--Boston merchant and King's Chapel communicant John Rowe noted in his diary.[52]

Chandler claimed that should bishops be sent to America they would be financed by the Society for the Propagation of the Gospel. To the Dissenters, this statement could only mean a further imperial infringement on American liberty.[53] And if his suggestions of the Society's further encroachments were not enough to make the Dissenters apprehensive, his claim that anyone opposed to a small tax being laid upon Americans to support a bishop could not be

---

who can command the Attention of the Public, to take the Cause in Hand, and set it forth to Advantage." Thomas Chandler to Bishop of London, Oct. 21, 1767, Fulham Papers, VI, 164.

[51] Thomas B. Chandler, An Appeal to the Public in Behalf of the Church of England in America, New York, 1767, p.28.

[52] Thomas Chandler, An Appeal, pp. 41, 115; John Rowe Diary, p. 146.

[53] The Society did have a Trust Fund for the support of American bishops when they should be appointed, to which Archbishop Secker left £1000 in his will in 1768. S.P.G. Journals, XVIII, 25.

considered loyal to the Crown, was sure to drive them to desperation. Furthermore, as if to contradict his claim that American bishops would have only ecclesiastical authority over the clergy, he concluded that "should the Government see fit hereafter to invest them with some degree of civil Power worthy of their Acceptance, which it is impossible to say they will not," it would mean only that powers were being delegated to "such Persons as are possessed of the greatest Abilities, Integrity and Prudence" who would, naturally not injure the colonists' rights. Chandler's language - - his use of capital letters making his intent formidably clear - - was certain to intensify fears that the proposed bishops were really only part of a general plan hatched in England, with the American Tories' support, to bring the American colonies under more direct Parliamentary control.[54]

Chandler's arrogant proclamations on behalf of the Crown soon brought the Dissenters down upon him, and early in the following spring "The American Whig" in Samuel Parker's New York Gazette and the "Centinel" in the Pennsylvania Journal launched into a savage, scurrilous attack upon Chandler's proposed colonial bishops, presenting their readers with the prospect of a politically powerful prelate, resplendent with the pomp and authority of a medieval prince. Particularly embarrassing was the Centinel's question: Why should Chandler be pressing the case for an American bishop, which would require an act of Parliament, at a time when Parliament's legislation was perceived as a threat to American liberties? One of the authors of the "American Whig" had sixteen years earlier been the leading figure in the opposition to the Anglicans' bid to control King's College. While he was sincere in his claim that Chandler and his associates were attempting to shackle the colonies with an "ecclesiastical stamp-act," he was also an expert propagandist. William Livingston knew full well that a "clamour" in the press was the best means of capitalizing upon the British ministry's recent capitulation over the Stamp Act in the face of

---

[54] The English Dissenter Thomas Hollis and his American correspondents were convinced that Chandler's pamphlet was largely the work of Thomas Secker. Thomas Hollis to Andrew Eliot, March 25, 1768; Thomas Hollis Papers; Thomas Chandler, Appeal, pp. 107-109, 115.

colonial opposition. [55]

Such a dangerous opponent as "The American Whig," of course, could not be allowed to go unanswered, and Myles Cooper provided "A Whip for the American Whig" in Hugh Gaine's Gazette, which was soon countered by a third series of articles signed "A Kick for the Whipper." John Dickinson was known for his "Letters from a Farmer," already printed in the various colonies, confuting the notion that Americans would accept taxation levied through duties upon their trade. He now joined with the Vice Provost of the College of Philadelphia, Francis Alison, to assume the role of the "Centinel" of America's political and religious liberties. They finally found themselves in controversy with Provost William Smith as the "Anatomist" in the Pennsylvania Gazette.

Though the newspaper controversy continued for over a year, Chandler's most damaging assailant was Charles Chauncey of the First Church in Boston. Chauncey had already launched an attack upon the indiscreet, misinformed Bishop of Landaff, John Ewer, whose anniversary sermon at St. Mary-le Bow the previous year had once again revived the cry on behalf of the Americans braving the seas for ordination, before he turned his attention to Chandler. Waving aside the scurrilous tone of the newspaper writers for a systematic analysis of Chandler's claims, Chauncey's answer to the Appeal ,in 1768, brought from Chandler a laborious defence, which in turn brought a further pamphlet from Chauncey. Finally, after four years of debate, Chandler, trapped between his denials and affirmations of the deliberately ambiguous language of his first pamphlet, made one more reply which he warned his opponent word be his last word.[56]

---

[55] William Livingston to Samuel Cooper, March 26, 1768, quoted in William Jones Seabury, Memoir of Bishop Seabury (New York, 1908), pp. 118-119; Richard James Hooker, "The Anglican Clergy and the American Revolution," pp. 175,178. For an account of the newspaper debate over the episcopate, see Arthur Lyon Cross, The Anglican Episcopate and the American Colonies, chapter 8.

[56] John Ewer, Bishop of Landaff, Anniversary Sermon, Feb. 20, 1767; Thomas Bradbury Chandler, An Appeal to the Public in Behalf of the Church of England in America (New York, 1767), The Appeal Defended: or, the Proposed Episcopate Vindicated . . . (New York. 1769), The Appeal Farther Defended . . . (New York, 1771); Charles Chauncey, The Appeal to the Public Answered (Boston, 1768), A Reply to Dr. Chandler's Appeal Defended (Boston, 1770).

He had written his last word to Chauncey, but he had much more to write in defence of the American episcopate, for while he had been occupied defending his Appeal, a letter which Archbishop Secker had written to Horace Walpole in 1750 had been printed. The letter, published posthumously in accordance with Secker's will, stating his case for a colonial bishop, brought an answer from the latitudinarian Archbishop Francis Blackburne to which Chandler felt obliged to reply. Chandler insisted that he had come off best, but even his fellow Anglicans were anxious to see the debate put to rest.[57]

Chandler's pamphlets were well received among the prelates in England (the Society eventually allowed him £25 to offset the cost of printing), though Archbishop Secker had felt uneasy about his suggestion in a publication of this nature, and at such a politically delicate time, that the Dissenters were potentially disloyal to the Crown. Nevertheless, the Bishop of Oxford, Robert Lowth, an admirer of Chandler, approved wholeheartedly of the work, which the bishops had printed in London. Thomas Hollis had received a copy of the Appeal from his Boston correspondent Andrew Eliot and he induced the Dissenting minister in London, Caleb Fleming, to reply to it.[58]

Among the American clergy, Chandler did have one supporter. Leonard Cutting wrote to the Society's Secretary, in December 1768, "it is with Pleasure, Sr. I observe, that the Disputes, which some evil minded Persons . . . have raised concerning our ernest Desire for Episcopal Government in the Church, has been a real Service, as it has opened, the Eyes of the People, made them examine more closely the Principles of the Church, habituated them to the Name of a Bishop, and taught them to reflect upon the Sacred Office, without Terror, or Suspicion." However, far from bringing the other American clergy together in defence of the Church, the controversy left them divided and frustrated. Even the arrogant rector of Trinity

---

[57] Thomas Secker's memorial is appended to Thomas Chandler's A Free Examination of the Critical Commentary on Archbishop Secker's Letter to Mr. Walpole (New York, 1774).

[58] S.P.G. Journals, XIX, 392; William Samuel Johnson to Thomas Chandler, Feb. 20, 1768, William Samuel Johnson Correspondence, 1744-1771; Andrew Eliot to Thomas Hollis, Oct. 17, 1768, Thomas Hollis to Andrew Eliot, May 25, 1768, Thomas Hollis Papers.

Church, who would normally have delighted in Chandler's supercilious indulgence towards the Dissenters, felt defeated at the drubbing the Church was receiving in the press. Many of the clergy felt that Chandler's stirring up the religious issue while the colonies were still up in arms about taxation was very unwise. Ebenezer Dibblee commented, in October 1769, after Chandler had published his reply to Charles Chauncy's Appeal to the Public Answered, that religion had become the tool of political party which bode ill for the Anglicans unless Parliament made concession to the colonies to bring about "a more happy union between our Parent Country and these remote Provinces."[59]

Across the Hudson River from New York, Isaac Browne, the only one of three Americans to survive the trip to England for ordination in 1733, was whole-hearted for the American episcopate, but was nevertheless, like William Smith, unhappy to see the matter brought before the public in such an arrogant manner as in Chandler's Appeal. He probably had the increased animosity between the Church of England and the

Dissenters in mind when he preached to his Newark congregation, in June 1767, on the text "Love one another." No doubt he wrote this sermon in reply to the bitter recriminations the Dissenters were levelling at the Church when they learnt that Archbishop Secker had prevented the Presbyterians from obtaining a royal charter of incorporation. But when he read the same sermon again in August 1769, he was more likely referring to the animosity raging over the Appeal. "All this Stir & bustle," he reminded his congregation, was over "some small Differences in opinion, some trifling Modes or ceremonies" between the contending groups which probably had "no real differences in their opinions" worth quarreling over.[60]

One week before Chandler's Appeal was published, John Rowe wrote in his diary that on the morning of June 17, 1767, the Anglican clergy attended Trinity Church in Boston where John Troutbeck read prayers and William McGilchrist preached "a sensible

---

[59] Leonard Cutting to Secretary, Dec. 28, 1768, B, II, 144; Ebenezer Dibblee to Secretary, March 27, 1769, B, XXIII, 110.
[60] Isaac Browne to William Smith, July 28, 1766, Hawks Papers, William Smith MSS, 8; Isaac Browne, MSS Sermon, John 13:35 (New Jersey Historical Society).

sermon." Following the service, fourteen Massachusetts and Rhode Island clergy met in annual convention where they prepared addresses to the Society and the Bishop of London. The urgency and militancy of their plea for American bishops reflected the tone of the New York-New Jersey addresses. Following the familiar arguments concerning the distance, expense and danger of facing Americans seeking ordination, they expressed amazement at the ministry's failure to provide a resident bishop for "such an extensive Territory as was here before possessed and hath since been added to the British Dominions by the Last War." They continued "the late popular Tumults in these Colonies we imagined woud (sic) have Strongly pointed out the Necessity of Such a Step towards the uniting and attaching the colonies to the Mother Country." Six weeks later Henry Caner wrote personally to the Bishop of London that if the American pleas for bishops were ignored, the Church of England "can have no long continuance in this part of the world ... considering the present disposition of people in these colonies."[61]

The pronouncements coming from the Boston clergy had been emboldened by the Bishop of Llandaff's anniversary delivered at St. Mary-le-Bow the previous February. Henry Caner, delighted with the Bishop's sentiments, had shared his copy with his colleagues in Boston. Bishop John Ewer had heard the pleas from America, and chose appropriately for his text Romans 10:14 "How shall they believe in him, of whom they have not heard? and how shall they hear without a preacher?" His sermon read like the litany of trials and sufferings replete in the correspondence from the clergy in the northern colonies. "The want then of Bishops in our colonies," he concluded, "appears in particular to be a fundamental cause of the want of native ministers." The Massachusetts Anglican clergy had found a friend; they had joined ranks with their neighbours to the south.[62]

On April 14, two months before the Boston clergy convention, the Rector of Trinity Church William Hooper died. Three days later, the

---

[61] John Rowe, <u>Letters and Diary</u>, June 17, 1767, p. 136; Massachusetts and some of the Rhode Island clergy to Secretary, June 17, 1767 B, XXII, 306; Clergy of Massachusetts and Rhode Island to Bishop of London, July 17, 1767, Henry Caner to Bishop of London, July 28, 1767, Fulham Papers, VI, 62, 64.
[62] John Ewer, Bishop of Llandaff, Anniversary Sermon, Feb. 20, 1767.

Society's missionaries Ebenezer Thompson and Edward Winslow, with John Troutbeck and William Walter, ministers at King's Chapel and Trinity Church, were bearers at his funeral. They were assisted by Congregationalist Ministers Charles Chauncy and Dr. Byles. This display of harmony between Church and Meeting House in Boston, and the mutual understanding with the Dissenters that had characterized the rural parishes of Weeks, McGilchrist and Wiswall was soon to end. The Bishop of Llandaff's sermon re-kindled indignation among the Dissenters, who often had access to the anniversary sermons before the missionaries. When Chandler's Appeal appeared a week after the Boston clergy convention, their ire became fury. Edward Bass commented that the Dissenters were "doing their utmost to prejudice the people in these parts against Bishops and the Church." Edward Winslow reported to the Society that "Amidst the present unhappy Commotions in the publick Affairs of this Province," the Braintree Dissenters' "Bitterness of Spirit" following the "Addresses on the Subject of resident Bishops" was indeed damaging. For Joshua Weeks and William McGilchrist it was merely a matter of time before the old animosities reappeared in Marblehead and Salem. "How long this harmony will continue, I know not," Joshua Weeks wrote from Marblehead, as "political matters begin already to poison and embitter the minds of the people." The people of Salem, McGilchrist reported, "are much enflamed at present on account of Parliament's taxes on Glass, paper etc." He continued "Last week their chief Demagogue declared vehemently in General Court . . . [and] asserted roundly that their Churches were in danger, inveighed bitterly against his Grace of Canterbury and the Bishop of London, and pursued a parallel between the former and Arch-bishop Laud."[63]

The absence of any defence of Chandler's publications from Massachusetts and Rhode Island can probably be explained by a letter addressed to the Society in September, 1768, signed by fifteen clergy from those provinces. They wrote "All that we are able to do in these times is only to cultivate among the people Committed to

---

[63] John Rowe, Letters and Diary, April 14 and 17, 1767, p.128; Edward Bass to Secretary, Sept. 29, 1768, Edward Winslow to Secretary, Jan. 30, 1768, Joshua Weeks to Secretary, June 20, 1769, William McGilchrist to Secretary, June 27, 1769, B, XXII, 31, 282, 252, 181.

our Care a spirit of peace & patience under the various insults, to which they are exposed for refusing to join in the popular clamours, that now prevail. We are neither allowed to speak nor scarcely to be silent unless we join with those, who we believe, to be labouring the destruction of our Constitution civil & religious. The civil Government is too weak to afford us protection; & ecclesiastical Superior we have none on this side the Atlantic, from whom we may receive timely advice or direction under our present trials."[64]

The Appeal could do little to heighten tensions between Connecticut's religious communities, and none of the clergy, besides Samuel Johnson, felt inclined to enter into printed controversy. However, one of the Society's missionaries was provoked into his own private retaliation against a sermon he found in his Simsbury parish. The Congregationalist Minister at Simsbury, Joseph Strong, published a sermon, in October 1768, in defence of Charles Chauncy's Appeal to the Public Answered. Roger Viets took the sermon home where he carefully annotated it. He had converted to the Church while studying at Yale College in preparation for the Congregationalist ministry, but he returned to his native Simsbury in 1763 as their Anglican priest. He was convinced of the validity of episcopal ordination. In the margin next to Chauncy's claim that he was well acquainted with the fathers of the Church "as any man in this country," Viets wrote that superior Anglican scholars were: Henry Caner, Thomas Chandler, Samuel Johnson, John Beach and Charles Inglis. Against Chauncy's claim that the Church was proselytizing in New England, he commented "just as if we mean to pervert them from Christianity to Heathenism." Nevertheless, he did not deny the charge, nor did he enter into public debate.[65]

In Philadelphia, William Smith regretted Chandler's publication as unfortunate and bad policy. The Church, he wrote to the Society, in May 1768, is being attacked "from one end of the Continent to the other" on account of American bishops. Smith wrote that he "never liked appealing to the Publick here about it." Neither did he "like

---

[64] Massachusetts and Rhode Island clergy to Secretary, Sept. 22, 1768, B, XXII, 309; Richard James Hooker, "The Anglican Clergy and the American Revolution," p.236.
[65] Roger Viets, "Annotations on a Copy of Joseph Strong's Sermon," Joseph Strong, Sermon, I Cor. 4:1, (Simsbury, Oct. 4, 1768) (Connecticut Historical Society); John Beardsley to Secretary, [Dec., 1762], B, XXIII, 51; S.P.G.Journals, XV, 348.

the too great zeal of our late Jersey Conventions." He would nevertheless have to defend the Church. In October, he wrote to the Society "We are at last obliged in this Province to bear our Part in the unluc[ky] War Commenced against the Church, on Account Dr. Chandler[s] Publication, which I wish had been let alone." The controversy only widened the gap between the ecumenical Philadelphia clergy and the country missionaries. George Craig considered the newspaper abuse of the Church to be "a great deal of Spunk & Noise" designed to weaken the Church and ultimately the British-American connection. "As soon as they [bishops] make their appearance on this Continent ye present Clouds will soon disperse" he assured the Society. From Reading, Alexander Murray spelled out his favourite lesson that the Dissenters dreaded the thought of bishops coming to America because they are "Friends of Monarchy & Subordination" as the civil wars in England had demonstrated a hundred years earlier. Thomas Barton wanted only "the natural Government & Discipline" of the Church and equality with all other sects. Smith's Anatomist had silenced the opposition. However, Barton wrote, and perhaps referring to William Smith's chameleon nature among his Proprietary Party friends and Presbyterian allies at the College of Philadelphia, even though the Anatomist had silenced the opposition in Philadelphia, "no Machinations, against the Church can prevail, unless betray'd by the Carelessness & Indifference of her own Sons." Nevertheless, he wrote, perhaps hinting at the country missionaries' suspicions of the city clergy's views, "there will always be a Virtuous Few, whose zeal, Fidelity, and Vigilence" will check the opposition.[66]

The longer the controversy dragged on the less inclined the clergy were to promote the sale of newly published pamphlets. William Smith in Philadelphia had difficulty selling the fifty copies of Chandler's first reply to Charles Chauncy, and by the time he published his second defence of the Appeal, the Connecticut Anglicans, who used to be fond of reading every defence of the Church, Chandler complained, had become "tired of the controversy." Jeremiah Leaming could only take two copies, which

---

[66] Wlliam Smith to Secretary, May 6, 1768, Oct. 22, 1768, B, XXI, 259, 261; George Craig to Secretary, April 17, 1769, B, XXI, 53; Alexander Murray to Secretary, Sept. 25, 1768, B, XXI, 106; Thomas Barton to Secretary, Nov. 6, 1769, B, XXI, 21.

he propably bought for himself, and Chandler had only slightly better success in the remainder of New England. When he set to work, in 1773, to reprint Archbishop Secker's sermons for sale in America, he found the missionaries' response to the proposed work very discouraging. "I have experienced their Backwardness in this Respect repeatedly," he wrote to William Smith, and "I shall be careful how I trouble them again" in the future. Having completed that project he began to prepare a biography of his old friend and mentor Samuel Johnson who had died a year earlier. But again he was put off by Johnson's son William, who called on the old and wise John Beach to help convince Chandler that he should not publish the biography at a time "so capricious & glutted with publications of every kind."[67]

Not only did the Anglicans fare badly in the controversy Chandler had begun, public opinion was even more hostile towards bishops than it had been during the Mayhew-Apthorp controversy five years earlier. The British ministry was even less willing to challenge the Dissenters at home or in America than before, and, as if to underline the High Church Americans' despondency, their most ardent English supporter had died in the midst of the furore. While Thomas Chandler waded deeper into controversy with Charles Chauncy, and as the "American Whig" lampooned the Anglicans, the clergy from Pennsylvania to Massachusetts mourned the loss of Thomas Secker whose death seem to signify the end of all hope of ever seeing a bishop in America. For the Dissenters, Secker's death was providential. Just before the Archbishop's death Thomas Hollis had learned that the ministry had dropped all thoughts of appointing bishops for the colonies, though he urged his correspondents in America to keep up their clamour. They did keep up their clamour, even extending it to Nova Scotia, usually considered a backwater. They sent a letter "from a Gent in London" to the German Lutheran-turned Anglican missionary at Lunenburg. The letter claimed that "Bishops are comming (sic) to America & all the Inhabitance (sic) will be obliged to pay the Tenth" part of their income to support him. Paulus Bryzelius sent the letter to Chief

---

[67] Thomas Chandler to William Smith, May 2, 1770 and June 14, 1773, Hawks Papers, William Smith MSS, 19,20; William Samuel Johnson to Thomas Chandler, April 15, 1773, William Samuel Johnson Correspondence, 1744-1771.

Justice Belcher, who had it printed in the Nova Scotia newspaper. The Dissenting "Gent's" seeds of discontent, however, fell upon thorny ground. Nova Scotia was not New England, even though many New Englanders had settled there.[68]

Though Chandler's work received a mixed reception among the clergy, there was one immediate success. Since 1766, Sir William Johnson had been trying to put into effect his scheme to establish missions for the Indians along the Mohawk River. He became a corresponding member of the Society and struck up a correspondence with William Smith and Richard Peters in Philadelphia, Thomas Barton in Lancaster and Samuel Auchmuty in New York. But his efforts failed to produce the devout, morally impeccable priests, prepared to live with the Indians at Fort hunter and Conajaharie, to learn their language and customs and to teach them Christian doctrine. The Society was anxious to assist missionaries, catechists and teachers on the Mohawk River, if suitable people could be found, for having prevented the New England Dissenters from incorporating their Society for Propagating Christian Knowledge among the Indians, in 1763, its own achievements were embarrassingly limited. The Society's missionaries had made a number of attempts but with little success. Thomas Barton had attempted to start a school for Indian boys in Lancaster, and the missionaries John and Matthew Graves in Rhode Island and Connecticut had made attempts which were no more successful. Thomas Wood had translated parts of the Book of Common Prayer into the Mickmack language for the Indians in his mission at Annapolis, Nova Scotia, and he had become so proficient that he could preach to them in their own language, but all these attempts were too scattered. However, the New York-New Jersey clergy's decision to urge the appointment of resident bishops in the mid-1760's turned Johnson's attention away from Philadelphia to New York, where the clergy were quick to see the political potential of his scheme. If the ministry were reluctant to risk offending the Dissenters, it would surely appreciate the strategic importance of attaching the Indians to the Church, work which could most

---

[68] Thomas Hollis to Andrew Eliot, July 1, 1768, Thomas Hollis Papers; Chief Justice Belcher to Secretary, Sept. 25, 1771, Paulus Bryzelius to Secretary, Nov. 30, 1771, B, XXV, 172, 176.

effectively be carried out under episcopal supervision.[69]

Therefore, Chandler sent Sir William Johnson a copy of his pamphlet, which pleased him so much that he offered 20,000 acres of land on the Mohawk River to support the proposed American bishop. In his haste to congratulate the author, who he had never met, on his "excellent performance," Sir William confused the American Churchman with the English Dissenter, Samuel Chandler. This letter, however, brought together the leading advocate of an American episopate, a most influential layman, and the cause most likely to win over the British ministry.[70]

The New York clergy were quick to seize Sir William Johnson's offer of assistance, and after visiting him at Johnson Hall on the Mohawk River, Charles Inglis drew up a memorial for presentation to the Lords of Trade. The clergy already had the Society's promise to provide £150 annually to support clergy and teachers for the Mohawk Indians, and now Sir William Johnson's reputation and his official access to the Secretary for the Colonies promised even weightier support for their plans. Inglis's memorial skilfully related the strategic importance of the Indians in upper New York to the value of civilizing them and securing them permanently for the Church. The memorial, complete to the last detail, received approval from both the Society and Sir William Johnson, and by the time Johnson had prepared Lord Hillborough for its reception, the clergy had found in John Stuart a missionary for Fort Hunter who soon proved himself worthy of the reputation he brought with him from the Presbyterians and Anglicans in Pennsylvania.[71]

Within a year of their success on the Mohawk River, the New York clergy received news of developments among the southern

---

[69] John Wentworth to Bishop of London, April 28, 1770, Fulham, Papers, VI,114; Thomas Barton to Sir William Johnson, July 22, 1767, Daniel Burton to Sir William Johnson, May 26, 1766, Sir William Johnson Papers, (Library of Congress); Thomas Wood to Secretary, April 1, 1765, Oct. 8, 1765, B, XXV, 63, 116.

[70] Sir William Johnson to Secretary, Dec. 23, 1767. B, II, 88; Sir William Johnson to Rev. Dr. Samuel Bradbury Chandler, n.d., Peter Force Papers, series D, Sir William Johnson Papers, 1755-1774; Myles Cooper to Sir William Johnson, Nov. 27, 1766, Sir William Johnson Papers.

[71] Charles Inglis to Sir William Johnson, May 25, 1771, Gratz Collection, case 9, box 10; S.P.G. Journals, XVII, 286, XVIII, 432; Charles Inglis to Sir William Johnson, July [-], 1772, Sir William Johnson Papers.

clergy that was very promising. Samuel Auchmuty had accurately analysed the attitude prevailing south of the Delaware River in 1765 when he advised Samuel Johnson to forget any attempt to involve them in the petitions to England because they were "quite Independent of the people, & therefore do not chuse a Master." Chandler, Cooper and McKean returned from Maryland two years later with much the same opinion, but in the following year, while the Dissenters in the northern colonies were up in arms over the proposed American episcopate, a number of Maryland clergy began to view the idea of having an American bishop more favourably. Hugh Neill had gone to St. Paul's parish in Queen Anne's county in the fall of 1766 where, he informed the Society, he had a living worth £300 sterling a year, which set him above the poverty of a missionary to the Pennsylvanians, and he had found Maryland to be a province "where the Church is established, and no man can be ruined by partial information" (such as William Smith might send to London.) and where "We have a Governor, who answers all the Ends of a Bishop, Except in Conferring Orders" and who, if he could perform that office, "would make as good a Bishop as we Could wish for." However, Neill's halcyon days were not to last long for a bill brought before the provincial assembly two years later threatened to place the clergy under a court of three clergymen and three laymen with powers to suspend any clergyman guilty of immorality or absenteeism. Neill wrote to the Bishop of London to put a stop to this "foundation for a presbyterian Government."[72]

This situation gave the Maryland clergy something in common with those to the north, and the recently formed Widows' Corporation could provide a very satisfactory basis for a union with them. Neill wrote to Smith, in November 1769, about the scheme, and invited him to visit him in Maryland so that they could discuss ways of creating a broader Church union. A month later, the Maryland clergy formed their own branch of the Widows' Corporation, with Henry Addison as president, and, at the same time, established a fund to employ legal aid against any further bills inimical to their interests. Having forged links with the northern

---

[72] Samuel Auchmuty to Samuel Johnson, Oct. 7, 1765, Hawks Papers, Samuel Johnson MSS., 7; Hugh Neill to Bishop of London, Sept. 20, 1768, Fulham Papers, III, 207; Hugh Neill to Secretary, June 9, 1767, B, XXI, 127.

clergy, the next move was for the individual clergy to follow Addison's example and become corresponding members of the Society.[73]

William Smith attended the first meeting of the Maryland Widows' Corporation in the summer of 1770, where a significant number of clergy expressed a serious interest in an American episcopate, because, apart from the threat to place them under lay jurisdiction, the assembly was now attempting to reduce their stipends by commuting their tobacco poll to a monetary payment. They drew up petitions to the King, the Archbishop of Canterbury, the Bishop of London and the proprietor, Lord Baltimore, urging the appointment of a resident bishop. Eight of the clergy present decided to become corresponding members of the Society, which so delighted the northern clergy that Myles Cooper visited them again, this time sure of a positive reception. He arrived in Annapolis in the fall of 1770, and in December, he, Inglis and Auchmuty recommended them to the Society for membership, with an encouraging word to the Secretary that more applications were almost bound to follow.[74]

To the New York clergy this Maryland conversion was providential. Thomas Chandler and Charles Inglis were convinced that it was the beginning of a general conversion in the southern colonies as the established Church came under criticism. Within days of hearing the glad news, Chandler set off for New York where he, Inglis and Cooper prepared a circular letter in favour of an American episcopate and sent it off with copies of the Appeal to leading clergy in Virginia and the Carolinas. The New York and New Jersey clergy convened at Samuel Auchmuty's house following the King's College commencement, in May 1770, determined to send off more addresses to England. Convinced that the rank and file were running into Presbyterianism, Auchmuty stopped their proceedings, and insisted upon his right as Rector of Trinity Church and Society corresponding member to read these "raw &

---

[73] Hugh Neill to William Smith, Nov. 10, 1769, Dec. 30, 1769, William Smith Papers, I, 65, 67(Church Historical Society); S.P.G. Journals, XIX, 25.
[74] Hugh Neill to Bishop of London, July 18, 1771, Fulham Papers, III, 215; Samuel Auchmuty, Myles Cooper, Charles Inglis to Secretary, Dec. 10, 1770, B, III, 339; S.P.G. Journals, XIX, 25.

inexperienced" missionaries a lesson in "Subordination" without which, he explained, "we are all upon a level, and therefore are plagued with the Folleys of those, who ought to mind their own Duty, and not turn Dictators." For the time being Auchmuty had his own way, but the missionaries were itching to take advantage of the promising news arriving from England.[75]

The controversy Chandler's pamphlet sparked in the colonies produced encouraging signs from England. The Society's anniversary lecturers in 1769 and 1770, echoing Chandler's arguments, claimed that it was time to send bishops to complete the American Church organisation, but what the young ordinand John Doty heard in London the following year made American prospects look much brighter. In February 1771, he had attended the anniversary lecture in which Robert Lowth, no doubt with the recent news from Maryland in mind, had delivered a scathing attack upon the American Dissenters who objected to the Society's work in New England, and who compelled young Americans to seek ordination in London from bishops who ought to reside in America. Conversations with the bishops, Doty reported, suggested that plans were afoot to give the missionaries what they wanted.[76]

With such encouraging news the clergy in New York decided now was the time to send an American "as a missionary" to "convert the guardians of the Church from the errors of their ways," for, as Chandler pointed out, "sending missionaries among them is almost as necessary as their sending missionaries to America." The missionary would be King's College President Myles Cooper, bound for England on a fund-raising tour on behalf of the College, and his numerous contacts among the Church hierarchy and politicians made him an admirable choice.[77]

---

[75] Thomas Chandler to Samuel Johnson, Dec. 14, 1770, Charles Inglis to Samuel Johnson, Nov. 10, 1770, Dec. 4, 1770, Dec. 22, 1770, Hawks Papers, Johnson MSS, 29, 40, 41, 42; Samuel Auchmuty to Secretary, June 8 and Aug. 16, 1770, B, II, 36, 37.

[76] Samuel Auchmuty to Samuel Johnson, March 27, 1771, Hawks Papers, Samuel Johnson MSS, 16; Charles Inglis to Samuel Johnson, April 30, 1771, Hawks Papers, Samuel Johnson MSS, 45; Robert Lowth, Bishop of Oxford, Anniversary Sermon, Feb. 15, 1771.

[77] Charles Inglis to Samuel Johnson, Nov. 6, 1771 and Feb. 5, 1771, Hawks Papers, Samuel Johnson MSS, 48, 43; Thomas Chandler to Samuel Johnson, Oct. 26, 1771, Schneider's Johnson, I, 482-483.

The Connecticut clergy, earlier reticent about Chandler's publications, were now in a jubilant mood. In May 1771, their convention of clergy thanked the Bishop of London for his "Readiness to exert [his] whole influence" for their cause. In America, they announced, "the Plan upon which Bishops are desired to be sent, has been fully explained, and it is universally approved, so that none oppose it, but those who do it out of Malice, or mere wantonness." Should the Church now be treated with "Neglect and are overlooked by Government" the result will damage "Religion and Loyalty." They also sent a petition to the Archbishop of Canterbury to present to the King. They also sent petitions to the Archbishop of York, the Bishop of Oxford, the Bishop of Litchfield and Coventry and to various ministers.[78]

Once again, however, divisions between Philadelphia and New York arose. Exactly who supported Cooper's mission, apart from the enthusiasts around Trinity Church, when the matter was discussed at Perth-Amboy, early in 1772, is not known, but the Philadelphia clergy certainly raised strong objections. Smith, as usual, claimed to speak for all the Pennsylvania and Delaware clergy when he wrote to the Bishop of London that they were refusing to support Cooper's visit because the missionaries were taking Church government too much into their own hands, especially at a time when the Virginia House of Burgesses had passed a resolution to oppose the appointment of American bishops. But by insisting that they had no fears that the visit "would be the means of raising so young a man" as Cooper "over the Heads of so many of his Seniors here, should the Episcopate take place," he betrayed their real intentions. The Philadelphia clergy, and various others in the middle colonies, feared that the Trinity Church zealots' influence on the appointment of an American bishop would mean continued religious hostility instead of the peaceful co-existence which had characterized Philadelphia and some of the country parishes.[78b]

However, on the surface at least, Anglican hopes seemed to improve in the early 1770's. Though the American Church had lost

---

[78] Jeremiah Leaming for the Connecticut clergy convention to Bishop of London, May 29, 1771, Fulham Papers, I, 317.

[78b] William Smith to Bishop of London, no date, William Smith Papers I, 75 (Church Historical Society)

its most influential advocates in England and America, Thomas Secker's successor to the Canterbury See was promising, and Thomas Chandler had already shown himself able to follow Samuel Johnson. The refractory St. Paul's congregation in Philadelphia appeared to be submitting to the Bishop of London's authority when they sent William Stringer to England, in November 1772, for ordination and license.[79]

Among the Maryland clergy, Henry Addison and Jonathan Boucher, in particular, were working enthusiastically for the American episcopate. Boucher's sermons educating his parishioners in the vital need for a Church establishment and resident bishops earned him an M.A. degree from King's College in 1771. In 1773, Myles Cooper paid a further visit to Annapolis to see what could be done to organize closer co-operation between their respective provinces. He then set out with Addison and Boucher to attend the annual Widow's Corporation meeting in Philadelphia.[80]

Boucher was delighted with William Smith's "very obliging Civilities" during his visit. Pennsylvania, he wrote to his friend in England, was "so rich, so cultivated a Country," and Philadelphia was "so large, so busy a City." Considering the support that Smith and the other Philadelphia clergy gave to the Second Continental Congress, it is understandable that twenty years later Boucher would write that "Dr. Smith's conduct on the occasion towards me was loose and false in the extreme." By that time Boucher "seemed not much to like either Philadelphia or its inhabitants . . . everything about it [had] a quakerly, or rather, a Republican, aspect."[81]

The following spring, events in Virginia seemed likely to create a Church union from New England to the Chesapeake when the conduct of two priests threatened to bring the clergy under the authority of the Virginia Council. To avoid the situation that was developing in Maryland, the president of William and Mary

---

[79] St. Paul's Church Minutes of Vestry, Nov. 2, 1772, Nov. 9, 1772, Dec. 4, 1772. St. Paul's Church's need for a regularly ordained minister in order to obtain a charter appears to be the motive for sending Stringer to London for ordination.
[80] Jonathan Boucher to William Smith, Feb. 14, 1774, William Smith Papers, II, 3(Church Historical Society).
[81] Jonathan Boucher to Mr. James, Nov. 16, 1773, Maryland Historical Magazine, VIII, 184; Jonathan Bouchier, ed., The Reminiscences of an American Loyalist (New York, 1967), pp. 100-101.

College, John Camm, called a convention of clergy to petition the House of Burgesses to request that the archbishops place the Virginia clergy under the supervision of a resident bishop. The Virginia clergy had cold-shouldered Camm's efforts to convene them for the same purpose in 1771, but now twenty four worried priests met, pledging the support of several others who could not attend. News of the Boston Port Bill and the dissolution of the House of Burgesses prevented them from presenting their memorial, but Camm assured Smith that they would renew their petition as soon as possible. In the meantime, they called upon Boucher to work as their liaison with the northern clergy.[82]

The attitude of the clergy in the southern colonies had alarmed one of the Connecticut missionaries who claimed to speak for many others. In October 1771, John Tyler wrote to the Society "We lament the Opposition which the Virginians and some others (where the Professors of the Church of England are the greater Part) have made to the British Government; and the coldness, or rather, utter Inattention of a great Part of them, to the cause of an American episcopate." He was afraid that the British ministry might be guided "too much by those unworthy and misguided" Anglicans "in some of the Southern Colonies" than by the professors of the Church of England in Connecticut who were "universally zealous for an Episcopate." John Tyler's purpose for writing at that time was to gain complete exemption from taxes to support the Congregationalist Church; hence his concern that the Society appreciate the support of Anglicans in Connecticut and in "these northern Colonies" for King and Parliament. Opposition in the southern colonies, he concluded, could possibly "withhold from us, that particular Favour and Protection which they [Parliament] would otherwise favour us with."[83]

John Tyler's fears could now be laid to rest. But the interest the southern clergy were beginning to show in the episcopate came too late to make any significant difference to the northern Anglicans' plans to strengthen the Church's position in the colonies, because, as the attitude of many Americans toward Parliament became more

---

[82] John Camm to William Smith, June 3, 1774, Hawks Papers, William Smith MSS, 12.
[83] John Tyler to Secretary, Oct. 9, 1771, B, XXIII, 364.

intransigent, their schemes were pushed into the background. The petition Myles Cooper took to England in 1772 were, in fact, the last formal requests from America for resident bishops, and like their earlier requests, they symbolized the factious nature of the American Church in the northern colonies. The New York High Churchmen's insistence on using political unrest in America to urge their own schemes upon the successive ministries had proved self-destructive, and they had driven a wedge between themselves and the other factions of the clergy, particularly those in Philadelphia. The degree of support the clergy had given to attempts to gain the episcopate suggests the extent to which they were prepared to accept the almost imperceptible changes America was forcing upon the Church of England. Between the hostility to compromise, that characterized the High Churchmen in New York, to the relative indifference of the Philadelphia clergy there was a spectrum of opinion reflected by the clergy in the various provinces which, in many cases, corresponded with their decisions for exchanging Presbyterian for Anglican ordination. Those differences continued to divide the northern clergy, and when armed resistance seemed to be the only option for many Americans, the individual priest's ecclesiastical position mirrored his view of the type of political and social community he wanted the American Church to be.

CHAPTER

V

Helpless Dependence Upon Britain

The developments that followed the closing of the Port of Boston, in 1774, caught the Anglican clergy totally unprepared. Apart from the few clergy who decided to join their congregations in rebellion, the majority of the clergy had no policy other than to wait for an initiative from Britain. As the radical members of the First Continental Congress led the colonies into outright defiance of Parliament, the Anglican clergy found themselves the dupes of ministerial policy and victims of American rebellion. Between the New York High Church Tories and the Philadelphia Low Church Whigs and spurious Whigs were the majority of clergy biding their time in hope of a constitutional reconciliation.

The clergy's position was made more difficult because many had privately expressed their disapproval of Parliament's proposals to tax the colonies during the 1760's and early 1770's. Particularly galling had been their duty as Anglican priests to urge submission upon their congregations which, of course, had given credence to the Dissenters' claim that the ministry had assigned them that role in its scheme to whittle away the colonists' liberties. Some clergy did express their disapproval of the taxes, though usually couched in praise for their congregations who remained aloof from the public clamour. Samuel Johnson confided in his autobiography, written between 1768 and 1770 and published posthumously, that the ministry "got two very ill judged acts to pass, to enforce severe stamp duty upon us." The fourteen clergy convening at Samuel Auchmuty's house in New York, in May 1766, listened to the Rector of Trinity Church "congratulate them upon the Repeal of the disagreeable Stamp Act," before proceeding to Church business.

They made no mention of the repeal of the Stamp Act in their addresses to Governor Moore, the Society and the Bishop of London. However, Auchmuty's comments were published in the New York Mercury and The Weekly Post-Boy. Leonard Cutting and Samuel Seabury, among others, when writing to England, took the opportunity to blame the new imperial legislation for their fiscal plight -- both had been forced to move to other parishes after their congregations had been unable to meet their monetary obligations.[1]

The clergy in New Jersey and New England had reacted in much the same way as the New York clergy. From his pulpits in Newark and Second River, New Jersey, Isaac Browne preached a number of sermons between 1765 and 1775 which reflected upon the troubled political times. The sermon he preached at Trinity Church, Newark, in October 1767, was poignant. Preaching from Hebrews 12:14 "Follow Peace with All Men" he urged that people (meaning Americans) should not insist upon "nice and rigorous Points of right, not to take all advantages in our Power, although the Law of the Land and Justice of the Case would determine the controverted point in our favour." Perhaps, he continued, "by denying yourselves of what perhaps you have reason to believe is your right" amicable relations could be restored. Andrew Morton had been compelled to draw his quarterly salary from the Society earlier than usual because of the trade depression, and in doing so he had warned that the stamp duty was "an intolerable Burthen" which could lead to "very serious Consequences." Thomas Chandler had naturally taken the opportunity of "mixing an Episcopate with almost every subject" in his letter to the Society in January 1766. Most people from Halifax to Georgia, he wrote, regard "some of the late acts of the British Parliament" as an "infringement of their essential rights." Every friend of the colonies and Britain "must wish that the Parliament would relax [the] severity" of these measures. Reading the Secretary a lesson on America's emerging national spirit he had suggested that the "present rebellious disposition" of the colonies was possibly "intended by providence as a punishment" upon the British people

---

[1] Schneider's Johnson, I, part 1, The Autobiography, p.44; Morgan Dix, ed., A History of the Parish of Trinity Church in the City of New York (5 vols.; New York, 1898), I, pp. 313-314; Samuel Seabury to Secretary, Oct. 1, 1765, B, II, 167; Leonard Cutting to Secretary, July 26, 1766, B, XXIV, 296.

for not paying greater attention to the needs of the Church of England in America, which, by its teachings would have produced "a general submission in ye colonies" to Britain.[2]

For Thomas Barton, in Pennsylvania, the political unrest had been perfectly predictable, since to his mind such disloyal behaviour was a natural projection of religious dissent. Even in November 1765, he insisted that the introduction of an American bishop "would not at present be disagreeable" except to a few who were raising the spectre of the episcopacy "when they knew the Minds of many were inflam'd" about the Stamp Act. It was typical that he called for the punishment of the opposition leaders in Philadelphia, while William Smith expressed sympathy for their resentment of the Stamp Act and the "ill-judged Restrictions" on American trade. He wrote to his acquaintance, the Dean of Gloucester, requesting that he help find "some happy Medium" between the colonists and the Ministry since he, himself, could only recommend "Decorum in our Remonstrances and Behaviour" in defence of the colonists' "essential Liberties." In New Castle county, Delaware, Philip Reading had become actively involved in the local opposition to the Stamp Act, and disenchanted with the attitude of many of his fellow clergymen who had assumed that the Anglican priesthood comprised their rights as Americans.[3]

The Stamp Act repeal had come as a relief to clergymen like Edward Winslow and Ebenezer Dibblee because it had served to justify their determination to continue preaching obedience even after factions of some of their congregations had deserted them. Others, like Samuel Andrews and James Scovil of Connecticut, who had made themselves the object of criticism and scorn by their opposition to the unlawful proceedings in their parishes, felt that

---

[2] Isaac Browne, MSS Sermon, Heb. 12:14, Psalm 14:1, Luke 8:18,; Andrew Morton to Secretary, Sept. 26, 1765, B, XXIV, 231; Thomas Chandler to Samuel Johnson, Feb. 1, 1766, Schneider's Johnson, I, pp. 357-359; Thomas Chandler to Secretary, Jan. 15, 1766, B, XXIV, 90.

[3] Thomas Barton to Secretary, Jan. 23, 1766, B, XXI, 16; William Smith to Dr. Tucker, Dean of Gloucester, Dec. 18, 1765, William Smith Papers, VI (Historical Society of Pennsylvania); Philip reading to Secretary, Sept. 5, 1766, B, XXI, 196.

the ministry in repealing the act had traded them for tranquility.[4]

The relief many of the clergy felt following the repeal of the Stamp Act was short-lived. Ministerial policy and episcopacy became so closely interwoven that relief and dismay followed in quick succession as plans to tax the colonies and American opposition to them inflamed political tempers and prolonged economic hardship. Thomas Davies wrote, in June 1765, that his New Milford mission in Connecticut was building a new church, though it would take years to finish because of "the present distressing Circumstances of this Country." In New Jersey, Andrew Morton found that even the wealthiest farmers, in 1765, could not pay their subscriptions because of "the want of paper Currency, and the Narrowness of our Trade" and lack of "Silver or Gold." The same problem plagued John Lyon in Taunton, Massachusetts, in 1768.[5]

With the repeal of the Townshend Acts and the subsequent collapse of the non-importation agreement, several clergy expressed relief at the improving financial and political outlook. However, there were those not so optimistic. William McGilchrist wrote to the Society, in late 1770, that "the ferment . . . wrought up . . . by the word liberty" was subsiding. But he cautioned that discontent could easily resurface as it had done with the acquittal of British soldiers involved in shooting at the crowd in front of the Boston customhouse, earlier that year.[6]

Nevertheless, the improving economic circumstances did not assuage the resentment some Dissenters felt toward the Anglicans. Their tempers were probably inflamed by comments from some tactless missionaries. The outspoken apostate priest Samuel Peters from Hebron was likely to upset any Dissenter. While visiting the

---

[4] Samuel Andrews to Secretary, June 25, 1766, B, XXIII, 12; James Scovil to Secretary, July 8, 1766, B, XXIII, 342; Ebenezer Dibblee to Secretary, Oct. 7, 1766, B, XXIII, 105; Edward Winslow to Secretary, Jan. 8, 1766, B, XXII, 277.

[5] Thomas Davies to Secretary, June 25, 1765, B, XXIII, 86; Andrew Morton to Secretary, Sept. 26, 1765, B, XXIV, 231; John Lyon to Secretary, April 12, 1768, B, XXII, 175.

[6] Samuel Auchmuty to Richard Peters, Sept. 9, 1770, Peters Papers, VII, 6 (Historical Society of Pennsylvania); Philip Reading to Secretary, May 18, 1770, B, XXI, 201; John Wiswall to Secretary, Nov. 5, 1771, B, XXII, 267; William McGilchrist to Secretary, Dec. 7, 1770, B, XXII, 183.

Hartford Anglican community, in 1770, he declared that the Dissenters had removed the foundation stone from the Anglican church being built there and "Sacreligiously placed [it] under a Dwelling House of a Puritan."[7]

Soon after his encounter with the stone robbers, Samuel Peters travelled to Litchfield where he sought advice from the clergy convened there, in June 1770. Ebenezer Dibblee was in attendance and wrote four months later that Samuel Peters preached the sermon before the clergy. Probably Peter's customary fulminations against the "Puritans" accounted for Dibblee's confusing him with Samuel Andrews, the Society's missionary from Wallingford. In his letter, Dibblee dwelt on the warring factions dividing the Connecticut Congregationalists. He wrote that the Church could gain greatly in those circumstances if it had "an effectual Establishment . . . an American Episcopate . . . cloathed with such powers and privileges as will support the Honor and Dignity of the Office."[8]

In his sermon before the Connecticut convention of clergy, Samuel Andrews also had the Congregationalists' factions in mind when he took as his text Matthew 16:6 "Take heed and beware of the Pharisees and of the Sadducees." Those ancient sects, he claimed, fearing the loss of their influence in Jewish affairs, united to turn upon Jesus. He contended that the present day was witnessing a similar challenge of sects against a legitimate authority. He claimed that the Connecticut Charter of 1662 "asserts the Supremacy of the British Parliament over the Colonies, in all Cases whatever" and has been accepted "by all even in the present Day, except in the instance of Taxation; which Exception seems trifling." And today, he continued, "multiformed Sects of Protestant –protesting Associators . . . have assumed the self-constituted Power of nullifying Acts of Parliament and the Statutes of this Colony." Our fathers never claimed independence of the Crown, he continued, and "nor did Israel make themselves a Calf until Moses [had led] them out of Egypt." And to make his analogy perfectly clear, he added a

---

[7] Samuel Peters to Secretary, June 26, 1770, B, XXII, 331.
[8] Ebenezer Dibblee to Secretary, Oct. 8, 1770, B, XXIII, 113.

footnote: "Canada was taken 1759."[9]

Some months before the Litchfield convention, Thomas Coombe, the ordinand from Christ Church, Philadelphia, wrote to his father from London. "All Ranks of People" in England "admire the calm Resolution with which the Pennsylvanians have proceeded to assert their Rights & Liberties," though he was troubled by the "Mob – Triumphs" in Massachusetts. In May 1770, he trembled to think of the consequences of two more regiments being sent from England. In October, he wrote "that obnoxious Act" remaining on tea bode ill for the future.[10]

Thomas Coombe's foreboding was confirmed when the British Parliament passed the Coercive Acts in early 1774. Nevertheless, the Connecticut missionary Ebenezer Dibblee's hopes remained high. In May of that year, he wrote to the Society that out of the American political disturbances "good will arise to the Church and a more effectual Indulgence and support" will be provided. "And as the Establishment of an American Bishop, or Bishops hath been the [sole] object of our desires and Requests, so if you Sir, [Dr. Hind, Secretary of the Society] Should have the Honour of being Appointed the first American Bishop . . . I believe it would not be disagreeable to the Clergy of the Church in this Province."[11]

On June 4, four days after Ebenezer Dibblee wrote his letter, Christopher Marshall recorded in his diary that with the blocking of Boston harbour, the bells of Christ Church in Philadelphia were muffled, and rung at intervals, a solemn peel from morning till night. Three days later, on George III's birthday, not one of the bells was rung. A compromise between the fourteen newly-elected vestrymen at Christ Church and the six remaining members of the old vestry appears to account for the entry in the vestry minutes of July 12: "The King's Birthday should be one of the Days included in the Agreement made by the vestry . . . and they should not for the

---

[9] Samuel Andrew, "A Sermon Preached at Litchfield, in Connecticut, before a Voluntary Convention of the Clergy of the Church f England of Several Provinces in America, June 13, 1770 (no place, July 1770).
[10] Thomas Coombe to his father, Nov. 1, 1769, May 5, 1770, Oct. 3, 1770, Thomas Coombe Papers.
[11] Ebenezer Dibblee to Secretary, Dr.Hind, May 28, 1774, B, XXIII, 119.

Future ring on King Charles Restoration Day."[12]

The controversy over taxation had left the Anglican clergy more closely associated with British ministerial policies than ever before, thus allowing the Dissenters to associate the Church and the proposed American episcopate with policies they claimed were inimical to America. The public debate over the American episcopate had served to crystalize the position of the two parties, and in the minds of many Americans it had exposed the Erastian nature of the Anglican Church. The religious and political disputes of the 1760's and 1770's had had a divisive affect upon the Church. Consequently the events of 1774 and 1775 caught the Tory clergy with neither plan to defend themselves nor to maintain the British connection which they knew was vital to their Church and their social philosophy.

On his way to attend the First Continental Congress in Philadelphia, John Adams stayed at the home of Peter Livingston in New York. Adam's host informed him that at the time of the Boston Port Bill, Thomas Chandler, Myles Cooper and other Anglican clergy had been employed night and day writing letters to the other colonies and to England. Peter Livingston believed they were trying to create an Anglican union in support of ministerial measures. Chandler, Cooper, Samuel Seabury and Charles Inglis had several years earlier pledged themselves to defend the Church and royal government in America. Now, with the First Continental Congress about to meet, defence of the Tory position became a very real burden. Even before the Congress's proceedings were made public, the leader of the moderates in Congress, Joseph Galloway, was transmitting the Congress's daily proceedings to Governor Franklin in New Jersey who relayed them to Lieutenant-Governor Colden in New York. This information proved useful. It enabled Charles Inglis to write several letters signed "A New-York Farmer" which he had printed in Hugh Gaine's New-York Gazette to warn Americans of the danger of independence and consequent civil war that could result from the direction the Congress was heading. When the

---

[12] William Duane, ed., Extracts from the Diary of Christopher Marshall kept in Philadelphia and Lancaster, during the American Revolution, 1774-1781.(Albany, 1877), p. 6; Vestry Minutes of Christ Church, Philadelphia, July 12, 1774.(Possession of the Rector)

Congress adopted the rebellious Suffolk Resolves he gave up writing about the benefits of the British Constitution in America, leaving Chandler and Seabury to expose to the public the Congress's abrogation of constitutional government.[13]

When the Continental Congress had published its resolves, Thomas Chandler sent to James Rivington's press a pamphlet entitled The American Querest, which he soon followed with another, A Friendly Address to all Reasonable Americans, condemning the Congress's denial of Parliament's right to tax the colonies. Though his pamphlets were unsigned, the style and sentiments identified the author, and public hostility compelled him to lie low for a while. Samuel Seabury now carried the Loyalist cause to the New York farmers in four pamphlets signed "A.W.Farmer." Using the rustic language that came naturally to him, he laboured the financial cost the farmer would have to bear for the Congress's usurpation of constitutional government. Moses Coit Tyler much later commented that Seabury's writings were "genuine English – pure, Saxon, sinewy . .every epithet a flash of fire." Indeed, Seabury's writings, Tyler wrote, for their "purely literary merits" entitle them to a high and a permanent reputation "in the literature of the era." Chandler soon followed the fourth Farmer Letter with a third pamphlet, What Think ye of the Congress Now, continuing Seabury's arguments against the illegal nature of the Congress, and its promotion of rebellion.[14]

Whatever posterity might decide about Samuel Seabury's literary merit, the Whigs were not for the present interested. Isaac Low's militiamen took the Westchester Farmer to New Haven, where he remained confined for six weeks, while the Elizabeth Town Committee of Correspondence (which included two of Chandler's congregation, John De Hart and John Chatswood) ceremoniously burnt his pamphlets, together with those Chandler had written. Thomas Chandler and Myles Cooper escaped the tar barrel aboard

---

[13] Memorial of Charles Inglis, Loyalist Claims, XXXXII, p. 541; Memorial of Joseph Galloway, Loyalist Claims, XXXXIX, p. 31; L.H.Butterfield, ed., Diary and Autobiography of John Adams (4 vols.; Belknap Press of Harvard U.P., 1962), II, p. 104.

[14] Thomas Chandler to Secretary, Feb, 22, 1775, S.P.G.Journals, XX, 362; Memorial of Thomas Bradbury Chandler, Loyalist Claims, II, 234; Moses Coit Tyler, The Literary History of the American Revolution, I, p. 349.

the man-of-war Kingfisher, in May 1775, together with printer James Rivington, whose press the Sons of Liberty had wrecked. A few days later, they transferred to another vessel bound for England. Aboard the Exeter, they met Samuel Cooke and his vestryman, Captain Kearney. Cooke had earlier gained the Society's approval to return to England in order to take care of his recently deceased uncle's affairs, and for that purpose he had booked his passage. However, his departure was probably opportune, since his delaying the appointment of a committee of observation in his Shrewsbury parish had resulted in physical violence. He did later return to New Jersey, before being driven to New York City. Ironically, Cooke and Chandler had first met soon after Cooke had arrived at his first mission in America, and Chandler had arrived home after ordination.[15]

Reverend Samuel Cooke 1723-1795, S. P. G. Missionary in New Jersey and later died in Fredericton, New Brunswick. (Courtesy The New Brunswick Museum, Saint John, New Brunswick, Canada. 1987.17.503).

---

[15] Thomas Bradbury Chandler, Memoranums, May 17 and 20, 1775; Samuel Cooke to Secretary, May 20, 1780, B, XXIV, 120; James Steen, History of Christ Church, Shrewsbury(privately printed, 1903), pp. 64-67; Henry Barclay to Secretary, Dec. 21, 1751, B, XIX. 66; Memorial of Dr. Seabury, Sept. 18, 1784, Notes of Daniel Coke, Loyalist Claims, p. 204; Loyalist Claim of Samuel Seabury, XXXXI, p. 559; S.P.G. Journals, XX, 331, 308; Edwin Francis Hatfield, History of Elizabeth, New Jersey, (New York, 1868), pp. 412-413.

Samuel Auchmuty took no part in the political pamphleteering, but his private correspondence, always full of venom for Whigs and Dissenters, finally caught up with him. When Washington's army arrived in New York, he decided it was time to go into hiding. He had offended some members of his congregation at Trinity Church a few years earlier, in 1769, with his sermon on the King's birthday. It had "been too loyal for some liberty Boys, that call themselves churchmen & has likely disgusted the Dissenters (in this I glory)." Many more of his congregation took offence at a letter he wrote to his son-in-law Captain Montressor with the British Army in Boston, which had been intercepted and printed in one of the Boston newspapers, early in 1775. Auchmuty's letter lamenting his misfortune at being born among America's "saints and rebels" and his contemptuous comment about "Hancock, Adams, and all their rebellious followers" was ill-timed because at that time a letter from exiled Samuel Peters had been intercepted and printed in the Hartford and Philadelphia newspapers. Peters' letter related to Auchmuty the views John Troutbeck, chaplain at King's Chapel in Boston, had expressed about the Whigs. Ridicule and insult, at which both Peters and Auchmuty excelled, were not for written communication, and several Anglican clergymen found these two men more burdensome than helpful. In particular, John Troutbeck, who was taking care of Samuel Peter's daughter in Boston, had cause for offence at their indiscretion because it was his house the crowd dismantled. When Chandler and Cooper left New York, in May, Auchmuty daily expected he might have to follow. To be safe, he burnt the correspondence between himself and the Society before taking refuge on his wife's farm at Piscataway in New Jersey.[16]

Of the New York Tories, Inglis fared better mainly because he was more discreet than the Rector. He later explained to the Commissioners to hear Loyalist Claims that he had been free from restriction, and he had served as liaison between the missionaries at Westchester, Elizabeth Town, Governor Franklin and Joseph

---

[16] Samuel Auchmuty to Secretary, July 4, 1775, B, II, 42; Samuel Auchmuty to Samuel Peters, Oct. 25, 1774, Samuel Peters to John Troutbeck, April 14, 1775 MSS of Samuel Peters, I, 5, 13; Samuel Auchmuty to Captain Montressor, printed in New York, April 19, 1775, Charles Evans, American Bibliography; Samuel Auchmuty to Secretary, July 4, 1775, B, II, 42; Samuel Auchmuty to [Samuel Johnson], [July, 1769], Hawks Papers, Samuel Johnson Mss, 17.

Galloway, conveying messages and pamphlets to Rivington's press. With Auchmuty's flight to New Brunswick, in the spring of 1775, the Revolutionaries interest in Trinity Church waned, thus allowing Inglis to remain in the city until the Battle of Long Island when he took cover behind the British lines. As acting rector at Trinity Church, Inglis continued to perform the Church service using prayers for the King and Parliament, even when General Washington attended. On May 17, a Continental Congress fast day, Inglis opened the Church and preached a sermon on "Peace and Repentance," carefully avoiding offence to the Revolutionaries while satisfying his own conscience. He continued in this manner, sermonizing on human weakness, and divine wisdom while maintaining liturgical correctness until the Declaration of Independence, when, on the advice of those members of the vestry and congregation still in the city, he closed Trinity Church and its two chapels. A young Bostonian serving with the Continental Army, sampling all modes of worship in the city, attended Inglis's service, but found his "Excellent Sermon" marred by the "Pedantick behaviour of the Priest, the Irreverent behaviour of the People, & the foolish parrade of Ceremonies." He decided the following week to return to the Dutch meeting, which, though he could not understand a word of what was spoken, showed far more devotion.[17]

Serious young Congregationalists were not the only people to regard Inglis as pedantic and pompous, for several of the junior clergy in New York and Connecticut held the same opinion. Perhaps his affectation and political discretion account for his being considered little threat to Revolutionary-controlled New York. Inglis's policy proved useful, however, for he was able to maintain a thread of organized Tory opposition in the middle colonies until the spring of 1776. When Thomas Paine's Common Sense appeared in January 1776, calling upon Americans to sever their connection with Great Britain, Charles Inglis published the only answer of any importance, which the New York Committee of Mechanics publicly burnt, without being able to identify its author. With the assistance of Isaac Ogden, a vestryman at Trinity Church in Newark, he

---

[17] Charles Inglis to Secretary, Oct. 31, 1776, B, II, 68; Edward Bangs, ed., Journal of Lieutenant Isaac Bangs, April 2—July 29, 1776 (Cambridge, 1890), p. 30.

transmitted another copy to George Panton at Trenton who finally got it printed in Philadelphia as The True Interest.[18]

The early departure of Chandler and Cooper reflected the degree to which their activities had aroused popular anger, even among some Anglicans. Their departure also reflected the difference between their views and those held by some of the other clergy. Chandler admitted two months before he left Elizabeth Town that a considerable part of his congregation were Whigs and were so opposed to his views that work on the new church that was being built had been brought to a halt. The clergy who had not approved of forcing the American episcopate into public debate in the 1760's felt that the pamphleteering had made matters worse. It seemed that once Chandler and his friends had raised the storm they had jumped overboard leaving the moderate clergy to bale the ship out. Isaac Browne in Newark, New Jersey, cast doubt on their need "to abscond in these Troublesome Times, or at least they tho't it necessary" - - a postscript the Society omitted from its Journals, and consequently from its yearly Abstracts of Proceedings. William Smith also claimed that their departure reflected negatively upon the other clergy. Some of Chandler's congregation, he informed the Society, insisted that he would have been safe in staying. With his penchant for recruiting others to bolster his claims, Smith also claimed that William Livingston, who became Governor of New Jersey after Independence, shared his view. A letter to Samuel Auchmuty, signed by a New York Anglican "C.J" claimed that Chandler and Cooper fled because they feared that some of their letters to England were among a batch that had been intercepted. Before Chandler left Elizabeth Town, however, he had learned from Thomas Pownall that the King had ordered the Lords of Treasury to grant him an annual £200 life pension for his services to Church and State, and both he and Cooper expected ecclesiastical elevation once the troubles were ended. The closer to those with the power of

---

[18] Memorial of Charles Inglis, Loyalist Claims, XXXXII, p. 541; Memorial of George Panton, Loyalist Claims, XV, p. 15; Evidence of George Panton before Commissioners to Hear Loyalist Claims in Nova Scotia in the First Report of the Bureau of Archives, Province of Ontario, 1903, vol I, p.5, quoted in A History of Trenton, 1679-1929 . . . 2 vols., vol. I Trenton Historical Society (Princeton, 1929), pp. 145-146.

preferment, the better the chances of success.[19]

While most Anglican clergy opened their churches on the fast days in 1775, the manner in which they met this "Tryal by Ordeal," as Luke Babcock saw it, differed. On June 30, William Smith wrote a letter to the Bishop of London, which all the Philadelphia clergy (including William Stringer) signed, to explain their position. Having attempted to keep their pulpits free from political disputes, their congregations now requested them to declare their sentiments on the fast day to be held on July 20, and fearing that their "Principles would be misrepresented," and even their "Religious Usefulness" destroyed among their people, they had decided to comply. But they made it clear in their joint letter that even if they were capable of influencing their congregations, they would never lead them into a "Criminal Resignation of their Rights," among which was the fundamental "Privilege of Granting their own Money."[20]

When John Adams arrived in Philadelphia to attend the First Continental Congress, in August 1774, Dr. Benjamin Rush gave him some advice. Dr. Smith, he said, "is looking up to Government for an American Episcopate and a Pair of lawn Sleeves." Rush continued that Smith was "Soft, polite . . . indefatigable, he has had Art enough, and Refinement upon Art" to impress the most worthy of the representatives to the Congress. Before William Smith wrote his letter to the Bishop of London, he had already obliged the Philadelphia militia. On June 23, Smith preached at Christ Church to the Third Battalion. He denied that he had heard talk of independence from Britain; he merely insisted that continued submission to taxation was unjustified. At Christ Church on July 7, before the First Battalion of militia, and on July 10, before the delegates to the Continental Congress, Jacob Duché pursued a

---

[19] Isaac Browne to Secretary, April 6, 1775, B, XXIV, 54; Memorial of Thomas Chandler, Loyalist claims, II, 234; William Smith to Secretary, July [10], 1775, B, III, 357; William Smith to Thomas Chandler, Aug. 28, 1775, William Smith Papers, VI (Historical Society of Pennsylvania); S.P.G. Journals, XX, 362; "A Letter to the Rev. Auchmuty" from "C.J." dated March 12, 1775, Charles Evans, American Bibliography.

[20] Luke Babcock to Secretary, March 22, 1776, B, III, 21; Philadelphia Clergy to Bishop of London, June 30,1775, William Smith Papers, VI (Historical Society of Pennsylvania).

theme similar to that William Smith had introduced. Independence, he claimed, was not an issue. Americans must preserve their liberties by banishing vice and by returning to "honest industry, sober frugality, simplicity of manners." By expanding on this theme, he avoided a detailed discussion of the conflict between Britain and its American colonies.[21]

On July 15, 1775, the vestry of Christ Church and St.Peters informed the Rector, Richard Peters, that they and their congregations expected him to observe the Fast Day, proclaimed by the Continental Congress, on July 20. He readily accepted. Christopher Marshall attended Christ Church on that day where he heard Thomas Coombe preach "an excellent sermon." Coombe had caused the Lord Chief Justice De Grey to "shed Tears" with his charity sermon, in London, in 1771, and on the July Fast Day at Christ Church Christopher Marshall wrote in his diary that his eloquence produced "numbers of wet eyes" among his listeners. John Adams also heard Thomas Coombe preach at Christ Church. He wrote in his diary that Coombe "is celebrated here as a fine Speaker. He is sprightly, has a great deal of Action, Speaks distinctly." However, Adams could not be brought to tears. He wrote in his diary "His Style was indifferent, his Method, confused" and he could not compare with several of the Congregationalist divines in Boston.[22]

William Smith sent copies of his own sermon with those of Duché and Coombe to London, explaining that all the clergy in the northern provinces, except two, had preached on the July fast day. He hoped to exculpate himself from the charge of disloyalty, and the more clergy he could claim to be of his opinion, the better, because

---

[21] L. H. Butterfield, ed., Diary and Autobiography of John Adams, (4 vols,; Belknap Press of Harvard U.P., 1962), II, p. 115; William Smith, "A Sermon on the Present Situation of American Affairs," at Christ Church, June 23, 1775" (Philadelphia, 1775); Jacob Duché, "The Duty of Standing Fast . . . ," at Christ Church July 7, 1775 (Philadelphia, 1775), "The American Vine," A Sermon Preached at Christ Church, Philadelphia before the honorable Continental Congress, July 10, 1775 (Philadelphia, 1775). Sermons in Charles Evans, American Bibliography)

[22] Vestry Minutes of Christ Church, June 15, 1775; The Diary of Christopher Marshall, p. 32; Joseph Hutchins to William Smith, June 19, 1771, Hawks Papers, William Smith MSS, vol. I, 42; Moses Coit Tyler, The Literary History of the American Revolution, II, pp. 285-286; L.H.Butterfield,ed., Diary and Autobiography of John Adams, II, p. 122.

he was sure that the émigrés in London would accuse him of being a rebel. In fact, before he left for England, Myles Cooper had written to him from New York that "since your Committeeship your Name has been roughly handled in England; and very Free Things have been said of you." He was referring to Smith's moderate role as a member of the Philadelphia committees of 1774. "Your Defence, however righteous and honest, has not had the Weight . . . you expected . . . you and Witherspoon are class'd together."[23]

Jonathan Odell wrote to the Society from Burlington, New Jersey, early in July referring to the Philadelphia clergy's letter to the Bishop of London as a "just and true representation" of Church affairs. He continued that the clergy believe that "by prudence & integrity of Conduct" they might help restore "harmony and peace, upon just and practicable grounds.".[24] Daniel Batwell preached to the York-Town militia, in Pennsylvania, on July 24, going even further than Smith and Duché in supporting resistance. He urged his company of Rifle-Men to defend America's rights in the knowledge that Congress was for reconciliation, not independence. "I have a commission . . . to bid you honour the King" he declared "but I have no Commission to bid you honour those, who wickedly stand between the throne and the subject."[25]

Among the other clergy in Pennsylvania and Delaware Smith could at least rely on support from Aenaeas Ross at New Castle and the Dover missionary Samuel Magaw. While there is no record of exactly what Ross preached on the Fast Day, the Pennsylvania Packet, on July 24, 1775, recorded that Ross preached from the text "When the House goeth forth against the enemy, then keep thee

---

[23] William Smith to Secretary, Aug. 28, 1775, B, III, 358; Extract of a letter from Myles Cooper to William Smith, Feb. 8, 1775, William Smith Papers, VI (Historical Society of Pennsylvania).

[24] Jonathan Odell to Secretary, July 7, 1775, B, XXIV, 146. In the Society's Abstracts of Proceedings for February, 1776, the Secretary, after learning of Odell's arrest by the Philadelphia Committee of Observation in October, 1775, ironically referred to Odell's earlier claim that the "prudence and integrity of the missionaries may contribute towards a recovery of harmony and peace, or at least secure them from the violence of the times," as having "met with a disappointment of his wishes in his own person." Quoted in George Morgan Hills, History of the Church in Burlington, N.J. (Trenton, N.J., 1876), pp. 309-310.

[25] Daniel Batwell, A Sermon, Preached at York-Town, before Captain Morgan's and Captain Price's Companies of Rifle-Men (Philadelphia, 1775).

from every wicked thing." The following month he preached a sermon at St. James Church urging resistance to Imperial encroachments. He had, in fact, preached the same sermon at his New Castle Immanuel Church a year earlier, during the agitation over the duty on tea. He urged his congregation to treasure virtue and simple faith when "we are reduced to the last Extremities...and the Sluices are opened, & the Floodgates broke up . . . so that we expect nothing but to be overwhelmed." Because, he claimed, "The mightiest & most victorious Prince that has not only lost nothing, but hath been gaining new Conquests all his Days" can be stopped. On October 8, Samuel Magaw preached at Christ Church, in Philadelphia, to the meeting of the Corporation for the Relief of Widows. All of the clergy attending gave their general approval to the Philadelphia clergy's preaching on the July Fast Day. As the occasion demanded, Magaw spoke of the spirit of benevolence. However, he concluded, "There is at this time more especially" a demand for disinterestedness in our bid to "re-establish PEACE and GENERAL WELFARE," adding that "Being united, in what we believe is a righteous cause" is an event "as important as ever mankind beheld."[26]

Thomas Barton, who had always been a stickler for royal government and the American episcopate, was a problem for Smith. In July, Smith sent the Lancaster missionary a copy of extracts from the Philadelphia clergy's letter to the Bishop of London, with a copy of the sermon he had preached before the militia, adding that "there is no man whose Sentiments upon it I would more regard than yours." Barton, however, replied that while he felt "absolute passive Obedience and non- resistance to be absolute nonsense," he could not approve of Smith's principles. Because politics was profound, he wrote, "I therefore paddle my Canoe, as much as possible, in quiet Waters, along the Shore; and so, by that Means, I hope to steer without Danger into the Port of Peace." Presumably, Thomas Barton opened his church on the Fast Day, possibly steering a course

---

[26] Aeneas Ross, MSS Sermon, Psalm 112:7 (Delaware Historical Society); John A. Neuenschwander, The Middle Colonies and the Coming of the American Revolution (New York, 1973), p. 124; Samuel Magaw, A Discourse Preached in Christ Church, Philadelphia, Oct 8, 1775 (Philadelphia, 1775).

similar to his neighbour Alexander Murray.[27]

When the "seditious" part of Murray's Reading congregation came to church, accompanied by militiamen, he preached from Jeremiah 4:19 on the "fatal causes of civil war," and when he declined to expand on the "merits" of the "pending" contest, they retired with "uncommon reverence, and the female part of the audience in tears." Having lost the first round, the Revolutionaries soon applied the test that would force all the Anglican clergy, sooner or later, to examine their beliefs very closely. When the Revolutionaries requested that in future he omit the prayers for King and Parliament, Murray closed the church and devoted himself entirely to his Mollatan congregation, fourteen miles away. There, he maintained the full liturgy until the following April when an angry crowd, egged on by rumours that Murray's house was being used as a Tory arsenal, destroyed his home and forced him into hiding. Alexander Murray and Thomas Barton were granted passes to proceed to New York City three years later.[28]

William Smith's private efforts to enlist the country missionaries' support for the Philadelphia clergy could only achieve limited success, so he began to prepare the ground for the annual Widows' Corporation meeting scheduled for October. There, with the aid of the city clergy, he would be able to influence those from the country to give the Church at least an outward show of unity. Eleven clergy from Pennsylvania, New Jersey and New York attended. They were joined from Maryland by William Thompson, who was Aeneas Ross's brother-in-law, and former missionary in Pennsylvania and New Jersey. They agreed on a joint letter to the Bishop of London. While Smith, in his memoirs, possibly compiled many years later, claimed that they "very unanimously adopted the Sentiments" contained in the Philadelphia clergy's joint letter of the previous June, their letter expressed considerable reservations. They agreed with their city colleagues that it had been necessary to comply with the Congress's request to preach on the Fast Day in order to keep

---

[27] William Smith to Thomas Barton, July 3, 1775, Thomas Barton to William Smith, July 10,1775, William Smith Papers, vol. VI(Historical Society of Pennsylvania).

[28] Memorial of Alexander Murray, Loyalist Claims, L, 137; Henry May Keim, "The Episcopal Church in Reading, Pennsylvania," Reprinted from The Pennsylvania Magazine of History and Biography, vol. IV (1880), p.11; Minutes of the Supreme Executive Council of Pennsylvania, vol. XI, p. 579 (Library of Congress).

their churches open, but they also insisted that they had "scrupulously" conducted themselves "as loyal Subjects and Ministers of the Church of England." They added, as a further mark of their distance from the Philadelphia clergy, "even were it proper for us to take any active Part in the Present Troubles, it would not be of any considerable Weight on either side of that fatal Dispute." These qualifications allowed Thomas Barton, Samuel Tingley, Alexander Murray and Charles Inglis to dissociate themselves from the Philadelphia clergy's approval of resistance to Parliament. By explaining their delicate position of wishing to preserve the British constitution in America, without actually expressing support for Parliament's right to tax the colonies, they were able to continue their fence-sitting for a little while longer.[29]

Ten days after the Corporation meeting, John Stuart wrote to the Society from Philadelphia where he was attending to what he termed "important Business," without giving any hint of what had brought him so far from the Mohawk River. A few days later he was in New York. It is likely that Stuart knew of the proposed joint letter which Smith had been organizing since the middle of the year, but refused to have anything to do with it. If he had arrived too late to attend the meeting, yet had approved of its deliberations, Smith would not have lost the opportunity to add another name to his list of supporters. Stuart's "important Business" might well have been an attempt to prevent the Philadelphia clergy from dragging the country missionaries into their Whiggish ways. The following January, John Stuart's letter to John Munro was intercepted. Munro was confined in Connecticut for enlisting men for the British army. The Albany committee of correspondence declared that Stuart had expressed "unfriendly sentiments to the American Cause," and ordered him confined to Fort Hunter.[30]

---

[29] Widows' Corporation members to Bishop of London, Oct. 6, 1775, Fulham Papers, VIII, 66; William Thompson to Secretary, Dec. 25, 1772, B, XXI, 290; Church Wardens, Trenton, New Jersey to Secretary, Nov. 8, 1773, B, XXIV, 184; "Memorandums . . . 1775-1803," William Smith Papers, VI, (Historical Society of Pennsylvania).

[30] John Stuart to Secretary, Oct. 17 and 27, 1775, B, II, 202, 203; <u>Minutes of the Albany Committee of Correspondence</u> (Albany, 1923), II,1039, 1081, I, 524, 526; Charles Hoadley, ed., <u>The Public Records of the Colony of Connecticut, May 1775-June 1776</u> (Hartford, 1890), p. 503.

William Smith informed the Society in August, 1775, that only two clergy in the four middle colonies had not opened their churches on the July Fast Day. Presumably, they were John Preston, who had left Perth-Amboy for few days to avoid making the decision, and Luke Babcock, who refused outright to tamper with the liturgy. He regretted that "The Battle of Lexington; then the affair of Bunker's Hill, followed by the Continental Fast, which may be confided as a Tryal by Ordeal" compelled most of the clergy to succumb. Finally, his "Refusal to bow down to an Alter, the Congress had raised" forced him into the confines of his parish, on pain of "Mutilation and Death," should he venture further.[31]

Perhaps Smith was doing some wishful thinking because at least two other clergy had defied the Whigs. William Ayers, after surviving several Patriot attempts to pull him from his pulpit for praying for the King, even before Independence, went temporarily insane at the end of 1774, shutting himself up in his church in New Jersey. He informed the Society, in 1780, that he had later recovered his health and, with the permission of his two vestries at Spotswood and Freehold, he had closed both churches when Independence was delared. Harry Munro, even before July 1775, had made himself unpopular with the Albany Whigs, who imprisoned him for a short while before allowing him parole in Albany. It seemed that fortune had turned full circle when, in October 1777, he was allowed to seek refuge in Canada. He had been present there at the capture of Montreal over fifteen years earlier, and once again he became chaplain to a British regiment until his return to England a year later.[32]

Poor communication between Philadelphia and the outlying parts probably accounts for Smith's exaggerating the numbers of clergy he claimed supported his position, but he probably did not look too carefully at the evidence. While he reported only two missionaries as having closed their churches in July 1775, Ayers and

---

[31] William Smith to Secretary, Aug. 28, 1775, B, III, 358; John Preston to Secretary, Jan. 12, 1777, B, XXIV, 284; Luke Babcock to Secretary, March 22, 1776, B, III, 21.
[32] William Ayers to Secretary, Nov. 16, 1781, B, XXIV, 12; Samuel Cooke to Secretary, Dec. 8, 1774, S.P.G. Journals, XX, 331; Abraham Beach to Secretary, Dec. 6, 1775, B, XXIV, 307; William Ayers to Secretary, Oct. 17, 1780, Nov. 16, 1781, S.P.G. Journals, XXII, 201, 401; Samuel Auchmuty to Secretary, July 4, 1775, B, II, 42; Memorial of Harry Munro, Loyalist Claims, vol. XXXXV, p. 51, vol II, p. 96.

Munro appear to have escaped his notice. Whether or not priests opened their churches on that July Fast Day is not as important as what they actually did. John Doty claimed that he had complied with Congress's request, but preached loyalty "to good Government" in and out of the pulpit. The Committee of Safety at Schenectady charged him with plotting against the State of New York; consequently, he was confined at Albany where he refused the oath of neutrality. Isaac Browne kept his church open in New Jersey, and he was still searching for compromise between American rights and Parliament's demands. His relations with the local Presbyterian minister McWhorter were sufficiently amicable for them to join forces in establishing an academy at Newark in 1775. However, Browne had never supported armed resistance to Parliament, he did not sign the joint letter from the Widows' Corporation meeting, in October 1775, and it was certainly wishful thinking if William Smith claimed him among his friends.[33]

Most of the Connecticut clergy also complied with the Congress in July 1775, and avoided persecution. Roger Viets, however, evidently suspected the Congress's proclamation of fast days was only the beginning of the Whigs' demands upon the Church when he wrote to the Society, in June, that he intended to persist in performing all his duties at the cost of his "Property, Liberty and even Life." James Nicholls and James Scovil fell foul of the local committee of safety for refusing to read proclamations against the King and Parliament on the fast day in August 1774. They were both subsequently driven from their missions in Northbury-New Cambridge and Waterbury. Samuel Andrews, who had already established his reputation for sermonizing against the Whigs and their notions of liberty, had a surprise in store for the Wallingford Sons of Liberty when they went to church to hear him preach on the Fast Day. His text was Amos, 5:21 "I hate, I despise your Feast days, and will not smell in your solemn assemblies." In the spirit of his text he examined the hypocrisy of feast days divorced from any

---

[33] Memorial of Rev. John Doty, Feb. 6, 1784, Hugh Edward Egerton, ed., The Royal Commission on the Losses and Services of American Loyalists . . . the Notes of Daniel Coke (Oxford, 1915), p. 72; Isaac Browne to Secretary, April 6, 1775, B, XXIV, 54; Nelson R. Burr, The Anglican Church in New Jersey (Philadelphia, 1954), p. 249; Joseph Fulford Folsom, ed., The Municipalities of Essex County, New Jersey, 1666-1924 (4 vols.; New York, 1925), I, p. 306.

attempt at a "reformation of manners." Persecutors of those who declined to join the popular movement of opposition to Parliament were as guilty of that oppression of which they accused Britain. Stressing the hypocrisy of the Congress Fast Day, he declared that if Americans could not reconcile the principle of liberty with their "detaining in captivity" the Black people, they should "let the oppressed go free." Andrews had his sermon printed because his name and text only had been published in the Gazette in order to represent him as being in contempt of Congress.[34]

The Massachusetts clergy were far more diverse in their response to the political crisis than those in Connecticut, possibly because several had been used to more amicable relations with the Dissenters. However, by 1775 the Massachusetts royal government no longer controlled political affairs, and the presence of British regiments heightened tensions in Boston. Any understanding remaining in 1775 between Meeting House and Church was shattered when the Bishop of Asaph Jonathan Shipley delivered his anniversary sermon at St.Mary-le-Bow Church in February 1773. His sermon appeared to many Anglican clergy as a betrayal of their pleas for toleration of Parliament's trade and revenue legislation. He took as his text Luke 2:14 "Good Will to All Men." He began on the promising note that the Society's mission to the Indians could not be successful until they were civilized, and, therefore, a more promising field for the Society's endeavours were the colonists

---

[34] Roger Viets to Secretary, June 24, 1775, B, XXIII, [395]; Roger Viets to Mr. Mitchelson, Dec. 6, 1776, Hoadley Collection, Box 12 (Connecticut Historical Society); Samuel Peters to Secretary, Dec. 7, 1779, Peters Papers, I, 42 (Church Historical Society); Samuel Peters, "A Narrative," Peters Papers, I; Samuel Andrews, <u>A Sermon Preached . . . before the Voluntary Convention of the Clergy . . .</u>, July, 1770; Samuel Andrews, <u>A Discourse shewing the Necessity of Joining Internal Repentance with the External Profession of it</u> (New Haven, 1775). Bishop Warburton, in his sermon before the Society in Feb. 1766, had delivered a scathing attack upon the Americans who defended their property so eloquently against Parliament, yet enslaved "vast Multitudes" to their "great idol, the God of Gain." The Society's anniversary lecturers in 1768 and 1769 tried to soften Bishop Warburton's devastating tirade upon the Americans. But in 1771 Robert Lowth used the occasion of the Society's anniversary meeting to hit back at the Americans for their "despotism beyond example" towards their slaves. Samuel Andrews' expression of concern for the slaves was not merely an attempt to confuse the Whigs' use of "liberty," for many of the missionaries made provision in their wills for emancipating their own slaves.

destitute of religion, especially the pioneers in the recently acquired territories. Bishop Shipley was possibly unaware that in recent years a great part of the Society's money had been spent in New England where "the colonists" were certainly not destitute of religious instruction. He then launched into imperial politics, in ignorance of the difficult situation the Anglican clergy had found themselves in since the early 1760's. The Society's "disinterested zeal" he suggested "may tend to revive that union and cordiality between the mother country and it's [sic] colonies." Britain should understand that the colonies were rising into states and nations, and, having tried to govern by force, should "have no reason to be proud of the experiment." He suggested, instead, that "the laws of justice and equity . . . must ultimately regulate the happiness of states as well as individuals." The Ministry should not ask "what are we to get by them; but, how we can best improve, assist, and reward them." The time will come, he concluded, "when the checks and restraints we lay on the industry of our fellow subjects...will be considered as the effects of a mistaken policy, prejudicial to all parties, but chiefly to ourselves." When the president of King's College Myles Cooper read this plea for sanity and understanding of the emerging national maturity of the colonists, he exclaimed "What a son of a b—h is this Bishop of Asaph! They say at Philadelphia that the sermon was written by Dr. Franklin."[35]

Bishop Shipley displayed an acute understanding of the Imperial conflict. He offered profound insight for an Englishman of his time, who, like most critics and commentators of American affairs, had never taken the trouble to cross the Atlantic. However, his comments served as fuel for the American patriots' fire. When Jacob Bailey travelled from his mission on the Kennebec River in Massachusetts to attend the Anglican clergy convention in Boston, in September 1774, he was "frequently insulted and mobbed." After returning home he was "obliged to flee from [his] house in the night, and to conceal [himself] for two days." He wrote "Nothing has inspired these opposers of government with greater resolution and fury than a speech said to be written by the Bishop of St. Asaph." From Boston to the Kennebec River every Anglican was

---

[35] Jonathan Shipley, Bishop of Asaph, Anniversary Sermon, Feb.. 19, 1773; Myles Cooper to William Samuel Johnson, Aug. 9, 1773, Schneider's Johnson, I, 488-489.

abused who would not subscribe to Shipley's sentiments "with the forced construction they [were] pleased to put upon his words." Bishop Shipley's sermon met with almost unanimous applause in the colonies. It was quoted in Rivington's New-York Gazeteer and in the Connecticut, Rhode Island and Philadelphia newspapers.[36]

Newbury Port missionary Edward Bass went too far with the Whigs for some Anglicans' liking. He was alleged to have prayed for the revolutionary cause on the Fast Day in 1775, and later he omitted from the liturgy prayers for the King and Parliament. The Society dismissed him from its service in February 1779, but his actual guilt was never unequivocally proven, though the Society certainly did all it could to do justice to him. He did open his church on the Fast Day in 1775, and he did later omit parts of the liturgy, but his alleged support of rebel activities was largely evidenced by Loyalists who had fled to England. In particular, Joshua Weeks, who had momentarily wavered when called upon to show his colours, was anxious to inform against Bass.[37]

Samuel Parker, William Walter's assistant at Boston's Trinity Church, joined with the Whigs. All the other clergy in Massachusetts were tested early. Moses Badger, who had gone to Haverhill in New Hampshire in 1767, resigned in 1774, after being pressured by the local committee of correspondence. He assisted Henry Caner in Boston until they both removed with the British army to Halifax in 1776. Ebenezer Thompson, who had always shown himself impartial to the Whigs, died at Scituate in November 1775, without having to face any political ordeal.[38]

---

[36] William S. Bartlett, ed., A Memoir of the Life of the Rev. Jacob Bailey, pp. 105-107; John Rowe's Diary, p. 285; Richard Hooker, "The Anglican Church and the American Revolution," p. 261; Rivington's New-York Gazeteer..., May 2, 1773.

[37] S.P.G. Journals, XXI, 415, 434; Edward Bass to Secretary, Oct. 30,1781, Feb. 27, 1782, March 15 and 17, 17[82], B, XXII, 44,45,46; Edward Bass to Samuel Hale, Nov., [--], B, XXII, 47; Account Given of Mr. Hale, [no date], B, XXII, 57; "State of the Evidence against Mr. Bass," B, XXII, 55; Joshua Weeks to Secretary, Sept. 7, 1775, "The State of the Episcopal Churches in the Province of Massachusetts . . . " [1778], B, XXII, 259, 260; Edward Bass to [Samuel Parker], Feb. 11, 1782, Edward Bass Misc. MSS, B.(New York Historical Society).

[38] [Mary Saltonstall Badger] to Mrs. Harrod, Aug. 10, 1778, Saltonstall Papers (Massachusetts Historical Society); Henry Caner to Secretary, May 10, 1776, B, XXII, 136; L.Vernon Briggs, History and Records of St. Andrew's Protestant Episcopal Church of Scituate, Massachusetts, 1725-1811 (1904), p. 8.

John Troutbeck, Caner's assistant at King's Chapel, and Robert Nicholls, McGilchrist's assistant and schoolmaster in Salem,, both ended their careers early. Troutbeck's association with Samuel Peters made him a target of popular abuse until he, too, left for Halifax. Nicholl's sojourn as assistant at Salem ended when he closed his school to join a British naval vessel after the fighting at Lexington. William Walter, Henry Caner, and Mather Byles left for Halifax with the British army in March 1776. Walter had preached a sermon a few days after the Boston port was closed to shipping, expressing his desire for compromise between Britain and America, but he was too much involved with the Governor's entourage to remain in Boston after the British left. Caner, having only six or seven hours notice of the army's evacuation on March 10, carefully packed up the King's Chapel register and vestry records, silver plate, linen and vestments, and hailed for Halifax. Mather Byles had no choice but to leave Boston because, even before his arrival at Christ Church, his congregation had been divided over the political disputes, and his outspoken defence of Parliament had driven a wedge between him and a large part of his congregation. By November 1773, he had decided to leave Boston. He secured an appointment to St. John's Church in Portsmouth, New Hampshire, but the trouble at Lexington prevented him from leaving the city. He then offered to officiate at Christ Church, without payment, but his former congregation refused to hear him.[39]

Several other clergymen were promptly persecuted for not doing the Whig's bidding. Gideon Bostwick at Great Barrington almost lost his life when his house was pulled down in October 1774, and both Joshua Weeks and John Wiswall were driven from their missions following Lexington. Weeks retired to a safe distance with his family to stay with his brother-in-law Jacob Bailey, on the Kennebec River until he thought it safe to return to his parish in Marblehead. John Wiswall suffered house arrest in Falmouth, before fleeing aboard the British warship Canceaux to Boston, at the end of

---

[39] John Breynton to Secretary, Jan. 13, 1776, B, XXV, 203; William McGilchrist to Secretary, May 29, 1775, B, XXII, 186; <u>John Rowe's Diary</u>, pp. 273, 292; "King's Chapel Vestry Records 1782"; Mather Byles To Secretary, Nov. 27, 1773, June 14, 1774, Dec. 7, 1776, B, XXII, 87, 89, 90; Robert Traill to Dr. Byles, June 15, 1775, B, XXII, 91a.

May 1775, where he was appointed chaplain to two regiments. Soon after his arrival in Boston, his nine year old daughter Elizabeth and his wife Mercy died within days of one another. The following January, as chaplain to the British warship Liverpool, and with his two young sons, he sailed for England. Finally, after serving as chaplain on a number of British warships, he found home in Nova Scotia.[40]

The Revolutionaries seized Ranna Cossit, along with Colonel John Peters, brother of the Hebron missionary, and several other Churchmen, in April 1775. They were ill-treated and held in jail for refusing to abjure the King. Eventually, Cossitt was confined to part of his mission in Claremont, New Hampshire until 1781. During that time he claimed to have conducted services without any alterations to the liturgy, though his congregations were badly distressed and reduced in numbers for refusing to join the militias. During his confinement in Claremont he evidently lived fairly freely, for he was allowed to visit New York City in 1779, and he visited lawyer William Pynchon in Salem, Massachusetts, in June 1781. Nevertheless, during his confinement, he continued to be regarded with great suspicion. Connecticut Governor Jonathan Trumbull urged the New Hampshire committees to "watch Mr. Ranna Cosset" who was suspected of being among "several evil-minded people" who had been carrying on "iniquitous designs." Winwood Sargeant had little time left in Cambridge after Lexington before he was forced to pursue a secret itinerary through New Hampshire, terminating in Newbury Port, while his church served as a military barracks.[41]

---

[40] John Tyler to Samuel Peters, Oct. 5, 1774, Peters Papers, I, 4; Memorial of John Wiswall, Loyalist Claims, XIV, 5; John Wiswall to Secretary, Aug. 11, 1775, May 30, 1775, B, XXII, 269, S.P.G.Journals, XX, 417; Rev. John Wiswall, Journal, 1731-1821 (Massachusetts Historical Society); Joshua Weeks to Secretary, June 2, 1775, B, XXII, 258.

[41] Ranna Cossit to Secretary, dated New York, Jan. 6, 1779, dated Claremont, May 10, 1782, B, III, 352, 353; Catherine S. Crary, The Price of Loyalty: Tory Writings from the Revolutionary Era (New York, 1973), pp. 69-70; Fitch Edward Oliver, ed., The Diary of William Pynchon of Salem: A Picture of Salem Life, Social and Political, A Century Ago (Boston, 1890), p. 99; Jonathan Trumbull to Hon. Meshek Weare, Feb. 13, 1779, Meshak Weare Papers, 1776-1780 (Massachusetts Historical Society); Henry Caner to Secretary, June 2, 1775, B, XXII, 132; Winwood Sargeant to Secretary, Aug. 3, 1775, B, XXII, 205.

In March 1776, Luke Babcock reported to the Society that his "Refusal to bow down to an Alter, the Congress had raised" on the Fast Day in 1775, led to his being confined to his parish. He was taken into custody in October 1776. Perhaps his privation and persecution were responsible for his death in March 1777. A fellow New York missionary, Epenitus Townsend continued to use the Church liturgy after Independence, before closing his church at Salem. Imprisonment at his own expense at Fishkill did not change his mind. His refusal to take the oath to the new State led to his exile on Long Island the following year. A Year later, his fortunes appeared to be improving when he was appointed chaplain to the Orange Rangers in Halifax, Nova Scotia. Thomas Brown, Samuel Peters' old friend, provided accommodation for him. However, in September 1779, when returning to Nova Scotia from New York City with his wife and four children, all were lost at sea. John Beardsley was forced to leave his Poughkeepsie mission to take refuge in New York City following Independence. Roger Viets, accused of assisting Loyalists who were imprisoned in the mines in his Simsbury mission in Connecticut, served time in the Hartford jail. Both he and Beardsley eventually sought refuge in the provinces under British control.[42]

Two Rhode Island clergy sided with the Revolutionaries. The Society dismissed Samuel Fayerweather from its service in April 1781, for having taken the oath of allegiance to the State of Rhode Island. Willard Wheeler had left the Society's mission at Georgetown in Massachusetts, in November 1771, to become assistant to George Bisset at Trinity Church in Newport. He was certainly not in sympathy with the Whigs as late as December 1774. Soon after Lexington, he left Trinity Church to live on his wife's farm near Boston. However, when John Graves refused to change the liturgy, Wheeler took his place at King's Chapel in Providence. Joshua Weeks was pleased to inform the Society, when he was in London in July 1779, that Edward Bass at Salem, Samuel Parker at

---

[42] Luke Babcock to Secretary, March 22, 1776, B, III, 21; Samuel Seabury to Secretary, March 27, 1777, B, II, 191; S.P.G.Journals, XXI, 192; Epenitus Townsend to Secretary, June [--], 1777, B, III, 57; Joshua Weeks to Secretary, May 17, 1780, B, XXV, 244; Thomas Brown To Samuel Peters, April 30, 1778, April 20, 1780, Peters Papers, vol. I, 33, 44; Samuel Seabury to Secretary, Dec. 29, 1776, B,II, 190.

Trinity Church, Boston, and Willard Wheeler had omitted the prayers for the King since Independence[43]

The Declaration of Independence compelled those clergy who were torn between their desire to continue the British connection and their concern for American rights to decide whether to side with the American resistance or to oppose it. While many clergy had been able to comply with the Congress's instructions concerning fast days, they found it impossible to evade its demands that they omit from the liturgy the prayers for the sovereign and Parliament. Here was cause for much deeper probing of their religious and social beliefs than ever before.

For clergy like George Panton at Trenton, New Jersey, who had never thought of temporizing with American society, the decision was clear-cut. But for Philip Reading it was a decision of monumental significance. In the 1760's he had kept an open mind in religious and political affairs. He had preached for the Methodists at St. Paul's Church in Philadelphia in 1762. Gradually he arrived at his own religious position. He wrote to Richard Peters at Christ Church in Philadelphia, in 1771, about the conclusions arising from his reading in religion and philosophy. "Systems of divinity and politics I have no taste for" he wrote. "My whole application now is to that grand system, My Bible." Sounding more like a minister of one of the more fundamentalist Dissenting sects than an Anglican priest, he continued "What need then of such a multiplication of Commentators?" Significantly, at no time did Reading support the call for an American bishop in his correspondence to the Society. While holding firmly to the Anglican form of worship, he wanted to live in peace with the other denominations.[44]

During his ecumenical journey he had wandered into political controversy. In September 1765, he had seriously considered a move to Trenton in New Jersey when Agar Treadwell died, as that parish was more compact than his own sprawling mission at

---

[43] S.P.G. Journals XXII, April 20, 1781, Nov. 15, 1782; Willard Wheeler to Jacob Bailey, Dec. 22, 1774, Jacob Bailey Papers (Library of Congress); Samuel Parker to William White, June 21, 1784, William White Papers, I, 34 (Church Historical Society); John Graves to Secretary, Feb. 12, 1782, S.P.G. Journals, XXII, 451; Joshua Weeks to Secretary, July 21, 1779, B, XXII, 261.

[44] St.Paul's Church Vestry Minutes, Nov. 15, 1762; Philip Reading to Richard Peters, Sept. 23, 1771, Richard Peters Papers, VII, 79.

Apoquiniminck. A fall from his horse five years earlier had left his right arm permanently injured, which, together with an old injury to his leg, made travelling difficult. The following year, the Society approved the move to Trenton, but by then he had changed his mind. The position had changed, he wrote, because he had become involved with a local committee appointed to oppose the Stamp Act, and he did not want to withdraw. He continued in this role as guardian of American liberties, though always insisting upon his "utter abhorrence of every opposition to higher powers." Soon after 1770, when he expressed his relief at the "seasonable repeal of the revenue acts," he began to realize that the movement he had supported would not stop short of using force. His change of heart about the resistance movement probably explains his disillusionment with "Systems of divinity and politics" about which he wrote to Richard Peters in 1771. Furthermore, at about the same time, he had begun officiating at the neighbouring vacant St. Augustine's parish in Cecil County, Maryland, when the Church establishment was coming under attack from the Assembly. He learned that he could not continue without becoming involved in the dispute. The difficulties in Maryland forced him to think carefully about his own part in opposing Parliament. When he was called upon to preach on the Fast Day in July 1775, he found it impossible "to avoid taking a part on one side or another." The following morning, his church door was scribbled over with "No More Passive Obedience and Non-Resistance." He had been confronted with this faceless, herd mentality in Philadelphia twelve years earlier when he had agreed to officiate at St. Paul's Church. On that occasion "an Anonymous Infamous & Scandalous Letter was left at the door of his Lodgings . . . impeaching his moral & Religious Character." For Reading, this behaviour in July 1775 was merely déjà vu. The following October, a letter he had written to the Society was intercepted. While attending the Widows' Corporation meeting in Philadelphia, he was summoned to attend the local committee of inspection. He was dismissed, but the committee noted him "as being of dangerous tendency."[45]

Eventually, Philip Reading resolved his political as he had

---

[45] Philip Reading to Secretary, Sept. 14, 1765, Sept. 5, 1766, Nov. 11, 1769, May 18, 1770, Dec. 2, 1773, March 18, 1776, B, XXI, 193, 196, 200, 201, 207, 195.

resolved his religious position. It finally came home to him "that the King's supremacy and the Constitution of the Church of England" were "intimately blended together" and that once the King's supremacy was suspended, the Church was destroyed. Clergymen like Reading now realized that their compromise with the environment, and with the Dissenters, had undermined the society they wanted to maintain. It was impossible to alter the smallest component without changing the whole, for even the slightest alteration would bring about a whole new structure. Clergy meant precisely that when they claimed that they had refused to change the liturgy rather than suffer a shipwrecked conscience. Continual demands that he stop praying for the King failed to impress Philip Reading, but with the declaration of Independence, he finally had to close his church. He remained in his mission. His old friend Thomas Barton, exiled to New York City, reported his death in January 1779.[46]

While attending the Widows' Corporation meeting in October 1775, Jonathan Odell began to reconsider his support for the direction the city clergy seemed to be taking. As the clergy met, he wrote a letter to Thomas Chandler in London explaining his diminishing respect for the Whigs as they appeared to be determined on independence. The letter was intercepted when Philadelphia merchant Christopher Carter was arrested while attempting to board an England-bound vessel in Chester, Pennsylvania. The letter (the more damning for being among a packet of letters from Philadelphia Tories Dr. John Kearsley, James Brooks and Leonard Snowdon) brought Odell before the Philadelphia committee, along with Philip Reading, and then the Burlington Committee of Safety. He was dismissed, but in June the following year he attracted his enemies' attention when he joined a group of paroled British officers on an island in the Delaware. Together, they had a grand Tory time singing some of Odell's verses to celebrate George III's birthday. When he closed the Burlington church after Independence, he was a marked man. On July 20, the Burlington committee of safety paroled him to an eight mile radius of the town east of the river. Here he attempted to remain on the

---

[46] Philip Reading to Secretary, Aug. 25, 1776, Thomas Barton to Secretary, Jan. 8, 1779, B, XXI, 211, 36.

sidelines, but his command of the French language thrust him forward as liaison with a regiment of Hessian soldiers to plead for the safety of the town, thus compounding his reputation as a Tory. After hiding in a tiny closet in his Quaker neighbour's home, he fled to Philadelphia. From there he made his way to New York where he attempted to save face with the Society by placing the blame for the Loyalist clergy's difficulties upon "indiscreet conduct" of the Philadelphia clergy.[47]

Daniel Batwell's position was more difficult than Odell's for he was an Englishman, and in his first flush of enthusiasm for American liberties he proclaimed the right to use force. When he realized that the resistance movement was heading for independence he tried to withdraw from it. Leading members of the community were seldom allowed to back out without drawing abuse from their former friends. When the Carlisle committee of correspondence demanded that he change the liturgy, in early 1776, he closed the church, and by the end of July he had also closed the churches at York and Huntingdon. Charles Inglis later commented that Batwell's desertion from the Whig ranks accounted for the severe treatment he received. Soon after independence, he was several times ducked in the river, and when a British regiment appeared on the Elk River, he was dragged from his bed in the early hours of a September morning in 1777, to spend six weeks in York Town jail. He became so emaciated and crippled with arthritis that he was removed to a private house. When the Provincial Congress finally allowed him to leave for Philadelphia, in February the following year, he was crippled and partly blind.[48]

---

[47] George Morgan Hills, History of the Church in Burlington, New Jersey (Trenton, 1876), pp. 310-311; Margaret Morris, Private Journal, Kept During a Portion of the Revolutionary War (Privately printed, 1836), pp. 6-13; Winthrop Sargeant, ed., The Loyal Verses of Joseph Stansbury and Dr. Jonathan Odell (Albany, 1860), p. 7; Christopher Marshall's Diary, pp. 45-46; Colonial Records of Pennsylvania, vol. X: Pennsylvania Provincial Council Minutes, Oct. 18, 1771-Sept. 27, 1775 (Philadelphia, 1851-1853), pp. 359-361; Jonathan Odell to Thomas Chandler, Jan. 7, 1777, Jonathan Odell to Secretary, Jan. 25, 1777, B, XXIV, 147, 148.

[48] Samuel Johnson [church warden] to Secretary, Nov. 25, 1776, B, XXI, 44; Daniel Batwell to Secretary, March 25, 1778, July 18, 1778, S.P.G. Journals, XXI, 312, 363; Memorial of Daniel Batwell, Loyalist Claims. LI, 12, III, 424; Daniel Batwell to Henry Lawrence, Nov. 7, 1777, Daniel Batwell to John Hancock, Oct. 1, 1777, Gratz Collection, Box, 21.

Some clergy, hoping to avoid the drastic choice of keeping their churches open on Whig terms or closing them completely, found comfort in the precedent set during the English Civil War. William Clark and Edward Bass met a month before independence was declared to discuss the possibility of using the English precedent. But Clark dismissed the idea since the American clergy, without a bishop to advice on any omissions from the liturgy, were not in the same position as the English clergy of the previous century. At Braintree, Edward Winslow also poured though his history books when the Scituate committee of safety confronted him when he continued for to pray for their enemy after independence. He finally decided that the liturgy must remain unchanged, and continued the Church services until his forced removal behind British lines a year later.[49]

The changes Edward Winslow had in mind were simple omissions from the liturgy, but Samuel Tingley managed to concoct a solution which suited the Lewes Whigs in Delaware, and satisfied his own inclinations. In the place of the words "O Lord save the King," he substituted "O Lord Save those, whom thou hast made it our special duty to pray for," with similar substitutions throughout the liturgy.[50]

The Connecticut clergy met in convention following the Declaration of Independence, and resolved to close their churches completely. They hoped that by following a common policy they could avoid the persecution that often resulted, in Pennsylvania for example, when clergy refused to make the same compromises as their colleagues elsewhere. Their decision was also prompted by the exploits of Samuel Peters, whose fanatic confrontation with

---

[49] William Clark's deposition to the Society, Feb. 23, 1781, B, XXII, 154; Edward Winslow to Secretary, Jan. 1, 1777, Jan. 4, 1779, B, XXII, 295, 296. The precedent referred to was set by Robert Anderson, later Bishop of Lincoln. After Parliamentary forces discharged him from his post as Regius Professor of Divinity at Oxford, in 1648, he retired to his parish of Boothby Pagnell in Lincolnshire, where he modified the liturgy in order to continue Anglican worship. His omissions did not satisfy the Puritans. He lost his living and served a term in jail, before the Restoration changed his fortunes. See Kevin T. Kelly, <u>Conscience: Dictator or Guide? A Study in Seventeenth Century English Protestant Moral Theology</u> (London, 1967), pp. 38-39.

[50] Samuel Tingley to Secretary, March, 5, 1782, B, XXI, 186.

Dissenters and Whigs had brought the Anglican clergy into bad light. His lordly denunciation of the Dissenters had earlier provoked a raiding party to remove the foundation stone from the Hartford Anglican church, which was in the early stages of building, for internment beneath the "dwelling house of a Puritan." But his flight from Hebron, in September 1774, brought a crowd upon the Anglican clergy convened at New Haven, compelling them to publish a declaration denying their complicity with Peters in a plot to subjugate the colonies.[51]

The Connecticut clergy's policy was successful in that, with the exception of a few clergy, the Church maintained a unity and resolution throughout the War years that saved many of them from persecution. According to Ezra stiles, John beach and Christopher Newton continued to use the full liturgy, at least for a while. Richard Mansfield, while not a fanatic like Peters, had spoken his Tory mind from the pulpit, and when his letter to Governor Tryon, estimating loyalist strength in Connecticut, fell into the wrong hands, only refuge on Long Island saved him from prison. James Nicholls had already been forced to go to the vacant Litchfield parish after he had refused to read the Congress's declaration in his own parish. John Marshall was ordered to appear before the Connecticut Assembly in October 1775, branded as inimical to American liberties, and Jeremiah Leaming spent a short time in jail during 1776. However, all of these clergymen, with the exception of Mansfield, Leaming and John Sayre, remained in Connecticut for the duration of the War, officiating in one parish or another, administering the sacraments, and reading sermons and parts of the scriptures as their convention had agreed.[52]

John Sayre came under surveillance in December 1775, when the Assembly passed a resolution to disarm the Loyalists. Early in 1776, when he refused to sign the Association, the Assembly directed the

---

[51] Franklin Bowditch Dexter, ed., The Literary Diary of Ezra Stiles (3 vols.; New York, 1901), II, p. 314; Samuel Peters' "Mobbing History" or "Narrative," Peters Papers I, 21; John Tyler to Samuel Peters, Jan. 9, 1784, Peters Papers, II, 2; Richard Mansfield to Samuel Peters, Jan. 12, 1776, Peters Papers, I, 21; Samuel Peters to Secretary, June 26, 1770, B, XXIII, 331.

[52] Richard Mansfield to Secretary, Dec.29, 1775, B, XXIII, 278; Samuel Peters to Secretary, Dec. 7, 1779, Peters papers, I. 42; Charles Hoadley, ed., Public Records of the Colony of Connecticut (Hartford , 1980), XV, pp. 159-159.

Fairfield township to refuse all dealings with the obstinate priest, and when that failed to bring him to heel, he was sent off to Farmington, sixty miles away. After seven months he was allowed to return to Fairfield, but his stay was short for, in July 1779, Governor Tryon bombarded Fairfield and neighbouring Norwalk driving both Sayre and Leaming to New York.[53]

In November 1778, however, the Connecticut clergy adopted a policy which many of the clergy who had taken refuge in New York City regarded as a betrayal of the Church and those clergy who had suffered for their loyalty. At the request of the Connecticut clergy, Thomas Chandler had approached the Bishop of London and the Archbishop of Canterbury for advice about how to cope with the new State leaders' demands that the clergy omit from the liturgy the prayers for the King. Chandler informed them that the prelates had advised that "if the clergy and communicants were unanimously of the Opinion that the life of the liturgy, with only the Omission of the Collects for the King and Royal Family was for the present necessary . . . they would not meet with the Censure of their Superiors at Home." Not long after Chandler's letter reached Connecticut, Ezra Stiles wrote in his diary, that this fall, the Bishop of London had written to the American Episcopal clergy to omit the offending parts of the liturgy and to open their churches. With that advice, the majority of the clergy agreed to follow the seventeenth century example of Bishop Sanderson. They omitted those parts of the liturgy that were offensive to the State leaders, and opened their churches. Jeremiah Leaming later commented that this policy had been largely responsible for the flourishing state of the Church in Connecticut at the end of the War, and he apparently made the omissions before leaving for exile in New York City. For John Sayre, a man who had been obstinate all along, it seemed that the clergy in Connecticut had "fallen into a method adopted by their Southern

---

[53] John Sayre's letter to the Committee of Safety, 1776, Charles Evans, American Bibliography; John Sayre's parole signed by Governor Trumbull, dated April 14, 1777, John Sayre to Governor Trumbull, Sept. 5, 1778, Trumbull Sr. Papers, IV, 1777-1786; Jeremiah Leaming to Secretary, July 29, 1779, B, XXIII, 257; Samuel Seabury to Secretary, Dec. 29, 1776, B, II, 190; John Sayre's Memorial to Loyalist Commission, submitted by his son, James, vol XII, 479.

brethren," in Philadelphia.[54]

The Connecticut clergy undoubtedly adopted this policy to keep their congregations together, but for part of surly old Matthew Graves' New London parish it was a means of declaring their church for the independent states, as well as an excuse to get rid of their royalist parson. On Saturday, November 14, 1778, the vestry met for the first time in three and a half years and resolved that "no Persons be permitted to enter the church, and as Pastor to it, Unless he openly prays for Congress, and the Free and Independant States of America, and there Prosperity by Sea and Land." Fourteen votes were cast in opposition to the resolution, eleven votes were in favour. After a challenge to the eligibility of persons present to vote, four of Graves' supporters and one of his opponents were disqualified. With a tied vote of ten persons for and ten against Matthew Graves, the vestry voted that the church wardens take the resolution to Graves, who predictably refused their offer. Persecution from the local committee followed, resulting in Matthew Graves exile on Long Island the following year.[55]

The Connecticut clergy's decision drew upon them criticism from many quarters, especially from the Loyalists in New York and England, who felt, like Samuel Peters and John Sayre, that it was a recognition of British defeat. But more to the point, as one bitter refugee in London pointed out to the Society, changing the liturgy meant that the refugee Loyalists' sufferings had been in vain. The bitter, anonymous refugee was probably Joshua Weeks who was specifically referring to Edward Bass, just then under discussion in London for his alleged disloyalty. Weeks was prolific in his condemnation of clergy who temporized with the Revolutionaries, even though he had wavered himself in the early years of the War. After taking refuge with Jacob Bailey on the Kennebec River, he returned to Marblehead where he continued to hold services in his church until January 1778. Sylvester Gardiner, one of the King's Chapel vestrymen, wrote to Bailey, in August 1776, that "Parson

---

[54] Abraham Beach to Secretary, Jan. 4, 1782, B, XXIV, 310; S.P.G. Journals, XXII, 141, 153; The Literary Diary of Ezra Stiles, II, 314; John Sayre to Secretary, New York, July 20, 1780, S.P.G. Journals, XXII, 153.
[55] Records of St. James Parish, New London, 1725-1850, I, Nov. 14, 1778; Charles Hoadley, ed., The Public Records of the Colony of Connecticut, II, p. 381.

Weeks is a conformist, but has behaved like a Gent;" presumably he was a gentleman because he was not praying for the Congress. At that time, William McGilchrist and Winwood Sergeant had closed their churches in Salem and Cambridge. Presumably, they would have been in danger if they had prayed for the King. Furthermore, Weeks was still performing the Church service for a year after McGilchrist had been forbidden to use the liturgy unchanged. Perhaps Weeks was the Marblehead "Vicar of Bray." William Pynchon wrote in his diary on Sunday, January 4, 1778, that Weeks' church was "shut up" and his congregation were being questioned about their non-attendance at the local Meeting House. Two months later, Joshua Weeks appeared before the local justice on a charge of "dining on board of a Flag of Truce at several times." Weeks' letter to the Society, in May 1777, accusing Samuel Parker and missionary Edward Bass of displaying rebel principles by changing the Church liturgy, sounds a bit like the pot calling the kettle black, for he had evidently not been as determined in his loyalty as he later claimed.[56]

Fifteen Anglican clergy in the colonies north of the Delaware River joined Bass and Parker in revising the liturgy. Of these, Samuel Fayerweather, Richard Peters and Aeneas Ross died during the War, and five others reconsidered their earlier conduct and joined the Loyalist ranks. As news of the imminent British arrival in Philadelphia spread, William Smith and Thomas Coombe were taken into custody with many others (most of them Quakers) suspected of pro-British sympathies. Significantly, the Rector of Christ Church Jacob Duché was not on the list of suspects. Thomas Coombe did not satisfy his captors of his trustworthiness; consequently he remained in custody. Smith was set free, under house arrest. Despite several protests from a Christ Church delegation, Coombe was sent to Virginia, on September 10 1777, two weeks before General Howe entered the city. Presumably, he satisfied the Patriots that he was no longer a danger, and he was

---

[56] "Reasons humbly offered why those missionaries who left out the prayers for the King and Royal family etc. should not receive any Salary . . . " B, XXII, 58; S.P.G. Journals, XXI, 264; Fitch Edward Oliver, ed., The Diary of William Pynchon of Salem. A Picture of Salem Life (Boston, 1890), pp. 24, 46, 51; Sylvester Gardiner to Jacob Bailey, Aug. 26, 1776, Jacob Bailey Papers (Library of Congress).

allowed to return to British-controlled Philadelphia.[57]

William White, Duché's Assistant at Christ Church, left town with the Revolutionary part of the congregation, while Duché, a man of no great conviction, became nervous, and as Charles Inglis commented, was soon "upon the stool of repentance." Christopher Marshall was probably mistaken in claiming that the day before the British arrived, Duché led a group of Tories to arrest the leading Whigs in Germantown. However, he drew contempt upon himself from both sides when, on October 8, 1777, he wrote a passionate appeal to George Washington pleading with him to have the Congress revoke the Declaration of Independence, and to acccept General Howe's surrender terms. In order to defend his earlier support for American resistance, he left for England to explain his views to the Bishop of London. Thomas Coombe and William Stringer, having refused to abjure the King, both left for England when the Revolutionaries retook Philadelphia.[58]

William Smith stayed on in Philadelphia, even after the Revolutionaries retook the city, but the Society had by then delivered its verdict. He had been officiating at the Oxford church for several years in addition to his work as Provost of the College of Philadelphia, and he had been drawing the Society's salary as missionary to that church. In October 1778, the Society, having considered his career since 1774, dismissed him from their service. Six months earlier, while the British were in Philadelphia, and while Jacob Duché was still Rector of Christ Church, the vestry voted to allow Smith permission to mow the grass on Christ Church burial ground for his own use. A year later, with Duché in England and the British army gone from Philadelphia, William White was elected Rector of Christ Church. Now, with thirteen vestrymen making their

---

[57] Minutes of the Supreme Executive Council of Pennsylvania, XI, pp. 283-284, 299-300; Christ Church Vestry Minutes, Sept. 6, Sept. 9, Sept. 10, 1777.

[58] Diary of Christopher Marshall, p. 132; "Copy of a letter from Rev. Jacob Duché to General Washington, dated Oct. 8, 1777, Charles Evans, American Bibliography; Jacob Duché's Memorial, Loyalist Claims, XXXXIX, p. 233; Hugh Edgar Egerton, ed., The Royal Commission on Losses and Services of American Loyalists 1783-1785 . . . Notes of Daniel Parker Coke (Oxford, 1915), p. 200; Christ Church Vestry Minutes, Dec. 9, 1777; Minutes of the Supreme Council of Pennsylvania, XI, pp.283, 284, 300, 527, 569; Memorials of William Stringer and Thomas Coombe, Loyalist Claims, L, p. 6, III, p. 432, III, p. 450.

first appearance, it was time to show William Smith how they felt. When he repeated his request to mow the grass on the Church burial ground, they unanimously refused. The following year, Smith, who had taken the oath to the State in order to keep his position at the College of Philadelphia, was not hired by the newly created Board of the University of Pennsylvania. In 1780, he accepted a call to a parish in Chester, Kent County in Maryland. Congress declared December 13, the following year, a thanks giving day for the surrender of Cornwallis at Yorktown. Smith displayed his patriotism at his church in Chester by preaching from Exodus 15:1 "I will sing unto the Lord, for he hath triumphed gloriously" over America's enemy. Ironically, the former incumbent of his church, John Paterson, a graduate of Smith's College of Philadelphia, had escaped imprisonment, and he had taken refuge in New York City, where he served as chaplain to the Maryland Loyalists.[59]

The Society dismissed both Robert Blackwell and Samuel Magaw at the same time as Edward Bass, in 1779. Robert Blackwell claimed that he was averse to independence and that he had remained silent in an attempt to reconcile his congregation who were divided over the issue. His mission at Glocester in New Jersey was in the path of American and British forces, and eventually he found it impossible to remain neutral. He had changed the liturgy at the beginning of hostilities and later he became chaplain to the First Pennsylvania Brigade. He served as chaplain and surgeon at Valley Forge. In March 1778, he closed his church, and later took the oath of allegiance to the State. He remained with the army until he went to Philadelphia to become assistant minister to William White at Christ Church. Magaw remained in Dover where he kept the church open, evidently conforming to the Congress's dictates until he replaced Loyalist William Stringer at St. Paul's Church in 1780. Aeneas Ross escaped the Society's notice, though the lack of any reference in his correspondence to the American disturbances should have aroused

---

[59] S.P.G. Journals, XXI, 358; Christ Church Vestry Minutes, April 27, 1778, April 12, 1779; William Firth Jones, A Pair of Lawn Sleeves, pp. 125-129; Horace Wemyss Smith, Life and Correspondence of the Rev. William Smith (2 vols.; Philadelphia, 1880), I, p. 573, II, pp. 18, 34, 49; Memorial of John Paterson, Loyalist Claims, XXXVI, p. 41; John Paterson to Secretary, Aug. 12, 1782, B, III, 354; William Smith to Secretary, June 17, 1778, S.P.G. Journals, XXI, 335.

their attention. While British forces occupied Philadelphia, he played safe by trying to please both sides. Lord Howe's secretary, Ambrose Serle, attended Immanuel Church in New Castle one October morning in 1777 and noted in his journal that an "odd kind of motley Service of Religion was exhibited. The Parson, one Ross, read the Liturgy, garbled of the Prayers for the King & Royal Family; after which, one of Mr. Wesley's Preachers mounted the Pulpit, and gave us a long & full Prayer for the King & and a Blessing on his Arms" which was followed by what the English visitor considered an illiterate sermon. Ross was evidently the New Castle Vicar of Bray for, in July 1781, he was at New London's St. James Church from which Matthew Graves had been expelled for refusing to pray for the American States.[60]

When the clergy in the northern provinces followed the example set by the Connecticut priests and opened their churches in 1782, the Church was in a sadly depleted state. Many of the country congregations were too poor to support their clergy; the privations of the War had reduced or dispersed others so that they could no longer constitute parishes. Where congregations still flourished, their ministers, in many cases, were in exile. Massachusetts was the most seriously affected province of all, having only one Anglican minister in Boston, Samuel Parker, and the Boston-born Whig, Nathaniel Fisher, at St. Peter's Church in Salem.[61] Nathaniel Fisher had gone to Granville, Nova Scotia, as the Society's schoolteacher in 1775. Three years later he was ordained for the Granville Anglicans. With so many Loyalist clergy in need of missions in Nova Scotia, the Society was unable to appoint him their missionary. That was probably reason enough for him to look elsewhere for a living.

---

[60] S.P.G. Journals, XXI, 415, 434; Vestry Minutes of Christ Church, Philadelphia, March 20, 1781, April 23, 1781, Sept. 12, 1781, Sept. 17, 1781; Copy of General Anthony Wayne's certificate showing that Robert Blackwell took the oath to the American States, dated Oct. 10, 1783, Wallace Papers, Vol. IV; Robert Blackwell to Secretary, Aug. 6, 1782, Aug. 3, 1784, S.P.G. Journals, XXII, 188, 394; Samuel Magaw to [unknown], Jan. 5, 1781, St. Paul's Church, Philadelphia, unsorted papers; Edward Tatum jr., ed., The American Journal of Ambrose Searle, Secretary to Lord Howe, 1776-1778(California, 1940), pp. 259-260; Aeneas Ross to Secretary, Oct. 10, 1781; S.P.G. Journals, XXII, 404

[61] William Bentley listed six Episcopalian clergy in Massachusetts on September 19, 1790. The Diary of William Bentley (4 vols.; Salem, Mass., 1905), vol. I, p. 196.

However, the friction his Whig sympathies caused among some of his parishioners was probably the motive that sent him back to New England in 1781. The arrival of a Nova Scotia Anglican priest in Boston aroused suspicions among the State authorities. Consequently, he was interned. With the help of St. Peter's Church in Salem, which had appointed him their minister, he was declared free of royal affection. Yet with the British capitulation imminent, the Anglicans reported improved relations with the Dissenters, even in Connecticut, now that the bonds between episcopacy and the Crown were sure to be severed. And the Tory clergy found themselves pondering over what the future would be.[62]

The War years had left them divided according to the social and political philosophies which had emerged from their contest with the Dissenters during the two decades following the fall of Quebec. Now they had to find out how to create the Church to serve the independent Sates. Already the Whig Episcopalians in Philadelphia were toying with the idea of forming a new constitution for the Church that omitted the episcopate. The Tory clergy were lost for an answer to their predicament: how were they to retain episcopal rule in a republican state, and how were they to secure the episcopal succession for America.

The Tories would put up a final struggle to save what remained of their philosophy, but the War had already decided what the future of the Episcopal Church would be. American lieutenant Isaac Bangs, enjoying the sights of New York City in 1776, commented on the elegance of the equestrian statue of George III, constructed of lead and gold, mounted on a white marble pedestal. The New York Assembly had erected it in 1770. Not long after Isaac Bangs wrote his description in his diary, he noted the destruction of the statue of "George Gwelph alias George Rex." He did not mention that the demolition on July 10 was carried out by the Black slaves of the patriotic devotees of freedom. Very soon a more devastating blow to George Gwelph's power was to follow. At about 1 A.M., on the

---

[62] Henry Caner to Bishop of London, [1777], Fulham Papers, XXIII, 130; Thomas Brown to Samuel Peters, April 30, 1778, Samuel Peters Papers, I, 33; The Diary of William Pynchon of Salem (Boston, 1890), pp. 79, 106-116; Minutes of the Nova Scotia Committee of Correspondence, April 11-Aug., 1775, B, XXV, 194; Nathaniel Fisher to Secretary, Sept. 30, 1778, B, XXV, 219.

morning of Saturday, September 21, a fire broke out in the lower end of Manhatten. A strong wind fanned the flames which destroyed several hundred houses, and with them, Trinity Church, symbol of British rule in New York. Some "rebels" were caught red-handed with combustible materials while they were sabotaging fire-fighting equipment. Several were given instant and final judgement. Charles Inglis was one of the fire fighters who saved nearby St. Paul's Chapel and King's College from the conflagration. As the fire engulfed Trinity Church, an officer of the Royal Welsh Fusiliers stood transfixed by the spectacle as the burning steeple appeared as "a lofty pyramid of fire" blazing in the sky, until finally the "whole fell with a great noise." Samuel Auchmuty returned from New Jersey to find his grand house and library nearby, completely gutted. All he could find in the rubble were a few trifles and the Church plate. Ten months later, as the British fleet was preparing to sail from New York to take Philadelphia, lightning struck the steeple on top of Christ Church, hurling the little crown from the top into Second Street below. The High Churchmen had nurtured a vision, which, like their Church in New York, was totally destroyed. They had depended upon support from overseas which never came, and even Trinity Church was lost while British troops were in command of the city. But lightening destroyed just enough of Christ Church to allow the Low Churchmen to begin anew as soon as better times prevailed.[63]

---

[63] Edward Bangs, ed., Journal of Isaac Bangs, April 1-July 29, 1776 (Cambridge, 1890), pp. 25, 56-57; Michael Kammen, Colonial New York, A History (NewYork, 1975), pp. 370-371; Edward H. Tatum Jr., ed., The American Journal of Ambrose Searle, pp. 110-111; Charles Inglis to Secretary, Oct. 31, 1776, B, II, 68; The Diary of Frederick McKenzie, (New York, 1968), Vol. I, p. 60; Minutes of Christ Church, Philadelphia, June 10, 1777; William Duane, ed., Diary of Christopher Marshall, p. 118; Samuel Auchmuty to Secretary, Nov. 20, 1776, B, II, 20.

CHAPTER

VI

Propagating Loyal Principles

The Anglican clergy in the northern colonies had believed that they could influence the development of American society, and with English aid they sought to lead their countrymen away from the troubled individualism of Dissent back to the orderly calm of the Prayer Book and sacraments. But America, with its boundless opportunities for self-assertion, denied them their ideal. Even during its infancy the Church had embraced clergy and laity whose distinctly American outlook would ultimately require them to demand greater autonomy in the management of their own affairs.

For most of the American clergy, religious dissent was their main enemy, for it seemed to encourage the egalitarian spirit they were determined to curb. The prelates, distinguished Churchmen, and the Anglican laity who directed and supported the Society's work, generally shared the Americans' view of religious dissent, and were prepared to provide the missionary clergy with the finance and guidance to foster the Anglican alternative. The Society's Secretary, Daniel Burton, informed Thomas Chandler following the Stamp Act riots that "the principal men of our Society have on every occasion, and particularly of late, strongly recommended the settlement of ecclesiastical matters and the protection of the Church of England, as the best security of duty and loyalty." The American clergy naturally played heavily upon the danger of religious dissent leading eventually to political independence. They were genuine in making such claims, but they were also aware of the need to supply information to the Society which was most likely to continue the flow of its considerable financial reserves in their direction.[1]

At its general meeting in September 1766, the Society clearly stated the purpose of its mission: "to provide Missionaries where no establishment is provided, or where the Provision for Ministers is mean, throughout the British Empire of America." Nevertheless, its proselytizing of Dissenters was plain for all to see. In its instructions to the missionaries the Society made it clear that the supply of money to America depended upon their fulfilling conscientiously their role as disseminators of Anglican culture. The notitia parochialis that the missionaries were required to submit twice each year to the Society's Secretary supplied statistics giving the total number of people in their parishes, specifying how many Dissenters, Roman Catholics, and Anglicans there were, and how many of the Churchmen were communicants or catechumens. Missionaries felt obliged to account for any period of stagnation in Church growth, while they related with pride any increase in their congregations, particularly among communicants. The Society's monthly general meetings recorded in their journals missionaries' apologies for failing to show increases in their congregations, and in the yearly Abstracts of Proceedings the Secretary lavished praise upon those missionaries whose congregations were on the increase.[2]

Proselytizing was as old as the Church in New England, but the American and English Dissenters were not the only people to resent the Society's activities there, for some of its own members were doubtful about the need to support clergy in those provinces. John Meadows, a Society member of eight years, wrote from Needham in Suffolk in 1743, asking the Secretary why the Society was so much engaged in New England when the other colonies seemed to be much more in need of assistance. The Secretary attempted to justify the Society's work referring to the large proportion of settlers in the middle and New England colonies. But twenty years later, when the Dissenters brought the matter before the public, large numbers of the Society's members refused to donate to its special collection.[3]

---

[1] Thomas Chandler to Samuel Johnson, Sept. 5, 1766, Schneider's Johnson, I, pp. 366-369.
[2] S.P.G. Journals, XVII, 110.
[3] John Meadows to Secretary, Oct. 25, 1743, Secretary to John Meadows, Nov. 6, 1743, B, XIII, part 1, 16, 17. The Society continued its assistance to King's Chapel and Christ Church in Boston, and to the wealthy churches in Rhode Island until the

Indeed, that so little had been done to reach the colonists south of the Chesapeake, or to instruct the Indians, became a real embarrassment by the end of the Seven Years War.[4] The anniversary sermons read before the Society's members each February at St. Mary-le-Bow Church were the only public declarations of the Society's aims, and judging by some of the lectures delivered it is not surprising that the Society should have wandered so far from its original purpose. If it was not sheer ignorance about America, then it was often total disregard of the American Dissenters that characterized the anniversary sermons. The lecturers very rarely showed anything like a real understanding of an Anglo-American society enmeshed in its own peculiar problems. In spite of the urbanity of Americans visiting Britain in the mid-eighteenth century, in the English mind, they were still the wild, independent and tough frontiersmen of popular imagination.[5]

During the 1750's until the conclusion of the War for Independence, the sermons defended the Society against repeated Dissenter accusations that it was neglecting its proper work of Christianizing the American Indians and Negroes. While a few bishops, like Edmund Keene, Bishop of Chester, in 1757, admitted that the Indians were the Society's primary concern, the anniversary lecturers, during the 1760's and 1770's, generally adopted the view that though the Indians were important, it was pointless trying to reach them when their immediate neighbours, the European Americans, were living in a state of religious and cultural

---

Revolution, even against the better judgement of some of its American members. On the advice of one of its corresponding members St. George Talbot, the Society did decline appointing Charles Inglis as catechist to the Negroes in New York City. Nevertheless, repeated requests from New York got the catechist's salary restored to Joseph Hildreth a few years later. Henry Caner to Secretary, April 9, 1771, B, XXII, 125a; Samuel Auchmuty to Secretary, Aug. 16, 1770, April 25, 1771, B, II, 37, 39; St. George Talbot to Secretary, July 3, 1763, B, II, 209; S.P.G. Journals, XVIII, 344; John Wolfe Lydekker, The Life and Letters of Charles Inglis (London, 1936), pp. 30-32; Archbishop Secker to Samuel Johnson, Sept. 27, 1758, Schneider's Johnson, III, pp. 256-260; S.P.G. Journals, XVI, 304.

[4] The Society did support clergy in the Carolinas and Georgia, but its attention was also focused on the royal governors and their attempts to have the Church function independently in those parishes where it was legally established.

[5] William L. Sachse, The Colonial American in Britain, (1956), p. 4.

degradation.[6]

In 1759, Anthony Ellis, the Bishop of St. David's, ignorance surpassed all others who followed him at St. Mary-le-Bow. Not only did he assume that all Americans were primitive backwoodsmen, he failed to understand that the colonists and the American Indians were different peoples. Furthermore, his failure to understand the importance of the Dissenters' churches and schools placed the entire burden of educating the colonists upon the Society's missionaries. The Bishop of Rochester John Thomas only failed to equal Anthony Ellis's ignorance by a small margin in 1780, when, after misreading the second volume of Thomas Hutchinson's History of Massachusetts Bay, he claimed that the Society had rescued the New Englanders from utter confusion following the Salem witch hunt of 1692. In 1754, the Bishop of London congratulated Samuel Johnson on his appointment as head of the Princeton Anglican College.[7]

A theme that the anniversary sermons consistently developed was the Church's role in fostering loyalty to the Crown. A few bishops continued in the mistaken belief that the Americans were in danger of being seduced into Roman Catholicism. But most of the sermonizers, as well as the Society's executive body, and the majority of the clergy in the northern provinces, assumed that the path to the colonies' independence lay in Protestant dissent. Richard Terrick, shortly before his promotion to the See of London, preached on the need to accompany the colonial administrative changes, then under consideration, with the appointment of American bishops and a more certain financial provision for the clergy. After the summer riots of 1765, he recommended to the Lords of Trade that "no clergyman should be preferr'd by the Governors in any of the

---

[6] Edmund Keene, Bishop of Chester, Anniversary Sermon, Feb. 18, 1757, (London, 1757). The anniversary lecturers wrote their addresses from information the American clergy and corresponding members sent to England; consequently, the sermons from St. Mary-le-Bow rarely offered any fresh insight into Americn society. For example, Roger Price wrote to the Society in 1740 that until the American masters were more concerned with their own souls, they would do little for their slaves, July 28, 1740, B, VII, part 2, 7.

[7] Anthony Ellis, Bishop of St. David's, Anniversary Sermon, Feb. 23, 1759 (London, 1759); John Thomas, Bishop of Rochester, Anniversary Sermon, Feb. 18, 1780 (London, 1780), pp. 16, 17; David C. Humphrey, From King's College to Columbia 1746-1800 (New York, 1976), p. 75.

Colonies, who has not given Security for a Bishop in England, that He is a Friend to the Establishment of a Protestant Church, and will Conform to its Doctrine and Discipline." This provision, he explained, was particularly important in light of recent experience "that they, who have given this Security, have shewn themselves in the late disturbances . . . the most decent and orderly in their Behaviour, and the firmest Friends of his Majesty's Government." The riots, he continued, must make it plain for all to see how urgent and necessary it was to appoint an American bishop with "a more compleat Establishment" to afford "Strength and Security" to government and religion in America. The Bishop of Worcester claimed at St. Mary-le Bow, in 1778, that the Anglican clergy and laity in America were being persecuted because, as members of the Church of England, they were assumed to be loyal to the Crown.[8]

The clergy in America had good reason to believe that their congregations were not necessarily the devoted Anglophiles the bishops appeared to believe them to be, but in their communications they concealed their suspicions. And the prelates could not know otherwise. Apart from the continually shifting parade of clergy the Society helped weather the uncertain financial support provided by the assemblies in Georgia and the Carolinas, their informants were the northern clergy, among whom those working for an American episcopate were the most vocal in their analysis of American society and the need for an established Church. It therefore became natural for them to equate Anglicanism in the colonies with loyalty to the

---

[8] Richard Terrick, Bishop of Peterborough, Anniversary Sermon, Feb. 17, 1764 (London, 1764), pp. 34, 35; Richard Terrickt to Lords of Trade, March 1, 1766, Fulham Papers, VI, 314; Brownlow North, Bishop of Worcester, Anniversary Sermon, Feb. 20, 1778. The Bishop of Worcester no doubt believed that the majority of American Anglicans were loyal; he could hardly believe otherwise when his informants were the frustrated Loyalist clergy crammed together in New York City, and those who had fled to London. Nevertheless, his lament for the American Anglicans was essential at this time because, since the Americans had taken up arms, the monetary contributions coming in to the Society had fallen so low that it had become necessary to take up special collections throughout the kingdom, with the King's blessing, in order to raise enough money to meet the Society's routine commitments. A few words from St. Mary-le-Bow could go a long way to convince the English members that their money was being used to help the "good" British Americans, instead of the rebels. General Meetings of the Society, April 16, 1779, April 30, 1779, May 21, 1779, S.P.G. Journals, XXI, 468, 481.

Crown. The prelates were well informed of the environmental problems, the ideas and traditions that the Dissenters could not shed when they conformed, but despite this knowledge, they continued in the mistaken belief that American Anglicans would remain loyal to Britain regardless of the cost. They had failed to understand that, for many Americans, the Church of England provided for a variety of needs that were often in no way concerned with their loyalty to the Crown.

Americans attracted to the Church during the Great Awakening had continued in their independent ways, dictating to their priests through the vestries and subscription lists. Many other congregations, like those at Glocester and Waterford in New Jersey, were Anglican mainly because the Society was prepared to pay their ministers, while those at Pomfret were even less concerned about theology or Anglican social philosophy than the man responsible for establishing that mission.

Godfrey Malbone had moved from his Rhode Island home to his property in Connecticut, in 1766, where he, like his father before him, continued to pay taxes to support the Congregationalist Teacher. There were only two other Church of England families in Brookline parish besides himself when the Congregationalists decided to build a new meeting house to rival that of the neighbouring parish, which Malbone described as a "Monstrous great, unformed new one and painted . . . all over with a very bright yellow." Brookline parish therefore decided their meeting house would be "a Newer, a larger, and a Yellower one" than their neighbour's. It would be financed by a tax levied on landowners. As about one-eighth of the total cost would fall on Malbone, he took to making "Proselytes" among other farmers who resented paying for a new meeting house when the old one could be repaired and enlarged. As the Congregationalists persisted in their scheme, Malbone, consumed with rage at their flippant dismissal of his objections, called upon his former Newport friends, Thomas Moffat, Joseph Harrison, John Robinson and Charles Paxton, customs commissioners in Boston and New London, to use their influence in the wealthy Boston and Newport churches to assist his scheme to build an Anglican church in Pomfret. In his letters to East Apthorpe, and to his old Oxonian companion, the Bishop of Bangor, he was quite candid about his motives for building the church at Pomfret. "I would not have you understand that I have been induced to this at present from a Religious motive only," he explained, for to mislead them would make himself as guilty of that "damnable Sin of Hypocrisy and Falsehood" as were his "Yankily" spoken Puritan opponents.[9]

His friends soon brought the matter before the Society which, clearly impressed with his endeavours on behalf of the Church, voted that "out of particular regard" to him, they would depart "from their established rule of not erecting any mission till a sufficient Glebe & House were provided" for the missionary. Even though he was averse to lay readers, without an Anglican priest, he read the sermons and conducted the services himself. At first, he held services in his home for a "modest Number of Hearers." He struggled with his congregation who, except for two or three, had never seen a Book of Common Prayer. With the help of Henry Caner at King's Chapel in Boston, he acquired the services of Richard Mosely, a Royal Navy chaplain. When the Congregationalists heard of Mosely's arrival, they visited Malbone's house to declare the Anglican minister an imposter. Godfrey Malbone was waiting for them. He presented them with his reply, which he read to them "as distinctly, emphatically and Yankily as [he] was able to do." Hearing about Malbone's victory over his opponents, the Society obliged him with a recently ordained young man, Daniel Fogg. Though Malbone, whose father had originally come from Virginia, and two other subscribers of the Pomfret church were Anglicans, all of the other fifteen subscribers were Congregationalists, whose major interest in the Church stemmed from their desire to resist their former co-religionists' attempts to squander their money.[10]

---

[9] Godfrey Malbone to Secretary, Sept. 28, 1769, Godfrey Malbone to East Apthorpe, Nov. 1, 1769, Godfrey Malbone to Charles Paxton, Nov. 13, 1769, Godfrey Malbone to Bishop of Bangor, Feb. 9, 1770, B, XXIII, 429, 430, 431, 432; GodfreyMalbone's statement written for the Committee of Brookline parish, Oct. 19, 1772, B, XXIII, 434; Vestry Minutes, Trinity Church, Brooklyn, 1771-1866, vol. I, page 1; The Literary Diary of Ezra Stiles, I, p. 94

[10] Godfrey Malbone to Secretary, May 20, 1772, B, XXIII, 435; S.P.G. Journals, XIX, 292. Anglicans who contributed to the salary of their own priest were exempted from the tax levied on inhabitants of a parish to pay the Congregationalist Teacher's salary and to maintain the meeting house.

Even genuine converts to the Church sometimes valued their special relationship with England more for the material benefits it brought them than for any philosophical attachment to the Anglican Church. However, poverty did prevent some parishes from supporting their ministers, and several missionaries made personal sacrifices on behalf of their congregations. In 1743, Addington Davenport donated his estate in Scituate, consisting of a house, barns and seven acres of land, to the Society. He had been the Society's missionary at Scituate until he resigned in 1736. That congregation's inability to provide a glebe had eventually led to the closure of the mission. Davenport's gift restored the mission which Ebenezer Thompson served until his death in 1775. During the depressed times of non-importation in the late 1760's, Samuel Andrews defended his parishioners in Wallingford, Connecticut, who, because of poverty, were unable to pay their subscriptions. In September 1769, he declined taking the rates "in these critical Days" from some of his people rather than see them go hungry. Inflation and an increasing family compelled him to request help from the Society, which added £10 sterling to his salary the following year. The St. James Church vestry in Derby, Connecticut, voted to commence an annual collection, in 1769, the interest to be used for the support of their minister, Richard Mansfield and his successors.[11]

Nevertheless, the attitude of some congregations towards the Society was too often mercenary. Many missionaries reported to the Society that without its help they could not exist, and missionaries naturally emphasized poverty in their correspondence to England. Samuel Peters, a source reputedly close to the fountain of knowledge in London, wrote to Jacob Bailey in Nova Scotia that "your Mission is to be docked next year [1786] to £40 –this hint is enough for you to improve upon in your future Letters of Complaint of Poverty." There is evidence that some congregations did not do as much as they could to provide for their priests as long as the Society would help support them. Each of the vestries at

---

[11] Addington Davenport to Secretary, June 24, 1743, B, XI, 115; Henry Caner to Secretary, June 2, 1775, Jan. 14, 1776, B, XXII, 132, 135; Samuel Andrews to Secretary, March 26, 1768, Sept. 4, 1769, Sept. 19, 1770, B, XXIII, 16, 18, 19; St. James Church, Derby, Vestry Records, vol. V, Easter, 1769.

Radnor, Chester and Lancaster in Pennsylvania at various times preferred to repair, enlarge or adorn their churches while falling short in their subscriptions to their clergymen. Other congregations that were prepared to admit to their ability to pay their priests, first tried to obtain assistance from the Society. When the Middletown vestry decided to send Abraham Jarvis to England for ordination, in March 1762, they proposed to pay him £66 per year Connecticut currency, in addition to the £20 sterling he could expect from the Society. However, they stipulated that if the Society gave more than the predicted £20, then they would deduct the difference from the amount they had agreed to pay. They did, however, pay Jarvis' travelling expenses to England for ordination. By the time he arrived in England, the Society had already decided not to open any more new missions in New England. When he returned to Middletown, the vestry voted him a salary of £70 sterling per annum. The vestry did attempt to meet their obligations to him, but by November 1767, Jarvis found it necessary to appeal to the Society to augment his income which had fallen well below what he had expected. Six years later, the Connecticut convention of clergy unsuccessfully appealed to the Society to relieve Jarvis' economic plight. Nevertheless, the Middletown vestry continued their efforts to support their minister. In April 1781, and the following year, the vestry voted to tax themselves at a higher rate in order to make up the arrears in his salary. They also paid him a fee for cleaning the church.[12]

---

[12] Vestry Book of St. James Church, Lancaster, 1744-1846: June 4, 1761, Oct. 18, 1762, Sept. 19, 1763 (Possession of the Rector); Thomas Barton to Secretary, Nov. 16, 1764, B, XXI, 14; Record Book of St. Paul's Church, Chester, 1704-1820, May 23, 1763 (Possession of the Rector); George Craig to Secretary, June 25, 1761, July 17, 1760, B, XXI, 45, 46; Vestry Minutes of St. James Church, Perkiomen of the Mission of Radnor, Nov. 12, 1764, Oct. 27, 1766, April 25, 1768 (Historical Society of Pennsylvania); Henry Pleasants, The History of Old St. David's Church at Radnor, 1715-1915 (Philadelphia, 1915), pp. 137-138; Vestry Minutes of St. David's Church, Radnor, April 22, 1765, May 16, 1769 (Photostats, Historical Society of Pensylvania); William Currie to Secretary, March 31, 1760, Sept. 29, 1763, March 27, 1771, XXI, 62, 69, 85; Records of the Church of the Holy Trinity, Middletown, Vol. B, March 29, 1762, March 21, 1763, Aug. 1, 1764, Jan 4 1779, April 16, 1781 (Photostats in Connecticut State Library); Abraham Jarvis to Secretary, Nov. 21, 1767, Jeremiah Leaming, Secretary of the Connecticut Convention of Clergy to Secretary, Sept. 26, 1773 B, XXIII, 182a, 183; S.P.G. Journals, XV, General Meeting, July 15, 1763, p. 392; Samuel Peters to Jacob Bailey, June 4, 1785, Samuel A. Peters Correspondence, (Connecticut Historical Society).

William Agar found his salary reduced, in 1766, when his church wardens at Christ Church in Cambridge, Massachusetts, learned that the Society was continuing its aid to that church. He was a little surprised at their parsimony because "all the proprietors of the Church" he wrote "are men of Fortune." He sent the Society a list of subscribers: six were "very rich," five were "esquires" while several others were prominent figures in the community. Perhaps the political and economic climate made his congregation cautious about spending their money. Agar commented to the Society that he was not surprised that clergy in England were "backward to take Missions, for the people here are of a very Capricious temper, & this Stamp Act, has made it Dangerous to preach Loyalty and Subjection." The Society allowed William Sturgeon £50 sterling per annum as its catechist to the Negroes at Christ Church in Philadelphia. The vestry deducted that amount from the salary they had promised him. In 1770, Mather Byles experienced similar treatment at Christ Church in Boston when the vestry deducted the Society's stipend from the salary they had agreed to pay him. Their decision to penalize him could have been caused by "the declining Circumstances of the Town in general" he informed the Society. However, he suggested it was more likely a reflection of "the political Principles, at present, prevailing in these Parts, which, you will know, are very unfriendly to Episcopacy & religious Establishments."[13]

It appeared that the Society's money was something Anglicans rich or poor expected as though it were a reward for listening to loyal principles that the Church emphasized so much. The wealthy town of Salem built additions to its church in 1773, and employed as assistant to missionary William McGilchrist an Oxford-educated Barbadian, Robert Nicholls at £100 sterling per year. McGilchrist hastened to urge the Society that because his congregation was poor,

---

[13] William agar to Secretary, May 1, 1766, B, XXII, 1,2; Minutes of Christ Church Vestry, Philadelphia, March 1761-April 1784, June 8, 1762; Mather Byles to Secretary, April 20, 1770, B, XXII, 79. The proprietors of Christ Church, Boston, did later agree to pay Byles the £100 sterling annually, though Henry Caner wrote to the Bishop of London that, in spite of their agreement, he suspected they would need the Society's help to meet their obligations. Thomas Ivers and Daniel Malcom, wardens of Christ Church, to Bishop of London, May 10, 1768, Henry Caner to Bishop of London, May 10, 1768, Fulham Papers, XXII, 185.

the Society should continue its assistance to Salem upon his decease. Ironically, the congregation was unable to live up to its agreement and Nicholls left for Boston a year later.[14]

When the Society's funds became scarcer as English benefactors began to take a longer look at money being spent among troublesome Americans, the American clergy also became more critical of the use of those much-needed funds. The Society resolved at its general meeting, in April 1766, that since so many congregations were failing to meet their financial obligations, each missionary should in future include with his half-yearly <u>notitia parochialis</u> an account of his congregations subscription payments, and in what manner they were paid, so that the Society could remove the missionaries' service from irresponsible congregations. When the Newport missionary Marmaduke Browne died, in March 1771, the Society received letters from Henry Caner in Boston and Samuel Auchmuty in New York, urging that support of that church was unnecessary and wasteful of the Society's funds. Auchmuty claimed that Trinity Church in Newport could comfortably support two ministers. Caner claimed that they were "apt to be sparing of their money" and were as wealthy as any Anglican congregation in New England. A third letter, anonymous, without date or place, sent the same message. Consequently, the Society's general meeting, in July 1771, resolved to discontinue its support to that church. At the same time, it adopted Myles Cooper's scheme to reduce its aid to new missions over a period of twenty years, after which they would be expected to assume full financial responsibility. No wonder the association between loyalist and Anglican often scarcely held true when many were attracted to the Church by such motives.[15]

The Anglican clergy were in a difficult position when they considered the Society's view of its mission in America. It claimed to be a body concerned only with the educational and spiritual wellbeing of Americans in need. It expressly instructed missionaries not to enter into political discussion. In 1753, the Society's directive stated that they were to take special care to give no offence to the civil government by meddling in affairs unrelated to their priestly

---

[14] William McGilchrist to Secretary, Dec. 24, 1773, May 29, 1775, B, XXII, 184, 186.
[15] Henry Caner to Secretary, April 19, 1771, B, XXII, 125a; Samuel Auchmuty to Secretary, April 25, 1771, B, II, 39; S.P.G. Journals, XVII, 59, XIX, 61, 65, 73, 224.

functions. Yet the 1756 Abstracts of Proceedings urged them to support "with the utmost care and zeal . . . his Majesty's Government." In practice, the Society's Secretary praised, the bishops preferred, and finally, the Commissioners appointed to examine the Loyalists' claims recommended to Parliament for preferential consideration clergy like Thomas Chandler who had deliberately mixed politics with religion. How to recommend submission to legal authority, and tolerance of apparently unjust Parliamentary legislation, without entering into political discussion was a quandary most clergy found themselves in. How are we to "discharge the Duties of our Office, and yet carefully to avoid taking any part in these Political Disputes?" Ebenezer Dibblee enquired in April 1775. Indeed, he spoke for most of his colleagues.[16]

After the First Continental Congress met in September 1774, the clergy's difficulties became immense. Boston's Christ Church was the most glaring example of laymen refusing to listen to their priest's pleas for patience with Parliament. After his conversion to the Church of England in 1766, Mather Byles found that Anglicans were often no more conducive to priestly authority than his former New London Congregationalists. The British-American controversy refused to die a natural death, and the majority of his congregation were determined not to keep their promise to pay his £100 sterling annual salary, claiming that as the Society was paying him £20 they were obliged to pay him only £80. This typically parochial squabble gradually assumed a political colouring, widening the wedge between Loyalist minister and the Whig members of his congregation. By the spring of 1774, he had given up hope with his native Bostonians, and had accepted an appointment to Portsmouth in New Hampshire.[17]

Loyalism certainly did not characterize the Anglican churches in Philadelphia. St. Paul's Church congregation refused to pay William Stringer's salary because of his loyalty to the Crown. When he left in 1778, they refused to pay him the £250 sterling they owed him unless he took the oath to the State. The Christ Church vestry had

---

[16] Arthur Lyon Cross, *The Anglican Episcopate and the American Colonies*, pp. 124-125; Ebenezer Dibblee to Secretary, April 5, 1775, B, XXIII, 121.
[17] Mather Byles to Secretary, April 29, 1772, Nov. 27, 1773, June 14, 1774, B, XXII, 84, 87, 89.

quite early decided in favour of resistance to Parliament. In September 1770, Jonathan Brown donated to Christ Church his £200 profit from trading in goods the Philadelphia Committee of Observation had confiscated from merchants breaking the non-importation agreement, an example several others followed. To be certain that Christ Church would support the Whigs, certain members engineered the election of several of their supporters to the vestry in 1774. Of the twenty vestrymen elected, fourteen were new members. At the first vestry meeting following the election, the old members "observing that the vestry consisted mostly of New-Members" thought it necessary to read them the laws of the church concerning payment of ministers and church funds. The new vestrymen lost no time in declaring their sentiments by voting that in future the church bells should not be rung to commemorate the restoration of Charles II. In September 1774, while the First Continental Congress was meeting in Philadelphia, the church wardens voiced their concern about persons who were not members of the church attempting to have the church bells rung on "public Occasions," presumably meaning those concerned with declarations of the Congress. The vestry, therefore, resolved that the bells should be rung only on days appointed for Church festivals, unless authorized by the Rector and wardens. At the Easter election of vestrymen, the following year, to prevent attempts to rig the vote, the number of ballots cast was compared with the list of eligible voters. They were found to match. Furthermore, in order that the result of the election was free from interference, and clear for all to see, the number of votes cast for each successful candidate was recorded in the vestry minutes. Seven of the vestrymen elected for the first time in 1774 were not re-elected, and appeared no more. After the British army left Philadelphia in June 1778, thirteen new names appeared on the vestry, presumably they had left the city with assistant minister William White when the British approached. The new vestry waived the unpaid pew rents for those "many of the Members of the Congregation who were absent during the time that the British army were in possession of the City." With the former Rector Jacob Duché having left for England, and Thomas Coombe also on his way there, the vestry unanimously elected William

White Rector on April 15, 1779.[18]

The political divisions in New York followed a similar pattern to those in Philadelphia. With the impending British evacuation of the City of New York in 1783, Charles Inglis, already under attainder and his property confiscated, resigned as Rector of Trinity Church. The Loyalist vestry appointed Benjamin Moore, who had been assistant minister at Trinity Church since February 1775. However, when the Whig Episcopalians returned, they cleaned the Tories out; Moore and his vestry were dismissed; Samuel Provost was installed as Rector with a completely new vestry. Many of those voting in the new order were strangers to Trinity Church. It was indeed a poignant moment for Samuel Provost when he accepted his Revolutionary friends' appointment, for he had spent the previous thirteen years virtually estranged from the Church of England.[19]

After graduating from Cambridge University in 1766, and after taking holy orders, Samuel Provost returned to New York to assist Samuel Auchmuty, John Ogilvie and Charles Inglis at Trinity Church. In the early years of the dispute with Britain over taxation, he clearly favoured submission to Parliament. He preached a sermon at Trinity Church and St. George's Chapel, on October 25 1767, and on his copy he wrote "King's accession." It was probably written for that occasion, and he appears not to have preached it at any other time. He entreated his congregation to heed "that great Duty of obedience to superiors whether kings or all that are put in Authority under them . . . now that we are commemorating a juncture of Time that I cannot but think it proper to enforce it upon your minds and Memories." Legal opposition, he said, is healthy in a free government, but opposition "from Indirect motives to measures which we see to be necessary, is itself immoral." In February and May 1768, at Trinity Church and the two chapels, he preached that a person who has good principles and virtue will "be loyal to his Prince, and true to his country." In June the same year,

---

[18] William Stringer's Memorial, Loyalist Claims, L, p.6; Vestry Minutes, Christ Church, Philadelphia, Sept. 10, 1770, April 14, 1774, April 11, 1774, July 12, 1774, Sept. 10, 1774, April 17, 1775, April 5, 1779, Oct. 22, 1778, Dec. 9, 1777, July 7, 1778, April 15, 1779.

[19] Trinity Church New York, Vestry Minutes, Nov. 1, 1783, Jan. 3, 1775, Feb. 7, 1775, Feb. 10, 1775, April 17, 1784, April 21, 1784, April 22, 1784; Morgan Dix, ed., A History of the Parish of Trinity Church, II, p. 14.

he preached a very strong sermon at Trinity Church and the two chapels on the duty of obedience to George III. Should a subject acknowledge his sovereign's rule, "yet withold his Obedience from him, and refuse to make the Due returns for Protection," he stated, would be unreasonable. Should a subject expect "profit or honor as a just reward of this [?] acknowledgement and empty declarations . . . but engaged in rebellion against" his king, then he is guilty.[20]

Perhaps Samuel Provost's political sentiments were not to the liking of some members of the congregation. His style of preaching certainly was not. There was a core of the congregation who had been afflicted by George Whitefield, and Provost was no evangelist. It appears that they had opposed his appointment in 1766, and they were the object of a very fiery sermon he delivered at Trinity Church in 1769. Taking as his text Psalm 140:3, "They have Sharpened their Tongues like a Serpent; adders poison is under their Lips," he launched into a carefully constructed denunciation of those who "pry into the Character of others – to discern their faults and infirmities." He continued "Let me tell you it is a Vice of the very blackest and most infernal Kind." Identifying his accusers more specifically, he continued "whatever Enthusiastick notions some may have embraced" such behaviour was contrary to the true doctrine.[21]

Provost's reference in his sermon to those who should "order themselves lowly and reverently to all their Betters" suggests that they were those whom Samuel Auchmuty called the "lower sort." However, they were not the only group he had upset. Even though his politics were in line with those of his clerical colleagues, they appear to have forsaken him, for there is no evidence that they came to his defence. In February 1769, he informed the vestry that he planned to visit England in May the following year. In response, the vestry "unanimously resolved" not to pay his salary in his absence. Trinity Church parishioners were feeling the pinch of the trade depression, aggravated by the cost of building a rectory and

---

[20] William Berrian, An Historical Sketch of Trinity Church, New York(New York, 1847), pp. 197-200; Trinity Church Vestry Minutes, Dec. 23, 1766; MSS Sermon, Matt. 6: 22-23, MSS Sermon, 1 Tim. 2: 1-2, MSS Sermon, James 2: 19 (MSS, Possession of the Rector);
[21] MSS Sermon, Psalm 140:3 (Possession of the Rector).

reconstructing the charity school house. Nevertheless, the tone of the vestry's resolution to discontinue his salary in October 1769, eight months after his announcement that he was going to England, makes it clear that economy was not the sole motive for their treatment of him. They voted unanimously that "if he [Provost] is continued that he be paid by an Annual Subscription only." Clearly, they wanted him out.[22]

Samuel Provost went to England and Ireland as he had planned, and when he returned to New York, he resigned from Trinity Church. He had to struggle to obtain his salary, which was two years in arrears. Those people who had agreed to subscribe to his support, declared that if they did pay what they had promised, they would reduce their support to Inglis and Ogilvie. While he was in England, or soon after his return to America, Provost's political views had changed. He was possibly disillusioned, as many Americans were, when confronted with English ignorance, arrogance and possessiveness towards the colonies. A letter he wrote to his brother, in 1775, testifies to his total conversion to the Whig cause.[23]

Loyalist clergy often found themselves before committees of public safety chaired by their own vestrymen. Alexander Murray was cross-examined by his vestrymen Edward Biddle and James Whitehead at Reading, while several others of his vestrymen held positions on revolutionary committees. Samuel Cooke came face to face with Josiah Hardy in New Jersey. In some congregations the Revolutionaries were only a minority, especially, it seems in Connecticut, but there too, some clergy, like James Nicholls, lost the majority of their congregations. But none were as hostile to their ministers as were the New London vestry towards Matthew Graves. Many of William Currie's congregation were Whigs. Anthony Wayne headed the Chester County committee of safety with vestryman Patrick Anderson. Laymen in other congregations almost to a man deserted their priests. Alexander Murray could number very few of the Reading parish on his side. The York Town laymen

---

[22] Minutes of Trinity Church Vestry, Feb. 22, 1769, March 25, 1768, Oct. 26, 1769, Nov. 6, 1769, Dec. 15, 1769.
[23] Trinity Church Vestry Minutes, May 27, 1771; Morgan Dix, ed., A History of the Parish of Trinity Church, II, p. 43.

in Daniel Batwell's parish requested that the notorious Tory Anglican Dr. John Kearsley, who had been arrested in Philadelphia on the same day as Jonathan Odell, be transferred from their jail because they considered his presence there an insult. When Kearsley died in the Carlisle jail towards the end of October 1775, the Anglicans were disgusted that he should be buried in their graveyard, and many declared that they would never again set foot in the church.[24]

Considering the independence that characterized the American Anglicans it is easy to understand why they should generally have shown little interest in the clergy's petitions for resident bishops, since such an appointment would have brought them under more direct English control. There were a few laymen who expressed an interest in resident bishops, but they were people who felt that the Society was not being properly informed about what was best for the American Church. The Dissenters were not far from the mark with their claims during the 1760's and 1770's that the Anglicans were opposed to the clergy's petitions for bishops.[25]

The Dissenters got hold of a copy of one of the petitions which the Shrewsbury convention sent to England, in October 1765, and passed it on to members of the congregation at Trinity Church in New York. They were considerably "stir'd up" and only after tedious explanation did Samuel Auchmuty convince "the better sort" of the need for such an appointment. He presumably failed to

---

[24] William Duhamel, ed., Historical Annals of Christ Church, Reading (Douglasville, Pennsylvania, 1927), pp. 10, 18, 19; Henry May Keim, "The Episcopal Church in Reading, Pennsylvania," The Pennsylvania Magazine of History and Biography, vol. IV, 1880; Samuel Cooke to Secretary, May 20, 1780, B, XXIV, 120; Memorial of Samuel Cooke, Loyalist Claims, XXXIX, p. 103; Harold Donald Eberlein and Cortlandt Van Dyke Hubbard, The Church of Saint Peters in the Great Valley, 1700-1940. The Story of a Colonial County Parish in Pennsylvania (Richmond, Virginia, 1944), pp. 78-79; James Steen, History of Christ Church (Privately Printed, 1903), p. 59; Vestry Minutes of Christ Church, Shrewsbury, New Jersey, April 2, 1771 through the Revolutionary Era; Samuel Peters to Secretary, Dec. 7, 1779, Peters Papers I, 42; Minutes of the Pennsylvania Provincial Council, X, 378, 773; Christopher Marshall's Diary, p. 144.

[25] None of the vestry records examined made any reference to the proposed episcopate. For laymen who did express interest in American bishops, see; Charles Ridgely to Secretary, Dec. 1, 1766, B, XXI, 150; Elihu Hall to Secretary, Oct. 2, 1764, B, XXIII, 415; John Ross to Secretary, July 6, 1771, B, XXI, 239; Henry Barnes to Bishop of London, Sept. 25, 1769, Fulham Papers, VI, 72.

reach those members he invariably termed "the lower sort." Samuel Johnson intimated to Archbishop Secker soon after the Shrewsbury convention that there some "Free Thinkers" among the laity north of Philadelphia who did not want bishops, and he could only claim that most of the Pennsylvania laity favoured the scheme - - a significant admission of dissent. Significant also was Samuel Auchmuty's choice of subject for his first sermon after his induction as Rector of Trinity Church - - the scriptural authority for bishops, and their important role in curbing false doctrines.[26]

Nevertheless, the general moderation the majority of the clergy and many laymen showed during the opposition to Parliament was sufficient to associate the Church with Toryism in the minds of the Whigs. Ezra Stiles, commenting upon Samuel Peter's departure for England in 1774, noted in his journal that Peters' "venomous" opposition to the Congregationalists and Whigs was typical of nine-tenths of Anglicans north of the Delaware to Nova Scotia. This association was further strengthened by a number of people who joined the Church during the troubled times of opposition to Parliament. Mather Byles left the Connecticut Congregationalists in the 1760's, and in his adopted role of Anglican priest, he spoke out against the opposition to the Stamp Act. Isaac Hunt left the Philadelphia legal profession for the Church in 1775. He had published a pamphlet in favour of the colonies' membership of the British Empire, following his defence of a client against the Philadelphia Committee of Observation. Ezra Stiles was shrewd to see that the Newport Tories in Rhode Island were associated with Godfrey Malbone's challenge to the Congregationalists in Pomfret. If the Whigs were inclined to dub Anglicans as Tories, they received ample assistance from Thomas Chandler who deliberately arranged for some of his writings on behalf of the American Church of England to be printed in London in 1774 "imagining it might be of service at that Critical Time, when a Plan was under Consideration for the future Regulation of the Colonies."[27]

---

[26] Samuel Auchmuty to Samuel Johnson, April 30, 1766, Hawks Papers, Johnson MSS, 8; Samuel Johnson to Archbishop, Oct. 17, 1766, Hawks Papers, Johnson MSS, [55]; Samuel Auchmuty, MSS Sermon, Cor. 2:4-5 (Possession of the Rector).

[27] Thomas Chandler to William Johnson, June 20, 1774, William Samuel Johnson Correspondence; Literary Diary of Ezra Stiles, I, 94, 466; Thomas Chandler to Bishop of London, Jan. 18, 1777, Fulham Papers, XXII, 15a; copy of letter from

There was a tendency for Tory Dissenters to join the Church of England as their political leanings in the 1760's and 1770's led to personal animosity towards them. Reports to the Society that the Anglicans' orderly conduct during the 1765 and subsequent political disturbances had won large numbers of converts to the Church, probably meant that Dissenters who were out of sympathy with the tone of colonial confrontation changed their religious affiliation. Samuel Peters had reported such acquisitions in 1767, and in 1771 he expected Hebron's leading citizen Alexander Phelps to conform to the Church as his moderate politics sent the "Puritans" in search of a new leader. The Loyalists in Halifax certainly lost no time in anointing Loyalist Dissenters honorary Churchmen. John Breynton reported large numbers of Dissenters attending St. Paul's Church soon after the first influx of refugees into Halifax in 1776, and the following year many were taking communion. When William Ellis arrived in Nova Scotia from England, in 1775, he found the "Lower order of people" were nearly all "Presbyterian or Fanatics." Two years later, he wrote "I suppose it is well known at home, that the Fanatics are Rebells to a man," but the Church was winning them over "and in the Same proportion, his Majesty acquires good Subjects." Jacob Bailey "could not recollect a single friend to government among the independents for the moment any person renounces his rebellious principles he commences either churchman or quaker."[28]

Anglicans who had frequently been reluctant to pay their priests found payment out of the question once the political issue intervened in parochial affairs. Many clergy had put up with their congregations' shabby performance in meeting their monetary obligations, but in the 1770's the subscription list became a tool with which the Whig members could lever their Tory priests. Samuel

---

[Philadelphia Clergy] to Bishop of London,; Oct. 2, 1775, Hawks Papers, William Smith MSS, 46; Christopher Marshall's Diary, pp. 40-41; Statement concerning Isaac Hunt and Committee of Inspection and Observation, David McNeely Stauffer Collections, VI, p. 493 (Historical Society of Pennsylvania); Memorial of Isaac Hunt, Loyalist Claims, LI, p. 20.

[28] Samuel Peters to Secretary, March 25, 1767, June 26, 1771, B, XXIII, 328, 333; John Breynton to Secretary, Jan.2, 1776, Jan. 13, 1777, B, XXV, 202, 212; William Ellis to Secretary, Sept. 14, 1776, Aug. 30, 1777, B, XXV, 208, 217; Jacob Bailey to secretary, July 26, 1779,B, XXV, 228.

Peters made no reference to his congregation's failure to pay until 1771, the year he expected Colonel Phelps to conform to the Church. He not only complained that the congregation were remiss, he also requested the Society to remove him to another mission. Similarly, William Clark found that as his parishioners in Massachusetts took sides in the dispute he depended more and more upon the Society's stipend. On April 7, 1775, he wrote that "in these troublesome and Distracted Times—Several [parishioners] have w'drawn on acc't of what is called the Toryism of the Church of England." And in a moment of unwitting prescience he continued that unless they can learn that their future "happiness is Connected with a subjection to King and Parliament of Great Britain" they face "the Horrors of Civil War!"[29]

The political disputes also had an unexpected affect upon some of the clergy. Scotsmen George Craig and Alexander Murray, during the 1760's, repeatedly accused their congregations of being no different from the Dissenters in their lack of respect for clerical authority, or, as the Delaware missionary, New Yorker Samuel Tingley, would have it, "Churchmen by profession, but Presbyterians by Trade." Craig's correspondence to London reeked with criticism of his mean Chester parish, which, sixty years after its founding, had still not provided "so much as a stable for their missionary's horse." However, from 1769 until the outbreak of war, his parishioners became "poor," rather than "mean," shining examples of loyal, peaceable subjects, whose numbers would have been greater had the Church been established in all the colonies. His change of heart coincided with the publication of Thomas Chandler's first pamphlet on behalf of the American episcopate. Although almost every letter George Craig wrote to the Society was a lesson on the dire need for American bishops, it should have occurred to him that his own descriptions of America's Anglican laymen contradicted the claims Chandler was making.[30]

Murray also approved wholeheartedly of Chandler's insistence that the Church of England made for loyal subjects, but a different

---

[29] Samuel Peters to Secretary, June 26, 1771, B, XXIII, 333; William Clark to Secretary, Feb. 3, 1774, April 15, 1774, April 7, 1775, B, XXII, 145, 147, 149.
[30] George Craig to Secretary, July 17, 1760, Nov. 10, 1769, Sept. 12, 1770, Aug. 16, 1775, B, XXI, 46, 54, 55, 58; Samuel Tingley to Secretary, March 5, 1782, B, XXI, 186.

motive influenced his change of mind regarding his congregations. He had been so dissatisfied with their failure to provide for his support that he applied for a transfer to the Indian mission on the Mohawk River, in 1767, but when the Society gave its approval, he withdrew his application. Soon, his tight-fisted, quarrelsome Pennsylvanians became an island of peaceful, orderly subjects in a sea of rebellious Dissenters. His change of mind was made possible by his marriage to John Ross's sister, a lady of independent means. Murray had finally achieved the financial independence of his congregations he had wanted since he first arrived in Reading.[31]

For years the correspondence from the American clergy had been hedged with doubts about the role of the Church as propagator of loyal principles, as long as it was left to flounder without bishops and political favour. The prelates were also well informed of the attraction Methodism held for many of the laity and clergy in Philadelphia; yet they continued to assume that all the American clergy would necessarily toe the line Parliament dictated, totally disregarding the diverse social and ecclesiastical backgrounds from which they were drawn. As long as the English Churchmen looked upon Americans as Colonial Englishmen, they were not able to understand that the path many of the clergy would take, if rebellion broke out, could have been predicted in the mid-1760's.

Those clergy who had been vocal in their bid to win the episcopate for the American colonies, and who were later active in opposing Congress, were driven into exile or behind British lines in New York. As the War continued, seventy seven clergy were to suffer for their loyalty. A few, like Thomas Coombe and William Stringer in Philadelphia, at first appear to have temporized, finally to refuse the oath of allegiance to the independent State. Others attempted to continue their pastoral duties without making themselves targets of "Patriot" persecution. Nevertheless, of the seventy seven clergy whose loyalism cannot be questioned, twenty were forced into New York City; twelve went to England; seven moved into the British-held provinces of Upper Canada and the

---

[31] Memorial of Alexander Murray, Loyalist Claims, L, 137; Richard Peters to Sir William Johnson, Dec. 7, 1768, Sir William Johnson papers; Alexander Murray to Secretary, [1767], Sept. 25, 1768, March 26, 1772, B, XXI, 105, 106, 108; S.P.G. Journals, XVII, 475.

Maritime Provinces. Thirty eight clergy managed to remain in their missions, though many suffered physical persecution and confinement.

Thirty one of these Loyalists were birthright Anglicans, twenty one of them were from Britain or Ireland. Clergy who converted from the Congregationalist Church numbered thirty; fourteen were from Connecticut, eleven were from Massachusetts. If we leave aside immigrant Anglican clergy, then clergy converted from the Congregationalists provided a substantial proportion of Loyalists.

The fare these Loyalists met differed considerably. For an Englishman like Matthew Graves, who had never accepted the colonists' right to be Americans instead of expatriate Englishmen like himself, life could be difficult. His determination to balance American clergy with immigrants from Britain, and his insistence that the first resident bishop should be an Englishman, set him apart from his colleagues. When the Connecticut Assembly finally allowed the Anglicans to collect the taxes levied upon them for the support of religious worship, Graves objected. He preferred to receive the money from the Congregationalist tax collector than from his own parishioners, fearing that his congregations might hold even more power over him than before. No wonder he was one of the three Anglican clergymen forced out of Connecticut. Perhaps his obstinacy and fastidiousness compelled a sneaking regard from his equally obstinate, fastidious Yankee parishioners, and possibly that is why he stayed so long in New London.[32]

His brother John, did little better in Rhode Island. Having refused to change the liturgy, his congregation at Providence suspended him, turned him and his wife and seven children out of the parsonage, and when the War ended, refused to have him back. Possibly Alexander Murray's alienation from his parishioners accounts for the rough manner in which his enemies handled him and his property, while Thomas Barton's long residence and deep involvement in local affairs allowed him to escape serious personal abuse.[33]

---

[32] Samuel Johnson to Secretary, Oct. 15, 1750, B, XVIII, 61; Matthew Graves to Bishop of London, July 20, 1750, Fulham Papers, I, 288.

[33] John Graves to Secretary, Feb. 12, 1782, S.P.G. Journals, XXII, 451; Samuel Parker to Secretary, Jan. 10, 1786, S.P.G. Journals, XXIV, 277; Samuel Parker to Secretary,

Barton had provided leadership for his York and Carlisle parishioners during the Indian uprising in 1755, and he then became chaplain to a local regiment on an expedition to the Ohio three years later, where he met Harry Munroe who was chaplain to a Scottish regiment. After his removal to Lancaster, he again assumed leadership of that community in demanding military protection for the frontiersmen against the Indians. He remained on very close friendly terms with his vestryman James Burd, who was commanding a Lancaster County battalion, exchanging hints on farming techniques, even after he had closed his church in 1776. For some, however, Barton's connection with the Society, and the alleged Toryism of many of his congregation was sufficient evidence to consider him an enemy to the State. Consequently, he was confined to his house until his refusal to abjure the King in 1778. His chaplaincy of a Loyalist regiment later in New York City gave the Whigs what they considered conclusive proof that they had judged him correctly[34]

Barton's Tory reputation spread like a mantle over all he associated with, including his brother-in-law Paul Zantinger. However, his son William had spent some time studying law in London during 1775-1776, and he returned to America "weaned of all fond attachment to that corrupted Country," as the Vice President of Pennsylvania George Bryan noted. Thus cleared of Tory sympathies, William was allowed to arrange a meeting with his father in Elizabeth Town, in 1780.[35]

Barton's refusal to support the Revolutionaries looked like betrayal to his former friends rather than defence of principle. The people at York and Carlisle felt the same way about Daniel Batwell who had gained their confidence when he proclaimed against Parliament from his pulpit. Unlike Barton, he had arrived from England only three years before and had not acquired a colourful

---

Jan. 1, May 10, 1783, S.P.G. Journals XXIII, 109; Samuel Parker to Secretary, June 3, 1783, S.P.G. Journals, XXIII, 172.

[34] Minutes of the Pennsylvania Supreme Executive Council, May 21, 1779-July 21, 1781, XII, 256,317; Thomas Barton to Colonel Burd, Sept. 12, 1776, Shippen Papers, VII, 209; Thomas Barton's MSS Journal of the Expedition to the Ohio . . .1758 (Historical Society of Pennsylvania).

[35] George Bryan to General Washington, March 5, 1779, Pennsylvania Archives, series I, VII, p.225 (Library of Congress).

reputation to defend him from physical abuse.

Released from prison, the weary, half-frozen Batwell, with his few remaining possessions in an old waggon crossed the ice-bound Susquehanna River to Lancaster where he called upon Thomas Barton. Six days later, he arrived at Radnor to find William Currie unmolested, though typhoid fever had claimed his wife, and an American general and his staff had taken his house. In May 1776, when Currie could no longer pray for the King, he discontinued Church services, contenting himself with performing baptisms and marriages. The vestry records substantiate his complaints to the Society that his vestries paid for church repairs, extensions, and a new vestry house, while neglecting to pay their part of his support. The congregations' neglecting to meet their obligations to him might have been their way of replying to their priest's strictly loyal principles. It was more likely another example of American Anglicans accepting a missionary for the value of the Society's stipend.[36]

William Currie refused to accept a penny for his services during the War years for he had declared on the day he heard of Independence he would never take money from any of his parishioners who had sworn allegiance to the rebel republic. He lived on his stipend from London, which he supplemented by selling some of his land. His congregations made no reply to his letters of resignation in 1776, apart from the Perkiomen vestry's comment scribbled on the bottom of his letter: "Let this be pinned in ye Vestry Book." However, they did continue a form of service with the assistance of a young man preparing for German Lutheran ordination. For his services they did pay. After forty years as their missionary, and sixty seven years residence among them, none of the vestries recorded any reference to the death of their ninety eight-year-old priest, in 1803, but he did have the last laugh. Of his three congregations, St. David's at Radnor appears to have appreciated his services the least, and to them he left £10 in his will to repair the

---

[36] Charles Inglis to Secretary, Oct. 24, 1778, Daniel Batwell to Secretary, March 25, 1778, July 18, 1778, S.P.G. Journals, XXI, 394,312, 363; Daniel Roberdean and William Clingan to President Wharton, Nov. 13, 1777, Pennsylvania Archives, Series I, vol. III, p. 770.

wall around their graveyard in which he requested they bury him.[37]

Three of William Currie's sons by his first wife, who joined the American army, and his second wife, the widow of one of his influential parishioners, might have made it possible for this old and infirm man to remain in Pennsylvania along with his neighbour and fellow Scotsman George Craig. Craig had also closed his churches in 1776, and remained in his parish until he died, in 1784. His parish was certainly divided over politics. One of his vestrymen John Morton signed the Declaration of Independence, and was buried in the St. Paul's Church graveyard in Chester. The sketchiness of St. Paul's vestry minutes appears to bear out Craig's complaints to the Society about his congregations' indifference to religion. The absence of any records of vestry meetings for 1774, 1775 and 1776, was followed by an unusual meeting on May 27, 1777, probably prompted by the imminent British advance upon Philadelphia, only fifteen miles away. That meeting of the "principle members" of St. Paul's Church, which Craig had called at the home of vestryman James Mather, suggests that the Revolutionary and Loyalist factions had been engaged in a struggle for control of the church. By 1782, George Craig had vacated the parsonage in Chester, and he was finally buried in a remote part of his mission.[38]

Enemies of this fiery Scotsman would have been hard put to drive him out of Pennsylvania, even if he had not married the widow of William Currie's son, the surgeon who had joined the American army. Craig's view of America remained unchanged until

---

[37] William Currie to Secretary, April 30, 1783, March 28, 1784, S.P.G. Journals, XXIII, 135, 345; William Currie to Secretary, Oct. 12, 1785, S.P.G. Journals, XXIV, 253; Vestry Minutes of St. David's Church, Radnor, April 22, 1765, March 27, 1765, May 16, 1769, Nov. 23, 1767, Nov. 17, 1788; Vestry Minutes of St. James Church, Perkiomen, Nov. 12, 1764, Oct. 27, 1766; Letter from William Currie to Vestry, dated May 20, 1776; Vestry Records of St. Peter's Church, Great Valley, Dec. 20, 1773; Chester County Wills and Administration Pennsylvania Abstracts, vol. IV, 1801-1825, William Currie's will, dated Dec. 28, 1794--Nov. 4, 1803; Penn—Physick MSS 1770—1796, Agreement between William Currie and William Godfrey for sale of land, March 14, 1777.

[38] George Craig to Secretary, Aug. 26, 1780, S.P.G. Journals, XXII, 202; Vestry Minutes, St. Paul's Church, Chester, May 27, 1777, April 1, 1782; Unnamed notes with St. Paul's Church Record Books; Harold Donaldson Eberlein and Cortlandt Van Dyke Hubbard, The Church of Saint Peter in the Great Valley, 1700-1940 (Richmond, Virginia, 1944), pp. 65, 81.

the end. His will provided only £250 for his wife in lieu of her dowry. His property in Philadelphia and Lancaster was sold to provide for his son's education in Scotland. Should the boy refuse to go to Scotland, or should his mother object to his going, then the will stipulated that he should receive only half the proceeds from the sale of the land. The remainder should go to a Scottish Episcopalian charity.[39]

William McGilchrist was the only Loyalist priest who was not driven out of Massachusetts, though most of his congregation deserted him when he refused to change the liturgy. The church windows donated by William Pynchon, vestryman and Loyalist, were broken on Christmas day in 1776, and the following Sunday, as McGilchrist approached the church, his enemies greeted him with prayers that he might drop dead as he entered the pulpit. Soon after, an act of the General Court compelled him to stop preaching. A month later, illness confined him to his home until he died in April 1780. On the day of his funeral the church was full of people, perhaps some were rejoicing at his death, but many were serious mourners - - some of whom had faithfully delivered their subscription payments throughout his illness. In his will he left his books and three years unclaimed salary to the Society as a gesture of appreciation for their unfailing support during his thirty four years of service.[40]

Parochial and personal conflicts exacerbated some clergy's problems. Jacob Bailey needed no lessons in drubbing the Dissenters, but from his arrival on the Kennebec River he had faced a situation not of his own making. Sylvester Gardiner, one of the settlement's leading proprietors, had induced the Society to support a missionary there, in spite of the Dissenter's demands that they should have a minister of their own choice. This explains much of Bailey's later trouble, which finally forced him to Nova Scotia. The

---

[39] William Currie to Secretary, July 1, 1784, S.P.G. Journals, XXIV, 71; Chester County Wills and Administration Pennsylvania Abstracts, vol. III, 1777-1800, George Craig's will, dated June 17, 1782- Feb. 27, 1784.
[40] William Pynchon, Diary, pp. 21, 22, 24, 60; The Diaries of Benjamin Lynde and of Benjamin Lynde, Jr. (Boston, 1880), p. 208; William McGilchrist to Secretary, Aug. 20, 1776, March 26, 1777, B, XXII, 189, S.P.G. Journals, XXI, 264; Dr. Edward Holyoke to Secretary, May 12, 1780, S.P.G. Journals, XXII, General Meeting, Oct. 20, 1780.

mission at Deadham and Stoughton had been established specifically to secure land donated to the Church in a Congregationalist community, a circumstance that left William Clark isolated when the Whigs, among whom he named members of his own congregation, began to persecute him.

Both Richard Mansfield and Samuel Cooke claimed that the Revolutionary members of their congregations were led by vestrymen who had come off second best in power struggles to dictate church affairs. These two missionaries would have become Loyalists anyhow, but they were probably pushed into a more extreme position by the personal animosities that arose from parochial disputes. Both ran foul of leading parishioners over the building of new churches. Mansfield named Captain John Holbrook, who developed a grudge "merely because [the minister and vestry] did not gratify some private views he had about the Place on which to build Oxford Church."[41]

Cooke named vestryman Josiah Holmes, a judge of Monmouth County, New Jersey. He had long ago left the Quakers to become one of the original Anglican proprietors who had built Christ Church directly across the road from the Friends' meeting house. Cooke challenged Holmes' leadership when the vestry decided to rebuild the church. Finally, after calling in Jonathan Odell from Burlington to arbitrate, Cooke and his supporters won their point, and the church was planned and the rebuilding was supervised by a committee they appointed. Holmes was appointed a member of the building committee, but, "not approving of the Method concluded in full the building of the church and for divers other Reasons" he had his name struck off both the committee and vestry, in 1769. He did, however, return to the vestry in 1771, and he served annually until 1784, long after Cooke had accepted his fate in exile. Cooke later recalled that the dispute over rebuilding the church was only a manifestation of Holmes' discomfort after being removed from the bench of magistrates by Governor Franklin, in 1770, for his part in closing the law courts.[42]

---

[41] Richard Mansfield to Secretary, Dec. 29, 1775, B, XXIII, 278.
[42] Vestry Minutes, Christ Church, Shrewsbury, May 5, 1767, Jan. 27, 1769, Easter, 1769, April, 2, 1771; Samuel Cooke to Secretary, May 20, 1780, B, XXIV, 120; Abraham Beach to Secretary, Oct. 1, 1782, B, XXIV, 311.

In July 1774, Holmes called a meeting of Monmouth County freeholders at the inn of Christ Church vestryman Josiah Halstead, and had himself elected to the New Jersey convention. The following January, Cooke succeeded in packing a meeting with Tories at Halstead's inn to prevent Holmes from having a committee of observation elected. But Holmes finally got the committee elected by calling another meeting at another inn, which he took care to load with his own supporters. Revenge came when Samuel Cooke left for England on private business, in 1775. The State Legislature proscribed Cooke with some of his congregation, and Holmes evicted the Tory's family from the Christ Church parsonage and occupied it himself.[43]

Such Tory Loyalists as these held a highly structured view of society. For them, society was cemented by divine decree. Just as the family was divinely instituted, so was kingship. That these men were Anglican priests was no accident. The appeal of episcopal rule was very real to them because it was the bulwark against emotional individualism; both royal and episcopal government meant authorized doctrine. The more these Tories saw of American society, especially after the Seven Years War, the more they were convinced that America's social cement was crumbling in the American crucible. John Locke's state of nature was hostile to them, they looked upon Society as God's refinement of nature, for in a state of nature passion ruled; the strong abused the weak. In society, mankind conducted himself with dignity, he was courteous to towards his neighbour; justice prevailed.[44]

Pennsylvania and Delaware presented the most uncertain Loyalists. Many of them did not at first deny the colonists' right to remodel society. Jacob Duché, William White and Thomas Coombe had been raised in the Church of England in Philadelphia where religious contention had been less evident than in the provinces to the north. The Quakers had proved more tolerant of dissent than the New Englanders, and the proprietors, while often favouring the

---

[43] James Steen, <u>History of Christ Church</u> (privately printed, 1903), pp. 59-67.
[44] Examples of this view are found in: William Frazer to Secretary, Jan. 4, 1780, Thomas Barton to Secretary, Dec. 17, 1770, George Craig to Secretary, June 25, 1762, B, XXIV, 247, B, XXI, 21, 52. The best discussion is found in Charles Inglis, <u>The True Interest of America Impartially Stated</u> (Philadelphia, 1776).

Church with bequests, since the they themselves in the eighteenth century were Anglicans, gave equal consideration to all religious denominations. The disputes between the Anti Proprietary Part and the Proprietary Party tended to array Churchman with Quaker against Presbyterian, but this division was by no means clear, for William Smith supported the Presbyterian party, while Benjamin Franklin, member of Christ Church, supported the Anti-Proprietary Party. Therefore, the Philadelphia Anglicans, unlike those of Congregationalist origin to the north, did not see the Church of England and its supposed social doctrines as the only possible future for America.

Consequently, from Philadelphia came three clergymen who, after supporting resistance to Parliament, finally refused to abjure the King, and left for England. Thomas Coombe and William Stringer chose exile when the British forces evacuated Philadelphia. Jacob Duché left for England during the British occupation of the city. William Smith, always an adept at political tight-rope walking, after weathering the British occupation, and then the American re-occupation, found himself estranged from both sides and removed to a Maryland parish.

It is little wonder that William Stringer should have become a belated Loyalist, because his association with Methodism was a reaction to the Church in England rather than a compromise with American society. Thomas Coombe had been perfectly at home in London during his preparation for ordination, and his subsequent career in England is almost unique among the Loyalists. His wife died in childbirth not long after he left America, and when his son was finally allowed to join him in England, he built up an exclusively English circle of friends, steering clear of the disgruntled Loyalist cliques in London. Jacob Duché conducted the ceremony when Thomas Coombe later married an English widow, whose family he had known during his earlier stay in London. At that time, he had waited for his twenty fourth birthday before receiving ordination so that he might one day take a living in England. His decision was wise. Soon after leaving America, in September 1778, he was officiating at two chapels in London. In 1781, in spite of his earlier criticism of noble patronage, curacies and pluralism, he became Lord Carlisle's junior chaplain in Ireland, "a sure step to a decent provision," he explained. Soon, he was Secretary to the Lord Lieutenant, with a living in Tyrone County, while keeping his chaplaincy. His income was further supplemented by his wife's dowry of £40 sterling per annum and his £200 sterling annual Loyalist pension. Living in Dublin Castle was quite a step up for the man from Philadelphia, now created Doctor of Divinity by the University of Dublin. There is little wonder that he had "no decided objection even to the fogs of November."[45]

The generous Quaker Samuel Shoemaker was called upon to give evidence in support of Jacob Duchés claim before the Loyalist Commission in London. He could only say that he preferred to look upon Duché's behaviour from "the most charitable point of view." But his description of the house Duché owned in Philadelphia more likely reflected his opinion of the turncoat priest's character. Shoemaker knew Duché and his house very well, he explained to the Commissioners. "It was a very good house it makes a great shew, but it was very shallow, and consequently not a reliable structure."[46]

The Church had also developed in a relatively free environment in Delaware. Aeneas Ross had succeeded his father as Rector of Immanuel Church in New Castle, and he appears to have lined his coat with Whig colours. Samuel Magaw had failed to satisfy the New Side element's questions about the work of grace in his soul when he applied to the Philadlephia Presbyterian Synod after graduating from William Smith's class at the College of Philadelphia in 1760. He had been attracted to the Church more by its dignified service than to the social and political tenets that appealed to the High Churchmen to the north, and he found solace in the Methodist doctrine of the itinerant Francis Asbury, whose open air meetings catered for all who would come to listen. Hugh Neill, also originally a Presbyterian, and Rector of a Maryland parish neighbouring that of Magaw, joined with Asbury in his meetings, along with the Virginian Sydenham Thorne who had taken part of Magaw's

---

[45] Thomas Coombe to his father, April 5, 1780, Jan. 29, 1781, May 22, 1781, Jan. 27, 1782, April 29, 1783, Jan. 19, 1785, July 28, 1790, July 17, 1798, Thomas Coombe Papers : Correspondence and Business, 1765-1803; Memorial of Thomas Coombe, Loyalist Claims, III, p. 432.
[46] Memorial of Jacob Duché, Loyalist Claims, XXXXIX, p.233.

mission in 1774.[47]

At the southern tip of the Delaware peninsula Samuel Tingley, who had been one of Samuel Johnson's students and later an assistant to Thomas Chandler in Elizabeth Town, refused to follow Samuel Magaw's example of joining with the Whigs. And the Philadelpia clergy's behaviour prompted him to pray "May the Cloak of Charity hide" their betrayal of the Church "from future ages." In 1782, a "friend," John Dickinson, now the Governor of Delaware, granted him a pass to visit New York City from where he was able to write to the Society. He explained that he had been able to keep his churches open throughout the War by making a number of innocuous alterations in the liturgy. In September 1779, he cautioned his congregation - - obliquely warning off evangelist Francis Asbury who was present in his church - - not to allow the current social and political ferment to send them into emotional disorder.[48]

The deterioration of religious and social bonds which accompanied the war years also found expression from John Tyler's pulpit in Norwich, Connecticut. Cut off from his colleagues, and the Society in England, he took to preaching the Universalist doctrine. He was troubled enough about his beliefs that he sought advice from Samuel Peters in London and his colleagues in Connecticut. Not the least of his concerns was his fear that dismissal from the Society would make his desperate financial situation even worse. He had lost most of his savings during the War, even though he had been driven to trade while his church was closed. He wrote Peters that his belief in a guaranteed salvation for all men was accepted by many of the Episcopalian laity in Connecticut, including many in Bishop Seabury's parish in New London. However, on advice from his colleagues, he wrote to the Society, in April 1784, explaining his behaviour. The Secretary informed him that he would have to decide between his new beliefs and the Church. Because his

---

[47] The Journal of Francis Asbury, Bishop of the Methodist Church, August 7, 1771 -- December 7, 1815 (3 vols.; New York, 1821), I, pp. 239, 241, 244, 252, 256, 272, 275, 320, 325.
[48] Journal of Francis Asbury, p. 251; Samuel Tingley to Secretary, March 5, 1782, B, XXI, 186; Harold B. Hancock, The Loyalists of Delaware, p. 64 claimed that Thorne ceased holding Church services for a time during the War. However, he gave no evidence.

livelihood depended on being received in Connecticut as a minister conforming to "the doctrines and discipline of the Church of England," he promised to conform, though his optimistic belief in a guaranteed salvation for all men was too dear to reject entirely. A year after receiving the Society's rebuke, Tyler was still going "thorough Stitch in that matter he denies not only the Eternity of future Punishment but the Existence of any punishment at all hereafter" according to Samuel Parker in Boston. At its general meeting on April 15, 1785, the Society resolved that it "cannot, consistently with their Charter, continue to employ" the missionaries in the Independent States, but that "their present salaries will be continued to Christmas next, and no longer." A large family and declining health prevented John Tyler from going to Nova Scotia. He was, therefore, free of the Society's restraint. In November 1787, Ebenezer Dibblee wrote to Samuel Peters that "Mr. Tyler remains inflexibly obstinate, he promises silence, except in his own Parish, and at Hebron, where he boasts of numbers of his converts." As late as 1791, Bela Hubbard reported that Tyler was still preaching Universalism, but that it was not gaining ground with clergy or laity.[49]

Uzal Ogden also drifted far from Anglican doctrine in his New Jersey parish. His family had been converted from the Presbyterian Church during the Great Awakening, and he had been brought up in Newark's Trinity Church. He was never as firmly convinced of the validity of royal and episcopal government as Thomas Chandler, his mentor. He had stopped using the liturgy after Independence, but continued preaching in his church at Newtown in Sussex County, an area still on the edge of European settlement. In 1777, he joined the refugees in New York City. Whatever he had done to offend the Revolutionaries in Sussex County did not prevent him from returning there the following year. At that time he began

---

[49] S.P.G.Journals, XXIII, 365; John Tyler to Secretary, July 1, 1785, S.P.G. Journals, XXIV, 166; John Tyler to Samuel Peters, Jan. 9, 1784, Peters Papers, II, p. 2; April 2, 1785, Peters Papers, II, p. 35; Samuel Parker to Samuel Peters, May 7, 1785, Peters Papers, II, 39; S.P.G. Journals, XXIV, General Meeting, April 15, 1785; John Tyler to Samuel Peters, Oct. 24, 1785, Peters Papers, II, 56; Ebenezer Dibblee to Samuel Peters, Nov. 16, 1787, Peters Papers, III, 61; Bela Hubbard to Samuel Peters, Jan. 9, 1791, Peters Papers, V, p.1; Franklin Bowditch Dexter, Sketches of the Graduates of Yale College, I, pp. 156-157.

preaching extempore sermons to crowds of people, though his church apparently remained closed. His popularity gained him an invitation to officiate at Isaac Browne's former mission in Newark where his father was church warden. With the other New Jersey missionaries, Abraham Beach and William Frazer, Ogden opened his church in 1782, following the Connecticut example. But, unlike them, he abandoned the Anglican service entirely since, he claimed, his Presbyterian audience was unable to make the necessary responses to the Church service. Reports reached the Society that he was preaching three-hour-long sermons seven days out of ten, sometimes three times a day. By the time the Society initiated enquiries into his unusual behaviour, he had accepted an invitation from the Methodists at Trinity Church in New York to join Samuel Provost as assistant minister.[50]

Uzal Ogden later accepted a call to Trinity Church in Newark, New Jersey, which had been without a rector since "the Dereliction there of by the Rev. Mr. Brown." No doubt by 1785, when Uzal Ogden followed Issac Browne, who was now in exile with part of his Newark congregation in Nova Scotia, the Newark parish had had time to repair the damage to the church wrought by the Continental Army. In 1779, Isaac Browne reported from New York that they had sold the church pulpit. Two years later they had repeatedly broken the church windows and, presumably the pews having been used for firewood, the empty space had become a place for ball games. The vestry did its best to secure the building but the soldiers again broke in and finally used the parsonage fence for firewood.[50a]

Joshua Weeks , William Walter and William Clark, who had

---

[50] Samuel Cooke to Secretary, May 1, 1777, May 7, 1782, B, XXIV, 118, 121; Uzal Ogden to Secretary, Oct. 5, 1776, Jan. 4, 1777, Feb. 24, 1779, B, XXIV, 159,160, 161; Uzal Ogden to Secretary, Feb. 24, 1780, S.P.G.Journals, XXII, 232; Abraham Beach to Secretary, Feb. 8, 1785, S.P.G. Journals, XXIV, 97; Uzal Ogden to Secretary, Oct. [?], 1783, S.P.G. Journals, XXIII, 258; Vestry Minutes of Trinity Church, Newark, New Jersey, April 5, 1779; Vestry Minutes of Trinity Church, New York, April 23, 1784, June 16, 1784; Uzal Ogden to Secretary, Sept. 17, 1784, S.P.G.Journals, XXIV, 132.

[50a] Isaac Browne to Secretary, Oct. 6, 1777, S.P.G. Journals, XXI, 278; Vestry Minutes of Trinity Church, Newark, New Jersey,(possession of the Rector) Nov. 3, 1785, Feb. 8, 1779, Feb. 16, 1779, Feb. 20, 1779, April 5, 1779, Sept. 6, 1779; Isaac Browne to Secretary, Oct. 6, 1784, S.P.G. Journals, XXIV, 10; Isaac Browne's claim lodged with Loyalist Commission, Nova Scotia, vol. XXVIII,469.

originally found the Church of England a fitting community for the Massachusetts elite, followed a pattern in Nova Scotia consistent with their earlier inclinations. After his minor excursion into Whig ways, Weeks left for England, and having failed to gain preferment, finally accepted the Society's mission at Annapolis. This rural backwater, one hundred and twenty miles distant from the provincial capital and its regimental balls, pageantry and the governor's entourage, proved unsatisfactory to Weeks who was determined to marry his three daughters into rank and fortune. His attempts to appoint a curate for Annapolis, while he lived in his fashionable house in Halifax, where he assisted John Breynton at St. Paul's Church and officiated as chaplain to Deputy-Governor Hammond's regiment, came to nothing. Finally, the Society had to dismiss him in order to find a mission for the rustic Bailey, who, unlike his brother-in-law Weeks, was never afraid of being "infected with the country air."[51]

When the British army evacuated Boston in March 1776, William Walter, Henry Caner and Moses Badger left with them. For a short while William Walter served as chaplain in Halifax before returning to New York, where he eventually became chaplain to General De Lancey's Brigade. At the end of the War he went to England where he submitted his claim to the Loyalist Commission, and gained the Society's appointment to Shelbourne in Nova Scotia. Unfortunately George Panton, former missionary at St. Michael's Church in Trenton, New Jersey, was already there as leader of a large group of refugees from New York City. Nova Scotia Governor Parr was infuriated at Walter's intrusion and Panton's group commenced legal proceedings against him. William Walter stayed in Shelbourne until he finally decided Boston was home. His wife's father had died there, leaving his daughter Lidia Lynde a considerable fortune. Mooted as possible bishop of Massachusetts, and after officiating at

---

[51] Jacob Bailey to Samuel Peters, May 3, 1782, Peters Papers, I, 62; Mather Byles to Secretary, Nov. 19, 1781, Deputy Governor A. S. Hammond, to Secretary, Nov. 25, 1781, B, XXV, 251, 253; General Meeting of the Society, Jan. 19, 1781, S.P.G. Journals, XXII; Jacob Bailey to Secretary, May 4, 1782, B, XXV, 259; Joshua Weeks to Secretary, Aug. 2, 1779, B, XXV, 234; Mather Byles to Secretary, May 7, 1781, B, XXV, 260; Joseph Peters to Samuel Peters, Oct. 17, 1791, Peters Papers, V, 39; General Meeting of the Society, March 19, 1784, S.P.G. Journals, XXIII.

a number of churches, he finally settled at Christ Church in Boston.[52]

William Clark finally arrived in England a very pathetic figure. The terrible persecutions he suffered in Massachusetts had left this partially deaf man almost unable to speak, "a case of great compassion," as the Loyalist Commission noted. When his wife died in Massachusetts, the lonely Loyalist left for Nova Scotia, where he boarded with Jacob Bailey at Annapolis. He soon married the widow of a Long Island Loyalist and moved into the house next door. However, being unable to officiate as a minister, and being incapable of turning farmer (he was bred to books, and sheltered from manual labour as a youth) it was not long before he grew bitter. He watched Bailey turning his glebe into a productive farm, making do with whatever came to hand in what some Loyalists sarcastically called "Hallelujah" country. His unfavourable stories about Bailey and Roger Viets, the pioneer farmer and missionary at Digby, ten miles away, soon found their way back to Bailey, and eventually Clark had no friends even among the Loyalists. He returned to Massachusetts a very disgruntled man to live on his Loyalist pension and the Society's salary, granted for life out of compassion for his sufferngs.[53]

The postwar years were very different for the Loyalists who would not remain in Connecticut. The two clergymen who had publicly expressed their disapproval of the Whigs, Samuel Andrews and James Scovil, left the Republic for British North America after the War. While these Loyalists could have remained in Connecticut, the security of the Society's employment, and a genuine attachment

---

[52] Henry Caner to Secretary, May 10, 1776, B, XXII, 136; Memorial of William Walter, July 15, 1784, Hugh Edward Egerton, ed. Daniel Parker Coke, The Royal Commission on the Losses and Services of American Loyalists (Oxford, 1915), p. 154; General Meeting of the Society, April 16, 1784, S.P.G. Journals, XXIII; Memorial of George Panton, Loyalist Claims, XV, p. 15; Governor Parr to Secretary, June 24, 1785, S.P.G. Journals, XXIV, 122; George Panton to Secretary, June 1, 1785, XXIV, 197; William Montague to Samuel Peters, Oct. 4, 1790, Peters Papers, IV, 94; Samuel Parker to Samuel Peters, Nov. 5, 1792, Peters Papers, V, 83.

[53] Memorial of William Clark, Loyalist Claims, IV, 114; Thomas Brown to Samuel Peters, Nov. 2, 1780, Peters Papers, I, 50; Roger Viets to Samuel Peters, Sept. 16, 1786, William Clark to Samuel Peters, Dec. 6, 1786, Peters Papers II, 105, 124; William Clark to Samuel Peters, April 10, 1788, Peters Papers, III, 77; William Clark to Samuel Peters, June 23, 1789, Peters Papers, IV, 26; Alexander Murray to William White, Dec. 26, 1785, William White Papers, I, 86.

to what they called "the sweets of British government" persuaded them to go. Scovil with nine children, Andrews with five, were so poor that the Society had to grant them a total of £75 sterling each to pay their removal expenses to New Brunswick. Both expected members of their former missions to join them. Richard Clarke's St. John's Church in New Milford went to great lengths to keep him there. They repaired the glebe house, they built a pew for his family, the subscribers struggled to meet their monetary obligations to him. The vestry called a special meeting with the other communities under Clarke's care to find a way of keeping him there. Finally Richard Clarke accepted the Society's gratuity of £50 sterling and a further £25 sterling to cover his removal expenses to a mission in New Brunswick. He sailed with Scovil and Andrews in the spring of 1787. His New Milford parish lost their minister, but they desperately wanted to keep what was left of their association with the Society. However, books were a treasure and Clarke took the Society's library with him to his new frontier home, even though his parish threatened him with legal action.[54]

After a period of exile in New York City, John Sayre also went to a mission in New Brunswick. There was nothing to return to in Fairfield. Everything he owned went up in flames when British forces bombarded the town, except a trunk he had carefully packed with the Church plate and the family's valuable belongings. With the Revolutionary soldiers close on their heels, Sayre's friends had to abandon the trunk in their dash to board the British vessels. What the Revolutionary soldiers did not take, the British soldiers, sent to recover the trunk, helped themselves to.[55]

The New Hampshire missionary Ranna Cossit also decided that the Republic was not for him, he took the Society's lonely mission on Cape Breton Island. Full of bitterness towards America, he later sent his two sons, one named after Lord George Germain, to the Church of England college at Windsor in Nova Scotia, swearing he

---

[54] Samuel Andrews to Secretary, Dec. 26, 1784, S.P.G. Journals, XXIV, 106; Samuel Andrews and James Scovil to Secretary, April 20, 1786, S.P.G. Journals, XXIV, 304; Richard Clarke to Secretary, May 5, 1786, Jan. 11, 1787, S.P.G. Journals, XXIV, 318, 391; Vestry Minutes of St. John's Church, New Milford, Conn., vol. I, 1764 -- 1848, Sept. 7, 1784 -- June 21, 1786.

[55] Memorial of John Sayre, Loyalist Claims, XII, 479; John Sayre to Jacob Bailey, March 1, 1784, Simon Gratz Collection, Case 9, Box 18.

would never have them educated outside the British provinces.[56]

The Connecticut clergy who made their homes in British North America were determined not to have anything to do with the Republic, and the clergy who remained in Connecticut were equally determined not to allow republican principles to infiltrate the government of their Church. Soon after hearing that the British government was considering peace terms with the American States, the Connecticut clergy met at Abraham Jarvis' home in Wallingford. At that meeting they decided to send one of their number to England for consecration. The following year, at John Marshall's home in Woodbury, they chose Samuel Seabury. Though he had never officiated in Connecticut, he was the logical choice. His forthright defence of the British constitution, and his support for an American episcopate had led to his persecution and exile in New York City. He would appear to be a more suitable figure than those Connecticut clergy who had opened their churches in 1778 with the liturgy changed - - albeit with the approval of the prelates in England.[57]

What Samuel Seabury did not know about the Connecticut Church, Samuel Peters would teach him. On October 30 1783, Peters sent him a very detailed summary listing ministers and their congregations, churches built and Connecticut's population, as they were in 1774. He even added a note that the Isle of Man, thirty miles long and eight miles wide, with a population of 2000 souls in seventeen small parishes, warranted a bishop; yet Connecticut, with 64,000 Anglicans, remained leaderless. Ironically, the first church that Bishop Seabury consecrated was St. Paul's Church in Norwalk. It was Jeremiah Leaming's church, burnt by British troops in 1779. Not only did a great part of his parish go up in flames, he suffered a personal loss of £2250 sterling.[58]

---

[56] Ranna Cossit to Samuel Peters, July 31, 1790, Peters Papers, IV, 90.

[57] John Tyler to Samuel Peters, Jan. 9, 1784, Peters Papers, II, 2; Bruce Steiner, Samuel Seabury 1729-1796 A Study in the High Church Tradition (Oberlin, Ohio, 1971), pp. 175-176.

[58] Samuel Peters to Samuel Seabury Oct. 30, 1783, Peters Papers, I, 75; Jeremiah Leaming to Secretary, July 29, 1779, Sept. 30, 1785, B, XXIII, 257, S.P.G. Journals, XXIV, 249; Bruce Steiner, Samuel Seabury, p. 318. It has become fashionable to write Samuel Peters off as an eccentric. He did get carried away when writing about his adversaries in the 1770's; however, from the "ravings" of eccentrics one can often

News from Philadelphia that the Episcopalians there were considering a proposal to adopt Presbyterian ordination until bishops could be consecrated for America prompted the Connecticut clergy to send Samuel Seabury to England without even first obtaining approval for their plans from England. Seabury's hasty departure also reflected the clergy's exasperation with the prelates. Jeremiah Leaming later remarked "the Bishops of England have always been averse to our having Bishops here; and had not a plan been carried into Execution by us, before any scheme could be formed to prevent it, we never should have had one." It appeared to many of the clergy that the English bishops had kept the American Church in a state of dependence to retain their loyalty to the Crown, and now that the Crown was forsaking the Loyalists, they must consecrate bishops or see the American Episcopalians absorbed into the Presbyterian Church.[59]

Samuel Seabury's attempts to gain consecration in England proved unsuccessful. Arriving in England while the Paris peace negotiations were still in progress destroyed any hope that Parliament could consider the special legislation that would be required to allow the Archbishops to consecrate bishops for a foreign state. He then applied to the non-juring Scottish Episcopalian bishops who consecrated him in Aberdeen, in November 1784. The English prelates naturally frowned upon Seabury's consecration from the non- jurors; yet to some American clergy it appeared to be but one more ironical twist to the Loyalists' fate. After working so hard in defence of the authority of the Crown, Samuel Seabury had to seek consecration at the hands of the Scottish Episcopalians who had not accepted the Hanoverian succession.[60]

The organization of the Connecticut Church followed from Connecticut's peculiar position among the Anglicans in the northern provinces. The rift between the Low and High Churchmen was complete. The ten clergymen who survived the War and remained in Connecticut acquiesced in the Republic, but they realized, as did

---

glean insight. Certainly, his collected papers contain valuable correspondence from some very level-headed people who were pleased to seek his opinion.

[59] Jeremiah Leaming to "The Reverend Abraham" [Beach], May 16, 1787, MSS No. 73364, Connecticut Historical Society.

[60] William Samuel Johnson to Samuel Peters, Dec. 3, 1785, Peters Papers, II, 61.

Ebenezer Dibblee, that "Episcopacy and Republicanism [could] not Coalesce." They, therefore, attempted to remain, according to John Tyler, in "a Kingdom of its own - - a religious Polity distinct from the civil." Thus they solved their problem of wanting to continue under monarchical, episcopal government, which would have meant the tremendous hardships of emigrating to the "American Siberia" or remaining at home under a political system to which they could give only passive support. They could at least preserve a vestige of their Tory philosophy in their Church. They could refuse to be part of the Philadelphia Church that had allowed the laity to reconstruct it, and in so doing had destroyed its divine fabric. Jeremiah Leaming summed up the situation succinctly: "The ministerial Authority is either from Heaven, or from men . . . If men give the authority to the minister, they must constitute all the Laws, by which that Chh is to be governed. In that case, the Chh would be nothing more than a meer human Invention." [61]

Two of the oldest Loyalist clergymen, Jeremiah Leaming and Ebenezer Dibblee, with Christopher Newton, believed so strongly in the relationship between royalty and episcopacy that they held reservations about Seabury's consecration from the Scottish nonjurors. Only old age and infirmity kept Dibblee and Leaming from going to the King's remaining American provinces. Nevertheless, the constitution of the Episcopal Church in Connecticut managed to retain the old-world order modified by American experience. The lay members elected their ministers, but in the State convention only clergy met, and changes in the liturgy were restricted to those political parts no longer consistent with the civil government. The final union of the Episcopal churches was due ultimately to their American nationalism which allowed them to overcome the bitter animosities between Loyalist and Revolutionary.[62]

In 1786, Parliament approved legislation to provide for the consecration of bishops for America. Consequently, when William White of Philadelphia and Samuel Provost of New York received

---

[61] Ebenezer Dibblee to Samuel Peters, Nov. 6, 1789, Peters Papers, IV, 47; Jeremiah Leaming to William White, Oct. 29, 1785, William White Papers, II, 99; John Tyler to Samuel Peters, Jan. 9, 1784, Peters Papers, II, 2.
[62] Ebenezer Dibblee to Jacob Bailey, May 15, 1786, Simon Gratz Collection, misc. papers; Ebenezer Dibblee to Samuel Peters, June 13, 1787, Peters Papers, III, 31.

consecration in London the following year, the American churches had the necessary three bishops to continue the episcopal succession. The bitterness Provost had felt for the Tory clergy during the War, however, almost prevented a reconciliation of the two branches of the Church. Finally, in October 1789, the efforts of Bishops Seabury and White for compromise resulted in the formation of the Protestant Episcopal Church in the United States, in Philadelphia. Samuel Parker of Trinity Church in Boston gave his support to the union. Samuel Provost gave his grudging approval.[63]

It was natural that from Philadelphia, where the mitre and sceptre had rested more lightly than among the clergy to the north, should come a scheme which would have finally Prebyterianized the Episcopal Church. William White's plan to meet the emergency that resulted from the American States' separation from Britain would have provided for ordination of candidates for the ministry by priests until a bishop could be consecrated. Parliament's special provision in 1786 to allow the bishops to consecrate Samuel Provost and William White made possible episcopal succession in America. But the Pennsylvania Episcopal convention reduced the bishop to a mere ex-officio member with only advisory powers to the presbyters. When the Pennsylvanians began to seek a broader union with the other states in 1785, Uzal Ogden and William Frazer who had remained in New Jersey during the War, and Abraham Beach, whose discretion had kept him safe at New Brunswick while the town changed hands between British and American forces, voted with White and Provost to accept the Episcopal constitution. They accepted the revised Prayer Book which finally omitted the Athanasian Creed, and which would have been drastically further revised had not the Archbishops of Canterbury and York required the Americans to modify their proposals before agreeing to consecrate American bishops. Thus, in the four middle states the Church constitution reflected the civil government, with clergy and

---

[63] Samuel Seabury to William White, Aug. 27, 1789, Samuel Provost to William White, Sept. 7, 1789, Jeremiah Leaming to William White, Oct. 29, 1789, June 16, 1788, William White Papers, II, 66, 95, 96, 99; Samuel Parker to William White, Sept. 15, 1786, William White Papers, II, 18; Samuel Parker to Samuel Peters, May 7, 1785, Oct. 23, 1786, Peters Papers, II, 39, 113; Samuel Parker to Samuel Peters, Sept. 29, 1787, Peters Papers, III, 45; Journals of the General Convention of the Protestant Episcopal Church in the U. S. A, 1785 – 1853 (Philadelphia, 1861), I, pp. 93-96.

laymen voting upon ecclesiastical affairs, while the bishops voted only as ex-officio members. The bishops could be removed from office by the State conventions if necessary - - a provision which also brought objections from the Archbishops. The Connecticut Church would not join the other States in a united Episcopal Church until the General Convention agreed to allow it to be represented by clergy without lay delegates. The State of Connecticut also gained the right to incorporate a house of bishops with legislative powers and the right of veto over the house of lay and clerical deputies.[64]

Samuel Provost tried hard to keep Seabury out of the general convention. He resorted to name-calling - - he reduced Seabury's name to "Cebra." He tried to have the convention refuse to acknowledge the validity of his consecration. He would have denied the ministers ordained by Seabury the right to officiate in the Church had it not been for the broadminded William White who placed a higher premium on a united American Church than upon personal vengeance. However, all Episcopalians in the northern States had one idea in common. Both Whig and Tory were concerned that the Church be restored as closely as possible to its primitive state. Even Thomas Chandler, perhaps with tongue in cheek, had stressed in his publications in the 1760's that the American Anglicans only wanted bishops with ecclesiastical authority, without civil powers or emoluments.[65]

Thomas Coombe, officiating in deacons orders in 1769, while very critical of America's subscriptions lists, expressed scorn for the "vicious noblemen" he saw in London who dispensed livings to clergy as though they were real estate. His postwar experience in England led him to betray his earlier feelings about the English

---

[64] Charles Inglis to William White, June 9, 1783, William White Papers, I, 19; Journals of the General Convention of the Protestant Episcopal Church in the U.S.A. (Philadelphia, 1861). 36, 41, 51-54, 58-60. Abraham Beach used the Widows Corporation as the basis for the general union of the Episcopal Church, see : Jeremiah Leaming to William White, July 30, 1787, William White Papers, II, 56; Abraham Beach to William White, Jan. 26, 1784, William White Papers, I, 25; Samuel Parker to Secretary, Jan. 1, May 10. 1783, S.P.G. Journals, XXIII, 109; William White, The Case of the Episcopal Churches in the United States Considered (Philadelphia, 1783); Samuel Parker to William White, Jan. 20, 1789, William White Papers, II, 78.
[65] Samuel Provost to William White, Oct. 25, 1785, Nov. 7, 1785, William White Papers, I, 73, 78; Journals of the General Convention, pp. 36-38.

Church and its trading in benefices, but his former colleague at Philadelphia's Christ Church found England no place for an American refugee. As soon as peace was declared, Jacob Duché set about making his own peace with his enemies. He wrote to his former assistant at Christ church for help in the business of returning to Philadelphia, and he gave some advice for the future of the Church. He warned White, who needed no advice: "Let there be no Archbishop, or Patriarch." And Seabury was "truly Primitive, unencumbered with any temporal Titles, or Honour or Interest" when Duché bade him farewell eighteen months later as the bishop boarded ship for home. Alexander Murray in London, Samuel Parker in Boston, and countless other clergy wrote page after page on the need for the American Church to purge itself of English corruption. The long years of waiting for the English ministry to appoint a bishop for the colonies; the frustration of having repeatedly warned their friends in England that independence would follow if the Church were not given official favour; and the final British surrender and desertion of the American Loyalists did much to make them think more kindly of their enemies. Even the Loyalists in British North America commented upon the futility of "the empty parade of military connexions" among the officers scrambling for the governor's favour instead of pursuing the enemy.[66]

Disillusionment among the Loyalists was naturally very common, but their determination to purify the Church of its old-world trappings has a familiar ring to it. Loyalists and Revolutionaries often viewed their world through the prism of war-torn seventeenth century England. The Loyalist clergy frequently referred to themselves as "Royalists," and their enemies as "saints," "puritans" or "Cromwellians." The Massachusetts Revolutionaries locked William Clark in a room for forty five minutes facing a portrait of Oliver Cromwell to contemplate his cavalier error in helping to destroy American liberties.[67]

So many Tory clergy were born in American and traced their

---

[66] Thomas Coombe to his father, June 6, 1770, Thomas Coombe Papers; Jacob Duché to William White, Aug. 11, 1783, William White Papers, I, 22; Mather Byles to Samuel Peters, Oct. 22, 1782, Peters Papers, 1, 70.
[67] William Clark to Secretary, Jan. 5, 1778, B, XXII, 150.

ancestry back to the early settlers in New England. The amazing conversion began with Samuel Johnson and his colleagues in 1722, and continued until the Revolutionary War. Johnson was speaking for scores of eighteenth century New Englanders when he claimed that as a young man he could not bear the egalitarian nature of the Congregationalist Church, and the low esteem its ministers were held in. Fifty years later, Jacob Bailey commented on how that egalitarian spirit had come to pervade almost every aspect of secular life. Having personally experienced the anger of mob action, and currently sheltering his brother-in-law Joshua Weeks from persecution, he wrote optimistically to the Society, in 1775, that he had "hopes in the success of his majestys forces, an happy prospect of which arises from the levelling principle which rages thro the Country - - from the contempt of all discipline and subordination which prevails" and will end in a splintering of opposition to legal authority. In the eighteenth century the Congregationalist clergy no longer commanded the leadership they had enjoyed earlier, and the elitists, dethroned, turned to the Church of England to regain their position. The Tory clergy's suspicions during the 1760's that Britain lacked sufficient vigour to arrest the colonies rush into social and religious chaos became a conviction as the War dragged on with only New York City firmly in British hands. Jeremiadic pronouncements came from the clergy that corruption in the Empire had brought the War upon them. When Britain finally withdrew from its American provinces they found comfort in the prospect of cleansing the Anglican Church in America of its Romish trappings.[68]

The energy expended in seeking an American episcopate and an establishment makes sense. The rebellion was precisely what the clergy had predicted, and almost every Loyalist clergyman offered his own pet scheme for improving the Church's position as soon as peace was restored. They wrote to the Society and the bishops, and the clergy cooped up in New York vented their frustrations in their joint letter to the Society, in 1777, expressing their conviction that

---

[68] Examples of the clergy's use of the Jeremiad can be found in : Isaac Browne to Secretary, Oct. 4, 1779, Samuel Andrews to Secretary, Jan. 7, 1766, B, XXIV, 58, XXIII, 11; Samuel Auchmuty to Richard Peters, May 16, 1770, Richard Peters,Papers, VI, 109; Sermon by C. H. Bogatzky, God's Thoughts on Peace in War, 1759, and reprinted for James Sayre in Brooklyn, 1780.

better times were ahead when they would receive their long overdue reward. And Loyalists in London attended the Society's meetings to offer expert advice on America and the Church.[69]

The Society had delayed extending its missions in Nova Scotia, and it had placed restrictions on the amount of aid it would afford the southern colonies, hoping to commit the Lords of Trade to provide for the Church there. Governor Benning Wentworth had long ago set aside between 200 and 300 acres of land in New Hampshire for the Church, part of which he signed over to the Society. In 1769, his successor John Wentworth, presented the Bishop of London with an elaborate plan to place clergy there. Consequently, Ranna Cossit settled at Haverhill in 1774, living on the Society's land. However, nothing more was done, though the Bishop of Oxford Robert Lowth, one of the most committed of the prelates to the American episcopate, informed Thomas Chandler, when he arrived in England in 1775, that the matter would be pursued relentlessly as soon as the colonies returned to order.[70]

Early in 1777, in New York City, Ambrose Serle listened to the "Fire-Brands," Auchmuty, Inglis, and Seabury pour out their plans for an establishment. They approved of a plan Serle had formed several years before, much the same as that which Governor John Wentworth had presented to the Bishop of London. With Robert Lowth only just promoted to the See of London they sent their plan to the Society, backed up by a joint letter from the New York clergy, both of which arrived in London with letters reporting the sudden deaths of Samuel Auchmuty, Ephraim Avery and Luke Babcock. There could be no better time for Lowth to urge theSociety to consider the future of the colonial Church, and a committee was established to review plans for an American bishop. Reports from America claimed that Auchmuty's death had been precipitated by the War. Paralysis, brought on by severe persecution and the death of his wife, reduced Avery to suicide. Luke Babcock had died soon after his release from the Hartford jail. Further losses at a time when it was impossible for Americans to seek ordination in London

---

[69] Joint letter of the clergy in New York to Secretary, Feb. 8, 1777, B, III, 343.
[70] Governor John Wentworth to Joseph Harrison, Sept. 24, 1769, Governor John Wentworth to Bishop of London, April 28, 1770, Fulham Papers, VI, 106, 114; S.P.G. Journals, XVII, 171, 268, 241, XX, 169.

would seriously damage any attempts to reorganize the Church after the War. Possibly Burgoyne's surrender later that year, and the prospect of a prolonged war, persuaded the Society to lay the committee's reports aside.[71]

The correspondence from the New York-New Jersey conventions during the 1760's had often contained the suggestion that the bishops and politicians delayed appointing American bishops in order to keep the American Anglicans dependent upon Britain. It was certainly a notion the Dissenters liked to spread. William Walter, with many others, returned from England of that opinion. When he applied to Bishop Osbaldeston for ordination in 1763, the prelate rather angrily commented: "You are like the rest always in a great haste to give people Trouble out of Season, & when you have got your twenty pounds, we never hear any more of you."[72]

John Sayre's "system without a centre," once completed with a resident bishop, could easily have resulted in a much weaker connection between the American and the English Church. William Knox, while Under Secretary of State during Lord North's administration, had proposed a plan, in co-operation with the Society, of which he was a member, to appoint a bishop for Nova Scotia. The Church of England would be established, there would be a gradation of benefices to provide an avenue of promotion for clergy - - the lack of which had caused concern during the American colonial experience. The bishop would hold office at the King's pleasure to safeguard him from popular dictate. Knox's scheme would provide Church schools and colleges, to keep the settlers within the British realm and to eliminate the attraction of republican schools. Knox also realized that if the clergy were not independent of their congregations, they would not be as active in defending British rule as they had been in the past. He explained that the need for Americans to go to England for ordination, and in some cases, for their education, was "one of the strongest bonds of Union between the colonies and Great Britain." His plan for a bishop in Nova Scotia with a British system of education would maintain the

---

[71] Samuel Seabury to Secretary, March 27, 1777, B, II, 191; S.P.G. Journals, XXI, 200, 214; Joint letter of the clergy in New York to Secretary, Feb. 8, 1777, B, III, 343; Journal of Ambrose Serle, pp. 191, 201, 209.
[72] William Walter to Bishop of London, Sept. 10, 1764, Fulham Papers, VI, 52.

union between Britain and its remaining North American Empire. Knox's plan to ensure that "peace might prevail between priest and people" sounds almost as though he had before him the report Isaac Browne sent to the Society in 1768. "The Church of England in this part of the World is truly Militant," he wrote, "and the clergy are more so than the other members of the Church" because they are dependent for their support upon subscription bonds "all of which are a perfect cheat in too many Instances." Consequently, the clergy's public declarations of loyalty to Britain might drive away their congregations, but their loyalty should finally bring about their cherished establishment. BishopTerrick's "compleat Establishment" was precisely what Knox had in mind.[73]

During the 1760's the clergy in convention had assumed a greater control of their own affairs, and as America's role in the Empire came under debate they came up with a solution of their own. The plan was Joseph Galloway's which would have provided for an American Council to share the legislative powers with Parliament. While accepting Parliament's supremacy, the plan would have allowed the colonists virtually full control of their own affairs. For Tories like the New York-New Jersey High Churchmen it was precisely what they wanted, for none of the Anglican clergy had approved of Parliament's bid to tax the colonies, but neither could they accept a dissolution of the constitution by denying the King's sovereignty.[74]

This refusal to be party to destroying the ancient concept of a divinely ordained society presided over by mitre and sceptre finally divided Tory from Whig. Thomas Coombe and William Stringer, who had been prepared to go further than the High Church men by changing the liturgy, chose exile rather dissolve their association with the Crown. If the King would dissolve the Anglo-American connection, Coombe told his vestry, he would be content to remain in Philadelphia, but as the State demanded he renounce his allegiance to the Crown, he would have to leave. Here was a man the Whig vestry at Christ Church held in very high esteem, and on

---

[73] Copy of a letter from William Knox to Mr. Pitt, 1786, Fulham Papers, I, 102; Isaac Browne to Secretary, April 6, 1768, B, XXIV, 40

[74] Joseph Galloway's plan is appended to Thomas Chandler's pamphlet What Think Ye of the Congress Now (New York, 1775).

his behalf they wrote a strong recommendation to the Bishop of London - - a very different treatment from that given to Duché and Smith.[75]

The same social philosophy drove John Andrews from St. John's parish in Maryland's Queen Anne County in 1776. He had been a friend of William White at the College of Philadelphia. They had both been part of the opposition to Parliament, but the two differed over the Whigs' optimistic belief that men could overthrow legal government and reconstruct another. Andrews finally had to leave his Maryland parish and return to his native York County in Pennsylvania where he had been the Society's missionary before Batwell arrived from England. Possibly the York Anglicans' hatred for Batwell prejudiced them against Andrews who they prevented from teaching school, finally facing him with the choice of abjuring the King or leaving the State. The tyranny of the people - - a basic Tory theme - - both Andrews and White agreed was a subversion of the Whigs' declared principles, but that nevertheless was how Andrews was treated. The Revolutionaries were not content, he wrote, until they should have as "lordly a dominion over his conscience, as they had already established, uninterrupted, over his person & property."[76]

Here then, lies the distinction between Low Churchmen and High Churchmen. The High Churchmen, most often of Congregationalist origin, were looking for the kind of society in which each individual knew the part he must play, not because he deemed it, but because his role was part of a plan that was above and beyond man's competency to alter. Thus they held firm to each tenet and sacrament of the Church as an outward manifestation of a divinely ordered society. The Low Churchmen might, like Thomas Coombe or Uzal Ogden, emphasize man's intimate relationship with God, and they might appeal to the emotional experience of a personal conversion, thus concerning themselves more with the individual's relationship with God than with society as a whole. Coombe's and Stringer's ultimate decision not to go one step further with William White or Samuel Magaw stems from the concept that unites the Tories of the Low and High Church philosophy. It was a

---

[75] Vestry Minutes of Christ Church, Philadelphia, July 7, 1778.
[76] John Andrews to William White, Dec. 14, 1779, William White Papers, I, 17.

lack of confidence in their own ability to lead America along the path they wanted. They wanted control of the Church to be vested in America, but with the ultimate authority in the Archbishops. They wanted to organize the western lands so that settlement would proceed according to their own social philosophy; they wanted political control to reside in America, but with the final veto in London - - in King and Parliament which tradition had placed sacrosanct above the law.

Frenchman J. Hector St. John de Crèvecoeur, traveling through the American colonies in the 1760's, pondering the almost imperceptible changes that were making America different from his native Europe asked "What is an American?" He described how the various Christian sects arriving from Europe when "mixed with other denominations, their zeal will cool for want of fuel, and will be extinguished in a little time" and "the strict modes of Christianity as preached in Europe are lost." In 1761, Thomas Chandler had also been alert to the insidious nature of ecumenism. He had expressed his fear that the distinction between the Anglican Church and Dissent might one day become "an Ecclesiastical Scarecrow." It appeared to have become a reality. Ezra Stiles, who had rallied the Dissenters to unite against the Anglican land-grab in the western lands in 1760, saw Chandler's point clearly fourteen years later. The Prayer Book adopted in 1784 had made the Philadelphia Episcopalians no different from the deists, and the Connecticut clergy were refusing to accept it, fearing that by giving up "one Thing after another they Shd at length give up all that distinguished Episcopacy, loose their Cause, & become Presbyterians." Ebenezer Dibblee, the Society's missionary for thirty-nine years, echoed Stiles' comment. "Every one thinks himself fit for a reformer," he lamented, "Omissions & alterations without the Bishops directions are made; the communion service, generally omitted, the form of administering the holy Eucharist varied, and other alterations offensive to steady friends of the Church" were now commonplace. Samuel Parker wrote to William White, in 1789, "the churches in Massachusetts have at present more the resemblance of Independent congregations than of Episcopal churches." There were only six Episcopal clergy in the State, two receiving ordination since the conclusion of hostilities. He continued that "two of the other four are so lax in their principles of Episcopal Government that I rather think them averse to uniting under any common head."[77]

The fraternizing between Anglican and Dissenter that Chandler had warned against was a portent of the end of the society that many Anglicans represented in America, and the War years gave the final nudge that sent a number of clergy along divergent paths. Uzal Ogden, laying aside the liturgy, praying extempore and preaching sermons lasting up to three hours, went to the Presbyterian Church. John Tyler chose the Universalist doctrine. From his pulpit in Norwich he delivered a eulogy on the life of George Washington, "our illustrious Moses - - our Deliverer from Oppression." King's Chapel in Boston was closed from March 1776. It was re-opened in 1782 under the guidance of a young Bostonian, James Freeman, as lay reader. In 1785, King's Chapel adopted a Unitarian liturgy; Freeman, having been denied Episcopal ordination because of his ideas, was ordained by his congregation. At that time, Samuel Parker, writing from Trinity Church in Boston to Samuel Peters in London, defended Samuel Seabury's consecration in Scotland. If you don't accept Seabury's solution, he wrote, what is the solution? More lay readers or Presbyterian ordination? "More injury has been already done to our churches by introducing lay readers than can be repaired in many years." The English Civil Wars the Tory clergy saw happening all over again in America had ended the divine right kingship in that country, had signalled the arrival of a new class of Englishmen who demanded to be heard. The American Revolution gave the death blow to the concept of divinely ordained society in civil, and for the majority of Episcopalians, in ecclesiastical government too. The American State and Church placed sovereignty in the people - - even Connecticut in the 1790's had to give in to lay representation in its conventions.[78]

---

[77] Albert E. Stone, ed., J.Hector St. John de Crèvecoeur, Letters from an American Farmer and Sketches of 18th Century America (Penguin Books, 1981), pp. 73-74; Franklin B. Dexter, The Literary Diary of Ezra Stiles, III,. 234; Ebenezer Dibblee to Jacob Bailey, May 15, 1786, Simon Gratz Collection, misc. papers; Samuel Parker to William White, Jan. 20, 1789, William White Papers, II, p. 78.

[78] Morgan Dix, ed., A History of the Parish of Trinity Church, II, pp. 64-65; Abraham Beach to Secretary, Feb. 8, 1785, S.P.G.Journals, XXIV, 97; Uzal Ogden to Secretary, Oct. 1783, S.P.G. Journals. XXIII, 258; King's Chapel Vestry Records, Book V; Samuel Parker to Secretary, Jan. 1, May 10, 1783, S.P.G. Journals, XXIII, 109;

The Revolution contained many ironies for the Anglican clergy. Samuel Seabury who had done so much for Church and State, refused consecration by the State bishops, had to accept consecration from the non-jurors in Scotland. The Tories had urged a complete establishment; yet Seabury returned to St. James Church in New London, which had been destroyed by fire after the dismissal of Matthew Graves. He delivered his first sermon to the clergy in the Dissenters' meeting house. His entire financial support came now from the laity - - he died possessing no land, a horse, two slaves, a bishop's mitre, two gowns, and a collection of old damaged books.[79]

In 1776, the Connecticut satirist John Trumbull had M'Fingal, his Tory prophet, predict the future of a number of New York Anglican zealots:

What solemn rows of bishops rise!
Aloft a Card'nal's hat is spread
O'er punster Cooper's rev'rend head!
In Vardell, that poetic zealot,
I view a lawn-bedizened prelate!
What mitres fall, as 't is their duty,
On heads of Chandler and Auchmuty!
Knights, viscounts, barons shall ye meet
   As thick as pavements in the street!

He omitted from his prediction the two clergymen who were to be consecrated bishops. Nevertheless, he did understand what some of the Anglican clergy wanted to see after hostilities should end. Myles Cooper, who had fled to England on the same ship with Thomas Chandler and Samuel Cooke, died in Edinburgh on May 22, 1785, the day Chandler sailed back to New Jersey. Samuel Cooke,

---

Henry Wilder Foote, Annals of King's Chapel . . . , ed. by Henry Edes (2 vols.; Boston, 1896), vol. II, chapter XXI; F.W.P. Greenwood, A History of King's Chapel in Boston; The First Episcopalian Church in New England (Boston, 1833), pp. 133-140; Frederick V. Mills, Sr., Bishops by Ballot: An Eighteenth Century Ecclesiastical Revolution (New York, 1978), pp. 167-168; Samuel Parker to Samuel Peters, May 7, 1785, Peters Papers, II, 39; John Tyler, "An Eulogy on the Life of General George Washington." (Norwich, 1800).

[79] Vestry Minutes of St. James Church, New London, Oct. 1781, April 23, 1783, Feb. 25, 1785, March 12, 1787; The Will of Samuel Seabury, dated Oct. 10, 1796, New London Probate District, Town of New London, No. 4722, (Connecticut State Library).

their old ally in the quest to gain the episcopate, drowned while serving as Bishop Inglis's commissary in New Brunswick. Thomas Chandler was offered the highest preferment in government's power, but failing health rendered him unfit to accept the Nova Scotia episcopate, and he returned to Elizabeth Town, where he died in 1790.[80]

Few Loyalists found the peace of mind that Thomas Coombe regained in England. It was just as well that he remained far from the other Loyalists, many of whom, whether in England or British North America, could not find sufficient reward for their loyalty, or sun to brighten their dreary days. Alexander Murray finally returned to visit his old Reading parish, and having cheated death at the Revolutionaries' hands, fell victim to yellow fever and was buried in Christ Church graveyard in Philadelphia. Jacob Duché could not find peace in London. In 1792, he informed William White, his friend and former assistant at Christ Church in Philadelphia, that he had written to President Washington about his wish to return to America. "The perpetual Fogs & Damps" will not let me live another winter here, he wrote. William White had offered his hospitality to Duché if he should return to Philadelphia. Duché asked White to plead his case for a pardon to the Governor of Pennsylvania, and on March 10, 1793, he sailed to America, a British subject.[81] Another Philadelphian, however, reacted quite differently from Duché. John Stuart had never vacillated in his loyalty to the Crown. He had been forced out of the Mohawk Valley during the War and he eventually became chaplain of the Kingston garrison in Ontario. In November 1798, he wrote to William White, who had studied with him at the College of Philadelphia. "Some years ago I thought it a great hardship to be banished into the wilderness and would have imagined myself compleatly happy could I have

---

[80] Samuel Peters to Jacob Bailey, June 4, 1785, Peters Papers in the Connecticut Historical Society; Ebenezer Dibblee to Samuel Peters, April 15, 1790, Peters Papers, IV, 76; Bela Hubbard to Samuel Peters, July 5, 1790, Peters Papers, IV, 87; John Lydekker, The Life of Charles Inglis, p. 250; Roger Viets to Samuel Peters, Aug. 24, 1798, Simon Gratz Collection, misc. papers; Moses Coit Tyler, The Literary History of the American Revolution, I, p. 439.

[81] William Duhamel, ed., Historical Annals of Christ Church, Reading (Douglassville, 1927), p. 15; Jacob Duché to William White, Feb. 1, 1792, Jan. 1, 1793, March 6, 1793, William White Papers, III, 14, 18, 20.

St. George's Cathedral, Kingston, Ontario
'A memorial to John Stuart's Mission'
(Courtesy Thousand Island Publishers, Ontario).

exchanged it for a place in the delightful city of Philadelphia. Now the best wish we can form for our friends is to have them removed to us."[82] The Loyalist clergy in British North America exemplify best the Loyalist plight. While they would not, or could not return to the United States, they resented the pomp and favouritism that seemed to govern preferment to ecclesiastical and civil office.

The final separation of the Protestant Episcopal from the Church of England was a tragic blow to many of the Tory clergy, for their association with the Anglican Church, its prelates and the Society had been dear to them. When Benjamin Moore wrote to the Society from Trinity Church in New York, he was struck by the sorrow among some of the American clergy. When Ebenezer Dibblee spoke to him about the Society severing its association with the former colonies, Moore noticed "a tear stealing down his furrowed cheek." Yet from their grief gradually emerged a feeling of relief at the freedom that had been thrust upon them. The relationship between the American clergy and the Society had always been one of warmth and mutual respect, but it had always kept them in a state of dependency. Their frequent requests for advice on liturgical and doctrinal matters, and even such simple, routine procedures as the removal from one parish to another, always required them to put their own initiative second to the verdict of their superiors in London. Even the corresponding society proved to be a disappointment to the colonials with North American interests. It had been designed to allow greater local control of colonial Church affairs. After it was rejected by the clergy in the middle colonies, it was introduced in Nova Scotia. Its authority was terminated when its members in Halifax began to assume more control over local affairs than the Society (which, after all, was paymaster) would tolerate.[83]

During its eighty-four year association with the American colonies, the Society's mission was a grand venture. It gave £350,000 sterling to provide 309 clergymen and schoolteachers, libraries,

---

[82] Quoted in Catherine S. Crary, <u>The Price of Loyalty: Tory Writings from the Revolutionary Era</u> (New York, 1973), p. 452.
[83] Benjamin Moore to the Society, Aug. 26, 1785, S.P.G. Journals, XXIV, 169; General Meetings of the Society, April 19, 1776, July 19, 1776, Nov. 21, 1777, S.P.G. Journals, XXI, pp. 51, 53, 91, 239.

Bibles and religious materials to support Americans, many of whom would have been destitute of religious guidance if left to their own devices. The Society offered a common focus with its directives, Anniversary Sermons and Abstracts of Proceedings to the scattered Anglican clergy and laity. It inadvertently helped prepare the ground for the union between the surviving parishes that became the independent American Episcopal Church after the Revolution.[84]

Unfortunately, the Society was never perfectly sure of what its American policy was. It professed to be non-political; yet its missionaries were expected to teach subordination to King and Parliament, and its greatest success was predominantly in gaining converts from among the Dissenters, an achievement the Society considered to have been a victory for the Crown. Archbishop Secker informed Samuel Johnson, in September 1756, that the Society's "charter was granted for the encouragement of an orthodox, that is a Church of England, ministry." While its aims were humanitarian, the Society's activities in the northern colonies played an important part in intensifying Americans' fears for their religious and political liberties. Few (if any) of the Society's members in England ever understood America, certainly no Church dignitary (apart from George Berkeley, Dean of Derry, who visited Rhode Island in 1724) ever took the trouble to visit the colonies. There can be little wonder that the colonials were generally considered to have been a fitting object of the Society's civilizing mission, whether they were Anglicans-turned-heathen, or Congregationalists expert in their own theology. The Society's historiographers from David Humphreys in 1730, Ernest Hawkins in 1845, C.F.Pascoe in 1893 and H. P. Thompson in 1951 have assumed that the American colonials were fast falling beneath the horizon of civilized Christendom. The Society's right to proselytize the Dissenters has been assumed by all of its chroniclers. Even H. P. Thompson, nearly 200 years after American Independence, refers to New England in the early eighteenth century as being a land "awaiting cultivation."[85]

---

[84] Charles T. Laugher, Thomas Bray's Grand Design: Libraries of the Church of England in America, 1695-1785 (Chicago, 1973), p. 63; John Calam, Parsons and Pedagogues: The S.P.G. Adventure in American Education (New York 1971), p. 199.
[85] Archbishop Secker to Samuel Johnson, Sept. 27, 1758, Schneider's Johnson, I, p. 257

Following the Seven Years War the Anglican clergy in the northern colonies were gradually edged into the position of an American Fifth Column. Their ordination oaths, their connection with the Society, and most of all, their dependence upon British support to establish the kind of society they felt was best for America, laid them open to suspicion and denied them the independent action the other denominations enjoyed. The Revolution destroyed the High Churchmen's ideal of a hierarchically structured society, tutored by clergy protected from popular whim by royal favour. But at last they were left free to make the best of what remained to them, without overseas help - - or hindrance.

The Tory clergy had turned to the Church of England to prop up their declining authority; yet they had remained plagued by their own distinctive notions of individual rights. Mather Byles' experience with the Boston Anglicans had been bitter, he nevertheless understood their peculiar way of thinking. The people he had come to serve in Halifax, Nova Scotia, were of the same strain. When the Rector of St. Paul's Church, Halifax, John Breynton, planned to visit England, in 1779, he appointed an itinerant missionary as his curate. The parishioners were so discontented with his neglecting to consult them that Breynton had to disembark his baggage and return to his church to pacify his congregation. Byles pointed out to the Society that their American informants kept them ill-informed about American affairs. He wrote that it is necessary that congregations "contribute largely to the Support of their Minister and will not readily relinquish the Privilege of choosing him." Therefore, he continued, "the choice of a Successor . . .ought to be left to a fair unbias'd vote of the parish." In 1767, Thomas Chandler had levelled this criticism at the proprietary governor's powers in Maryland. The American clergy wanted to rule their people, but not in so arbitrary a fashion as the English.[86]

The War years had brought the American Anglican clergy into a closer relationship with Britain than ever before. Whether as refugees in London, New York or Halifax they were compelled to experience the situation they had hoped to force upon the American

---

[86] Mather Byles to Secretary, Oct. 15, 1779, B, XXII, 95; Thomas Chandler to Samuel Johnson, June 9, 1767, Schneider's Johnson, I, pp. 406-409.

Dissenters. The Loyalists, in general, were treated fairly. The commissioners, appointed by Parliament to examine the Loyalists' claims for compensation, refused remuneration so that their work would be above reproach. In London and Halifax they waded through thousands of petitions and letters, and listened to nearly as many claimants and their witnesses seeking compensation for their losses arising from their loyalty to the Crown. They were meticulously disinterested and fair in their judgements. But the American clergy, searching London for persons with influence to help them gain preferment or perquisite, nevertheless, felt the indignity of being second class citizens; they were neither Englishmen, nor were they Americans anymore.

New York offered a similar fate to the clergy whose function had been reduced to officiating as chaplains to royal regiments that were slowly losing their grip on America. It was during this waiting period that many of them began to give expression to the dissatisfaction that had remained latent for many years. In fact, Jacob Duché had claimed in his sermon at Christ Church, Philadelphia, in July 1775, that Britain's policies were designed to check the colonies' economic growth and their drive to independence. Now, in London, Duché, and the other Loyalists wherever they were waiting, began to see themselves as Americans, no longer an appendage of Britain. The curt treatment from some of the bishops they waited on while seeking ordination; the frustration, after having thrown in their lot with the National Church, to be left without even a bishop in America was humiliation, not a reward. Samuel Peters, eccentric, yet frequently perceptive, wrote to Samuel Seabury, in October 1783, that several Dissenting ministers had told him in 1774 that "the Church of England would in five years become the majority [in Connecticut] and seven of them, foreseeing their danger, asked [him] <u>'why in the name of God do not English Bishops send you a Bishop, who might do more Good here, than the whole Army & Navy of Great Britain?</u> ' " Finally, the disillusionment that dawned upon them as they waited, totally dependent upon Britain that could ultimately only keep control of that bleak part of its North American provinces which so many of the city-bred Loyalists could not bear, convinced them that their future no longer lay with the mother country.[87]

The Anglican Tories of the New World had made an alliance with the Old World. They believed they could keep the colonies loyal within the Empire if only England's National Church could transplant some of its privilege across the Atlantic. The matter was not for them to decide. The Dissenters' dogged opposition to colonial bishops forced the prelates and successive ministries to put off the scheme. Finally, when the High Churchmen were sure that Providence had appointed the hour for their success, their proposed bishops became interminably associated in the colonists' minds with Stamp Taxes and the encroaching power of Parliament.

With the power of the Crown destroyed in the colonies, all that remained was to create a purely ecclesiastical Church, divorced from politics, and shorn of its pomp and inequalities; a task the War years had made almost as palatable for the Tories as for the Whigs. The Whig clergy, like the Tories, had sought the harmony and grace of the Anglican Church. The difference between them was that the Whigs had confidence in their own ability to lead the Church in the direction they wanted. They believed that they could command respect, and maintain control by working with their congregations in free competition with other denominations, without royal favour, and if necessary, without English money. They were unafraid of America's egalitarian spirit. They did, however, understand that the dignity and harmony of the Anglican Church would be lost unless order were secured through the separation of lay and clerical powers.

Even those clergy who had unhesitatingly taken the Revolutionary side early in the revolt against Britain often found themselves at odds with their congregations in the post-War years over the same problems that both Whig and Tory had faced before the Revolution. Samuel Magaw, who had been called to St. Paul's Church in Philadelphia in 1780, fought a continuous battle with his vestry for twenty years over his right to vote with the vestry. And if he had not given way to the vestry's demand that it be allowed to disobey the constitution of the Protestant Episcopal Church by calling whoever they chose to their pulpit, even while they had a properly inducted rector, St. Paul's Church would have gone their

---

[87] Samuel Peters to Samuel Seabury, Oct. 30, 1783, Peters Papers, I, 75.

own independent way. Samuel Magaw was finally forced to resign, beaten by the same independent spirit that he had supported in Delaware during the years of the Revolution. Similarly, Uzal Ogden resigned from his New Jersey parish after a protracted debate over the question of whether the rector should be merely a hired preacher or a pastoral leader.[88]

It is ironical that the Whig clergy should have had to fight back the democratic movement within the Church which they had been prepared to accept before the Revolution. The Tory clergy in Connecticut, however, who opposed democratic encroachments upon their authority, unilaterally elected and sent to London their own candidate for the English prelates to consecrate as their bishop. Even the Connecticut clergy and other Loyalist refugees in Britain's remaining provinces busied themselves with letters and petitions which they proposed to dispatch to London in the vain hope of electing their fellow countryman Samuel Peters to the Nova Scotia episcopate. Peters was in London, and he appeared to have the ear of influential people. But their concern for Samuel Peters was also partly motivated by their dislike, or jealousy, of Charles Inglis, the most likely candidate for that office. "We want no Resurrection Bishops here," one of Peters' supporters wrote about "Charley of Nova Scotia." Richard Clarke, formerly missionary at New Milford, writing from New Brunswick, considered Inglis to be "a Boil & a Hibernian Redemptioner." Samuel Peters' own resentment sprang from his having been overlooked for the Nova Scotia episcopate in favour of Inglis who had been "droped on the backside of Belfast," a man who "was not Educated any where." Ebenezer Dibblee prayed "God forbid" that the "Hibernian Doctor" might "obtain the Mitre." He was not alone in disliking Charles Inglis for his apparent "pride Covitiousness & haughtiness." It was difficult for New Englanders to see a redemptioner, or indentured servant, consecrated Bishop of Nova Scotia. They would probably have been more indignant if they had known that when Inglis was sentenced to a "second Transportation" he took with him to Nova Scotia £200 Sterling from the Society's fund that had been intended for the support of an

---

[88] Records of St. Paul's Church, 1760-1835; Trinity Church Minutes, 1778-1804, Newark New Jersey. (Possession of the Rector)

American bishop.[89]

Nevertheless, the Nova Scotia clergy finally accepted, albeit with sarcastic resignation, the pompous pronouncements and visitations of their new diocesan. Charles Inglis signed his name in the style of his old ally, the "Westchester Farmer," who had now become in the English tradition, "Samuel, Connecticut." William White did away with even this appellation, which seemed to him to echo more the princely gift of a medieval benefice than the episcopate trimmed to suit the American Republic.

The Episcopal Church that finally emerged from the Revolution contained something of both the Whig and Tory dogmas. The suggestion of authority beyond human interference was maintained in the episcopal succession. The preservation of clerical authority was secured while allowing the laity a voice in the government of the Church. Finally, the freedom allowed the State conventions in choosing whether or not to allow lay representation in the General Convention of the Church meant that the Episcopalians had at last learnt to tolerate dissent, even among themselves.

---

[89] Joseph Peters to Samuel Peters, January 31, 1788, Sept. 3, 1789; Richard Clarke to Samuel Peters, Jan. 19, 1791; Samuel Peters to Colonel [Simcoe], Aug. 30, 1791; Ebenezer Dibblee to Samuel Peters, June 13, 1787; Samuel Peters Papers, III, 70; IV, 39; V, 4; V, 33; III, 31; Samuel Peters to William Samuel Johnson, Feb. 12, 1786, William Samuel Johnson Correspondence, 1772-1817 (Connecticut Historical Society); S.P.G. Journals, XXV, 28.

Notes

*

Bibliography

*

Index

NOTES ON THE MAJOR PRIMARY SOURCES

The most important sources used in this study are the voluminous correspondence and Journals of the Society for the Propagation of the Gospel in Foreign Parts. The twenty five volumes in series "B" of the correspondence consist of letters from the clergy in the northern colonies to the Society's Secretary from 1701 to 1786. There are also a small number of letters from the Secretary to the clergy. While the letters to London were primarily concerned with parochial affairs they naturally contain valuable reflections on almost every aspect of colonial American life. Because each missionary was required to write to the Society's Secretary twice each year, the correspondence offers a continuous commentary on the lives of the Society's missionaries, in some instances, for as long as sixty years.

The fifty volumes of Journals of the Society's monthly general meetings are a necessary supplement to the missionaries' correspondence. The decisions reached after discussing the correspondence from America reveal the Society's evaluation of the missionaries' work, and frequently its own policy in America. Unfortunately, there is no record of the discussion or the voting divisions that took place at the meetings, but the Journals do contain abstracts of all correspondence received from America —sometimes very useful because the letter files are incomplete. Both the correspondence and the Journals are housed in the Society's archives in London and have been available on microfilm.

The Library of Congress has copies of the Society's anniversary sermons and abstracts of proceedings which were published every February. The sermons are the only public indication of the Society's policies.

The vestry minutes of the churches are a logical complement to the S.P.G. correspondence and Journals. They throw further light upon parochial affairs, and often help in understanding how the laity felt about the Society and its missionaries.

A number of manuscript collections in the Church Historical Society in Austin, Texas, provide a more personal understanding of some of the clergy, and reveal the conflicts and striving for authority among them. They are: the William White Papers; the William Smith Papers; the Samuel Peters Papers; the Hawks Manuscripts.

"The Transcripts of the Manuscript Books and Papers of the Commission of Enquiry into the Losses and Services of the American Loyalists," available in the New York Public Library, are valuable for the submissions the Loyalists presented to the Commissioners in London and Halifax, Nova Scotia. They provide details of their own careers, and many of them were also called upon to witness to the character and loyalty of other claimants. Many of the Loyalists were naturally bewildered by events in America, and in their claims for compensation many of them took the opportunity to present their own personal views of the causes and success of the Revolution.

BIBLIOGRAPHY

Manuscripts

Jacob Bailey Papers, 1756-1781. Library of Congress.

Byles Family Papers, 1728-1835 and 1753-1865. Massachusetts Historical Society

Thomas Coombe Papers; Correspondence and Business, 1765-1803. Historical Society of Pennsylvania.

Commission of Enquiry into the Losses and Services of the American Loyalists. 60 vols.

Transcripts in the New York Public Library.

Duane Papers. New York Historical Society.

Fulham Papers in the Lambeth Palace Library. Copies in the Library of Congress.

Simon Gratz Collection. Historical Society of Pennsylvania.

Hawks Papers. Manuscript letters of Samuel Johnson, William Smith and miscellaneous Papers. Church Historical Society, Austin, Texas.

Hoadley Collections, Box 12. Connecticut Historical Society.

Thomas Hollis Papers. Massachusetts Historical Society.

Peter Force Papers, Series D. Sir William Johnson Papers, 1755-1774. Library of Congress.

William Samuel Johnson Correspondence, 1744-1771. Connecticut

Historical Society.

Lambeth Palace Manuscripts, vol 1123. Copies in Library of Congress.

Richard Peters Papers, 8 vols. Historical Society of Pennsylvania.

Samuel Peters Papers, 8 vols. Church Historical Society.

Samuel Peters Correspondence. Connecticut Historical Society.

Saltonstall Family Papers. Massachusetts Historical Society.

hippen Family Papers. Historical Society of Pennsylvania.

William Smith Papers, 2 vols. Church Historical Society.

William Smith Papers, 6 vols. Historical Society of Pennsylvania.

David Mc Neely Stauffer Collections, vol. VI. Historical Society of Pennsylvania.

Wallace Papers, vol. IV, Papers of Robert Blackwell. Historical Society of Pennsylvania.

William White Papers, 3 vols. Church Historical Society.

Journal of John Wiswall, 1731-1821. Copy in Massachusetts Historical Society.

Printed Primary Sources

Albany. Minutes of the Albany Committee of Correspondence. 2 vols. Albany, 1923.

Connecticut. The Public Records of the State of Connecticut, Oct.

1776 – Feb. 1778. Edited by Charles J. Hoadley. Hartford, 1894.

Diocese of Connecticut. The Records of Convocation, 1790 – 1848. Edited by Joseph Hooper. New Haven, 1904.

Samuel Johnson, President of Kings College. His Career and Writings. 4 vols. Edited by Herbert and Carol Schneider. New York, 1929.

New Jersey. Journals of the Convention of the Protestant Church in the State of New Jersey, 1785 – 1816. New York, 1890.

New York. Journals of the Convention of the Protestant Episcopal Church in the State of New York, 1785 – 1802. New York, 1861.

Pennsylvania. Colonial Records of Pennsylvania. 16 vols. Harrisburg, 1851 – 1853.

Jounals of the Meetings which led to the Institution of Conventions of the Protestant Episcopal Church in the State of Pennsylvania. Philadelphia, 1790.

Journals of the General Conventions of the Protestant Episcopal Church in the U.S.A., 1785 – 1808. I vol. Edited by Francis L. Hawks and William S. Perry. Philadelphia, 1861.

Stowe, W.H., ed. "The Seabury Minutes of the New York Clergy Conventions of 1766 and 1767." Historical Magazine of the Protestant Episcopal Church, X (1941), 124 - 162.

Pamphlets

Apthorp, East. Considerations on the Institutions and Conduct of the Society for the Propagation of the Gospel in Foreign Parts. Boston, 1763.

[Barton, Thomas] The Conduct of the Paxton-Men, Impartially

Presented. Philadelphia, 1764.

[Caner, Henry] A Candid Examination of Dr. Mayhew's Observations on the Charter of the Society for the Propagation of the Gospel in Foreign Parts. Boston, 1763.

Chandler, Thomas B. An Appeal to the Public in Behalf of the Church of England in America. New York, 1767.

The Appeal Defended. New York, 1769.

The Appeal Farther Defended. New York, 1771.
An Address from the Clergry of New-York and New Jersey to the Episcopalians in Virginia. New York, 1771.

The American Querist: or, Some Questions Proposed Relative to the Present Disputes between Great Britain, and Her American Colonies. New York, 1774.

A Friendly Address to All Reasonable Americans, on the Subject of our Political Confusions. New York, 1774.

What Think Ye of the Congress Now. New York, 1775.

Chauncy, Charles. The Appeal to the Public Answered. Boston, 1768.

A Reply to Dr. Chandler's "Appeal Defended." Boston, 1770.

Inglis, Charles. The True Interest of America Impartially Stated, in Certain Strictures on A Pamphlet Entitled Common Sense. Philadelphia, 1776.

Leaming, Jeremiah. A Defence of the Episcopal Government of the Church . . .. New York, 1766.

Mayhew, Jonathan. Observations on the Charter and Conduct of the Society for the Propagation of the Gospel in Foreign Parts.

Boston, 1763.

Paine, Thomas. Common Sense. Philadelphia, 1776.

Stiles, Ezra. A Discourse on the Christian Union. Boston, 1761.
Vance, Clarence H., ed. Letters of a Westchester Farmer. New York, 1930.

[Welles, Noah] The Real Advantages which Ministers and People May Enjoy Especially in the Colonies, By Conforming to the Church of England. No place, 1762.

Collections of Manuscript Sermons

Samuel Auchmuty. Corporation of Trinity Church, New York.

Isaac Browne. New Jersey Historical Society.

Samuel Provost. Corporation of Trinity Church, New York.

Aeneas Ross. Delaware Historical Society.

Printed Sermons

Andrews, Samuel. A Sermon Preached at Litchfield, Connecticut, before the Convention of Clergy. New Haven, 1770.

A Discourse Shewing the Necessity of Joining Internal Repentance with the External Professions of it. New Haven, 1775.

Batwell, Daniel. A Sermon Preached at York-Town, before Captain Morgan's and Captain Price's Companies of Rifle-Men. Philadelphia, 1775.

Beach, John. A Modest Enquiry into the State of the Dead. New London, 1755.

Bogatzky, C. H. God's Thoughts of Peace and War. London, 1759.

Duché, Jacob. The American Vine, A Sermon Preached in Christ Church Philadelphia Before the honorable Continental Congress, July 10, 1775. Philadelphia, 1775.

The Duty of Standing Fast in our Spiritual and Temporal Liberties. Philadelphia, 1775.

Magaw, Samuel. A Discourse in Christ Church, Philadelphia, on Sunday, October 8, Philadelphia, 1775.

Sayre, John. A Sermon Preached before the Convention of Clergy of the Provinces of New-York and New Jersey. New York, 1773.

Smith, William. A Sermon Preached on the Present Situation of American Affairs. Philadelphia, 1775.

Strong, J. Let a Man Account of us, as the Ministers of Christ. Simsbury, Connecticut, 1768.

Vestry Records

Connecticut
Brooklyn. Trinity Church Records, 1771-1866.(formerly Trinity Church, Pomfret). Vol. I. Connecticut State Library.

Stratford. Christ Church Records 1722-1932. 12 vols. Vol. II, Church Accounts and Meetings, 1726-1834. Connecticut State Library.

New London. St. James Church. Vol. I, 1725-1782. Connecticut State Library.

Milford, St. Peter's Protestant Episcopal (formerly St. George's Church) Records 1764-1869. Connecticut State Library.

New Milford. St. John's Church. Connecticut State Library.

Middleton. Church of the Holy Trinity (formerly Christ Church). ConnecticutState Library.

Delaware.
New Castle. Immanuel Church Minute Book, 1710-1858. MSS in possessionof the Rector.

Massachusetts.
Boston. King's Chapel Vestry Records, 1782. In the custody of the Massachusetts Historical Society.

New Jersey
Newark. Trinity Church Vestry Minutes, 1778-1804. MSS in possession of theRector.

Shrewsbury. Vestry Minutes of Christ Church. MSS in possession of the Rector.
New York.
Corporation of Trinity Church in the city of New York. Minutes of Vestry.Vol. I. MSS in possession of the Rector.

Poughkeepsie. Christ Church Vestry Minutes. Vol. I. MSS in possessionof the Rector.

Pennsylvania.
Chester. St. Paul's Church Record Book, 1704-1820. MSS in possession of theRector.

Great Valley. Saint Peter's Church Records, 1744-1885. MSS in the HistoricalSociety of Pennsylvania.

Lancaster. St. James Church Vestry Book, 1744-1846. MSS in

possession of theRector.

Perkiomen. St. James Church Vestry Book, 1739-1799. MSS in the Historical Society of Pennsylvania.

Philadelphia. St. Paul's Church Records, 1760-1835. MSS in the Historical Society of Pennsylvania.
Christ Church and St. Peter's Church Vestry Records, 1761-1784. MSS
in possession of the Rector.

Radnor. Vestry Minutes of St. David's Church. MSS in the Historical Society of Pennsylvania.

Manuscript Diaries

Barton, Thomas. Journal of an Expedition to the Ohio. Pennsylvania Historical Society.

Chandler, Thomas B. Memorandamus, 1775-1785. Transcript of the first part in theNew-York Historical Society.

Shoemaker, Samuel. Diary, 1783-1785. MSS in the Historical Society of Pennsylvania.

Printed Diaries, Journals and Memoirs

Adams, John. Diary and Autobiography. Edited by L. H. Butterfield. 4 vols. Cambridge, Massachusetts, 1962.

Asbury, Francis. Journal, 1771-1815. 3 vols. New York, 1821.

Bailey, Jacob. The Frontier Missionary. Edited by William S. Bartlett. New York, 1853.

Bangs, Isaac. Diary, April 1776- July 1776. Edited by Edward Bangs. Cambridge,
Massachusetts, 1890.

Bentley, William. Diary. 4 vols. Salem, Massachusetts, 1905.

Chandler, Thomas B. The Life of Samuel Johnson, The First President of Kings College, New York. New York, 1805.

Coke Daniel P. The Royal Commission on the Losses and Services of American Loyalists, 1783-1785. Being the Notes of Mr. Daniel Parker Coke, M.P., one Of the Commissioners During that Period. Edited by
Hugh Edward Egerton. Oxford, 1915.

Holyoke Diaries, 1709-1856. Salem. Mass. 1911.

Lynde. The Diaries of Benjamin Lynde and of Benjamin Lynde, Jr. Boston, 1880.

McKenzie, Frederick. Diary. 2 vols. New York, 1968.

Marshall, Christopher. Extracts from the Diary of Christopher Marshall, 1744-1781. Edited by William Duane. Albany, 1877.

Morris, Margaret. Private Journal, Kept During a Portion of the Revolutionary War. Privately Printed, 1836.

Pynchon, William. Diary. Edited by Fitch Edward Oliver. Boston, 1890.

Rowe, John. Letters and Diary, 1759-1762, and 1764-1779. Edited by Anne Rowe Cunningham. Boston, 1903.

Serle, Ambrose. The American Journal of Ambrose Serle, 1776-1778. Edited by Edward H. Tatum, Jr. Calif., 1940.

Stiles, Ezra. Literary Diary. Edited by Franklin B. Dexter. 3 vols. New York, 1901.

Wills

Craig, George. Chester County Wills and Administration Pennsylvania Abstracts. Vol. III, 1777-1800. Historical Society of Pennsylvania.

Currie, William. Chester County Wills and Administration Pennsylvania Abstracts. Vol. IV, 1801-1825. Historical Society of Pennsylvania.

Seabury, Samuel. New London Probate District, Town of New London. No. 4722. Connecticut State Library.

Parish Histories

Berrian, Willam. An Historical Sketch of Trinity Church, New York. New York, 1847.

Briggs, Vernon L. History and Records of St. Andrews Protestant Episcopal Church of Scituate, Massachusetts, 1725-1811. No place, 1904.

Carter, William C. and Glossbrenner, Adam J. History of York County, 1729-1834. Harrisburg, 1930.

Clarke, Samuel. History of St. James Church, Elizabethtown, New Jersey. New York, 1857.

Dix, Morgan, ed. A History of the Parish of Trinity Church in the City of New York. 5 vols. New York, 1898.

Duhamel, William., ed. Historical Annals of Christ Church, Reading, Pennsylvania. Douglassville, 1927.

Eberlain, Harold D. and Hubbard, Cortlandt Van Dyke. The Church of Saint Peters in The Great Valley, 1700-1940. Richmond, Virginia, 1944.

Foote, Henry Wilder. Annals of King's Chapel. 2 vols. Boston, 1896.

Greenwood, F.W.P. A History of King's Chapel in Boston. Boston, 1833.

Folsom, Joseph Fulford, ed The Municipalities of Essex County, New Jersey 1666-1924. 4 vols. New York, 1925.

Hanson, Willis T. A History of St. George's Church in the City of Schenectady. Schenectady, 1919.

Rightmyer, Nelson Waite. The Anglican Church in Delaware. Philadelphia, 1947.

Raum, John O. History of the City of Trenton, New Jersey. Trenton, 1871.

Steen, James. History of Christ Church. Privately Printed, 1903.

Stubbs, Alfred. A Record of Christ Church, New Brunswick. New York, 1850.

Webb, Edward A., ed. The Historical Index of Sussex County, New Jersey. No place, 1872.

General Secondary Sources

Albright, Raymond W. A History of the Protestant Episcopal Church. New York, 1964.

Bridenbaugh, Carl. Mitre and Sceptre, Transatlantic Faiths, Ideas, Personalities, and Politics, 1689-1775. New York, 1962.

Cities in Revolt: Urban Life in America, 1743-1776. New York, 1964.

Burr, Nelson R. The Anglican Church in New Jersey. Philadelphia, 1954.

Calam, John. Parsons and Pedagogues: The S.P.G. Adventure in American Education. New York, 1971.

Crary, Catherine S. The Price of Loyalty: Tory Writings from the Revolutionary Era. New York, 1973.

Cross, Arthur Lyon. The American Episcopate and the American Colonies. Hamden, Conn., 1964.

Curti, Merle. The Roots of American Loyalty. New York, 1968.

Dexter, Franklin Bowditch. Biographical Sketches of the Graduates of Yale College. 6 vols. New York, 1885-1912.

Grant, Alfred. Our American Brethren: A History of Letters in the British Press During the American Revolution, 1775-1781. North Carolina, 1995.

Gaustad, Edwin. The Great Awakening in New England. Gloucester, Mass., 1965.

Hall, Michael G. Edward Randolph and the American Colonies 1676-1703. New York, 1960.

Hancock, Harold B. The Loyalists of Delaware. Cranbury, New Jersey, 1977.

Hawkins, Ernest. Historical Notices of the Missions of the Church of England in the North American Colonies. London, 1845.

Hawks, Francis Lister. Collections of the Protestant Episcopal Society. 2 vols. New York, 1851-1853.

Hooker Richard J. The Anglican Church and the American Revolution." Unpublished Ph.D. Dissertation, University of Chicago, 1943.

Humphrey, David C. From King's College to Columbia 1746-1800. New York,1976.

Humphreys, David. An Historical Account of the Incorporated Society for the Propagation of the Gospel in Foreign Parts. London, 1730.

Kammen, Michael. Colonial New York: A History. New York, 1975.

Lydekker, John Wolfe. The Faithful Mohawks. Cambridge, 1938.

Lydekker, John Wolfe. The Life and Letters of Charles Inglis. London, 1936.

Jones, Thomas Firth. A Pair of Lawn Sleeves: A Biography of William Smith (1727-1803). Philadelphia, 1972.

Laugher, Charles T. Thomas Bray's Grand Design: Libraries of the Church of England in America, 1695-1785. Chicago, 1973.

Malone, Henry Thompson. The Episcopal Church in Georgia, 1733-1957. Atlanta, Georgia, 1960.

Manross, William Wilson, ed. The Fulham Papers in the Lambeth Palace Library. Oxford, 1965.

A History of the American Episcopal Church. New York, 1950.

McCaughey, Elizabeth P. From Loyalist to Founding Father: The Political Odyssey of William Samuel Johnson. New York, 1980.

McLachlan, James. Princetonians 1748-1768: A Bibliographical Dictionary. New Jersey, 1976.

Mills, Frederick V. Sr. Bishops by Ballot: An Eighteenth-Century Ecclesiastical Revolution. New York, Oxford University Press, 1978.

Nelson, William H. The American Tory. Boston, 1961.
Neuenschwander, John A. The Middle Colonies and the Coming of the American Revolution. NewYork, 1973.

Norton, Mary Beth. The British Americans. The Loyalist Exiles in England 1774-1789. Boston, 1972.

Pascoe, Charles F.,ed. Classified Digest of the Records of the Society for the Propagation of the Gospel in Foreign Parts, 1701-1892. London, 1893.

Two Hundred Years of the Society for the Propagation of the Gospel: An Historical Account, 1701-1900. London, 1901.

Perry, William Stevens. The History of the American Episcopal Church 1587-1883. Boston, 1885.

Reed, Susan M. Church and State in Massachusetts. Urbana, Illinois, 1914.

Rightmeyer, Nelson. Maryland's Established Church. Baltimore, 1956.

Sargeant, Winthrop, ed. The Loyalist Verses of Joseph Stansbury and Dr. Jonathan Odell. Albany, 1860.

Sasche, William L. The Colonial American in Britain. Connecticut, 1956.

Schlesinger, Arthur M. Prelude to Independence: TheNewspaper War on Britain, 1764-1776. New York, 1965.

Seabury, William Jones. Memoir of Bishop Seabury. New York, 1908.

Shipton, Clifford K. Sibley's Harvard Graduates: Biographical Sketches of those who attend Harvard College. Boston, 1970.

Silverman, Kenneth. A Cultural History of the American Revolution. New York, 1976

Smith, Horace Wemyss. Life and Correspondence of the Rev. William Smith, D.D. 2 vols. Philadelphia, 1880

Sprague, William Buell. Annals of the American Pulpit. 9 vols. New York, 1857-1869.

Steiner, Bruce E. Samuel Seabury 1729-1796. A Study in the High Church Tradition. Athens, Ohio, 1972.

Sykes, Norman. Church and State in England in the Eighteenth Century. Hamden, Connecticut, 1962.

Thompson, Henry Paget. Into All Lands: The History of the Society for the Propagation of the Gospel in Foreign Parts 1701-1950. London, 1951

Trinterud, Leonard J. The Forming of the American Tradition: a Re-Examination of Colonial Presbyteriansm. Philadelphia, 1949.

Tyler, Moses Coit. The Literary History of the American Revolution. 2 vols. New York, 1966.

Warch, Richard. School of the Prophets: Yale College 1701-1740. New Haven, 1973.

Worrall, Arthur J. *Quakers in the Colonial Northeast.* Hanover, New Hampshire, 1980.

INDEX

A.W.Farmer, 220
Abstracts of Proceedings, 6, 32, 109, 174, 185, 224, 227, 254, 264, 306
Adams, John, 219, 220, 222, 225, 226, 324
Addison, Henry, 205
Agar, William, 166, 175, 262
Alison, Francis, 48, 195
Allen, William, 61
Alling, Enos, 41
American Bishops Trust Fund, 30
'An Appeal to the Public in Behalf of the Church of England', 80, 118, 193, 195, 320
Anderson, Patrick, 268
Andrews, John, 94, 107, 299
Andrews, Samuel, 34, 124, 176, 177, 178, 183, 186, 187, 215, 216, 217, 232, 233, 260, 287, 288, 295
Andrews, William, 34, 58, 94
Andros, Edmunds. Governor of Massachusetts, 16
Anti-Proprietary Party, 49, 144, 281
Apthorp, East, 46, 67, 166, 168, 169, 170, 171, 175
Archbishop of Canterbury, 23, 25, 31, 37, 38, 39, 42, 44, 45, 60, 63, 78, 121, 147, 167, 177, 206, 208, 245
Arnold, Jonathan, 26
Asbury, Francis, 282, 283
Auchmuty, Samuel, 25, 26, 33, 45, 46, 47, 51, 52, 56, 58, 63, 75, 76, 89, 95, 106, 115, 124, 125, 127, 139, 140, 145, 146, 148, 150, 151, 152, 153, 154, 155, 156, 168, 180, 181, 182, 183, 186, 189, 203, 205, 206, 207, 213, 216, 222, 224, 231, 252, 255, 263, 266, 267, 269, 270, 295, 296, 321
Avery, Ephraim, 76, 174, 175, 296
Ayers, William, 36, 64, 107, 161, 231
Babcock, Luke, 33, 74, 76, 225, 231, 238, 296
Backhouse, Richard, 21, 29, 44
Badger, Moses, 98, 235, 286

Bailey, Jacob, 33, 36, 38, 39, 66, 67, 73, 83, 98, 234, 235, 236, 239, 246, 247, 260, 261, 271, 278, 286, 287, 288, 291, 295, 301, 303, 317
Bangs, Isaac, 223, 251, 252
Barclay, Henry, 53, 54, 58, 59, 83, 95, 96, 153, 154, 221
Barclay, Thomas, 53
Barton, Thomas, 40, 49, 51, 52, 54, 55, 56, 58, 60, 86, 104, 105, 135, 144, 152, 159, 183, 201, 203, 204, 215, 228, 229, 230, 241, 261, 274, 275, 276, 280
Bass, Edward, 108, 199, 235, 238, 243, 246, 247, 249
Batwell, Daniel, 227, 242, 269, 275, 276
Beach, Abraham, 76, 186, 231, 246, 279, 285, 292, 293, 301
Beach, John, 33, 69, 75, 76, 77, 96, 97, 110, 111, 124, 127, 163, 167, 168, 174, 200, 202
Beach, William, 65
Bearcroft, Philip, 26, 38, 106, 110, 143
Beardsley, John, 65, 84, 93, 124, 200, 238
Becket, William, 20
Belcher, Governor Jonathan, 70
Bennett, Joseph, 101, 117, 118
Berkeley, George, 306
Bernard, Governor Francis, 133, 187
Biddle, Edward, 268
Blackburne, Francis, 196
Blackwell, Robert, 249, 250, 318
Blair, James, 30
Bloomer, Joshua, 73, 74, 75, 76, 126
Bostwick, Gideon, 236
Boucher, Jonathan, 6, 92, 131, 209
Bours, Abigail, 37, 38
Bours, Peter, 29, 51, 52
Braddock, General Edward, 51
Bradstreet, John, 68
Bray, Thomas, 17, 30, 306, 329
Breynton, John, 41, 118, 236, 271, 286, 307
Brockwell, Charles, 20

333

Brooks, James, 241
Brown, Jonathan, 265
Brown, Thomas, 26, 94, 238, 251, 287
Browne, Arthur, 98, 116
Browne, Isaac, 20, 35, 50, 51, 69, 70, 91, 93, 96, 97, 101, 102, 118, 145, 151, 152, 155, 183, 186, 197, 214, 215, 224, 225, 232, 285, 295, 298, 321
Browne, Marmaduke, 168, 263
Bryan, George, 275
Bryzelius, Paulus, 60, 98, 104, 202, 203
Bunker's Hill, Battle of, 231
Burd, James, 105, 106, 275
Burton, Daniel, 89
Byles, Mather, 34, 66, 70, 71, 72, 175, 176, 236, 262, 264, 270, 286, 294, 307
Calvinists, 8, 59, 61, 69, 103
Cambridge University, 42
Camm, John, 190, 210
Camp, Ichabod, 94, 100
Campbell, Colin, 68, 137, 140, 145
Campbell, William, Governor of Nova Scotia, 41
Caner, Henry, 23, 28, 31, 32, 38, 39, 70, 73, 106, 114, 134, 135, 146, 165, 166, 167, 168, 170, 171, 172, 173, 187, 198, 200, 235, 236, 237, 251, 255, 259, 260, 262, 263, 286, 287
Carter, Christopher, 241
Chandler, Samuel, 60, 61, 62, 171, 204
Chandler, Thomas Bradbury, 19, 24, 26, 37, 45, 64, 75, 79, 80, 91, 92, 115, 116, 117, 127, 133, 138, 145, 148, 149, 151, 152, 156, 158, 176, 177, 186, 188, 190, 191, 192, 193, 194, 196, 200, 202, 206, 207, 209, 214, 215, 219, 220, 225, 241, 242, 245, 253, 254, 264, 270, 272, 283, 284, 293, 296, 298, 300, 302, 303, 307
Chapman, Walter, 22, 23
Charlton, Richard, 95, 140, 145, 154, 156, 192
Chauncey, Charles, 195
Checkley, John, 23, 101, 102, 186

Christ Church, Boston, 34, 39, 70, 71, 254, 262, 287
Christ Church, Philadelphia, 16, 22, 40, 66, 86, 107, 131, 163, 171, 218, 239, 262, 303
Clap, Thomas. President of yale college, 44
Clark, William, 37, 38, 94, 99, 185, 243, 272, 279, 285, 287, 294
Clarke, Richard, 288, 310, 311
Coercive Acts, 218
College of New Jersey, 74, 125
College of Virginia, 190
commissaries, 30, 41, 42, 132, 138, 145, 148, 149, 150, 156, 190, 193
Commissioners to Hear Loyalist Claims, 68, 222
Compton, Bishop Henry, 17, 30
Congregationalists, 7, 9, 16, 18, 19, 20, 21, 45, 65, 67, 68, 73, 74, 87, 94, 103, 110, 115, 130, 155, 165, 217, 223, 258, 259, 264, 270, 274, 306
Continental Congress, 209, 213, 219, 220, 223, 225, 226, 264, 265, 322
Conventions of Anglican Clergy, 160
Cooke, Samuel, 36, 37, 140, 145, 148, 149, 183, 221, 231, 268, 269, 279, 280, 285, 302
Coombe, Thomas, 40, 80, 81, 90, 93, 122, 218, 226, 247, 248, 265, 273, 280, 281, 282, 293, 294, 298, 299, 303, 317
Cooper, Myles, 45, 56, 75, 148, 149, 150, 152, 156, 158, 159, 190, 195, 204, 206, 207, 209, 211, 219, 220, 227, 234, 263, 302
Corporation for the Relief of Widows and Children, 149
Corresponding Members of the S.P.G, 40
Corresponding Society, 136
Cossit, Ranna, 67, 237, 288, 289, 296
Craig, George, 64, 85, 87, 88, 97, 101, 201, 261, 272, 277, 278, 280
Crèvecoeur, Hector St. John, 300, 301
Cummings, Archibald, 22, 23, 85
Currie, William, 20, 34, 35, 68, 261, 268, 276, 277, 278

Cutler, Timothy, 18, 19, 41, 93, 106, 108, 146, 185
Cutting, Leonard, 34, 81, 85, 87, 145, 182, 183, 196, 197, 214
Davenport, Addington, 260
Davies, Thomas, 66, 177, 178, 216
Dean, Barzillai, 23
DeLa Roche, Peter, 34
Dibblee, Ebenezer, 23, 33, 34, 65, 82, 93, 101, 155, 172, 173, 174, 176, 197, 215, 216, 217, 218, 264, 284, 291, 300, 301, 303, 305, 310, 311
Dickinson, John, 195, 283
Dickinson, Jonathan, 74
Doty, Doty, 58, 119, 207, 232
Doty, John, 207
Duche, Jacob, 39
Dummer, John, 19
Dutch Reformed Church, 6, 47
Eagleson, John, 118
Elliot, Andrew, 127
Ellis, Anthony, Bishop of St. David's, 256
Ellis, William, 100, 101, 102, 271
Evans, Nathaniel, 37, 81, 130
Fayerweather, Samuel, 91, 101, 238, 247
Fisher, Nathaniel, 250, 251
Fleming, Caleb, 196
Fletcher, Governor Benjamin, 16
Fogg, Daniel, 259
Fowle, John, 106
Franklin, Benjamin, 40, 61, 62, 74, 144, 160, 281
Franklin, Sir William, 158
Frazer, William, 36, 64, 107, 280, 285, 292
Freeman, James, 301
Friendly Address to all Reasonable Americans, 220
Frinck, Samuel, 119, 171
Fulham Palace, 39
Gaine, Hugh, 195, 219
Galloway, Joseph, 219, 220, 223, 298
Gardiner, Sylvester, 246, 247, 278
Germans in Pennsylvania, 49
Gibbs, William, 23, 97, 98
Gibson, Bishop Edmund, 31, 123

Giles, Samuel, 181, 182
Godfrey, Thomas, 130
Graves, John, 97
Graves, Matthew, 71, 79, 88, 89, 95, 97, 98, 102, 108, 109, 110, 152, 203, 246, 250, 268, 274, 302
Great Awakening, 7, 19, 21, 22, 69, 116, 166, 258, 284, 328
Greaton, Charles, 38
Green, John, Bishop of Lincoln, 189
Grenville, Grenville, George, 173
Griffith, David, 81
Grotius, Hugo, 159
Hall, Jacob, 58
Halstead, Josiah, 280
Hamilton, James, 61
Hancock, John, 222, 242, 283, 328
Hardy, Josiah, 268
Harrison, George, 40
Harrison, Joseph, 41, 71, 72, 258, 296
Harvard College, 66, 71, 72, 166, 170, 331
Hawkins, Ernest, 306
Holbrook, John, 279
Hollis, Thomas, 31, 32, 42, 43, 127, 169, 170, 171, 172, 188, 189, 194, 196, 202, 203, 317
Holmes, Josiah, 279
Hooper, William, 74, 198
Hopkinson, Francis, 81, 82, 119, 130
Hubbard, Bela, 73, 76, 119, 124, 177, 178, 284, 303
Hubbard, Daniel, 71
Hubbard, William, 71
Hughes, John, 89, 90, 139, 144, 173
Humphreys, David, 306
Hunt, Isaac, 270, 271
Hutchinson, Thomas, 256
Illing, Traugott Frederick, 105
Indians, 34, 49, 52, 53, 54, 55, 56, 58, 59, 103, 106, 142, 154, 164, 165, 169, 177, 188, 203, 204, 233, 255, 256, 275
Inglis, Charles, 50, 51, 56, 96, 97, 107, 114, 120, 138, 140, 148, 149, 158, 181, 182, 183, 191, 200, 204, 206, 207, 219, 220, 223, 224, 230, 242,

335

248, 252, 255, 266, 276, 280, 293, 303, 310, 311, 329
Iroquois, 53, 54, 58, 102
Jacobites, 173
James, John, 131
Jarvis, Abraham, 76, 119, 146, 148, 172, 177, 178, 183, 186, 261, 289
Jenny, Robert, 90
Johnson, Samuel, 9, 19, 20, 21, 22, 23, 24, 25, 26, 27, 30, 34, 41, 42, 44, 45, 46, 47, 48, 54, 56, 63, 65, 69, 70, 72, 73, 75, 76, 77, 78, 82, 83, 88, 89, 91, 95, 96, 97, 99, 100, 101, 106, 108, 109, 110, 111, 115, 124, 125, 127, 128, 133, 134, 141, 142, 146, 148, 149, 150, 151, 152, 153, 154, 155, 158, 163, 164, 166, 168, 169, 170, 171, 172, 173, 177, 178, 179, 180, 181, 182, 183, 184, 185, 186, 188, 189, 190, 191, 192, 196, 200, 202, 205, 207, 209, 213, 215, 222, 234, 242, 254, 255, 256, 270, 274, 283, 290, 295, 306, 307, 311, 317, 319, 325, 330
Johnson, Sir William, 54, 55, 56, 58, 89, 106, 144, 149, 159, 203, 204, 273, 317
Johnson, William, 48, 56, 91, 270
Johnson, William Samuel, 106
Kearsley, John, 241, 269
Keene, Edmund, Bishop of Chester, 255, 256
Keith, George, 17
King's Chapel, Boston, 7, 16, 28, 29, 31, 32, 38, 45, 50, 66, 72, 78, 80, 108, 109, 110, 114, 146, 166, 171, 187, 193, 199, 222, 236, 238, 246, 254, 259, 301, 302, 323, 327
King's College, New York, 26, 29, 42, 46, 47, 48, 56, 58, 75, 83, 96, 111, 123, 152, 171, 182, 190, 192, 194, 206, 207, 209, 234, 252, 256, 329
Kneeland, Ebenezer, 38, 119, 155
Knox, William, 297, 298
Lambeth Palace, 20, 34, 38, 41, 78, 111, 114, 120, 121, 133, 134, 144, 148, 164, 165, 166, 167, 168, 170, 173, 179, 317, 318, 329
Lamson, Joseph, 23, 124, 185

Langman, John, 101
Lay Readers, 9, 24, 25, 30, 75, 109, 152, 184, 259, 301
Leaming, Jeremiah, 23, 76, 106, 124, 148, 154, 155, 177, 178, 179, 201, 208, 244, 245, 261, 289, 290, 291, 292, 293
Lexington, Battle of, 231
Libraries, S.P.G, 34
Lindsey, William, 28
Livingston, Peter, 219
Livingstone, William, 47
Llandaff, Bishop of, 31
Locke, John, 280
Low, Isaac, 220
Lowth, Robert, Bishop of Oxford, 188, 196, 207, 233, 296
Lutherans, 8, 52, 59, 61, 69, 105, 144
Lynde, Lidia, 286
Lyon, John, 32, 93, 94, 108, 119, 187, 216
Lyons, James, 25, 26, 27, 28, 29, 87, 91, 101, 102, 130, 151, 154, 155
Magaw, Samuel, 82, 96, 107, 227, 228, 249, 250, 282, 283, 299, 309, 310
Maillard, Monsignor, 59
Malbone, Godfrey, 19, 28, 45, 46, 102, 103, 258, 259, 270
Malcom, Alexander, 29
Mansfield, Richard, 23, 244, 260, 279
Marshall, Christopher, 218, 219, 226, 242, 248, 252, 269, 271, 325
Marshall, John, 119, 244, 289
Mather, James, 277
Mayhew, Jonathan, 32, 43, 50, 165, 167, 168, 169, 170, 171, 172, 179
McClennachan/ McClennaghan, William, 63, 66
McDowell, John, 35
McGilchrist, William, 35, 74, 146, 166, 169, 187, 197, 199, 216, 236, 247, 262, 263, 278
McKean, Robert, 81, 95, 98, 107, 133, 138, 140, 145, 183, 190
McSparran, James, 27, 78, 79, 106, 108, 109, 110, 184
Meadows, John, 254
Methodists, 50, 139, 144, 159, 239, 285

Miller, Ebenezer, 67, 168
Milner, John, 93, 94, 125, 145
Miner, Richard, 23, 185
Ministry Act 1693, 47
Moffat, Thomas, 258
Mohawk Indians, 53, 54, 95, 154, 329
Moore, Benjamin, 266, 305
Moore, Henry, Governor of New York, 45, 47, 63, 89, 147, 184
Moore, Thomas Lambert, 92
Morris, Theophilus, 20, 25, 26, 44, 98, 102, 103, 108
Morton, Andrew, 97, 137
Morton, John, 277
Mosely, Richard, 28, 259
Mühlenberg, Henry, 61
Munro, Harry, 68, 151, 231
Munro, John, 230
Murray, Alexander, 36, 37, 51, 52, 60, 64, 68, 69, 77, 78, 103, 106, 201, 229, 230, 268, 272, 273, 274, 287, 294, 303
Nationalism, 30, 132, 291
Negro Americans, 23, 52, 53, 95, 120, 143, 153, 255, 262
Neill, Hugh, 42, 83, 93, 94, 120, 121, 138, 139, 140, 142, 143, 145, 148, 181, 182, 183, 205, 206, 282
New York Mercury, 192, 214
Newton, Christopher, 66, 124, 244, 291
New-York Gazette, 219
Nicholls, James, 232, 244, 268
Nicholls, Robert, 153, 236, 262
Nicholls, William, 155
Odell, Jonathan, 74, 75, 76, 227, 241, 242, 269, 279, 330
Ogden, Isaac, 223
Ogden, Uzal, 64, 284, 285, 292, 299, 301, 310
Ogilvie, John, 51, 52, 54, 65, 182, 184, 266
Ordination into Anglican Orders, 22, 23, 24, 29, 36, 37, 38, 39, 40, 52, 54, 56, 58, 60, 69, 70, 72, 73, 74, 75, 76, 78, 81, 85, 90, 92, 100, 105, 106, 107, 108, 115, 116, 117, 118, 119, 120, 123, 131, 133, 134, 144, 147, 151, 155, 157, 159, 160, 161, 168, 171, 177, 178, 182, 184, 185, 186, 187, 189, 192, 193, 195, 197, 198, 200, 207, 209, 211, 221, 261, 276, 281, 290, 292, 296, 297, 300, 301, 307, 308
Orrery, 135
Osbaldeston, Richard, Bishop of London, 131, 164
Oxford Universitiy, 42
Paine, Thomas, 223
Palmer, Solomon, 35, 70, 93, 124, 167, 168
Panton, George, 224, 239, 286, 287
Parker, Samuel, 192, 194, 235, 238, 239, 247, 250, 274, 275, 284, 287, 292, 293, 294, 300, 301, 302
Pascoe, C.F., 306
Paterson, John, 249
Paxton, Charles, 71, 258, 259
Penn, Thomas, 48, 49, 107, 108, 131, 132, 135, 136, 138, 144, 158
Peters, John, 119, 237
Peters, Richard, 40, 45, 56, 58, 62, 89, 103, 122, 123, 131, 136, 142, 148, 149, 150, 153, 159, 160, 171, 172, 203, 216, 226, 239, 240, 247, 273, 295, 318
Peters, Samuel, 91, 119, 155, 172, 185, 216, 217, 222, 233, 236, 237, 238, 243, 244, 246, 251, 260, 261, 269, 271, 272, 283, 284, 286, 287, 289, 290, 291, 292, 294, 301, 302, 303, 308, 309, 310, 311, 316, 318
Phelps, Alexander, 271
Philips, Colonel Frederick, 41
Pierson, John, 33
Plant, Matthias, 108
Pownall, Thomas, 224
Presbyterians, 6, 7, 8, 9, 11, 15, 16, 17, 19, 21, 47, 48, 49, 67, 69, 92, 103, 107, 135, 138, 142, 144, 149, 157, 188, 191, 197, 204, 272, 300
Preston, John, 75, 86, 87, 231
Price, Roger, 18, 23, 24, 26, 27, 28, 29, 35, 44, 45, 66, 72, 78, 79, 80, 81, 108, 109, 110, 133, 256
Prince, Nathaniel, 72, 73
Prince, Thomas, 72

337

Proprietary Party, Pennsylvania, 48, 49, 201, 281
Proselytizing, 34, 116, 147, 200, 254
Provost, Samuel, 153, 266, 267, 268, 285, 291, 292, 293, 321
Pufendorf, Samuel, 159
Pugh, John, 100, 101
Punderson, Ebenezer, 20, 41, 70, 84, 100
Pynchon, William, 237, 247, 251, 278
Quakers, 6, 8, 15, 17, 48, 49, 71, 74, 85, 128, 136, 144, 247, 279, 280, 332
Randolph, Edmund, 16
Reading, Philip, 33, 34, 99, 120, 139, 159, 160, 175, 215, 216, 239, 240, 241
Revolutionary War, 35, 178, 242, 295, 325
Ridgely, Charles, 96, 269
Rittenhouse, David, 135
Rivington, James, 220, 221
Robinson, John, 41, 258
Roe, Stephen, 28
Rogerines, 70
Ross, Aenas, 37, 38, 103, 228, 229, 247, 249, 250, 282, 321
Ross, John, 52, 107, 121, 139, 140, 142, 143, 144, 269, 273
Rowe, John, 38, 90, 171, 193, 197, 198, 199, 235, 236
Rush, Benjamin, 225
S.P.G General Monthly Meetings, 32
Sargeant, Winwood, 237
Sauer, Christopher, 61
Sayre, John, 129, 130, 131, 132, 244, 245, 246, 288, 297
Schuyler, John, 45
Scotch-Irish, 11, 21, 49
Scott, John Morin, 47
Scovil, James, 88, 100, 124, 133, 134, 173, 174, 175, 176, 177, 178, 183, 186, 187, 215, 216, 232, 287, 288
Seabury, Samuel, 8, 79, 184, 220, 290, 301
Seabury, Samuel, the elder, 24
Secker, Samuel, Archbishop of Canterbury, 40, 122, 124, 133, 142, 147, 163, 167, 169, 185, 187, 189, 192, 193, 195, 196, 197, 202, 255, 270, 283, 289, 306, 331
Secker, Thomas, Archbishop of Canterbury, 34, 42, 43, 63, 114, 133, 148, 163, 166, 167, 194, 196, 202, 209
Serle, Ambrose, 250, 296, 297, 326
Seven Years War, 50, 160
Sharpe, Gregory, 190
Sharpe, Horatio, Governor of Maryland, 93, 191
Sherlock, Thomas, 31, 91
Shipley, Jonathan, Bishop of Asaph, 233, 234
Shirley, William, Governor of Massachusetts, 23, 29, 45, 59, 66
Shoemaker, Samuel, 282
Skene, Colonel, 40
Smith, William Jr, 47
Smith, William, Provost, College of Philadelphia, 37, 195
Snowdon, Leonard, 241
Society for the Propagation of the Gospe, 16
Sons of Liberty, 84, 174, 221, 232
St. George's Chapel, New York, 45, 51, 63, 266
St. Mary-le-Bow Church, 31, 53, 92, 255
St. Paul's Chapel, New York, 63, 252
St. Paul's Church, Philadelphia, 22, 23, 59, 85, 118, 120, 121, 122, 123, 124, 139, 140, 142, 149, 159, 160, 209, 239, 240, 249, 250, 261, 264, 271, 277, 286, 289, 307, 309, 310, 324
St. Peter's Church, Philadelphia, 44, 49, 63, 65, 68, 75, 78, 250, 251, 277, 324
Stamp Act, 32, 71, 72, 88, 125, 134, 146, 151, 159, 173, 174, 175, 176, 179, 183, 187, 189, 193, 194, 213, 215, 216, 240, 253, 262, 270
Stewart, Duncan, 71
Stiles, Ezra, 7, 114, 115, 116, 166, 167, 244, 245, 246, 259, 270, 300, 301
Stringer, William, 121, 123, 209, 225, 248, 249, 264, 266, 273, 281, 298

Strong, Joseph, 200
Stuart, John, 56, 58, 103, 204, 230, 303
Sturgeon, William, 23, 52, 89, 90, 120, 121, 139, 143, 144, 148, 262
Suffolk Resolves, 220
Talbot, John, 17
Talbot, St. George, 33, 41, 65, 255
Temple, John, 71
Terrick, Richard, Bishop of London, 121, 131, 141, 145, 146, 149, 156, 177, 179, 180, 256, 257
'The American Querest', 220
The College of Philadelphia, 48
The Weekly Post-Boy, 214
Thomas, John, 93
Thomas, John, Bishop of Rochester, 256
Thompson, Ebenezer, 23, 27, 199, 235, 260
Thompson, H. P, 306
Thompson, Thomas, 85
Thompson, William, 85, 86, 94, 229, 230
Thorne, Sydenham, 282
Tingley, Samuel, 75, 130, 230, 243, 272, 283
Townsend, Epinetus, 238
Treadwell, Agar, 37, 239
Trinity Church, New York, 6, 16, 25, 33, 35, 36, 45, 47, 48, 52, 54, 56, 63, 65, 66, 83, 90, 95, 96, 107, 115, 118, 129, 131, 132, 133, 138, 139, 140, 142, 146, 150, 153, 154, 156, 167, 182, 184, 186, 197, 198, 199, 206, 208, 213, 214, 222, 223, 235, 238, 239, 252, 259, 263, 266, 267, 268, 269, 270, 284, 285, 292, 301, 305, 310, 321, 322, 323, 326, 327
Troutbeck, John, 74, 197, 199, 222, 236
Trumbull, Governor Jonathan, 237
Tryon, William, Governor of New York, 41, 45
Tyler, John, 102, 127, 128, 210, 237, 244, 283, 284, 289, 291, 301, 302
Tyler, Moses Coit, 74, 82, 220, 226, 303
Ulstermen, 49
Usher, John, 29, 102, 103, 185

Vardill, John, 92
Vesey, William, 23, 95, 132, 153
Viets, Roger, 65, 66, 102, 124, 157, 174, 181, 182, 200, 232, 233, 238, 287, 303
Vincent, Robert, 98
Walter, William, 131, 132, 199, 235, 236, 285, 286, 287, 297
Warburton, William, Bishop of Gloucester, 187, 188
Washington, George, 223, 248, 275
Watkins, Hezekiah, 23, 83, 87, 88
Wayne, Anthony, 250, 268
Weeks, Joshua Wingate, 33, 37, 74, 104, 176, 177, 199, 235, 236, 237, 238, 239, 246, 247, 285, 286, 295
Welles, Noah, 77, 78, 127, 167, 168
Wentworth, Benning, 46, 296
Wentworth, John, 41, 47, 204, 296
Wesley, John, 121
West, Benjamim, 130
Wetmore, James, 18, 19, 70, 82, 93, 102, 132, 133
Wetmore, Timothy, 93
What Think ye of the Congress Now, 220
Wheeler, Willard, 131, 132, 238, 239
White, William, 81, 239, 248, 249, 265, 266, 280, 287, 291, 292, 293, 294, 299, 300, 301, 303, 311, 316, 318
Whitefield, George, 19, 20, 22, 23, 117, 120, 121, 142, 267
Whitehead, James, 268
Widows' Corporation, 205, 206, 229, 230, 232, 240, 241
William and Mary College, 210
Wilson, Hugh, 181, 182, 183
Winslow, Edward, 38, 67, 111, 113, 114, 172, 175, 199, 215, 216, 243
Wiswall, John, 37, 38, 216, 236, 237, 318
Wood, Thomas, 58, 59, 99, 203, 204
Yale College, 19, 20, 22, 23, 44, 69, 73, 76, 115, 128, 133, 186, 200, 284, 328, 331
Yeates, Jasper, 173
Zantinger, Paul, 275

Printed in the United States
75629LV00004B/45